Bel Canto Bully

Bel Canto Bully

*The Life and Times of
the Legendary Opera Impresario
Domenico Barbaja*

PHILIP EISENBEISS

First published in Great Britain in 2013 by
Haus Publishing Ltd
70 Cadogan Place
London SW1X 9AH
www.hauspublishing.com

A CIP catalogue record for this book is available from the British Library

ISBN 978-1-908323-25-5

Typeset in Caslon by MacGuru Ltd

Printed and bound in China by 1010 Printing International Ltd

CONDITIONS OF SALE

To my mother, who knew I had a voice, but not for singing

Contents

Preface and Acknowledgements

Five years ago, I had never heard of Domenico Barbaja. Nor had I ever been to Naples. Today, when I look at this first biography of the legendary opera impresario, I sometimes think it is a miracle. Professor Paologiovanni Maione, musicologist at the Conservatorio di Musica Domenico Cimarosa, near Naples, summed up my feelings perfectly: 'In the 19th century, Barbaja caused miracles in our city and in the world of opera. I guess he is still causing miracles.'

Professor Maione was categorical about the enormous impact Barbaja had on the development of opera, and he was as puzzled as I was as to why Barbaja had become all but forgotten. He was also perplexed about my interest in the 19th-century impresario. 'And *why* are you doing this?' he asked me repeatedly, not hiding his surprise that somebody who was neither a musicologist nor a musician was trying to hunt down the traces of Barbaja.

It was a question I was to be asked many times during my quest, for it was surely an unusual (to say the least) pursuit for a financial headhunter from Hong Kong. Yet the simple truth was that I have been hopelessly hooked on this unique art form since my parents took me to see my first opera in Switzerland when I was barely 13. While many opera aficionados speak of the wonderfully harmonious interaction of drama, music, costumes and scenery that coalesces to create a perfect and complete artistic expression, it was the singing voice that captured me. As a young teenager I even considered pursuing an operatic career, but a retired Argentinean baritone brought in to train me to become the next Caruso quickly disabused me and my parents of this notion: my vocal talent was decidedly modest.

Instead, after several years of journalism, I started a career as a banker, eventually finding my way to Hong Kong and becoming a financial headhunter. It was a job I enjoyed (and still enjoy) but I missed the easy access to great opera that Western cities provide. I found myself spending an ever increasing amount of time chasing around the world for selected performances and performers, spending endless evenings listening to rare recordings of operas, and voraciously researching operatic esoterica. I was especially drawn to the so-called *bel canto* composers of the early 19th century, finding their music oddly addictive. As I worked my way through the literature of the time, Barbaja caught my attention, and this interest soon grew into an obsession.

This book seeks to shed light on the life and times of Domenico Barbaja, the most colourful and influential impresario of the *bel canto* age, one of the most exciting periods of music and history. Barbaja's times were dominated as much by Napoleon and the Bourbon royalty as they were by the composers Rossini, Bellini or Donizetti.

While every effort has been made to be accurate, *Bel Canto Bully* is neither a work of academic scholarship, nor is it aimed at a specialist audience of musicologist researchers whose enormous efforts working through primary sources far surpass anything I have set out to achieve. A particular challenge was the reconstruction of Barbaja's life and travels in view of the paucity of original written records. As Barbaja was nearly illiterate, he did not leave behind a lot of revealing correspondence. Writing this book in Hong Kong, I relied principally on publicly available secondary sources, but I did spend seemingly endless days in the civic, operatic and banking archives of Milan, Naples and Rome.

This book would never have been possible without the help, patience and support of an operatic-sized cast of people. Their help and influence on this book has been enormous. Any mistakes there might be, however, are entirely my own.

Above all, I want to express my deepest gratitude to Professor Paologiovanni Maione, whom I contacted out of the blue. He put his faith in me without having any clue what I was going to do. In fairness, nor did I. He encouraged me, opened my mind and showed me the true heart of Naples and the world that Barbaja inhabited.

My special thanks to Sergio Ragni and Luigi Cuono, whose scholarship, generosity and gentility was an enormous inspiration. Their museum and home dedicated to Gioachino Rossini and Isabella Colbran is perhaps the most magnificent sight in Naples. My appreciation also to Bruno Cagli, President of the Accademia Nazionale di Santa Cecilia, who made this introduction possible.

I am deeply grateful to Reto Mueller who lives, of all places, in Switzerland where, a prolific scholar of Rossini, he runs one of the most complete archives of the composer's documents. Barbara Gariboldi at the Civic Archives in Milan was extraordinarily patient, persevering and helpful in discovering many of the sources to which I had no access from Hong Kong. Likewise, I was privileged to enjoy the help of La Scala in Milan, especially its Archivist, Matteo Sartorio. My thanks also to the Fondazione Rossini in Pesaro for allowing me to quote extensively from Rossini's letters and documents, as well as to Alma Books for permission to quote from Stendhal's *Life of Rossini*.

On the ground in Naples, I was helped by Carla Ceccere who runs Napoli Città Visibile, Professor Alfredo Buccaro of the Università degli Studi di Napoli Federico II, as well as the staff at the archives of the Teatro San Carlo. A special thanks to Luciana Florio, who demonstrated the inimitable Neapolitan warmth and genius for cooking. I also enjoyed the hospitality of Dr Domenico Barbaja – the dentist, not the impresario – and his sister Maria-Esther Contocalakis. Direct descendants of the great opera (and gambling) impresario, they warmly received me in their Neapolitan bridge club.

Steve Freeman, publisher of *HK Magazine* in Hong Kong, deserves my very special appreciation for his advice and services as a red wine-swilling Svengali. Among my friends and patient readers/editors/advisors, my thanks goes to Anna Esaki-Smith, Peter Shay and Marysia Juszczakiewicz in Hong Kong, Ken Krimstein in New York, Kate Whight in Melbourne and Tom Preston, Katie Fried and Wanda Whitely in London. My special thanks to my father for editing and commenting on the text with the critical yet caring eye that only a parent can have. Furthermore, Annick Medard in Strasbourg provided valuable help with translation, my niece Naomi Eisenbeiss sourced some of the rare materials via the internet, and David Secar in New York scoured American libraries. John Nugee, Juan Flores and Marc Flandreau answered my questions on historical currencies and values.

Astrid Angvik at Naxos Records merits particular mention for picking up the idea of launching a CD on Barbaja-related operas, a beautiful musical memento of the composer's legacy. My thanks also for the support and encouragement of Nicolas Soames of Naxos AudioBooks, Ashutosh Khandekar of

Opera Now, Rahul Jacob of the *Financial Times*, Stephen Revell of *Opera Rara* and Razia Iqbal of the BBC.

Above all, I must thank my friend and college roommate Arne C Wasmuth, who read and re-read the manuscript, gave me much-needed moral support throughout the project, and finally came up with the all-important title. He also introduced me to my publisher, Dr Barbara Schwepcke of Haus Publishing. To Barbara my extraordinary gratitude for her vision, trust, support and guidance, as well as her enormous courage. I would also like to extend my thanks to all the helpful and able staff of Haus Publishing in London, especially Harry Hall and Ellie Shillito, as well as my incredibly patient, detailed and attentive editor Jaqueline Mitchell.

Lastly, I would like to thank my friends and family, as well as my colleagues at Executive Access Ltd, who put up with me and my weird obsession. It was passion that drove me, and passion cannot be stopped. Barbaja would have understood. Though he would have made more money doing it than I ever will.

Hong Kong, 2013

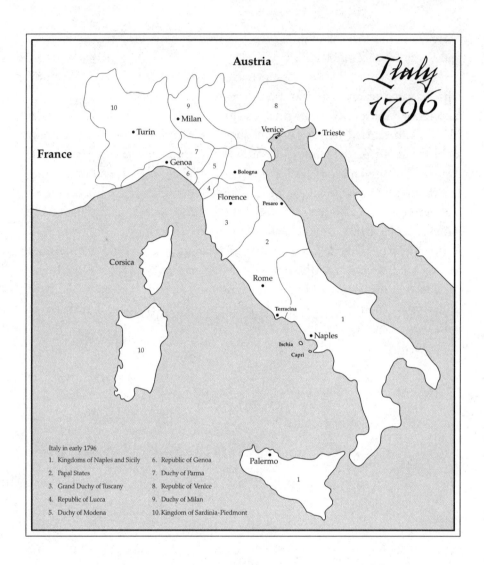

Austria

Italy
1796

France

10

9
• Milan

8

• Turin

Venice
•

• Trieste

7

• Genoa

5

6

• Bologna

4

Florence
•

Pesaro •

3

2

Corsica

Rome
•

Terracina
•

1

10

• Naples

Ischia ○

Capri ○

Palermo
•

1

Italy in early 1796

1. Kingdoms of Naples and Sicily
2. Papal States
3. Grand Duchy of Tuscany
4. Republic of Lucca
5. Duchy of Modena

6. Republic of Genoa
7. Duchy of Parma
8. Republic of Venice
9. Duchy of Milan
10. Kingdom of Sardinia-Piedmont

Introduction

In search of Barbaja

As far as obsession with opera goes, I would rate my condition as 'extreme'. I therefore had no hesitation whatsoever in flying from Hong Kong to Milan to see the only known painting of the legendary opera impresario Domenico Barbaja.

I started what would become a three-year quest to find the story behind Barbaja at the Teatro alla Scala, which is considered by most to be the world's leading opera house. La Scala dominates the square it faces and is immediately recognisable, with its cream and grey façade, triple-arched portico and distinctive, almost exaggerated triangular lintels. The oversized programme boards fronting the rusticated base of the building are famous as the cover designs of hundreds of historical opera recordings from La Scala. The Museo Teatrale alla Scala, slightly to the left of the porticos, is much less well known and houses the theatre's historic treasures. It was here that I first saw Barbaja.

The museum features paintings, marble busts and memorabilia of the great artists of the past and present, with a heavy emphasis on the golden years of La Scala, when superstars such as Maria Callas and Renata Tebaldi cemented the theatre's pre-eminence in the world of opera. These names and their portraits still draw tour groups to the Museo Teatrale alla Scala, where visitors question the tour guides as to who the modern-day successors of 'La Divina' Callas are, and admire the depictions of Enrico Caruso, Arturo Toscanini, Luciano Pavarotti and other operatic legends.

I was looking for someone equally legendary (apparently I was the first to do so), but without assistance I could not even find him. I asked the guards and attendants at the museum to show me the portrait of Domenico Barbaja, but mostly got blank stares. After some confusion and chatting amongst the guards, one of them showed me to the second room of the portrait gallery. She pointed to a portrait hanging high on a wall above another painting. The reflected light coming in from the open windows and the painting's remote position made it hard to read the plaque at the bottom of the frame. But here he was.

In the three-quarter-length portrait, Domenico Barbaja stands tall, proud, his hands folded and gently resting on a walking cane, which was certainly more for decoration than for assistance. Leaning on a cabinet with a piece of cloth thrown over it, he wears an elegant, dark, embroidered overcoat with a thick, black fur collar. His striking clear blue eyes glow with an unmistakable twinkle, as if he is about to flash a mischievous grin. Gently arched eyebrows are set off by a pronounced bulbous nose, distracting from his thin lips. The chin and jaw are covered with a narrow, trimmed beard which goes up to his ears. His glance is peaceful, content, self-satisfied without looking smug.

Looking at the portrait, the only documented painting of Barbaja, I reflected on some of the descriptions I had read about the great impresario. The French novelist Alexandre Dumas (père) described Barbaja as of medium height, but 'built like Hercules, wide chest, square shoulders, and with an iron wrist. His head was rather common, and his facial features were not regular. But his eyes bubbled with spirit, intelligence and malice'.[1] Gioachino Rossini called him the 'most bald and most ferocious director',[2] but he appears to be neither in this painting. The anonymous artist portrays the rich, elegant and influential impresario in a room overlooking the main auditorium, with three small disembodied heads behind him – the composer Gioachino Rossini and the celebrated opera singers Giovanni Battista Rubini and Giuditta Pasta – almost like a puppeteer in front of his performing puppets.

While the fact that his portrait was hanging in La Scala's museum proved the impresario's importance to the opera world, it struck me as odd that his portrait was so unknown, even hidden. The epithet 'the legendary impresario Domenico Barbaja' frequently appears in the history of opera and in the histories of the great opera composers of the 19th century, but mostly as a mere footnote. Even the booklets that accompany recordings of the operas he commissioned have little to say about him, other than that he was 'legendary'. But that was enough to pique my interest: who was this 'legendary impresario', and how did he come to acquire such a reputation? If he is always referred to as 'legendary', why is there so little information about him?

My investigations began with the encyclopaedias of opera, which outline the bare facts of Barbaja's life, mentioning only his interaction with the great Italian composers of the early 19th century. As an *impresario* – a producer and promoter of commercial musical entertainment – he rose to run the most important opera houses in Europe, including the fabled Teatro alla Scala of Milan, the Teatro San Carlo of Naples and, finally, the Kaern-tnertortheater in Vienna. He helped discover and worked closely with the composers Gioachino Rossini, Gaetano Donizetti and Vincenzo Bellini, three of the greatest names in music and the protagonists of the operatic period generally referred to as *bel canto*. He also managed the careers of many legendary opera singers, such as Isabella Colbran, Maria Malibran and Giovanni Battista Rubini, and worked with the leading ballet dancers of the time, including Antoine Paul. From the encyclopaedias' descriptions, he sounded like an early version of a Hollywood movie mogul running a 19th-century 'studio system'.

A more detailed account of Barbaja can be found in the 1937 novel *Der Impresario* by the Austrian writer Emil Lucka (1877–1941), who is better known for his treatises on sexuality (*The Three Stages of Love*). In Lucka's description, Barbaja emerges from poverty in Naples to become a waiter in a Neapolitan coffee shop, accidentally invents a drink called the 'Barbagliata', joins the circus, then becomes a gambling entrepreneur, and ultimately – by seducing an aging and unattractive but influential society lady – takes over an opera house as a scheming, womanising and ambitious manipulator. He escapes a murder attempt and is uncomfortably close to the inept King of Naples. Lucka's colourful but completely inaccurate tale was based on the urban legend that was Barbaja, further embellishing the stories that had been told and retold over time.

I hoped my first visit to Naples would shed some more light on his story. At the Teatro San Carlo in Naples, Europe's most important opera stage during the impresario's years and the centre of Barbaja's activities, there was, however, scant information about the man. A marble bust stands without any prominence in the rather soul-less modern foyer where patrons go for drinks during the interval of an opera performance, rather than in the magnificent 19th-century foyer where Barbaja actually worked his magic. Professor Paolo-giovanni Maione from the Conservatorio di Musica Domenico Cimarosa in Avellino, a picturesque hill town some 60 kilometres east of Naples, seemed to be the only one who had done any recent work on Barbaja; he and a colleague had written several academic articles about Barbaja's innovative business model and his revolutionary impact on the world of opera.

Professor Maione generously showed me all around the city, pointing out the real landmarks of Barbaja's life. He then sent me to explore the little-known archives of Europe's greatest opera houses, the hidden 18th-century document collections of long-defunct Neapolitan banks, the catacombs beneath baroque southern Italian churches, and threw me into a world of scholars, musicologists and musicians.

What gradually emerged from my research was a man who had been the greatest impresario of his time. Through sheer willpower, astounding energy, fearless gumption, and more than a fair share of bullying, Barbaja changed and shaped the world of opera. Womanising, foul-mouthed and illiterate, he led a life as cosmopolitan and decadent as that of any modern-day movie mogul, and romanced the leading prima donna of the era. He built some of the best-known buildings in Naples, and became one of the richest men in the kingdom.

Today, few may know his name, yet his legacy lives on in the operas he commissioned, the landmarks of Naples and in the very way we enjoy opera.

The Italian impresario

A century before Italian unification in 1861 there was no such thing as an Italian nation-state. Italy was a mere geographic area, and a true Italian consciousness had barely started developing. The peninsula was fragmented into many different city states, most of which fell to foreign domination. 'Italy' consisted of three major political entities controlled by the Austrian Habsburgs, the Neapolitan Bourbons, and the Pope. Milan, Lombardy and the formerly independent Venice were part of the Habsburg Austrian Empire run from Vienna. Naples (Campania), the southern tip of Italy (Calabria) and Sicily were part of The Kingdom of the Two Sicilies ruled by the Neapolitan branch of the Spanish Bourbon royal family. The Papal States (stretching from the Adriatic and including Bologna) and Rome were controlled by the

Pope from the Vatican. There were numerous other, smaller duchies, such as Parma.

Opera developed as an art form in Italy and France in the 17th century, and opera houses run by impresarios were first seen in Venice in 1630,[3] and from there spread all over Italy. By the 19th century there were literally hundreds of opera houses. From the large cities of Naples, Rome, Venice, Genoa, Milan and Turin, to secondary cities such as Bologna, Parma and Bari, all had one and sometimes two opera houses.[4] The Teatro alla Scala in Milan and the Teatro San Carlo in Naples were merely the largest and most famous. It is fair to say that 19th-century Italy was completely addicted to opera. The opera houses were owned by a monarch, a municipality, a group of nobles, or in some cases by an eccentric and wealthy individual. Loathe to manage the opera seasons themselves, the owners generally contracted an impresario to handle this on their behalf.

The impresario's was a rather unusual profession. In fact, strictly speaking, it was not a profession at all, as there was no training, preparation or typical career trajectory. People slid into the role from various backgrounds. To begin with they were noblemen, merchants, tailors or even thugs. Later they increasingly came from the arts, being musicians, singers, dancers or music critics.

The term impresario derives from *'impresa'* (pl. *imprese)*, loosely translated as 'enterprise'. Many Italian records refer to an *'appaltatore'* (who holds an *appalto*, or several *appalti*), with the more exact meaning of 'concessionaire' or a 'lessee', though this term usually refers to the entrepreneur leasing part of the opera house, for instance the public foyers or concession stores. In today's parlance, an impresario would probably be called a producer, promoter or simply theatre director, though these terms do not capture the full implications of the word. In the 18th century the term impresario was also accompanied by a whiff of deceit, opportunism, risk and speculation, not least because many found themselves forced into financial ruin. In an 18th-century parody of the opera business the archetypical impresario was named 'Signore Fallito' (Mr Bankrupt).[5]

The impresario functioned as an independent producer who assumed the financial risk of an opera season ('*stagione*') at one or sometimes several opera houses. The *stagione* was the carnival season from 26 December until Lent, but later additional *stagioni* were added, including spring and autumn seasons. Both artistic and administrative director, the impresario was responsible for putting together the season's performances, choosing the composers, the music, the librettists, singers and set designers, and deciding on all other issues to do with the enormously complex productions.

Typically, theatre owners would open a bidding process to those impresarios interested in taking on a season. The winning impresario was signed on and given an endowment (a '*dote*' consisting of the government or municipal subsidy), as well as receiving the revenues from the season tickets of the box-holders. He also kept the take from ordinary ticket sales. But putting on operas was an extremely expensive undertaking and the theatre was often left with a deficit at the end of the season. Opera house owners sometimes needed to make up the shortfall in moneys owed, and it was not unknown for the impresario to flee from the city.

Opera house owners had no certainty of making a profit, but they seemed to tolerate the reality of frequent losses in their theatres. Owning and supporting an opera house carried prestige and provided the proprietors with a place to socialise, host guests and be entertained, and this seems to have been regarded as sufficient reward alone. Though it has never been a venue of entertainment for the masses, the opera house was at this time the single most important meeting place for the city's high society: 'The Neapolitan quality rarely dine or sup with one another,' wrote the English surgeon and travel writer Samuel Sharp in 1765, 'and many of them hardly ever visit, but at the opera; on this account they seldom absent themselves, though the Opera be played three nights successively, and it be the same opera, without any change, during ten or twelve weeks.'[6]

An evening in the boxes at the opera took on a life of its own. Guests would eat, drink, chat, entertain and not infrequently block off the performance by closing the box curtains. The social element took priority over what was happening on stage. The boxes could become quite messy, with servants running between them and an ante-chamber to prepare and serve food. The rules of La Scala demanded that box-holders clean their own boxes during the day and not leave behind piles of rubbish in the aisles, but this rule is unlikely to have been rigidly enforced.[7]

Such behaviour came as a shock to the many northern travellers to Italy. On his visit of 1831, the German composer Felix Mendelssohn-Bartholdy was taken aback by the audience's habits, their lack of interest in the performed music and general rowdiness, commenting that Italians 'treated music like any ordinary object of fashion, regarded with coldness and indifference'.[8] The French composer Hector Berlioz regarded his southern neighbours' theatre habits with disdain. The audience, he complained of a performance in Milan, 'spoke as loud as at a stock exchange and the canes on the floor made a noise as loud as a large cash register'. There is 'nothing more humiliating' for an artist.[9] But visitors also recognised that Italian opera was hugely glamorous, and was produced for pleasure, not profit.

By the middle of the 19th century, the fervour and fashion for opera saw composers', dancers' and especially singers' fees spiral out of control, and far from hoping to break even or even make a small profit, owners of opera houses faced losses on a broad scale. The opera house was increasingly seen as the playground of the rich, an indulgence few could afford. Democratic voices clamoured that grand opera was 'a genre bound up with absolutist courts and sung by extravagantly rewarded castrati' in 'a place where "lascivious harmonies" had lulled the people to sleep.'[10] It comes as little surprise then that in 1867 the Chamber of Deputies of a newly united Italy swiftly abolished all central government subsidies for opera, and instead imposed a tax on all theatre takings.

The loss of government sponsorship was to sound the death knell for the independent impresario. Yet, for a period until Italian unification, under the sovereignty of Bourbon Southern Italy and Habsburg Northern Italy, the grand opera world of the impresario flourished. Juggling a demanding sovereign, status-conscious and venal nobility, composers under extraordinary creative pressure, demanding and egotistical singers, difficult and overly precious dancers, not to mention the hundreds of front and back office staff of greater or lesser integrity, was a formidable task. Many impresarios were stage-struck chancers who were simply not up to the job, and more often than not disappeared into oblivion, leaving a *stagione* in shambles and reputations ruined. But there were some who rose to the challenge and the opportunities presented, and among them was one man in particular who emerged to transform the profession and turn opera into a large-scale, multinational and profitable business: Domenico Barbaja.

1

From Coffee Waiter to Croupier

(1778–1806)

Domenico Barbaglia was born on 10 August 1777 in the small rural community of Ponte Sesto about 16 kilometres south-west of the Milanese city centre. As his birth was so difficult and his health so precarious, it was decided that the boy should be immediately baptised in the house of the midwife, as he was unlikely to survive. His parents Carlo Giuseppe Barbaglia and Maria Stabilini were working as farmers, moving around the area according to the work opportunities offered to Carlo, mostly in the rice or vegetable fields. Ponte Sesto, with a population of only 350, had little to offer anyone and would face a large population outflow towards Milan. A few years later, the Barbaglias would be working in Romano Banco, a town of 700 souls, which saw the number of inhabitants dwindle to just over 100 by 1805. Like all the peasants in the area, the Barbaglias would have had a keen eye on the opportunities and happenings in Milan, a city to which they were to move around the turn of the century.

Milan was the capital of the Duchy of Milan and a small part of the enormous Austro-Hungarian Habsburg Empire. Stretching from Austria and Hungary, through Bohemia to the Duchies of Milan, Modena and Reggio, the huge empire was run from Vienna by the Empress Maria Theresa, the first and only woman to head the Habsburg dynasty. She put her various relatives in charge of the satellite territories, and it was Maria Theresa's son Ferdinand, the 14th of her 16 children, who governed the Duchy of Milan on her behalf. Fashioned as Archduke of Austria-Este, he enforced his mother's will with the support of the Austrian army, the police and a network of spies and informants.

Few Milanese had actually been to Vienna, but they had all heard stories of the splendour and wealth of the city at the heart of the Habsburg Empire. And the heavy tax burden imposed by the Austrians on their Italian territories served as an unpleasant and regular reminder of the power of Vienna.

Two branches of the Habsburg dynasty had dominated Milan for most of the last 300 years, since the Sforza dynasty had gained control and turned the Duchy of Milan into a centre for arts and commerce during the Renaissance. From 1525 the city-state was ruled by the Spanish line of the Habsburgs, which hung on to Milan until 1701 when they were once again replaced by the French. In 1706, the Austrian line of the Habsburgs took control of the city, retaining it through to 1796.[1]

By the time of Barbaja's birth in 1777, Milan was again a thriving city, its Austrian rulers revitalising it and endowing a new flowering of Milanese culture. The Austrians also made great efforts to improve the hygiene, sanitation and medical infrastructure. The centre of Milan was dominated by the Duomo, the largest church in Italy after St Paul's in Rome. Building of the magnificent Gothic cathedral had started in the 14th century, and it remained a work in progress for the next 400 years. In the late 18th century, the famous Madonnina spire was erected, at a height of nearly 110 metres. At that time, a visitor standing on the roof-top and looking through the veritable forest of spires and pinnacles would have had a clear view of the entire city. Surrounding the city walls were fields and small villages like Ponte Sesto, with marshes and rice fields to the south, which contributed to the regular outbreaks of malaria in the hot and humid summers. Winters were wet and damp.

The view from the Duomo would have shown a clear outline of the city walls, the countless covered canals criss-crossing the city and in focal position the large square in front of the Duomo. Streets radiated outwards from the square and larger roads formed concentric circles around it. Looking north-east from the Duomo, one would also have seen the Church of San Babila, which dated back to the 11th century and was once considered the third most important church in the city.

San Babila was the parish responsible for the neighbourhood of Porta Orientale, the Eastern Gate of the city, the area to which Domenico Barbaglia would later move. Like the rest of the city, it was a mixed neighbourhood. Facing the street, with wide avenues stretching in front of them, were grand houses with imposing frontages, but behind these were a warren of small streets, most not even big enough for a carriage to pass through. Here, four-or five-storey buildings were literally stuck one against another and the streets buzzed with activity from the inhabitants of countless small homes, stores, workshops, textile manufacturers, simple rooms for rent and modest inns.

Directly north of the Duomo, and just a stone's throw away, stood the city's magnificent opera house, the Royal Ducal Theatre. The theatre was a wing of the ducal palace and it was accessed through the spacious palace courtyard. In 1776 all Milanese were shocked to hear of the destruction of the Royal Ducal Theatre by fire. The destruction of the city's main theatre was a devastating event for the city's population, and nearly 100 wealthy box-owners petitioned Ferdinand of Austria-Este to reconstruct it. It was quickly decided that the Ducal Theatre would be rebuilt under the auspices of the Habsburg Empress, Maria Theresa of Austria, and it would be far bigger and grander than its predecessor. In fact, the decision was taken to build two theatres: the Teatro alla Scala, as well as the Teatro Cannobbiana. The Scala would be north of the centre of the city and the royal palace, and the Cannobbiana – which took its name from the building it replaced, which had been inhabited by an order of nuns – would be to the south. The Scala was the main theatre, the Cannobbiana smaller and less grand.

The new, larger theatre was to be built on nearby land of the Church of Santa Maria alla Scala, which had been demolished and deconsecrated. Its cost was borne by the Milanese nobles who had owned boxes in the old Ducal Theatre, in exchange for possession of the land on which the church had once stood, and entitlement to a box in the new theatre. In their discussions with the authorities, the nobles made sure to press for continued permission for gambling in the theatre's spacious foyers. Gambling had long been a popular pastime pursued in salons all over town, but especially by patrons of the opera in the foyer of the Ducal Theatre. The new theatre was called the Nuovo Regio Ducale Teatro alla Scala (New Royal Ducal Theatre alla Scala), but everyone just referred to it as La Scala. La Scala opened its doors in 1778, a year after Domenico Barbaglia was born.

La Scala immediately became the centre of much of the city's social life. Performances of operas and ballets were offered nearly nightly. The theatre's layout with its private boxes, ante-chambers and horseshoe-shaped auditorium was perfect for socialising, chatting and seeing and being seen.

In the first few months of La Scala's operations, gambling was indeed still offered in the foyer; but at the end of 1778 Maria Theresa issued a personal edict forbidding any gambling whatsoever either in public at La Scala or in any private location. Yet even without the gambling, La Scala became a larger and more active social centre for the moneyed and noble classes than the old theatre had ever been.

For the Milanese commoners, attending La Scala would have been completely out of reach, both financially and socially. Observing the nobles entering and leaving the opera house was exciting, however. Servants were often seen at the opera peering through the grilles at the back or in the upper gallery stalls where the traditionally black-cloaked family servants and porters were permitted to watch the opera for free.

There are virtually no records of Domenico Barbaglia's first 18 years, nor is much known about his three sisters.[2] As a matter of fact, Domenico's date of birth is not certain. The certificate of baptism states 10 August 1777, yet the population census conducted by the French in 1811 states his birth date as 7 December 1775. All later records indicate his birth as being in 1778, which is likely what he considered it to be.

With the population outflow from Ponte Sesto and Romano Banco to Milan, it is safe to assume that Domenico moved to the city in search of work as a young teenager, certainly ahead of his parents. There is no evidence of his having had much schooling or religious inculcation. While the Habsburgs introduced elementary schools in their territories in the 1790s, these were neither free nor compulsory (education in Italy did not become compulsory until 1877), and were mostly entrusted to religious orders. More prosperous and talented children could have entered a conservatory, enjoyed private tutoring or been taken under the wing of a tradesman or academic. Poorer students might have attended classes, earning their keep by providing services for the religious order that ran the school. But according to all later accounts of his contemporaries, Domenico demonstrated little enthusiasm for school and showed no interest in learning proper Italian; the Milanese vernacular must have seemed sufficient to him. His classroom was probably the street, where he was most comfortable arguing at full pitch with his friends, or really with anyone, in his native Milanese dialect. They must have noticed, too, that Domenico was 'gifted by God with the loudest and most dissonant of voices'.[3]

The young Domenico would have worked at odd jobs without learning any profession. It is possible that the Barbaglias encouraged their son to start working at a coffee-shop in the city, washing crockery, cleaning, serving, and generally helping out. They might have been hopeful that Domenico, just like their relatives Gaetano Barbaglia and Cristofforo Barbaglia, would grow up to be a *caffetiere*, a coffee-shop operator.

But the relative tranquillity of Milanese life was severely interrupted by news from Paris in 1789. All of Milan was shaken by the stories of a popular revolution that had deposed the royal family of France and brought to an end an absolutist regime that had run the country for as long as anyone could remember. The Milanese press and pamphleteers had given full play to the revolutionary ideas coming from France. The ideals of liberty, equality and fraternity fell on fertile ground and were a subject of heated debate in the coffee-shops. The Italian youth in particular responded enthusiastically to the reports from Paris. Though less so in Milan, Piedmont, Bologna and Palermo witnessed youth-driven attempts at revolutionary upheaval, which were brutally suppressed.

The uprising of the masses against the ruling classes, the opposition to the King and the unspeakable violence that was occurring all over the country became topics of fascination all over Milan; the goings-on at the opera house suddenly seemed much less enthralling. Then, in early 1793, barely four years after the beginning of the French Revolution, the Milanese were shocked to learn of the execution of King Louis XVI, the first time they had ever heard of such a thing happening. The instrument of death, the so-called *guillotine*, was something so novel and gruesome it dominated many evenings' discussions at the noisy coffee-shops.

All year, stories of violence in France reached the ears of the Milanese. But one event brought the turmoil much closer to home: the execution by guillotine of King Louis' wife, Queen Marie Antoinette.[4] Marie Antoinette was the daughter of their own ruler, Maria Theresa of Austria.

In just a few short years the French Revolutionary government had become established, and predictable. French expansion into Italy appeared to be just a matter of time, and plenty of Italians would welcome it. The upstart Corsican-born general Napoleon Bonaparte moved quickly up the ranks in the French Revolutionary army and he led the French troops to invade Milan in 1796, once again displacing the Austrians. The invading French promised a fairer and more prosperous society, and were warmly welcomed by the

Milanese, with the exception of the aristocracy.

The 18-year-old Domenico Barbaglia joined the youths from the lower and middle classes in welcoming the French troops, who brought ideas that appealed to the young and under-employed. Domenico and his friends also enjoyed seeing their city moving centre stage in world politics, as Napoleon spoke of creating a Kingdom of Italy with Milan at its centre.

In honour of the arrival of the victorious General Napoleon himself in November 1797, the French ordered dramatic torch lighting to be placed at the entrance to La Scala, and entry to the theatre was granted free of charge. This was the first chance for Domenico and many other Milanese finally to glimpse the spectacular La Scala from the inside. It was a sight nobody would ever forget.

Coffee-shop waiter

The row of small buildings right in front of La Scala was home to the first generation of major coffee-shops in the city, attracting French troops, patrons of the theatre, musicians and the many people who passed through from the stores in the streets behind. It was here that Domenico worked in the Caffè dei Virtuosi (Café of the Virtuosos),[5] a small and modest establishment directly opposite La Scala that faced into a side-street, and was principally patronised by the less affluent choristers and orchestra members. It's more popular moniker, Caffè dei Pompieri (Firemen's Café), was earnt by its being the preferred meeting place for musicians to congregate pre-and post-theatre to light their cheap cigars, probably from a gas-lamp: matches were still not widely available and remained too expensive for many.

Over the years, as a coffee-shop culture developed, the market became enormously competitive and each establishment cultivated its own market niche and style. Many years later, the grand Caffè Cova would open only a few doors away. Founded in 1817, it is now a franchised coffee-shop chain, even in distant Hong Kong. Cova became so dominant it ran many of its nearby competitors out of business. Some 40 years later, it also became the chief meeting point for conspirators against the Austrian regime (that again had replaced the French) and was therefore equally well attended by the omnipresent spies working for it. An Austrian diplomat wrote in 1840 that 'The Café Cova is the breeding place of conspirators and we still have not the courage to close it down.'[6]

A direct competitor to Cova was the Caffé del Gran Teatro, located on the side-street leading directly to La Scala, which made a business of serving wine and food directly to patrons in the boxes inside the opera house, its delivery boys running in and out of the theatre during performances. It went out of business after only eight years, probably unable to keep up with the popularity of Cova.

But 20 years before Cova opened and impressed its patrons with its magnificent architecture, the smaller coffee-shops competed principally on product. Creating new and exciting drinks and playing up their originality, by whatever means, was a way for smaller coffee-shops to raise their profile and fight their larger and more glamorous competitors. In 1800 at the Caffé dei Virtuosi, the strident and irreverent Domenico was struck by the simple idea of mixing coffee with cream and hot chocolate and he started serving the drink to guests. It had the sweetness from the chocolate, possessed the kick of the coffee, and the cream on top provided richness and a substance for decorative swirls. When guests asked what they were being served, the self-confident young Milanese quipped in his inimitable loud voice, 'But Sir, it's a Barbagliata! I invented it.'

The Barbagliata proved a sensation. The drink became a household name around the turn of the century, and helped the Caffé dei Virtuosi remain competitive. Cynical observers pointed out that the loud-mouthed coffee-shop waiter took credit for it and insisted on claiming naming rights for something as simple as mixing three ingredients that were routinely placed on the same table in coffee houses. They also noted that his ground-breaking invention was launched in the same year that Alessandro Volta unveiled the voltaic pile, the world's first battery, also named after its inventor.[7] Certainly this was a more important discovery, but the Barbagliata proved its value, and the 22-year-old waiter milked his sudden notoriety in Milan for everything it was worth. The Barbagliata helped establish his credentials for innovation and sheer nerve.

The drink has also demonstrated remarkable longevity. To this day, older Milanese will refer to what we might call a 'café mocha' as a Barbagliata. They would probably not, however, know the origin of the term; many think the name is derived from the white foam cap, which might look like a white beard, a 'barba'.

Around the time of the launch of the Barbagliata, the young man changed the spelling of his name to the more marketing-friendly 'Barbaja'. It was also around this time that with great excitement he began to romance the 16-year-old Rosa Gerbini, whom he would eventually marry.[8] We know little of Rosa, as she is never mentioned in Barbaja's correspondence, but she does not seem to have shared her husband's ambition or sense of adventure, nor to have had any desire ever to leave Milan.

Rosa bore Domenico two children: Pietro, born in 1799, and Carolina, born in 1801. As was common then, her principal occupation was caring for the children. Barbaja, meanwhile, worked in the coffee-shop and spent time drinking and playing cards with his friends, something for which he discovered he had a natural ability. But with the creation of the Kingdom of Italy, Domenico's world as a coffee-shop waiter and young father was soon to become a whole lot more exciting.

Napoleon created the Kingdom of Italy in 1805, originally consisting of the Duchies of Milan, Modena and Mantua, later expanding through his military advances to include parts of the Republic of Venice in 1806 (previously an independent city-state), and the Marches in 1807. All told, the Kingdom of Italy encompassed around seven million subjects. At its centre, the city of Milan had a population of 150,000.[9] The thousands of French troops brought new political ideas and, as importantly, new money and business opportunities. Shortly before his coronation, Napoleon gave orders to have the façade of the Duomo finished, a project which was finally completed seven years later.

On 26 May 1805, amid much pomp and ceremony, Napoleon declared himself the King of Italy and had himself crowned in a packed Duomo. Keen to remain in the good graces of the Church, the ceremony was held with the full cooperation of the Cardinal Bishop of Milan.[10] In a heavily symbolic gesture, Napoleon bestowed upon himself the Iron Crown of Lombardy. Being reportedly beaten from one of the nails used in the crucifixion, the crown is not only a venerated reliquary, but is also laden with historical significance, having been used to crown Holy Roman Emperors since the 10th century. Napoleon appointed Eugene de Beauharnais, his stepson and adopted child, his viceroy to rule the Kingdom of Italy in his absence.

Milan was the narrow end of the wedge of Napoleon's Italian conquest. From here he would direct various forays – some successful, others less so – into other parts of Italy. It would also be the staging ground from which the French would spread their ideals and their views of the world.

Napoleon would introduce French-style Republican ideology, the Napoleonic code, the Italian lire (same weight, size and metal as the French franc, and essentially pegged 1:1 to the French currency) and such useful things as the Population Census of 1811.

Domenico had other distractions from the coffee-shop. He was increasingly interested in the goings-on across the road in the opera house. It was not so much the music that interested him, however. He was attracted to the activities once again going on in the foyer of the theatre: gambling.

Spinning the wheels

Of the many changes brought by the French, the introduction of legalised gambling was of greatest interest to Barbaja. Traditionally, the Austrian government had prohibited gambling all over the city with the exception of the opera houses, where it granted an operator a monopoly concession. These monopolies were intermittently abolished by the sovereign.[11] While the abolition would prohibit high-stakes gambling, milder games, such as backgammon, were normally not affected by the interdiction.

The French shared the Austrians' negative attitude towards gambling. By the early 1800s, however, the French government had begun to recognise the economic value of gambling and it was keen to obtain the tax revenue it provided, not least to help support the heavy financial burden brought by the expansion of Napoleonic Italy. So it was that from 1802 to 1810 gambling in Milan saw its heyday, creating many gambling millionaires and even more gambling paupers.

Games of chance were pursued by the upper classes in the opera house, which had been purpose built for gambling with its large foyers. Unlicensed gambling dens of course proliferated, then as at most other times in history. La Scala became the preferred meeting place, not least because it was well heated and well lit,[12] something that was particularly appreciated in the damp and unpleasant Milanese winters. Gambling, not music, became the building's biggest draw.

The game of choice was initially backgammon until faro gained in popularity later on. A simple and easy-to-learn card game, faro (also known as Pharaoh or pharaon, and played between a banker and several players) was an early French export that enjoyed widespread popularity due to the good odds for the players. It even spread as far as the American Wild West where it was known as 'Bucking the Tiger'.

The *appaltatore* holding the concession controlled the venue, provided the cards and dice and collected the revenues, part of which went directly to the government. The job of working within the opera house and serving as a casino operator catering to the gambling nobility demanded somebody entrepreneurial, thick-skinned and not averse to risk. It was the perfect environment for Barbaja.

Without hesitation, Barbaja turned his back on the small and smoke-filled coffee-shop, and started working in the Milan gambling halls as a card dealer. He swiftly picked up the game and gradually accumulated significant amounts of cash by holding the bank at faro. As a card dealer he was also well positioned to make invaluable contacts, not only with Milanese high-rollers but also with a 'host of French army-contractors who were making and losing fortunes every six months in the wake of the battalions'.[13] Barbaja also occasionally secured assignments as a go-between or gun-runner, giving him plenty of opportunity to make a quick franc, or lire as the case may be.

Shrewd and calculating as well as loud and brash, Barbaja made a name for himself in gambling circles as a thriving table operator in the opera foyer. His talent was not lost on the opera house management. After much badgering and argument, Barbaja managed to convince Francesco Benedetto Ricci, the impresario of La Scala, to sub-contract to him the gambling in the opera house for the carnival season of 1805.[14]

Ricci was one of a handful of impresarios among whom the management of La Scala, and the Cannobbiana from 1789 onwards, rotated. These impresarios ran both the theatre and the concessions in the foyers. From 1808 to 1814, the number of concession operators in Milan became so numerous it is hard to know truly who ran what at what time.[15] Many worked in syndicates or in silent partner arrangements.

Ricci was a businessman from Genoa with a solid reputation,[16] and he specifically moved to Milan to assume the *impresa* of La Scala in 1799, hoping to strike it rich. But the demands made by the local government on the impresarios became increasingly onerous and challenging. Even for the smaller Teatro Cannobbiana, for example, the government demanded the establishment of a permanent comic company, the maintenance of a drama school and the commissioning and performing of operas, ballets, comedies and tragedies.[17] It became increasingly difficult for Ricci to keep La Scala afloat, let alone make a profit.

He and his colleagues had lobbied the French government to reintroduce gambling. In recognition of these financial difficulties, as well as the afore-mentioned financial pressures from the military campaigns, the French government finally conceded and re-admitted gambling in the opera houses in February 1802.[18] This completely changed the financial equation. In just five years, Ricci was able to amass a fortune, all thanks to gambling. This made the *appalto* more interesting, and numerous contenders emerged to bid for the concession of La Scala, including Barbaja.

Ricci was impressed by the young man's enthusiasm, but he did not fully understand what Barbaja proposed to do: introduce a new game of chance called roulette. In the early 1800s, France spawned the game that was destined eventually to take over gambling salons worldwide: *roulette*, the 'little wheel', where a croupier rotates the wheel in one direction, while spinning a ball in the opposite direction around a circular numbered track.

Barbaja had heard about this novelty from the many Frenchmen he had talked to at the gambling tables, and quickly recognised the capacity of roulette to permit a far larger number of participants to play at one time than the more common card games. The game required no skill to participate and the odds were stacked in favour of the house, unlike faro. Roulette, with its elegant and colourful wooden wheel that was dramatically spun by a stylish croupier in front of a captivated crowd would also have appealed to Barbaja's sense of drama; and was possibly his first lesson in showmanship.

Barbaja was not the only person attempting to lease the concession from Ricci, however. A young man from Piedmont, Carlo Balochino, had also set his eyes on the potentially lucrative gambling contract. Balochino had started his career as a faro croupier in Milan, and then run a (probably unlicensed) gambling den with links to the French government. The two men were completely different in style and background, and yet somehow they clicked.[19] Balochino was educated, obstinate yet restrained, and wrote correct and florid Italian. Barbaja was exuberant, vulgar and uneducated.

By all accounts Barbaja was practically illiterate. His surviving written correspondence is relatively meagre, and consists principally of business letters dictated by him to secretaries. Barbaja himself wrote in colloquial terms with frequent spelling errors, interjected curses and strange turns of phrase. His letters are hard to decipher, with upper and lower cases chosen at random. Names are mis-spelled and the texts are peppered with '*coglioni*' (bollocks) used as noun, verb or exclamation. His favourite forms of address were *assassino* (assassin),[20] *mariolo* (rogue) and *ladro* (thief),[21] though he used them with such abandon that they were often even considered terms of endearment. He also referred to himself in the third person, usually as a 'beast', and would finish a letter by apologising for writing 'bestiality upon bestiality'.

The two impresarios formed a lasting and lucrative partnership, though Barbaja alone won the gambling contract for La Scala in 1805.

Courtesy of roulette, within one season at La Scala Barbaja had earned a fortune, investing some of the money in property. His wealth was certainly significant enough that in the first population census of Milan, conducted by the French in 1811, Barbaja was mentioned as 'prosperous' and his occupation was stated as 'gambling operator'.

Barbaja and Balochino banded together, and jointly expanded their gambling operations in the wake of the advancing French army. As Napoleon's armies expanded southwards, so did Barbaja's and Balochino's business. Balochino moved to Venice in 1806 where he took over the gambling monopoly. A year later, he became impresario of the legendary Teatro la Fenice of Venice.[22] Barbaja, on the other hand, had his eyes on the gambling monopoly of Naples, the largest metropolis in Italy and a city that was legendary for its gaming habits.

By the end of the decade, and closely following the pattern of French military conquests, the Barbaja Syndicate (including Balochino, Ricci and various other *appaltatore*) controlled the gambling monopolies in Milan, Venice and nearly 20 other towns in Northern Italy, in addition to numerous former Papal and Austrian cities. By 1806 Balochino and another *appaltatore*, Giuseppe Crivelli, held gambling concessions not only in Milan, but also in Laibach (today's Ljubljana), Klagenfurt (in today's Austria), Gorizia (in today's Italy, on the border with Slovenia) and Fiume (Rijeka in today's Croatia).[23] All of the gambling venues were attached to the main theatre of the cities.

The jewel in Barbaja's network of gambling businesses was to be Naples, a city to which he found himself inextricably attracted. For Barbaja, the move south was a big step. The French novelist and travel writer Stendhal said that 'in Italy, civilization stops on the river Tiber. Midway across that river you will start seeing the energy and the extroversion of savages.'[24]

Barbaja arrived in Naples by horse-drawn carriage in 1806. The 28-year-old Milanese travelled to the city alone. Naples was not the right place for a wife with young children. The city had just been through a very tumultuous decade.

2

Naples, the only Capital of Italy

Since 1734 the Bourbon dynasty had held sovereignty over the southern Italian Kingdom of Naples, one of the Italian peninsula's many independent states and princedoms. As the leading European royal house, the Bourbons controlled much of 18th-century Europe, with relatives on the thrones of Spain, France, Naples, Sicily and Parma. Just as the Habsburgs were centred on Vienna, the Bourbons were headquartered in Madrid.

The Spanish influence on Naples was significant. Even before the arrival of the Bourbons, Naples spent many centuries under foreign domination, including that of the French house of Anjou, the Spanish Kings of Aragon, and then a series of viceroys appointed by Spain in the 16th century. The most important Spanish viceroy was Don Pedro Alvarez de Toledo (1484–1553). While he was intensely religious and unashamedly partial to the ideology and methods of the Inquisition, he also paved streets, erected many buildings and palaces, and ensured – courtesy of the heavy taxes he imposed on the population – that Naples was one of the most heavily fortified cities in the Spanish empire. He also opened up the principal road from the royal palace into the city – Via Toledo – Naples' most important street.[1]

The Bourbon Charles III became the first King of Naples and Sicily (1735–59), choosing not to fully integrate Naples and Sicily under the Spanish throne, and marking the real beginning of the Neapolitan Bourbon branch. Eager to establish his place in history and strengthen the image and position of Naples and his dynasty, Charles III embarked on a construction spree which included the palaces of Capodimonte, Caserta and Portici, the Biblioteca Nazionale (library) and the opera house, the Teatro San Carlo, named after his own name saint. Personally, Charles III had limited interest in opera, but as opera houses were sprouting all over Europe he understood that his capital needed something comparable. He attached the theatre directly to the royal palace, accessible by an internal tunnel. More interested in antiquity, Charles III also sponsored the early excavations of Herculaneum and Pompeii, the ancient Roman cities outside Naples that were buried by the volcanic eruption of Mount Vesuvius in AD 79.

With the royal court at its centre, the Spanish Bourbons created and encouraged a society that adulated pomp, ceremony and pageantry and was steeped in religiosity, superstition and an exaggerated sense of honour. In 1759, Charles III left Naples for Madrid to ascend the Spanish throne and appointed his third son, Ferdinand, as King of Naples and Sicily.[2] Ferdinand's concurrent ascension to the Neapolitan and Sicilian thrones – at the age of eight – marked the beginning of the reign of the Naples-born Bourbons.

The young King inherited a teeming, vibrant and dynamic city with an enormous, festering underclass of poverty, grime and crime. Before the unification of Italy, the Kingdom of Naples was Italy's largest political state, accounting for a third of its population and about 40 per cent of the territory. Naples was more than twice the size of Rome or Milan, and among European cities smaller only than London or Paris. The city was an overpopulated hodge-podge of about 300,000 Neapolitans, 30,000 provincial immigrants and 7,000 foreigners, with about half the population living in grating poverty and squalor.[3]

The capital city of the kingdom was marked by intransigent social structures: a venal and self-contented nobility and upper class, a virtually absent middle class and an enormous lower class, consisting of economic refugees from the countryside, disenfranchised urban poor with neither profession nor permanent address and the two overpowering establishments of Church and Government. But early 19th-century Naples was also among the leading cities in Europe in terms of culture. It is with good reason that Stendhal was to call Naples 'the only capital of Italy, compared to which the other big cities are merely like a reinforced Lyon'.[4] While Lyon was France's largest city after Paris, it was recognised as a proverbial second-tier city.

Styled as Ferdinand IV of Naples[5] and as Ferdinand III of Sicily,[6] King Ferdinand oversaw some of Naples' most tumultuous years, with the city constantly engulfed in revolution, uprisings, wars, foreign occupation and general chaos. The various interruptions in his reign were caused by his frequent flights from the capital whenever there was sign of trouble.

Ferdinand had never been meant to rule. His father, Charles III, had had limited choice when he was called back to Madrid. His first son was mentally retarded, his second son was destined to assume the Spanish throne from Charles himself, which left to his third son, Ferdinand, the duty of remaining in Naples and assuming sovereignty of the unruly, if attractive, Kingdom of Naples. Charles' daughters were not, of course, considered: their destiny was marriage to a suitable royal household elsewhere in Europe according to political expediency. As Charles had not originally thought that Ferdinand would assume any throne, he had left his education largely in the hands of the Chief Minister, Bernardo Tanucci. However, Tanucci had deliberately neglected the young Ferdinand's education in the skills of monarchy, encouraging him instead to pursue his youthful passions of hunting, sporting and playing with other youths: a distracted and unprepared sovereign would give Tanucci the run of the court.

On coming of age in 1767, Ferdinand's first act was the expulsion of the Jesuits from Naples. This was not in and of itself a particularly noteworthy event, as Jesuits were being expelled that year from Portugal, Parma and the entire Spanish Empire. What would be done with the Jesuits' property, however, would be of greater interest for Naples' subsequent operatic history.

One year into adulthood, in a purely political arrangement, Ferdinand married Archduchess Maria Carolina of Austria, 13th child of Empress Maria Theresa of Austria, then Europe's most influential monarch. Maria Carolina was the sister of Joseph II (the future Emperor of Austria) and of Marie Antoinette. With this union the Neapolitan branch of the Bourbons cemented their pan-European credentials. In honour of the royal marriage in 1768, the Teatro San Carlo underwent a renovation.

Unlike her husband, who was of merely mediocre intelligence, Maria Carolina was educated, clever, ambitious, and probably also quite attractive until smallpox took its toll on her features. She was well read, while Ferdinand despised reading and disapproved of others doing so. Maria Carolina was also politically interested and took on an integral role in the Neapolitan royal household, claiming for herself significant responsibilities and rights, which her husband gladly devolved to her. Initially, she focused on introducing some reforms, which included the revocation of the ban of Freemasons and the modernisation of the Neapolitan navy, a task she assigned to Lord Acton.

Sir John Francis Edward Acton, 6th Baronet (1736 –1811) had been recruited by Maria Carolina for this very task, the success of which he parlayed into a career in Naples. He was soon promoted to commander-in-chief of both the army and the navy of the Kingdom of Naples, subsequently minister of finance, and finally Prime Minister. Lord Acton devised his policies in coordination with the English ambassador to Naples, Sir William Hamilton, with the aim of strengthening the influence of Great Britain in the important Southern Italian kingdom. Acton worked nearly seamlessly with Maria Carolina and had easy access to King Ferdinand.

King Ferdinand's persona did not please many of his foreign visitors. Maria Carolina's brother Joseph remarked on his course manners, darkened and dirty hands (from never wearing gloves while riding or hunting), his 'pig's eyes' and weak lower body. Joseph also remarked on his constantly loud 'piercing voice like a shrill falsetto'. 'Although an ugly Prince', he reported in a letter to Vienna, 'at least he does not stink.'[7] Hunting was his overriding passion and Stendhal remarked that the sovereign 'remains a being utterly devoid of the least semblance of moral consciousness, as indeed it becomes a true huntsman to be.'[8]

Yet, being Naples-born and thoroughly Neapolitanised, the King spoke the Neapolitan dialect fluently and shared many of the attitudes and values of his citizens, especially the lower classes and menial workers, the so-called *lazzaroni*. His very simplicity endeared him to the Neapolitan people and he enjoyed enormous popularity amongst his subjects, earning him the nickname *'Re lazzarone'* (King of the *Lazzaroni*), or *'Re Nasone'* in reference to his protruding and beaming nose. They supported their king and welcomed him back with open arms after his various flights from the city, his tragically wrong decisions and, ultimately, his brutal repression and reprisals.

The first of those flights from the dangers of Naples came in the aftermath of the French Revolution, which caused Maria Carolina's policies to swing from liberal reforms to suppression and expansion of the police surveillance of citizens. With her sister Marie Antoinette under direct threat in Paris, the actions of the French rebels profoundly disturbed Maria Carolina and her husband King Ferdinand. The popular uprising had drawn in thousands, only to be followed by the brutal repression of the Terror. The truly revolutionary social and constitutional changes introduced by the new Republic were seen as a direct challenge to autocratic rule all over Europe.

After some initial interest, Maria Carolina showed little sympathy for the causes of the French Revolution and found its objectives abhorrent. But as in many cities in Europe, the republican ideals found support among Naples' intellectuals, students and journalists as well as from the liberal elements in the army and the aristocracy. And in 1793, the queen's worst fears were confirmed when news of the guillotining of her sister, Marie Antoinette, reached Naples.

Wishing that France 'could be pulverised with all its inhabitants,'[9] Maria Carolina's paranoia about France turned into a 'burning obsession'[10] as the following letter from her demonstrates:

> I should like this infamous nation to be cut to pieces, annihilated, dishon-oured, reduced to nothing for at least fifty years. I hope that divine chas-tisement will fall visibly on France, destroyed by the glorious arms of Austria.[11]

Her fear was to have many fateful consequences during Ferdinand's reign. Maria Carolina, heavily influenced by Lord Acton, encouraged Ferdinand to enter into the First Coalition of 1793. This was the first initiative of European nations to contain the expansion of France and was led by Austria, Prussia, Spain and Great Britain. The Kingdom of Naples sent troops to support the British and Spanish to keep the French harbour city of Toulon from falling into French Republican hands. This campaign proved a disaster. French troops were moving with determination into Italy and occupied the Holy City of Rome, the capital of the Papal States.

Ferdinand, advised again by Maria Carolina and Lord Acton, ordered 50,000 troops to Rome. The campaign scored some initial success as Ferdinand and Acton triumphantly entered Rome in order to defend the Holy Church. But the French soon reassembled and routed the Neapolitan troops, quickly moving towards Naples.

Fearing the advancing French armies and terrorised by images of what the Jacobins had done to their relatives in Paris, the Neapolitan royal family made its bid for safety, boarding the English Admiral Nelson's flagship, the *Vanguard*, in December 1798 in order to escape to Palermo, the capital of Sicily. The ship was commanded by Nelson himself, who ferried King Ferdinand,

Queen Maria Carolina, their three-year-old son, Lady Emma Hamilton (the wife of the English Ambassador to Naples, who had been conducting a well-publicised affair with Nelson) and various other members of the royal entourage. The departure was a scene of chaos, with the royal family frantically removing coffers of gold from the palaces, and the ship setting out to sea into a storm. The royal couple's son did not survive the journey and he was buried upon their arrival in Palermo. Ferdinand wasted no time in quickly setting out to explore the wonderful hunting Sicily offered, however.

While saving himself and his family, and possibly even the Neapolitan Bourbon dynasty, Ferdinand left behind an edict appointing a Vicar General of the kingdom, and commanded the people to fight the French invaders and defend their Church and State, threatening reprisals for those who supported the French. The King's appeal to his supporters unleashed the working classes, the *lazzaroni* and the clerics into a frenzied witch-hunt for traitors, Frenchmen and their supporters. The masses stormed the Teatro San Carlo and the city's arsenals, taking possession of arms and ammunition. When the French armies reached the city they faced a heavily armed but undisciplined and chaotic population. Naples descended into utter chaos and violence. The more disciplined and better equipped French armies soon won the upper hand, not least since King Ferdinand failed to send his promised reinforcements.

With many parts of the city laid to waste and rotting corpses littering the streets, the French proclaimed a ceasefire, installed order and on 21 January 1799 declared the Parthenopean Republic. King Ferdinand was officially no longer in power. The Republic was named after Partenope, the mythological siren who allegedly threw herself into the sea after failing to bewitch Ulysses with her song, and gave the city of Naples its first name.

The new Provisional Government consisted of educated members of the upper classes and intellectuals who had been handpicked by the victorious French General Championnet. It introduced new freedoms for the citizens and a republican constitution (the first of many attempts to introduce a constitution to Naples), provoking immediate enthusiasm from the city's liberal and middle classes. The *lazzaroni*, however, could not forgive the French invaders, and their support for their King and Church remained unshakable. The intellectually tinged Provisional Government was more alien to the *lazzaroni* than the populist King Ferdinand, who shared their language, interests and habits. And their hatred for the French occupying troops grew with the spreading stories of violence, rape and disrespect for the Neapolitan lower classes and their Church. Not least, a new tax imposed by Paris led to a popular backlash and set the stage for a counter-revolution.

A retired Calabrian Cardinal, Fabrizio Ruffo, was the central figure of the Bourbon counter-revolution. He pulled together a 'Christian and Royal Army' and, benefitting from British artillery support, moved towards Naples, his armies committing their own share of atrocities on the way. The French, now showing fatigue with their Neapolitan adventure and needing their troops up north, had withdrawn many of their soldiers by the spring, effectively bringing the five-month-old Parthenopean Republic to a rapid end on 23 June 1799.

The returning royal family were determined to wreak vengeance upon their enemies. Admiral Nelson, treated as part of the inner circle of the Neapolitan royal court, was dispatched from Palermo by the king and queen to do their handiwork, and entered the harbour of Naples with a large fleet, launching a campaign of unmitigated repression and retribution. Jacobins and many members of the city's intellectual and aristocratic elite were mercilessly executed by firing squad, beheaded or hanged, usually in front of a large audience of bloodthirsty *lazzaroni*. Even the leading Neapolitan composer Domenico Cimarosa found himself on the wrong side of the political upheavals and was sentenced to death. He was later pardoned and his sentence commuted to banishment.

In June 1802 Ferdinand finally felt it was safe enough to return to his homeland himself, and dramatically entered Naples on horseback, to an enthusiastic welcome from royalists and *lazzaroni*. He was soon followed by his much weakened wife. Elsewhere, however, Napoleon had been consolidating his power. The Battle of Marengo in June 1800 effectively saw the military defeat of the Austrians, and was followed by France's political victory with a peace treaty within a year.

But both Milan and Naples soon came under renewed threat. Napoleon, whom Maria Carolina had learned to despise, calling him 'Little Despot' or the 'Little Corsican', had been voted First Consul, and in 1804 made himself Emperor of France. No longer willing to tolerate the transgressions of the royal family in Naples, he continued to tighten his grip on the kingdom. Ferdinand and Maria Carolina played a dangerous game with Napoleon, at once agreeing to keep British and Russian ships out of Neapolitan harbours, and then suddenly repudiating the agreement in a public about-face, allowing British and Russian soldiers to enter the kingdom.

By 1805 Napoleon had had enough. Bolstered by his victory over the Russians and Austrians at the Battle of Austerlitz, he issued the Declaration of Schoenbrunn on 27 December 1805, announcing the end of the Bourbon dynasty in Naples. Napoleon correctly pointed out the ineptitude, treachery and instability posed by the Neapolitan Bourbons.

> Shall we trust a fourth time a court without faith, or honour, or intelligence? No! No! The Neapolitan dynasty has ceased to reign, its existence is incompatible with the tranquillity of Europe and the honour of my crown.[12]

While Maria Carolina wrote pleading and ingratiating letters to Napoleon, begging him to let the monarchy survive, King Ferdinand was furiously preparing once again for flight to Palermo. He fled his capital for the second time on 23 January 1806, leaving behind an undefended city, and thousands of *lazzaroni* disappointed by the cowardice of their King. Napoleon made his elder brother, Joseph Bonaparte (Giuseppe Napoleone), King of Naples, launching the *decennio*, a decade of French domination of Naples.

Il Decennio

The relative political peace of the *decennio* made it possible for Barbaja finally to move to Naples. The spectacular beauty of the city must immediately have revealed itself to him, just as it does to the visitor today. The large square dominated by the royal palace is now the Piazza del Plebiscito, the sprawling main square of the city and the best known tourist attraction of Naples, with stunning views over the Mediterranean, Mount Vesuvius and the harbour. Flanking the piazza is the monumental neoclassical basilica of the Church of San Francesco di Paola to one side, with the ochre complex of the royal palace on the other, while to the left of the royal palace, and attached to it, is the Teatro San Carlo. Seemingly an extension of one wing of the palace, the Teatro juts into the Piazza di Trento e Trieste, and opens onto the Via San Carlo. Its dramatic façade has a rusticated ash-grey stone base with five great arches. Marble freezes on the architrave depict mythological scenes (today somewhat eroded by salt and pollution), while the upper floor is dominated by a row of white columns with, above, a pediment. The royal palace, the church and the open view from the Piazza del Plebiscito appear practically untouched by 200 years of development.

The city that greeted the young Domenico was thriving, bustling and noisy. Naples had once again become an essential stop on the young aristocrat's 'Grand Tour', drawing visitors by the score. This educational 'rite of passage' undertaken by European men of means in the 18th and 19th centuries was designed to educate them in classical civilization. Following a standard itinerary, it included cities in France, Switzerland and Italy. Grand Tourists would generally reach Italy via the Alps. The first stops were Genoa or Milan, followed by Venice, then Florence and Rome, with Naples as the last main stop. From Naples visitors would go to Pompeii, Herculaneum and Mount Vesuvius. They looked at the antiquities, visited the sights, museums and libraries, and admired the scenery. In the 1780s the German poet Johann Wolfgang von Goethe wrote of the city's extraordinary physical setting and – somewhat naïvely – reported on the carefree and happy people.

The artistic and especially musical scene of Naples had been developing steadily since the days of Charles III and was a key attraction for these tourists. Travellers would always take in performances at the famous Neapolitan theatres, in addition to enjoying the spectacular setting, mild climate and the historical antiquities. The city boasted four major conservatories and with untold numbers of singers, musicians and composers was considered the pre-eminent centre of music in Europe. The 18th-century philosopher Jean-Jacques Rousseau referred to Naples as the 'capital of the musical world', and urged serious musicians to travel there to improve their skills.

In her *Directions for Travellers on the Continent* of 1828, Mariana Starke describes Naples as the 'most captivating city of Italy'.[13] The streets were packed with entertainers, singers of folk songs, puppeteers performing stories of the great Neapolitan heroes, and readers reciting tales to the passing audience. But there were also beggars and thieves everywhere. Not everyone found the city so enchanting and its economic and social problems were blatant. The traditional English view was that the Neapolitan lower classes were 'cunning, rapacious, profligate and cruel'. The upper classes were considered 'ignorant, licentious and revengeful.'[14] At the same time the common classes were considered 'open-hearted, industrious, charitable and though passionate, so fond of drollery'.[15]

The Neapolitan carnival became an attraction in its own right, and guidebooks warned of higher hotel prices during the season. Carnival was marked by merrymaking and unbridled feasting, with much of the upper-class social life in carnival season circulating around the opera house and the operas performed.[16] At the opera house, the opening of the carnival was the most important day in the year's social season. Stendhal wrote: 'When at last the 26th of December does arrive, I honestly do not believe that the news that Napoleon himself had risen from the dead would cause a single mind to abandon its passionate preoccupation with music.'[17]

At the end of the carnival in Naples, the citizens dressed in costumes and masks and packed into the Via Toledo where they engaged in mock battles. They would throw small pellets of gypsum at one another, some carrying spoons to fling the projectiles further. Some people carried tin shields to protect themselves. There were no actual fights, visitors noted, however.[18]

The German composer and musician Louis Spohr, once considered an equal of Beethoven but now practically forgotten, wrote an autobiography that covers his eight-month trip in 1816 (financed by regular concert performances on the way) to the country 'where the lemon trees bloom',[19] and gives amusing and perceptive insights into the world to which Barbaja had now come. Naples, he wrote, was a deafeningly noisy city, with more and louder people in the street than anywhere else he had been. The streets were busy with carriages and carts, and they tended to drive double-file in their lanes. The contrast between rich and poor shocked Spohr in Naples even more than in Rome:

> More noticeable than in any other city in the world is the contrast between the luxury of the carriages and the elegant clothes of the rich, and the filth and the nakedness of the poorer classes, especially the so-called *lazzaroni*. These one sees right in the middle of the elegant people sitting in the streets and picking off the vermin from their half-naked bodies. I have never witnessed such a disgusting scene![20]

On his return trip to Rome, he and his family were accompanied by another carriage with an Englishman who had 'a machine that threw a picture of the landscape in small scale onto paper'.[21] It was the first camera he had ever seen.

The new French King of Naples, Joseph Bonaparte (reigned 1806–08), was immediately captivated by the city and its spectacular beauty, and he took pains not to wreck the royal pageantry or its cultural infrastructure: he would not treat Naples as a vanquished colony of France. He launched a series of reforms, including the abolition of the feudal rights of the nobility, the elimination of the nobility's separate law courts and their right to impose feudal taxes. Yet he did not address the serious underlying social and economic issues, and he was unable to break the *lazzaroni's* allegiance to the Bourbons. Much to his brother's dissatisfaction, he also failed to raise an efficient home-grown army that could have eliminated the threat of the English from their stronghold in Sicily.

The violent restoration after the Parthenopean Republic of 1800 had left its mark. The theatre scene was nearly dead, and the Teatro San Carlo barely functioned. The theatre had gone through a period of short-lived impresarios including Francesco Porta (1801), Lorenzo d'Amico (who aborted his three-year contract after less than a year), and finally the Società dei Cavalieri, a cooperative of nobles that tried to keep the management of the theatre afloat under the supervision of the Real Deputazione dei Teatri e degli Spettacoli (Royal Deputation of Theatres and Performances), which in turn reported to the Ministry of the Interior. The German writer August von Kotzebue described the difficulties the Teatro San Carlo faced:

> The Teatro San Carlo is normally let out to an impresario. But since the artists are demanding and receiving such incredible fees, and also raise their outrageous demands every year, it is therefore practically impossible for an impresario to satisfy the audience without taking a personal financial loss. Therefore this year nobody could be found to take up the challenge. Several noblemen were forced to cooperate and jointly step up to run the theatre.[22]

It was widely known that the theatres also encountered difficulties in attracting good performers because of the ever-increasing financial demands upon them. Kotzebue wrote with astonishment about this poor state of affairs in his travel journal of 1803:

> The gentlemen Cavaliere, the operators [of the theatre] talk with much optimism … but the audience makes it painfully clear that they are wrong. No theatre is emptier than the beautiful San Carlo, and they try in vain to attract the audience, either through some Illumination, or through a new pas de deux. The reason the boxes remain empty is probably due to the

unbelievable prices, which the Cavaliere have raised this year in order to pay for their mediocre and smug Parisian dancer ...[23]

Kotzebue's impressions of the sub-standard operas at the Teatro San Carlo sum it up: 'The prima donna, Signora Perotti, is an ugly, fat old person, whose voice is not able to let you forget her figure.'[24] He also commented with bewilderment on the habits of the theatre-goers, who 'only attend the theatre to chit chat and whose employees set up makeshift tables at the doors of [the box of] their employers, which they keep open for better ventilation, constantly emerging for refreshments'.[25]

It did not appear an auspicious time for a young impresario to make his name and his fortune. But Barbaja sensed enormous opportunity in this political state of flux and in some of the addictions of the Neapolitans.

3

Feeding Naples' Twin Addictions

(1806–1813)

When Joseph Bonaparte ascended the throne in 1806, he inherited a royal theatre whose coffers had been emptied by the fleeing Bourbons, who had also removed furniture, paintings, the famous mirrors in the boxes of the theatres and seemingly everything of value down to the 'lead in the drainpipes'.[1] One of his first acts therefore was to reinstate the police to help control the press and the theatres. He lavished money on the city and its theatres, including the Teatro San Carlo, continually badgering Napoleon for additional funds until he tried the Emperor's patience. 'Naples is richer than Vienna, and not so exhausted,' responded Napoleon. 'Expect no money from me.'[2]

The King was also aware of the reliable source of income that gambling might provide and he made an early attempt to establish rules and regulations for the gaming industry, aiming to bring it fully under control of the state. Unlike Milan, gambling had been running out of control in Naples for years, a fact that was well noted by many travellers including Kotzebue:

The elegant Neapolitans are the savages of Europe. They eat, drink, sleep and gamble. Their only business is gambling. The nations of Europe are in turmoil; Naples gambles. Pompeii emerges from its grave; they gamble. The earth trembles, the Vesuvius spits flames; they gamble. The magnificent ruins of Paestum, just a few miles from here, needed to be discovered by foreigners; the Neapolitans were busy gambling. The leading dukes and princes of the city are the hosts of gambling. A Prince Ruffano, one of the most respected of the country, runs the leading casino in Naples, and there are twenty additional such venues. All of elegant Naples goes to the gambling halls in the evenings.

… generally no words are exchanged during gambling. One goes gambling like going to a coffee house – worse than a coffee house, since there you can at least get something for your money. Here there are no refreshments, maybe a glass of water which you have ordered ten times from a waiter. A large, poorly decorated hall is the centre of Rouge et Noir. Chairs piled high in the corner are testament to the large numbers of guests that are expected. As soon as the colourful society has entered, it immediately assembles at the tables glistening with gold. These reunions are called Conversations, but dare anyone who actually starts a conversation.

… Women, especially old women with long boney fingers, their protruding eyes fixed on the rouge and noir, are collecting money with green sparkling eyes, or are crying through their missing teeth in lamentation of the disloyal Goddess of Fortune. Even members of the clergy play, as does the nine year old daughter of the Marchese Berio, one of the most enlightened Neapolitan cavaliers. Some claim that Prince Ruffano makes 50,000 ducats on the gaming.[3]

King Joseph decided to rein in the city's addiction and attempted to impose some structure on the literally hundreds of largely unregulated gambling salons around Naples. He realised that a system of organised and legalised gambling concessions would offer much needed tax revenues and help bring some order to the city's nightlife.

Domenico Barbaja's track record of successfully running large-scale gambling enterprises in the north brought him to the attention of the King. So in March 1806, just weeks after Barbaja's arrival in the city, King Joseph granted the loud-mouthed gaming entrepreneur the first large gambling concession for a legalised gambling salon in the city, situated above the Caffé della Meridionale in the centre of town, nearby but not inside the Teatro San Carlo. This loosely defined licence entitled Barbaja legally to offer most commonly pursued games of chance in what was the principal gambling establishment in town. The King simultaneously cracked down on unlicensed gaming dens, forcing gamblers into the few licensed salons.[4]

As operator of the city's largest regulated gambling venue, Barbaja had a unique opportunity to cash in on the enormous appetite for gambling during his first two years in Naples, and he did not hold back. The Neapolitan nobles and the French troops and administrators provided a large, affluent audience that immediately took to large-scale professionally run gambling, especially roulette. Better than anyone in Naples, Barbaja understood the dynamics and economics of gambling and knew how to run profitable roulette tables. He was literally raking in the ducats until his first concession expired in July 1808, just before there was a change in government.

King Joseph's short assignment in Naples was brought to an abrupt end when Napoleon urgently summoned him to take over the throne in Spain, where Napoleon was about to remove another Bourbon king. Encouraging his brother to accept this important assignment, Napoleon wrote: 'At Madrid you are in France; Naples is the end of the world.'[5] Joseph had grown fond of Naples and was far from happy about the decision, but ultimately he ceded to his stronger brother's will. As a replacement for Joseph, Napoleon chose his brother-in-law Joachim Murat.

Joachim Murat was married to Napoleon's youngest sister, Caroline, and was serving as the French commander in Madrid, by all accounts doing a creditable job. He had been hoping eventually to take on the crown of Spain, but there was no arguing with Napoleon. Murat and his wife moved to Naples to assume the throne of the kingdom on 6 September 1808.

Colourful, outspoken and a flamboyant dresser, Murat's style and his glamorous though less than faithful wife appealed to the Neapolitan sense of drama and grandeur. He quickly established himself as a capable ruler and administrator, and went on to become perhaps the most popular and effective ruler in Neapolitan history.

Murat quickly addressed the issue of gambling regulation and, after initially banning it, he soon introduced precise legislation that defined the exact roles and responsibilities of the gambling hall operators and the activities conducted in the salons. He settled the official timetable of the gambling foyers, the ability of operators to run several gambling establishments, what could be offered in terms of entertainment, and who was permitted to attend these foyers. Members of the clergy, for one, were no longer allowed.

In terms of regulating the theatres, Murat signed a decree on 31 January 1809 that put the theatres' administration directly under the Commissione dei Teatri e degli Spettacoli (Commission for Theatres and Performances), reporting to the Ministry of Interior. In March Murat placed the Frenchman Charles de Longchamps in the role of Commissioner, a role usually referred to as Superintendent. Longchamps took a hands-on approach to the theatres and tried to exploit the political value of the stage. He specifically requested, for instance, that the Teatro San Carlo present Mozart's *La Clemenza di Tito* (The Clemency of Titus) in May 1809 because of its theme of sovereign clemency.[6]

Murat and Longchamps also realised that managing the theatres was administratively too challenging and fiscally too onerous for the government and understood that theatres needed other income in order to raise their standards of production. They also appreciated that revenue from the gambling foyers in the theatres could help fund the theatres themselves. Murat therefore allowed gambling once more in the royal theatres.

While legislation had long provided for the possibility of joint administration of gaming and theatres, it had never been done before in Naples.[7] King Joseph, like all his predecessors, had kept the gambling licences and the administration concessions for the theatres completely separate. The best solution, Murat concluded, was to hand over *both* the gambling and the theatre concessions to one person, and the choice was clearly Barbaja.

Barbaja had long understood that gambling and theatre would be better administered together, and had been lobbying both Murat and Longchamps to allow him to do so. He negotiated intensively with Commissioner Longchamps for the concessions of the Neapolitan royal theatres until agreement was reached on 7 July 1809. Charles Longchamps, on behalf of Murat, offered Domenico Barbaja a three-year renewable contract for the management of the two royal theatres (the Teatro San Carlo and the Teatro del Fondo), effectively laying the cornerstone of Barbaja's Neapolitan empire.

The contract was extensive and precisely drafted. On the gambling side, the impresario attained the license for the Teatro San Carlo, but was required to extend the building to accommodate a larger scale *ridotto* (foyer) suitable for gambling. Barbaja was also given several restricted sub-licenses for other gambling venues in Naples. This concession cost Barbaja 100,000 ducats, an enormous amount of money at the time and a clear indication of the profit he had been making in the earlier years.

On the theatre side, the Government imposed a long list of responsibilities for the new impresario. The contract stipulated how many new operas had to be commissioned specifically for the Teatro San Carlo, how many revivals of older operas could be staged, and how many balls could be given. The impresario was expected to put on no fewer than 110 performances annually.

The contract also stipulated the number of principal singers and choristers the royal theatres should employ. The orchestra was to have 78 permanent members (and was one of the first fully professional orchestras in Italy). The Government put nine stage-sets at the impresario's disposal. Barbaja invested in 60 more from his own funds. Ownership of, and responsibility for, the stage machinery, accessories, tools and costumes passed to him.[8] This was no mean task: the costumes alone could constitute a very considerable cost.

As well as being required to meet these conditions himself, Barbaja was also expected to pursue via the courts any members of the ensemble who failed in their obligations, were late for rehearsals or otherwise were in breach of their contracts. The impresario was offered the Government's full support, including if necessary military or police force, in enforcing payment from box-holders or subscribers late in paying their dues.

The contract of 1809 featured a clause that was useful in ensuring the royal theatres were well attended. It prohibited all other small theatres such as the Fenice, San Carlino and Sorte theatres from having performances on evenings when the Teatro San Carlo was staging something new. This rule throttled the competition and ensured sold-out opening nights at the royal theatres.

Finally, the contract spelled out the impresario's responsibility to ensure that the Superintendent, who supervised the censors and authorised productions, would be afforded the final word over the themes, stories and characters featured in the performances.

At the age of 31, Domenico Barbaja was a full impresario, in charge of the largest opera house in Italy, the Teatro San Carlo, as well as the smaller Teatro del Fondo, in addition to the city's principal gambling halls, including the spectacular *ridotto* of the Teatro San Carlo. The only dampener came when Ricci, his erstwhile boss at La Scala, who no doubt regretted having missed out on the enormous success of the roulette tables in Milan, demanded that Barbaja repay the favour and grant him a stake in the tables of the Teatro San Carlo. Barbaja acquiesced to his former boss' request. He did, after all, consider himself a man of honour.

Barbaja's contract had a renewal clause which the Murat government exercised twice, in 1812 (for the season 1812–15) and in 1815 (for the season 1815–18). These years saw a constant 'tug of war'[9] between Barbaja and the authorities on structure, definition, limitation and taxation of the concessions he controlled. Barbaja was always seeking to expand his ways of making money from the gambling concession by adding new games, extending the hours and reducing the concession fees. As the largest single gambling operator in the city, his negotiations were of significant importance to the Government.

Barbaja was unhappy that the theatre absorbed so much of the profits he made on the gambling side, and demanded the concession fee be lowered and the licences expanded, so that he would be able to make a more significant return for his risk, rather than just be the 'cashier of gaming and theatres'.[10] The Government took a narrower view on the gambling, seeing it simply as 'a panacea for resolving the loss-making of theatrical events'.[11] As Barbaja's operations expanded, his demands on the Government grew and he took on a more challenging – even arrogant – tone with it. When push came to shove, Murat tended to side with the impresario. Barbaja's confidence was riding so high that in 1811 he even attempted to take over the lottery of the Kingdom of Naples for six years, though this venture never took off.[12]

While Barbaja was consolidating his hold on Neapolitan gambling and theatre, Murat had other worries. Only a few weeks into his Neapolitan regime, Murat decided to do something about the thorn in his eye that was the island of Capri. Smack in the middle of the Bay of Naples, and therefore close to the Bourbon royalists camping in Palermo, Capri remained resolutely under British control, something that never ceased to rile him.

Murat tried to win more autonomy for his kingdom by issuing a decree on naturalisation, forcing all senior government posts to go to Neapolitans: if a foreign public official chose to take up a post he would have to become a Neapolitan citizen. Although ultimately this legislation was overturned by Napoleon, its instigation was enough to cause many to rethink their position. Many decided to leave Naples, including Longchamps, and in 1812 the Frenchman was replaced as Superintendent by Giovanni Carafa, the Duke of Noja. The Duke of Noja was not new to the job, having previously chaired the Commissione dei Teatri e degli Spettacoli in 1808 for a short time before Longchamps. But he would stay in the Naples post for 14 years, and Barbaja would have a great deal of contact with him.

Barbaja's third contract renewal was dated 8 March 1815 and was nego-tiated between the Duke of Noja and Barbaja. It was the last contract for Barbaja under Murat, and was particularly blunt in its financial demands due to the near bankruptcy of the Murat regime. It stated that Barbaja would have to pay the royal household a 156,000 ducats concession fee (in monthly instalments)[13] as well as 7,000 ducats for the police,[14] and this was in addition to the personal financial security Barbaja was required to provide. As the sums became greater, the French were determined to ensure their main impresario did not do a runner from the city.

The security Barbaja posted included his by now extensive property holdings, his houses on the Via Toledo and in the village of Mergellina on the outskirts of Naples. In addition to these, he pledged the rental income from about half a dozen shops he owned on the Via Toledo, warehouses, houses, flats and numerous *bassi* dwellings he owned around the city.[15] Small, cramped, dark and mostly windowless, *bassi* were the ground-floor inner-city dwellings which usually served as homes for the poorer families in Naples.

Under this new contract, Barbaja obtained additional gambling licenses that were outside the theatres, though the Government tightened the rules on how Barbaja reported the gambling revenues. Barbaja also now gained control over the city's third major theatre, the Teatro dei Fiorentini, where he could build a bench of back-up artists for the two leading houses.[16]

Benefitting from the full artistic and military support of the royal family, he was now in total control of the city's artistic resources. He had manoeuvred himself into the position of one of the most important men in the city, respected by gamblers, opera patrons and certainly large numbers of admiring women. He controlled a spectacular money-machine and was at the helm of the greatest and most glamorous opera house in the world. Domenico must surely have looked at himself in the mirror, his blue eyes glistening with excitement, and muttered to himself, *che coglione avrebbe mai pensato?* Which idiot would ever have imagined this? The world of being a waiter in a coffee-shop must have seemed a lifetime away.

While these years saw Barbaja greatly strengthening his position under French rule, Murat was increasingly at odds with Paris. His naturalisation law and other efforts to give Naples autonomy were rejected by Paris and they also deepened the rift with Napoleon, who at this time was heavily involved in the Russian campaign[17] and had little patience for Murat.

Much of Murat's reign in Naples was defined by the to-ing and fro-ing of negotiations between himself and Napoleon over the freedoms the kingdom would be allowed. Napoleon, burned by Joseph's incipient independent tendencies during his time on the Neapolitan throne, had pre-arranged a constitution for Murat which gave him limited autonomy, settled his line of succession in favour of the Bonaparte family and codified the tributary nature of the

Neapolitan kingdom. Napoleon viewed Naples not only as a good source of soldiers for the many armies around his empire, but also believed – erroneously – that the kingdom was cash-rich and could easily afford his taxes and levies.[18]

The tensions between Napoleon and Murat only affected Barbaja to a limited extent, however: he was not bothered by the political and military goings on in Paris, Capri, Palermo or the Bay of Naples, which had little influence over the artistic goings-on in the city. His concerns were the theatres he had to run, and especially the Teatro San Carlo, which Barbaja had taken over for the first time for the 1809/10 season when it was at its nadir.

The royal theatres

The Teatro San Carlo in Naples is one of the oldest opera houses in Europe. Built by Charles III to replace the dilapidated Teatro di San Bartolomeo, the theatre was inaugurated only eight months after construction began, on 4 November 1737. The theatre is justifiably proud of its long history which dates back 41 years longer than La Scala, and 5 years longer than the Teatro la Fenice in Venice.[19] Today its repertory programme is rather thin compared with other major European opera houses, but it continues unabated.

By far the largest theatre of its time, with nearly 1,400 seats and 184 boxes, seating 2,500 altogether, the splendour of the house with its blue upholstery set off with gold ornamentation, echoing the Bourbon colours, created a sensation and controversy in Europe. The boxes were decorated with monumental wooden carved sconces backed with plate mirrors that reflected the flickering candlelight, casting a lively and elegant glow throughout the theatre.

All guests were impressed by the visual splendour. 'It is not easy to imagine or describe the grandeur and magnificence of this spectacle,'[20] wrote the visiting English composer Charles Burney when he attended a San Carlo gala at the invitation of Lord Hamilton. 'The house was not only doubly illuminated, but amazingly crowded with well-dressed company ...' The candles in the boxes, reflected in the mirrors and multiplied by the lights on stage made 'the splendour too much for the aching sight'.[21] He further commented that the San Carlo 'as a spectacle, surpasses all that poetry or romance have painted: yet with all this, it must be owned that the magnitude of the building, the noise of the audience are such, that neither the voices nor instruments can be heard distinctly'.[22]

Kotzebue visited the San Carlo on the occasion of a performance attended by the royal family and reported that each box had a golden candelabra with three 'torches' (not candles, he wrote), though he was highly critical of the ceiling paintings and the other decoration, which he described as mediocre. 'The curtain's decoration is beyond any criticism and no one can guess what it actually depicts.'[23]

Operas were performed to a fully lit auditorium, which made it easier for patrons to see the many interesting goings-on in the other boxes, unless they had closed the curtains to their own. Each box had a large mirror facing towards the middle of the theatre, so everybody could see the royal family in their box:

> The King's Theatre [the San Carlo], upon the first view, is, perhaps, almost as remarkable an object as any a man sees in his travels: I not only speak from my own feeling, but the declaration of every foreigner here. The amazing extent of the stage, with the prodigious circumference of the boxes, and height of the ceiling, produce a marvellous effect on the mind, for a few moments; but the instant the Opera opens, a spectator laments this fine coup d'oeil [sight]. He immediately perceives this structure does not gratify the ear, how much forever it may the eye. The voices are drowned in this immensity of space, and even the orchestra itself, though a numerous band, lies under a disadvantage: It is true, some of the first singers may be heard, yet, upon the whole, it must be admitted, the house is better contrived to see, than to hear an opera.[24]

As for nearly all visitors on the Grand Tour, the behaviour in the theatre was the utmost surprise for the 18th-century writer Samuel Sharp:

> … it is so much the fashion at Naples, and, indeed, through all Italy, to consider the Opera as a place of rendezvous and visiting, that they do not seem in the least to attend to the musick [sic], but laugh and talk through the whole performance, without any restraint; and it may be imagined, that an assembly of so many hundreds conversing together so loudly, must entirely cover the voices of the singers.[25]

Unsurprisingly, Sharp wrote that 'witty people, therefore, never fail to tell me, the Neapolitans go to see, not to hear an Opera'.[26]

The etiquette at the opera also raised a few observers' eyebrows. Kotzebue wrote with particular spite about the royal family who arbitrarily decided the time of a performance's beginning, and blocked all the carriageways with their extensive security detail. He compared this unfavourably to 'our dear Prussian King', who travelled with limited security and whose 'only escort home were his loving citizens'.[27] Of special annoyance to Kotzebue were the dragoons that blocked the streets leading to the theatre, forcing other theatre-goers to walk home past the King's carriages and to face the indignity of being spattered with the excrement of the royal horses.

Stendhal shared much of Kotzebue's disdain for the unnecessary pomp of the Neapolitan theatre.[28] He resented being stopped by a guard who enjoined him to take off his hat because a member of the royal family was in the audience (he had not noticed), and complained about having to wait in front of the theatre upon exiting, because 'the six horses of some princess block the door and keep you waiting for an hour; and that's when you catch a cold'.[29]

Spohr complained about the severe Spanish etiquette at the San Carlo, which stipulated that the curtain had to be raised as soon as the King entered the royal box. This forced the singers to stand idly and awkwardly on the stage during the entire overture. Likewise, any expression of appreciation or criticism was forbidden, which, however, did not stop the audience from jeering and whistling when they disliked the performance:[30] this seems to be where the Neapolitans drew the line regarding the sovereign's authority. The English singer John Orlando Parry described his experience in 1833:

During its performance His Majesty Ferdinand II & his royal Consort & suite entered in their Private Box on the left hand side of the house, looking at the stage. It is three small Boxes, thrown into one, and hung with blue silk & chandeliers &c. He bowed to the house: when all the officers in the Pit rose, touched their foreheads with the back of their hands 'a la militaire'; but they do not applaud or make the least sign of approbation to the performance 'till the King leaves. – It appears so odd to see the most beautiful dances, scenery, effects &c going off without a hand ! – ... Such splendid dress! Such scenery! Such beautiful Dancing. It was really superb!! – It is in fact one of the most splendid and gaudy things imaginable.[31]

This extraordinary pomp and pageantry was with good reason. The royal theatres served a political function: the splendour and spectacle of the performance reflected the wealth and magnificence of the royal family. The dignified

behaviour of the audience, which turned out in its best garb and fully bejewelled on gala nights, was an expression of the population's deference to the
sovereign, and their acceptance of the social structure he represented and
protected.

The boxes were leased by members of the nobility and upper merchant
classes. Then, as today, the location of the box mattered. While today's opera-
goers are mostly concerned with which box or seat offers the best view of
the stage, 19th-century Neapolitans wanted to be as close as possible to the
royal box, located right in the middle of the second tier. These were therefore
the most coveted and expensive boxes. The third and fourth tiers were less
desirable.[32] Prices dropped, the higher the tier.

The first three rows of seats in the boxes were only sold as season tickets.
The fourth to sixth row box seats were sold for individual performances. Box
seats in the San Carlo cost around 4 ducats a performance, almost as much as
a manual labourer earnt in a month. In those theatres owned by the monarch
(Turin, Naples), 'the question of which families should be allowed to rent a
box (or for that matter to give it up) was an affair of state',[33] and the King was
able to reallocate boxes if tenants fell into arrears with their subscriptions. The
stalls, very different from today, were the cheapest seats in the house, and were
only used by commoners or by the military, who attended the opera in large
numbers. Numbered seats in the stalls were sold for 5 carlini, the equivalent
of half a ducat.[34]

That the theatre was much more than simple entertainment for the upper
and middle classes was also reflected in the structure of the supervisory board,
the Commission for Theatres, as well as in the board's concern about how a
performance, its décor, its story and especially its message might reflect on
the Crown. While in the 17th century, opera storylines mostly had a happy
ending, frequently with a monarch demonstrating clemency by forgiving
anyone who had thought of conspiring against him, the French *decennio* made
the idea of a despotic sovereign more publicly acceptable. Once back in power
after the restoration in 1815, however, the Bourbon government was keen to
re-establish a more respectful vision of the monarchy. It therefore took pains
to police the plots of operas, and stories of regicide such as that of Mary
Stuart or Anne Boleyn were forbidden.

Avoiding any potential damage from the dramatic plots of what was
staged in the theatres was a complex undertaking, and demanded diplomatic
finesse by the lynchpin of the operation, the impresario. The impresario was

accountable to the theatre owner, in Barbaja's case reporting directly to the Superintendent of the Theatres and Performances, who ran the Commission for Theatres. The Superintendent, always a member of the nobility, was assisted by two deputies, also nobles. Their office coordinated all the issues between Barbaja in his role as impresario, the Ministry of Interior, the Ministry of Police and the censors.

To help the Superintendent, opera houses were classified according to the type of work they were permitted to perform, and were expected to adhere to certain guidelines. The San Carlo, for instance, adjacent and connected to the royal palace, was deemed only suitable for operas of a dignified and momentous nature, and it therefore focused on *opera seria;* it was forbidden from showing *semi-seria,*[35] though occasionally the Superintendent would misinterpret a work and an *opera buffa* (comic opera) could sneak into the repertory. As the name suggests, *opera seria* were serious, often tragic operas, followed or interspersed by elaborate ballet performances, and they were usually attended by the upper classes. In contrast, the lighter fare of the *semi-seria* consisted of more frivolous stories of a popular nature, and catered to more pedestrian, simple tastes.

The Superintendent was the impresario's point of liaison with the censors, the critical arbiter over the life and death of a libretto, the very first step in gaining permission for performance of a new opera. The Superintendent and the censors took their roles very seriously as the King would frequently become personally involved with the decisions made by them. Different Neapolitan Bourbon kings took a different line, though all of them shared a vivid interest in opera, most of all King Ferdinand I.

The other royal theatre that Barbaja controlled in conjunction with the Teatro San Carlo was the much smaller Teatro del Fondo di Separazione, commonly known as the Teatro del Fondo. The Teatro del Fondo was euphemistically named after the source of the funds that permitted its construction, the Fondo di Separazione dei Lucri (the Fund for the Separation of Profits). This referred to the proceeds confiscated from the forcibly dissolved Jesuit Order. The expulsion of the Jesuits, as we know, had been King Ferdinand's first executive order as an adult.

Opened in 1779 with an opera by Domenico Cimarosa, the Teatro del Fondo offered a wider range of performances than the San Carlo. It specialised in more popular fare, such as *opera semi-seria* or even *opera buffa. Opera buffa* was aimed at the masses. Produced with lower budgets and less splendour, the tickets were cheaper, with admission costing one-third less than *opera seria*.[36]

The Teatro del Fondo was a focus of politically charged cultural activity during the upheavals of the Parthenopean Republic, and in 1799 was temporarily renamed the 'Patriotic Theatre'. It was inaugurated with a performance in the presence of the victorious French General Championnet. While it languished in the early days of the Bourbons, its fortunes were revived under Barbaja, when the stage put on Italian and French works, as well as *opera semi-seria* and *opera buffa*. In 1870 the theatre was again renamed, this time in honour of the composer Saverio Mercadante, and it continues in operation today as Teatro Mercadante on the Piazza Municipio.

The Teatro Nuovo was the smallest of the main theatres that Barbaja would eventually control and did not benefit from royal patronage. It was restricted to *opera semi-seria* and especially the more frivolous *opera buffa*, as well as the most pedestrian form, the *farsa* (farce). *Opera buffa* had largely been developed in Naples and drew heavily on Neapolitan popular stories. It had greater parts sung or even spoken in Neapolitan dialect without musical accompaniment and was therefore easily accessible to the masses. Being a great *buffo* singer meant being a great actor and entertainer. Singers of *opera seria*, on the other hand, were principally expected to sing well.

Controlling a variety of different theatres, Barbaja was able to put on a wide range of cultural events, catering to differing socio-economic classes and interests. The Teatro del Fondo, for instance, proved a useful testing stage for young opera singers. Many of the greatest sopranos under Barbaja's management had their Neapolitan debuts at this small theatre. It also hosted visiting opera companies and offered a venue for the *accademie* (academies). *Accademie* denoted a wide range of performance art ranging from great contemporary virtuosos to child prodigies, from outright curiosities such as ape men and ventriloquists to gymnasts, conjurers and magicians, or even performers with exceptional mathematical skills. At times, the Teatro del Fondo resembled a 'circus tent rather than an opera house'.[37] Its dance performances were more risqué than those at the San Carlo, as witnessed by John Orlando Parry in 1833: 'The most nonsensical thing I ever beheld! Two or three of the ballet – girls – seemed to have left all their modesty (!) at the great St Carlo! – judging by what we saw at the wings!! (Excuse me!).'[38]

One thing Barbaja obviously did not bother improving was the interior condition of the Teatro del Fondo, as Parry noted:

I must observe, this was the first time I had seen the Fondo Theatre, (which is next in the size to the St Carlo) & in fact belongs to Barbaja. – The same people, dancers, actors, singers perform here – as at St Carlo – and it is opened alternate nights. Of all the horrid, dirty, filthy, mean, poor despicable, shabby places I saw, this beat them!! – It is really dropping to pieces for the want of a bit of paint &c – Dreadfully dark! – the ceiling – with holes knocked thro' it – ! Cobwebs hanging from it &c &c dirt & filth too much to name – However the Neapolitan gentry suffer it to remain in such a shocking state – is a great wonder![39]

Barbaja also opened food and beverage outlets at the theatres which he controlled, including a trattoria, ice-cream stores and coffee-shops where, one can safely assume, he also served the Barbagliata. The unusually varied sources of income from these more or less regulated professions gave Barbaja a relatively easy way of generating tax-free revenue.

Management Barbaja-style

Barbaja quickly set about raising the standard of the royal theatres, changing the style and structure of the management and administration, focusing on the development and engagement of top artistic quality and improving the repertory. Coupling 'his despotism as impresario … with the stolid cynicism of a gambler',[40] he was determined to turn round the fortunes of the legendary theatres.

Barbaja made short shrift of any obligations that he inherited from previous impresarios. He invoked a cancellation clause on the commissioning of a new work by the Neapolitan composer Giovanni Paisiello (1740–1816), considered a living monument to the Neapolitan school of music, because of the high 'levels of Napoleonic compensation the musician had been accustomed to,'[41] and relegated the reprise of one of the composer's operas to the smaller Teatro del Fondo. Rather than solely relying on expensive new operas, Barbaja brought to the San Carlo revivals of works by the composers Gaspare Spontini and Christoph Willibald Gluck, weaning audiences off their expectation of newly composed operas. Keeping a tight watch on the finances, he also recycled productions between the Teatro San Carlo and the Teatro del Fondo, and cut down on expensive scenery and costumes, which had been a mainstay of the productions of the San Carlo's distant glorious past.

At his theatres, Barbaja wooed talented young singers, raised the production quality, and improved the choice of works. Skimpily dressed dancers found their way into many a production: Barbaja made every effort to ensure full houses, even if this meant testing the limits of what was considered decent at the time. Commentators started to complain that the theatres were 'in the hands of an immoral man like Barbaja, who pays the police millions in order to impoverish the nation and who cares little who enters the theatre, and allows the committal of all sorts of debauchery.'[42] But people started flocking to the opera and the financial results spoke for themselves. In just over two years, Barbaja had the funds to refurbish the run-down auditorium and upgrade the exterior of the San Carlo. For this first renovation, he chose to work with Antonio Niccolini, a young Tuscan architect who had been making a name for himself with assignments for the Bourbon royal household.

December 1812 saw the relaunch of the refurbished theatre with the opera *Ecuba*, composed specially for the San Carlo by the promising young Neapolitan composer Nicola Manfroce (1791–1813). It was a stunning success. The opening showcased not only the revived splendour of the Teatro San Carlo, albeit on a tight budget through making use of students from the ballet school attached to the theatre, but also emphasised the continuation of the line of great Neapolitan composers from Giovanni Battista Pergolesi (1710–36) in the early 18th century through to Niccolo Piccini (1728–1800), Domenico Cimarosa (1749–1801), Giovanni Paisiello (1740–1816) and Niccolo Zingarelli (1752–1837) in the later 18th and early 19th centuries. Barbaja had quickly sensed that in order to gain acceptance from the proud Neapolitan audience, he needed to pander to the respect for the Neapolitan school of music: composers who were Naples-born or trained in one of the great conservatories of Naples.

The audience saw Manfroce as the big hope of a resurgence of great Neapolitan composers, and Barbaja was delighted by his tremendous creative and commercial potential. But Manfroce's premature and unexpected death at the age of 22 in July 1813 forced Barbaja quickly to find a replacement. With a lack of suitable new talent in Naples, he would need to go beyond the borders of the Kingdom of the Two Sicilies to find new composers to reinvigorate his opera houses. In this search, he would not be constrained by having to use Neapolitan-born or trained talent.

The influence of the French on cultural trends and tastes during the *decennio* saw the introduction of many new stylistic elements. On the operatic scene, the French style advocated modernisation of composition forms, leading to the disappearance of the more traditional *recitative*. The spoken *recitativo secco* (the dry recitative) common in 18th-century operas and usually accompanied by harpsichord, served to drive the action forward, set up the story for the song about to be sung, or introduce characters, but it also disrupted the singing. They thus became increasingly unpopular to Neapolitan taste.

Perhaps more on the grounds of humanitarianism than style, the French also frowned upon the use of castrati. This practice, whereby young boys were castrated before the age of puberty to retain their juvenile voice, was required to fill the ranks of high voices in the all-male church choirs. The Roman Catholic Church condoned it on the grounds that St Paul had enjoined that women should remain silent in church, forcing men to sing all parts. The Church introduced castrati into the Sistine Chapel Choir as early as the mid-16th century. The use of castrati soon crossed over to secular music, where they enjoyed roaring popularity, especially in the baroque period. The castrati's voices were exceptionally powerful, flexible and capable of remarkable tonal homogeneity. In the absence of the carnal distractions suffered by more normal mortals, the castrati spent most of their waking hours either performing, practising or teaching. As such, their technique was superbly honed.

Today, it is of course hard to imagine what castrati really sounded like, though some recordings exist from 1902 of the last castrato, Alessandro Moreschi, in his waning years.[43] Eerie and odd-sounding, the recording does not come close to the historical descriptions of the castrati's capabilities. Charles Burney described his encounter with the Naples-born Carlo Broschi, known as Farinelli.[44] Farinelli was reportedly able to out-sing a strong trumpeter with the sheer power of his lungs. The emerging notes, that seemed never to want to end, sounded practically supernatural. His unrivalled ability to start gently singing a note in a near whisper, and gradually increase the volume to an unbelievable force, and then just as easily pull back the sound in a slow *diminuendo* without any apparent effort, transfixed the courts at which he sang. It is no wonder that the audience burst out screaming '*Evviva il coltellino!*' (Long live the little knife).

As superstars of the operatic stage with the ability to mesmerise their audience, the castrati commanded hefty fees and lived very comfortable lives. Charles Burney, for one, wrote in awe about the lifestyle and décor of Farinelli's home.[45] This visible affluence often prompted parents to consider castrating a son if he showed vocal promise as a way of ensuring him future prosperity. Gioachino Rossini's parents considered long and hard whether they should castrate their son, who had a fine singing voice, but common sense fortunately prevailed.

While Barbaja was focused on turning around the Neapolitan theatres and adjusting to the stylistic changes brought by the French, the political stage during the last years of the *decennio* was also witnessing tremendous change. Napoleon needed Murat's support in the difficult Russian campaign, and he drafted him into the *Grande Armée* in 1812. Murat would lead an army including 25,000 Neapolitan troops through the battles of Borodino and Moscow. He returned safely to Paris, but the horrors of the disastrous Russian campaign, and the bitter winter retreat that saw hundreds of Napoleon's forces die from starvation, illness or cold, left him more determined than ever to liberate the Neapolitan throne from the shackles of his powerful brother-in-law. He rejoined the Napoleonic cause in 1813, but after the decisive Battle of Leipzig in October, which saw massive losses on the French side, and sensing a turning of the tide against Napoleon, Murat threw his support behind the Austrian Chancellor Klemens von Metternich and sided with the Austro-British coalition. The coalition now invaded France, forcing Napoleon's abdication. Exiled to Elba, Napoleon escaped and made one last attempt to recover his empire, but his 'Hundred Days' ended at Waterloo. The Vienna Congress of 1815 divided the spoils of Europe at the end of the Napoleonic Wars, and though Murat had been given an Austrian guarantee to protect his position on the Neapolitan throne in return for his earlier support, it did not rule in his favour.

Returning to Italy, Murat wagered his future on the Italian nationalists, leading his army into central Italy and issuing the Rimini Declaration, which called for an independent state, and aimed to establish his image as a true patriot and defender of Italian independence. However, the Neapolitan armies were defeated by the Austrians, and in 1815 the allies restored the Bourbon royal family to Naples. Murat led a last-ditch effort with an insurrection in Calabria aimed at retaking Naples. But he was captured, sentenced to death by military tribunal and executed by firing squad in Calabria on 13 October 1815. Murat chose to face his death standing and without blindfold.

With the defeat of Napoleon came the restoration of the pre-Napoleonic order in much of Europe. Louis XVIII was installed on the French throne, the Papal States were returned to the Pope, Northern Italy went to Austria, and Naples once again was restored to the Bourbon monarchy.

The French *decennio* had left Naples much altered: it had a strong penal and legal codex, the Napoleonic code and regulated taxation. Feudalism had been eradicated and the clergy weakened, with an accompanying hope by the people for greater liberalism and modernity. Kingship was no longer seen as a divine right, and the Neapolitans were impressed by the French approach to government and royalty. Stendhal (though exaggerating as usual), had a point when he remarked, 'Thanks to Napoleon's government, Italy leapfrogged over three centuries of development.'[46]

Culturally, too, there had been great change. Thanks to Barbaja, the theatre scene was much improved, wiping out much of the memory of the dark period from 1780 to 1805, and returning the royal theatres to the efficiency and splendour of their more glorious moments. Above all, Barbaja managed to raise the quality of the performances and to shift the focus away from the auditorium and the boxes, back to the stage. He moved the stage from being a sideshow of a social event to the focal point of a cultural venue. The impresario had successfully exploited the dual addictions of the Neapolitans: opera and gambling. The enthusiasm over Joachim Murat's support of the arts and the relative stability the Frenchman brought all came to an end in 1815, as the Austrians and reactionary forces gained the upper hand in Europe. Barbaja would need to reassess his alliances.

4

Rossini and Roulette

(1813–1816)

Barbaja's resolution to bring Gioachino Rossini to Naples, in spite of the volatile and uncertain political times, would prove to be the single most important decision of the impresario's life. With Rossini at his side, Barbaja would lead the Neapolitan theatres to their greatest artistic heights, and fully develop the gambling franchises, enabling him to acquire immense riches.

It is unclear when Barbaja first heard of the Pesaro-born Rossini. In 1810, aged just 18, Rossini had his first success in Bologna, and by 1812 his first operas were being staged in northern Italy. He scored dazzling triumphs with his opera *Pietra del Paragone* (The Touchstone) at La Scala in 1812, the farce *L'Inganno Felice* (The Fortunate Deception) in Venice the same year and *L'Italiana in Algeri* (The Italian Girl in Algiers) in Venice in 1813.

In October 1812, Barbaja wrote to Gaetano Gioja (Italy's leading choreographer as well as an occasional impresario), responding to his description of Rossini's huge success with *Pietra di Paragone*: 'that maestro rosini [sic] you are proposing, I have already engaged all the composers for the Teatro San Carlo as well as for the fiorentini [sic] for this year and for next year, but we can talk about the following year.'[1] Clearly, Barbaja was not yet familiar with Rossini.

It was possibly the success of the opera *Tancredi*, which opened in February 1813 at the Teatro la Fenice in Venice, that changed Barbaja's approach to the young composer. Known principally for his *opere buffe*, *Tancredi* was Rossini's first attempt at an *opera seria*. The aria 'Di tanti palpiti' ('with a beating heart') became a hit and Barbaja must also have heard many reports of the promising new talent from his correspondents, agents or friends in Milan and Venice, possibly even from Carlo Balochino, who was working in Venice from 1813 and remained in contact with Barbaja.

How these operatic arias became popular hits in the absence of recorded music or radio is hard to ascertain. As the population at large did not usually gain access to the opera houses, it is unlikely that they would have heard the tunes directly. Perhaps they overheard them during rehearsals, or possibly from outside the theatre. Singers occasionally gave stand-up performances outside the theatres in the piazza, where many locals would have gathered. Also, popular arias were quickly transcribed – with or without permission – as sheet music for piano or smaller ensembles and were performed in house concerts and less formal events.

Part of the fame of this particular aria of Rossini's, however, comes from a probably apocryphal story surrounding its creation. The contralto chosen for the title role in *Tancredi* was reportedly uncomfortable with the music and asked the composer to make some changes. Rossini returned to his lodgings and when he sat down to rewrite the music at the dinner table, the waiter asked if he was ready for his rice, which would take about four minutes to cook given his preference for it to be served *al dente*. By the time the waiter returned with the cooked rice, the composer had the new version of 'Di tanti palpiti' written. It was dubbed the 'rice aria'. This all sounds a bit far-fetched, and probably is, but the sheer volume of work Rossini produced in a short period of time demonstrates his astounding creative speed.

In any case, by 1813, Barbaja was dead-set on engaging Rossini and travelled the 600 kilometres to Bologna to meet him.[2] By horse-drawn coach this would have taken several uncomfortable and unsafe days. Rossini must have been flattered by this personal attention from Barbaja, who unlike most other impresarios he would have met, was not a fly-by-night speculator on the brink of bankruptcy, but a surprisingly wealthy and self-confident businessman. Barbaja offered Rossini the platform the composer needed to expand his musical horizon: the large stage of the San Carlo as well as smaller stages for a different audience, a stable opera company with high-quality singers, and a certain amount of autonomy. Nevertheless, Rossini took his time negotiating with the impresario, eventually committing to compose two new operas a year for the royal theatres under Barbaja's management. He would also act as Musical Director of the theatres, helping to arrange and make adjustments to other operas that Barbaja wanted to produce at the theatres he controlled, which included the smaller, more intimate Teatro dei Fiorentini.

Barbaja also requested that Rossini assume occasional administrative and managerial duties for his theatres. Clearly, Barbaja intended to keep Rossini very busy: 'If he had been able to,' Rossini would joke later on, 'Barbaja would have also put me in charge of the kitchen.'[3] As principal Musical Director of the Teatro San Carlo, Rossini was paid 12,000 francs (the equivalent of around 2,300 ducats) per year. As importantly, in a totally novel compensation structure, he was given a cut of the takings from the gambling operations in the royal theatres that Barbaja controlled, amounting to at least another 1,000 ducats.[4]

Like all other composers working for Barbaja, Rossini was at liberty to leave Naples occasionally and take on assignments at other opera houses, provided he had the impresario's explicit approval. During these absences, Barbaja would suspend the monthly payments.

Although many details of the terms under which Rossini was employed at the Naples theatres are found in his letters, no complete contract between Rossini and Barbaja has been traced, and accordingly there is much speculation among musicologists and historians as to whether his initial contract was a long-term one or a three-year renewable agreement, and whether his title was Musical Director or something less precise. A letter from Rossini of 9 January reveals that by 1818 Barbaja had asked him to become Musical Director of all his theatres for a period of four years.[5]

He now became Barbaja's business partner in both the opera and gambling concessions of the royal theatres. As a true partner, he even placed a sum of money with Barbaja, which he raised by taking out a loan from a Bologna banker.[6] The exact amount of his financial participation is not stated. But from a little regarded footnote in the correspondence between Rossini and his bankers, we can deduce that Rossini had a financial investment equivalent to about 21 per cent of Barbaja's theatre and gambling operations.[7]

It also seems that Barbaja managed much of Rossini's earnings, even after the composer's departure from Naples.[8] At the very least it is established that Rossini deposited 100,000 francs with Barbaja 'at seven and a half [per cent interest] a year'.[9] The money that Barbaja administered on Rossini's behalf would become a bone of contention between the two some years later. It is worth stressing that this financial arrangement set Rossini apart from any other composer of his day – he was perhaps the first Italian composer to make any serious money.

Within a few years, Rossini's role had further evolved so that he was both close advisor and confidante to Barbaja. When Rossini arrived in Naples in 1815, Barbaja laid out the red carpet for him, offering the composer all facilities and comforts so as to encourage him to deliver his operas on time. In keeping with the habits of the day, Rossini was offered housing and full board during his years in Naples. Barbaja put up the composer in his palazzo at 210 Via Toledo.

The two men soon became close companions. Barbaja even offered to cook for the famously gluttonous Rossini whose real intention in coming to Naples, the composer joked, had been to 'eat macaroni and sip ices'.[10] Barbaja and Rossini certainly shared an enormous appetite for food, wine and also women. Rossini's enthusiasm for women is well documented. Barbaja's escapades were an open secret. The impresario had the run of the house at the Teatro San Carlo, and dancers, singers and musicians, as well as the many socially ambitious young ladies who frequented the theatres and gambling salons, were within his reach. Barbaja did not hold back; there was nobody to stop him. His wife Rosa had remained in Milan with the children and had shown no interest in following her husband to the chaotic south. Barbaja could and did behave like a bachelor.

King Ferdinand returned to his native Naples on 17 June 1815, to a large, though less enthusiastic homecoming crowd than he had faced back in 1802. Dramatic as always, he entered the city on horseback followed by columns of Austrian soldiers, supported by British, Hungarian and Sicilian troops. Cannon were fired from the Fort of St Elmo at the top of the city.

Austrian support, which continued in some form until 1818, would cost the sovereign dearly. Ferdinand was forced to make payments to Austria to compensate the Austrian Chancellor Metternich for his aid in the restoration of the Bourbon regime as well as the posting of troops, putting a constant strain on the resources of the Neapolitan monarchy.[11]

On 19 June 1815, the king triumphantly entered his box at the San Carlo to deafening applause, at a performance which Barbaja stage-managed:

By universal assent such brilliant illumination had never been witnessed, nor such a spectacle, nor a keener, more perfect and more seemly joy. The King was moved to tears ... the theatre resounded with applause and continued cheering for half an hour.[12]

The returning King wisely respected all existing contracts for the running of the theatres, including Barbaja's own, which had recently come up for renewal and which Barbaja had been able to renegotiate successfully.[13] King Ferdinand certainly had no reason to make any changes. He had returned from exile to find that Barbaja was in firm control of the theatre scene, had turned around the fortunes of his beloved opera house and had just attracted one of the most talked about young composers to the city.

King Ferdinand and Barbaja had more in common than was immediately apparent. Neither was a heavyweight intellectual nor was encumbered by an excessive education; neither was terribly interested in politics; both had a roving eye; both preferred speaking in the vernacular, the King in the Neapolitan dialect, Barbaja in Milanese; both had oversized voices, the King a piercing shriek, Barbaja a stentorian roar; and both were entranced by opera. King Ferdinand could get quite carried away while sitting in his royal box, as one contemporary commented: 'He speaks very loud and laughs uproariously; at the theatre, and especially at the Italian opera, he applauds with a ringing voice and beats time vigorously on the ledge of his box.'[14] Just like the hunt, the opera house proved a welcome respite for the King from the annoying tedium of government.

The King's advisors were adamant that he should not unleash vindictive reprisals as he had done after the previous restoration in 1799, but instead play a part in reshaping a more harmonious society based on the legal system that had been established by the French. Initially Ferdinand appeared quite amenable to forgive and forget and move forward, perhaps helped by the fact that his obdurate and vindictive wife Maria Carolina had died the previous year, on 10 September 1814.[15] The King ordered all theatres to close for a month and imposed a six-month mourning period, which he himself broke when he married his mistress, Lucia Migliaccio, the Princess of Partanna, less than three months after Maria Carolina's death.

The King quickly reverted to form, letting his Chief of Police, Prince Canosa, unleash a wave of terror, seeking retribution from all those seen as having been disloyal to the royalists – but Barbaja was safe. King Ferdinand also now promulgated the union of the two Crowns of Sicily and Naples, by taking as his title 'Ferdinand I of the Kingdom of the Two Sicilies'.[16] This was not only in accordance with the decisions of the Congress of Vienna, but also because it offered Ferdinand the opportunity to break with an often difficult past history and re-launch his territories as a glorious new kingdom.

Barbaja's choice of Rossini was as prescient as it was courageous, both politically and artistically. Rossini's arrival in Naples came at the same time as the return of the Bourbon sovereign and the demise of Murat, who had been a strong backer of Barbaja and his management. Before his departure from Bologna for Naples, Rossini had sailed close to the political wind, attracting some unwanted attention which now caused him some concern in view of the turn of political events. He had composed a hymn to independence, which was performed in Bologna in the presence of Murat in 1815. But the experiment with French revolutionary ideals was short-lived in Bologna, and Rossini found himself politically wrong-footed. He reset the hymn to new lyrics praising the Austrian troops, who were now once more in control: he needed to ensure that he would be given the necessary papers to travel in Austrian-controlled areas.

Keeping on the right side of the current political regime was not easy given the frequent changes, and nobody was sure of the reception Rossini would receive, least of all the composer himself. Rossini was also entering a formidable musical arena. The Teatro San Carlo was again considered one of the great stages of Europe, and Barbaja had put together one of the best orchestras in the country. The city also had an extremely demanding audience that had been spoiled by the masterpieces put on by popular composers such as Giovanni Simone Mayr, Domenico Cimarosa and Giovanni Paisiello.

The local newspaper *Giornale delle due Sicilie* (Journal of the Two Sicilies) wrote in September 1815 that 'at this moment there is a lot of movement in our theatre world'. That 'Signor Rubini[17] is due to sing at the Teatro dei Fiorentini', and a 'so-called Signor Rossini, maestro di cappella [musical director], is said to be coming to put on Elisabetta Queen of England on the very same stage of the Teatro San Carlo, where the melodious tunes of the operas *Medea* and of *Cora* of the respected Sign. Mayr are still resounding'. This deliberate slap in Rossini's face was not so much about his relative lack of fame or his young age of 23. What bothered the journalist was that Rossini was not Neapolitan, and had no link to the Neapolitan school of music. Up until then, with the notorious exception of the German-born Mayr (who was considered nearly an honorary Neapolitan because of his popularity in the city), the Neapolitan stage had been dominated by Neapolitan-born or -bred talent: and Rossini was neither.

At the same time, the legendary Neapolitan composer Nicola Zingarelli, Director of the Naples Conservatory, banned his students from studying Rossini's music, considering it unworthy of their standards. He was equally keen to stave off a future competitor. The conservative and deeply religious Zingarelli, it should be noted, was himself not without his critics. The German musician Louis Spohr complained that under his guidance the Conservatory of Naples fell into a terrible decline. In his memoirs, he describes Zingarelli as pompous and ignorant:

> He has very confused ideas of the achievements of our German composers. During my visit to Zingarelli he spoke extensively and with much admiration of Haydn and other composers, without even as much as mentioning Mozart. So I directed the discussion to Mozart, whereupon Zingarelli said: 'Oh yes, that one also had some talent, but he did not live long enough to fully develop it. Had he lived another ten years, he would have been able to write something decent.[18]

Spohr finished the sentence with the only illustration in his book:

Two stars are born

Rossini's first Neapolitan opera, *Elisabetta*, based on the story of England's Elizabeth I, was to premiere at the Teatro San Carlo on 4 October 1815. Barbaja gave full support to his new composer in his first Neapolitan production, assembling a top-notch cast including the tenor Manuel García, his compatriot and rising star the soprano Isabella Colbran, and the Bergamasc tenor Andrea Nozzari. There was much correspondence back and forth about the finer points of the leading singers' contracts in the weeks running up to the premiere, especially with regard to the frequent absences and tardiness of Manuel García. This included the threat of legal action on all sides, including from Barbaja and the Superintendent, the Duke of Noja.

The opera's subject appealed to the recently restored Bourbon monarchy as it celebrated royalty (albeit the English one) and highlighted royal clemency. The story focuses on the queen, who learns that the man she covets, the Earl of Leicester, has secretly married a young commoner. When the queen fails in her attempts to have Leicester give up his wife, she throws him in jail and sentences the earl to death. In the end the queen unravels the plots of the intriguing courtiers and pardons Leicester.

The chosen librettist, Giovanni Schmidt, was a poet employed by the royal theatres and therefore an uncontroversial choice for the Bourbon government. He was, however, notoriously morose, and Rossini begged Barbaja to keep the depressing librettist away from him.[19] Rossini put tremendous thought into this opera and clearly set out to impress. The score, with its grandiose arrangement and use of extensive and large-scale orchestration, proved a turning-point in his musical direction, since in it he redefined the structure of the *opera seria* and developed a new artistic and musical vocabulary.

Elisabetta was to prove a tremendous influence on the look and sound of opera for the next generation of composers. It introduced the use of musical patterns repeated throughout the work to allude to a theme or dramatic context, laying down a lot of the groundwork for the structure and techniques of operas of the late 19th century, including the thematic motifs associated with the German composer Richard Wagner (his 'Leitmotiv'). The opera also did away with the *recitativo secco*, thus making it much more like the through-composed operas of composers such as Giuseppe Verdi or Giacomo Puccini, rather than the previously more familiar ones of Mozart, Gluck or Paisiello.

Rossini also perfected one of his trademark melodic signatures, the *crescendo*. The classic Rossini *crescendo*, often positioned at the end of an aria and regularly adopted in his overtures, features a gradual increase in volume with a repeating phrase structure and the gradual addition of new instruments. The build-up to a climactic *crescendo* is one of the composer's key identifiers, and still today is one of the reasons for the addictiveness of much of his music.

Of further historical note was Rossini's scoring of vocal embellishment. Traditionally, singers provided their own vocal ornamentation, adding in trills, scales and other elements to demonstrate their vocal agility. *Elisabetta* was one of the first operas where these were written into the score. While stripping the singers of their autonomy in giving *fiorituri*,[20] Rossini helped create a more consistent and probably more pleasant performance, if one is to believe accounts of some of the vocal aberrations that some singers committed. The vocal difficulties incorporated into the score became a testament to the ability of the original singers, especially Colbran, creating what some writers refer to as a 'biography of voices'. Rossini tailored the score for the voices that Barbaja had put at his disposal. In particular, he calibrated the opera to suit Isabella Colbran perfectly, well aware that in order to gain his paymaster's favour he must please the impresario's favourite singer as she 'held Barbaja in the hollow of her hand'.[21]

The choice of Colbran for the lead of *Elisabetta* turned out to be a momentous one. In 1810, needing to recruit a new prima donna, Barbaja had hired the 'Queen of La Scala', Teresa Belloc, but she had only stayed for one season.[22] Barbaja decided to replace her with a home-grown talent, the young Spaniard Isabella Colbran. Barbaja knew both Isabella and her father, a musician who was frequently in Naples, and had first heard her giving private recitals in the city. Impressed by the young singer, he had recruited her to the Teatro San Carlo, where her first performance was on 15 August 1811.[23] Although her early performances at the San Carlo met with some criticism from competitors and audiences alike, after a short absence in 1812, Colbran returned to command the stage in 1813 as the uncontested leading soprano of the Teatro San Carlo, a position she maintained until 1822, one of the longest periods at the top for a prima donna of the time.[24] Her contract from 1817, a pre-printed document where only name, title and special conditions were inserted by hand, clearly stipulates Colbran's role as the *'prima donna assoluta'*.[25] In Barbaja's time, this was a contractual and functional title, designating her role as the 'absolute principal singer' of the company, with no competition among the opera house's company (today, it is largely an honorific).

Colbran's contract, like that of every other singer under Barbaja's management, prohibited her from making use of her talents in any other theatre, concert or performance, either public or private, without the impresario's written consent.[26] While rigidly enforcing this rule, Barbaja could be relaxed about performances elsewhere when properly asked, and he certainly made use of his own contractual right to loan singers to other houses or impresarios. Colbran's contract also gave her adequate housing, and she was billeted at Barbaja's Palazzo at 210 Via Toledo, as well as at Mergellina, Barbaja's seaside villa.

During the first few years of her employ by Barbaja, Colbran's fame spread and she emerged as the greatest opera singer in Europe. Her voice was reputed to be nothing short of magical, possessing an unrivalled agility and lightness, and she was able to tackle the most challenging *fiorituri*, as well as effortlessly slide up and down chromatic scales. She had an extraordinary range reaching nearly three octaves and for the quality of her trills knew no rival; except for one – Crescentini, the great castrato.[27] Stendhal reported that 'it is impossible, without having watched Signora Colbran ... to understand the furore which she inspired in Naples, and the mad things which were done in her name at the time'.[28]

She was by all accounts an artist of exceptional beauty with a strong dramatic presence. One of the greatest admirers of her art was none other than King Ferdinand himself. The English impresario John Ebers wrote:

> Madame Colbran was a wonderful favourite with the King of Naples ... [Colbran's] name was a party word and the royalists shewed their attachment to the monarch, by applauding the singer. A gentleman from this country went to the Theatre with a friend, a Neapolitan. On coming away, the Englishman asked his friend whether he liked Madame Colbran: 'Like her! I am a royalist,' was the reply.[29]

Barbaja and most of the audience were smitten. Given both her growing status as a prima donna and the physical proximity in which the impresario and his leading lady found themselves, it is easy to understand how it was more than her voice that soon caught Barbaja's attention. Colbran quickly became his favourite singer, and a romance soon ensued that would last well over seven years. The prima donna became the impresario's mistress as well as his biggest marquee star: no major opera would be premiered at the San Carlo without Colbran, no role would be written without Colbran's voice in mind.

Barbaja's attraction to Colbran was part social and part sensual, probably not unlike the more recent affair between the Greek shipping billionaire Aristotle Onassis and Maria Callas. Colbran was the talk of the town in Naples, the leading prima donna in Italy, and eventually also the muse to the greatest composer of her time. In contrast to the many young ingénues and ballerinas Barbaja normally mixed with at the opera house, Colbran was to him much more akin to a peer.

A slim, very tall woman, with aquiline features and long, gracious limbs, Colbran clearly also appealed to the impresario's senses. Having a keen eye for the ballerinas, Barbaja is unlikely to have been as attracted to the curvaceous type.

While 19th-century ideals of beauty were very different from today, with admiration for the corpulent, the curvaceous and the voluptuous far more common, Barbaja was not alone in his predilection. King Ferdinand, too, was known to admire the dancers and singers,[30] and he had a particular weakness for women with long and well-shaped arms, especially when they were adorned with fitted elbow-length white gloves.[31]

Colbran clearly enchanted the impresario. Stendhal suggests that he was actually 'under the thumb of his mistress', and other novelists imply that she had the gruff impresario wrapped around her little finger and that he showered her with valuable gifts. Without doubt, Barbaja was Colbran's biggest and most vocal supporter. He was known to scream vehemently 'brava, brava' at the end of her arias, and if the audience expressed its disapproval of her performance, he would just as vociferously dress down the detractors from his box, his voice bellowing through the theatre.[32]

While she took artistic advice from Barbaja, and later – to an even greater extent – from Rossini, Colbran was a woman of independent means. She was among the best paid prima donnas of her time and, after the death of her father in 1820, she became a wealthy woman. She inherited a country estate in Castenaso outside Bologna, which her father had acquired at a discount during the land price depression brought on by the Napoleonic Wars, as well as land in Sicily and a substantial amount of cash. Barbaja and Colbran were a 'power couple' on the social circuit in Naples, the likes of which the city had rarely seen. The fact that they were not married was of little consequence to Neapolitan society.

The opening night of *Elisabetta* was accompanied by considerable pomp and pageantry, since this was a double premiere (for the composer in Naples and his new opera), the opening night of the 1815/16 season, and the name day of Prince Francis, eldest son of Ferdinand I. The Teatro San Carlo was completely sold out and, with the royal family in attendance, the audience turned out in their finest clothes and jewellery.

The evening started slowly, with much hostility and sceptical anticipation towards this 'northern' composer. But as soon as Colbran began singing her opening aria, the audience was seduced, breaking into thunderous applause at the end of the first act. At the end of the opera, the young Rossini was fêted on stage.

Isabella Colbran was a natural for the title role. Her tall stature and chiselled, classical features gave her a regal bearing and, with a natural command of the stage, she made Elisabetta her own. 'In all the huge arena of the San Carlo, there can scarcely have been a man who had not, at that moment, thought death an insignificant price to pay for a glance from so beautiful a queen' commented Stendhal,[33] while a Spanish newspaper reported that the audience exclaimed, 'you are the real queen'. This was a politically tricky statement, as the King had not only just returned from exile, but was also accompanied to the performance by his second wife, the Princess of Partanna.

Perhaps it was the contrast with her offstage appearance that made Colbran such an appealing opera singer and actress. She must have been an unusually strong example of the transformative power of an accomplished operatic voice. Stendhal described how, 'Offstage, she possessed about as much dignity as the average milliner's assistant; but the moment she stepped on the boards ... she inspired involuntary respect' and 'radiated majesty'.[34]

On the back of the overnight sensation of *Elisabetta*, the sceptically received northerner soon became known as the 'Swan of Pesaro'. Rossini's fresh style put pressure on all Italian composers and theatres, having introduced new musical trends and set a new standard for performances.[35] King Ferdinand, waxing lyrical about the composer, immediately and personally rescinded Zingarelli's ban on Rossini's music at his city's conservatories.

Rossini went on to compose ten more operas specifically for Colbran's voice between 1815 and 1823 and she created the title role in many of the operas that were to become the cornerstone of the composer's success. At her peak, she so dominated the Neapolitan stage that one could be forgiven for thinking that only the sopranos mattered at this time.

Collecting singers

While Barbaja controlled costs with an iron fist, he was committed to offering standards of production higher than ever before, and this included the stage sets and design. He recruited Antonio Niccolini, the Tuscan architect and engineer who had worked with him on the San Carlo's refurbishment several years earlier, contracting him in 1813 to create stage sets of 'maximum luxury'.[36] Barbaja was perhaps the first impresario to use prominent architects and artists for the opera stage, over a century before the Metropolitan Opera House in New York was hiring artists such as Marc Chagall to design its stage sets.

But far more important than the stage design, productions, and even the compositions themselves were the singers. Barbaja knew well that star singers draw a bigger audience, and he was willing to pay big money to attract the best voices. But he also realised that it would be financially more rewarding if he groomed his own troupe of high-quality singers.

While he was unable to differentiate style, pitch or harmonies, his instinct was spot on when it came to the quality of voices, and he could quickly sniff out a potentially successful singer. Barbaja had such a keen sense for new talent that the latter-day impresario Gino Monaldi (1847–1932) likened it to the 'sense of a fox who smells the odour of chicken in the air and cannot stop himself from seizing upon it and devouring it'.[37] That Barbaja was considered an authority on operatic voices and their market value is shown by the French novelist Honoré de Balzac's (1799–1850) reference to him in his novella *The Girl with the Golden Eyes*. Balzac describes one of the protagonists as owning 'a voice which would have been worth fifty thousand francs a season to Barbaja'. Written in 1833 without any explanation of who Barbaja was, the passage demonstrates not only Barbaja's reputation as a talent-spotter, but that his name was well known throughout Europe.

Correctly managing his stable of singers – his '*cartello*' – took finesse and skill. During the Colbran years, there could be no other major soprano or mezzo-soprano at the Teatro San Carlo. Barbaja reported with satisfaction to the Duke of Noja: 'With Colbran we have acquired an extremely useful linchpin of the [royal] theatres, and her enormous talent will compensate any of our sacrifices.'[38]

Consequently, Barbaja relegated the talented and popular soprano Margherita Chabrand, a rival of Colbran's, to the Teatro dei Fiorentini, and made sure he kept her appearances at the San Carlo to a minimum. He also pushed Chabrand to accept engagements at other theatres, often against her wishes, to ensure Colbran did not need to share the limelight in Naples.[39] Barbaja had a freer hand with the tenors, and he recruited four promising ones: Giovanni Battista Rubini, Andrea Nozzari, Domenico Donzelli and Giovanni David. These tenors would weave through Barbaja's entire professional life and heavily influence composition and singing style.

But the very first tenor to have a real impact was Manuel García, the Spanish tenor who featured in *Elisabetta*, and who had been signed by Barbaja and debuted at the Teatro San Carlo on 20 January 1812.

Manuel García I[40] is often referred to as the 'father of modern singing'.

Born in Seville in 1775, he first moved to Madrid, and then Paris, until he settled in Naples, where Murat made him lead tenor of his private chapel choir. In Naples, García studied under the legendary teacher and composer Nicola Porpora.[41] Later, García himself would become the teacher of many of the next generation of the finest operatic singers.[42] A tough taskmaster known for his furious temper, he drove many of his students to despair. García had three children, all of whom achieved degrees of operatic celebrity, the most famous being Maria Malibran, who would be a key member of Barbaja's stable in the post-Colbran years. In his later years García and his troupe travelled to the United States and Mexico, where he was one of the first to introduce Italian-style opera to the New World.

Of the generation after García, the first of the great Barbaja tenors was Giovanni Battista Rubini, later known as the 'King of the Tenors'. Like the other three contemporary leading tenors, Rubini was from Bergamo in the north. He had a difficult start and left Bergamo at a young age to try his luck in Milan and Venice, but found no success until he moved to Naples where he came to Barbaja's attention. Barbaja recognised the prodigious talent of the 22-year-old singer and agreed to put him on his roster, though only at reduced rates. Rubini agreed, knowing what Barbaja could do for him, but he also made it clear he would remember the harsh deal once he was famous.

Barbaja signed on the tenor in 1816 and soon sent him to Rome, where Rubini had his first big success in Rossini's *La Gazza Ladra* (The Thieving Magpie) in 1817. His international breakthrough came only when he performed at the Théâtre-Italien in Paris in 1825, where he starred in a large selection of Rossini's operas. Barbaja, who still had him under contract, pulled back the now famous singer after six months in Paris. He could not risk losing him to a competing impresario.

Rubini on stage must have been quite a revelation. Short, stout, unattractive and with a face scarred by pock marks, he was notoriously awkward and clumsy as an actor. But the minute he opened his mouth, strong, melodious sounds emerged, transforming the singer and enthralling the audience. Rubini would eventually fall out with Barbaja, however. He finally severed his contract with him in 1830, then went on to enjoy an international singing career in London and Paris.

Rubini was one of the very first superstar tenors, and probably the first to raise the importance of the tenor in Italian opera to the level of the prima donna, a status previously only enjoyed by the *castrati*. Very unusually for his profession, he pulled back at the first sign of vocal decline, though he did then go on a concert tour with Franz Liszt, before fully retiring a very rich man. He chose not to become a professional teacher as so many of his peers did; he once said, 'Monsieur, le chant ne s'enseigne pas'.[43]

Realising that his singers were key to his success, Barbaja took care in managing them. His approach is perhaps best summarised by Dumas (père): 'He is at once a skilful exploiter and an indulgent father, an absolute teacher and a loyal friend, an enlightened guide and an incorruptible judge.'[44] But Dumas did not mince his words. He also described Barbaja as someone with a great heart but with 'brusque manners, with the most violent character … it is impossible to translate into any language the dictionary of insults and curses he used with his artists.'[45]

Indeed, Barbaja's approach to his singers was much like that towards any product he represented: efficient, profit-oriented and, with the exception of Colbran, emotionally uninvolved, cold and calculating. Over the long duration of their contracts, his attitude was one almost of ownership of the singers. He saw them as assets he could move around at will, and referred to them as 'my dogs'.[46] Barbaja regarded the relationship with his singers as one in which they were to be subservient and owed him obedience, while he would provide them with a livelihood, guidance and career management.

But the singers sometimes refused to cooperate, and provided a good many challenges to his legal and moral authority. In 1812 Manuel García showed up drunk for a performance and was unable to perform the full opera. As it was a *prima* (premiere) and was attended by the King, his antics occasioned the intervention of the police. García had another argument with Barbaja after his refusal to attend rehearsals for Rossini's first Neapolitan opera, even though the composer had written the part specifically for García's voice. This was principally his revenge for Barbaja blocking the production of an opera García had himself written.[47] A year later García had a public spat with Isabella Colbran during a concert performance at the Teatro del Fondo, hurling vulgarities and insulting the singer. Again, the police were called in.[48]

Indeed, litigation and police intervention seems to have been almost standard procedure at the time. It also to some extent explains why the impresario was by contract obliged to pay the police force a monthly stipend, as Dumas (père) describes:

The impresario did not only have the law on his side, he also had the force.

He has at his command a detachment of cavalry and a platoon of infantry, a police commissioner and police captain on the spot, henchmen, the carabinieri, and the gendarmes. He can immediately send to prison any singer who threatens to become capricious or members of the audience who dare to whistle for no reason.[49]

Barbaja certainly did not hesitate to use the police. In 1822, the impresario had a minor singer arrested for refusing to sing in the chorus.[50]

But the wrath of the authorities could be dispensed in both directions. When Donizetti's opera *Adelia* premiered in Rome in 1841, the over-zealous impresario Jacovacci over-sold the theatre seats. Throngs of dissatisfied ticket-holders unable to enter caused a riot, forcing the performance to be stopped, and the authorities stepped in and arrested Jacovacci, who was forced to spend the night in jail.[51] Likewise, the impresario of the opera at Palermo,[52] a colleague and competitor of Barbaja, was arrested and thrown into jail for a day in 1825 after the Superintendent received audience complaints about the poor quality of the performance during Donizetti's sojourn. Indeed, the condition of the orchestra was reportedly quite shocking. The second bass at the opera also had an argument with Donizetti during rehearsals and insulted the visiting composer. When he refused to apologise for the slight, he too was taken away for a day in jail.[53]

For many years, it seems that all Barbaja was doing was either defending or initiating law suits against singers, dancers, publishers, copyists or composers. He furiously argued, fought, debated and sued. It is no surprise that Dumas saw him as regent, writing that 'the reign of Domenico Barbaja 1st was complete and absolute for 40 years'.[54] Stendhal was a bit more to the point: '… in Naples, the rule is one of unmitigated despotism – a despotism based upon pure favouritism, which, in the matter of Signor Barbaja and the Teatro San Carlo, was to be seen in all the effulgent glory of its unredeemed absurdity.'[55]

Collecting properties and art

With his successes at the theatres, and the returns from his gambling concessions, Barbaja was flush with cash, and the years of his first *appalto* awakened in him a taste for collecting; not just singers, but also houses and art. Barbaja's principal residence, his palazzo at 210 Via Toledo, had been his city home from his earliest days in Naples. It was also one of the properties he put up as security for his first *appalto* with the Government. The five-storey building, sub-divided into apartments, was just a few minutes' walk from the San Carlo. Barbaja lived on the second floor. The apartments (other than one reserved for gambling) were let commercially, or used to accommodate visiting artists for whom lodging was part of their contracts. He often held dinners in the apartment's generous reception areas, hosting the visiting artists during their stay. He also used the palazzo for business meetings. The English singer John Orlando Parry called on him in 1834:

> We were up by 8 and at a ¼ 9 were in the anti-room at Barbaja Palace waiting to see the 'great lion'! We stood trembling as we heard him roaring out his vengeance on some unfortunate scene shifter or other, fearing he would deny me [the singer Luigi] Lablache's licence, and everything else! At last the door burst open and Barbaja stood before us! 'Che volete, giovani?' (what do you want young man [sic]) was the first expression we heard from his lips. My friend Negri then went forward and said in a very humble tone of voice 'if your Excellency would allow Signore Lablache to sing at a little concert I was giving on Monday evening next.' The moment he heard this he shouted out in his shrill voice 'don't you know Malibran leaves on Monday and shan't I want Lablache & c. to play every night to supply the deficiency eh?' (pinch of snuff). After this rencontre we stood for some while perfectly silent until Barbaja had finished looking over a play bill. Presently he turned round and, after taking another pinch of snuff, said 'where's this thing to be eh?' 'At the grand Trattoria House in Strada Nuovo, Signore.' 'You'll have all Inglese [Englishmen] there I suppose, eh?' Upon this he turned, looked at another bill, when suddenly a smile darted over his countenance. He took off his green velvet cap, scratched his head, took an extra extraordinary pinch of snuff (which fell and almost covered his waist coat) then placing his hands behind him came slowly towards us – we standing like two culprits not knowing what to do or say. After looking at me for some while he said 'young man, I'll tell you what I'll do for you! you know my Casina or Villa at Possilipo [sic]?' Yes, Sigr. 'Well, you shall come with me today to see it. If you like it you shall give me your concert there, you shall have the whole house at your disposal – you shall have the gardens and the Theatre open – you shall have all the Opera singers (!) you shall have the bills and tickets arranged for you. You shall have the police permission obtained and you

shall not have a farthing of expense!!' Was the like ever heard – we thought he was joking. We knew not what to make of it. I was going to make an observation about troubling him when he burst out again 'But why in the devil did you not come to me before! Eh Ha!' (pinch of snuff) then almost in the same breath he said 'come here at twelve and I'll take you in my carriage there. Avete Capito. Good morning! Addio!' (At the same moment turning round to a poor man who was waiting with some papers: 'Now sir, what do you want staring there!')[56]

Much more than his city palazzo, Barbaja conceived his seaside home in Posillipo as somewhere for his personal pleasure, as well as a place to entertain and impress visitors. While strictly speaking in Mergellina, a sleepy and picturesque fishing village a few kilometres outside Naples, most of the literature refers to the legendary villa as being in the chic suburb of Posillipo. In the early 19th century, however, Posillipo was still very rural, with terraced vineyards, the wine from which – along with that of Capri and Ischia – was thought to be 'palatable and wholesome'.[57] Posillipo is derived from the Greek Pausilypon meaning 'respite from worry', and the impresario's villa seems to have been exactly that.

Barbaja commissioned Antonio Niccolini to draw up some designs for the villa. Niccolini's designs featured a seigniorial palace of relative rigid, boxy, neoclassical forms. Ignoring his architect's suggestions, Barbaja chose to follow his own designs, opting for something more multi-functional, but also much showier, which would impress his guests and provide a monument to his extraordinary wealth. He also wanted something that had the potential to bring in further revenue.[58]

Barbaja had recognised the tremendous tourism potential of the seaside village and its wonderful location. Naples had a significant number of long-term visitors, many of them on the Grand Tour, and the prices for hotels and lavish apartments were the highest in Italy.[59] He consequently split the building into several apartments, some of which he intended to let as short-term luxury flats, mostly in the winter when he spent less time in Mergellina.

The villa overlooked the beach and the small fishermen's huts, and beyond these had a picture-perfect view over the Bay of Naples and Mount Vesuvius. The composer Francesco Morlacchi, who visited the villa in 1817, said that it had 'the most beautiful view in the world'.[60] Indeed, the rental apartments would prove quite popular, the librettist and sometime essayist Emmanuele

Bidera writing that 'nothing is more enchanting than a summer dinner on a loggia of the Villa Barbaja'.[61] A dinner party at the Villa became a veritable marketing event for prospective tenants, and Barbaja had brochures printed (even in French) to promote the rental of the luxury apartments.

Adjoining the right side of the Church of Santa Maria del Parto, the house had entrances on both the lower street level near the beach, as well as on the much higher road up the hill. This was common in many seaside villas outside Naples, which had both an upper-level street entrance and one at shore level, the latter sometimes combined with access to a private boat berth. Barbaja chose to site his villa right on the seaside, rather than up in the hills, where some of his stars, such as the singer Luigi Lablache, would build their villas.

The villa had running water, an unusual feature at that time. The lower floor had six rooms, the dining-rooms comfortably able to accommodate 60 guests. This lowest level opened out onto the garden with at least one date tree, which gave the villa its name, 'Villa Dattero' (Villa of the Date Tree).[62] There were also grottoes, a garden fountain, and a fully equipped theatre for small-scale productions. The coach house could hold up to 20 carriages and their horses. The middle floor featured 20 rooms, kitchens, offices and servants' quarters. The third and top floor was split into two apartments with 20 rooms, kitchens, offices and servants' quarters. The interior of the villa had neoclassical columns and elaborate mouldings and was decorated in the Pompeian Revival style dominated by the terracotta-coloured 'Pompeian red'. Elaborate mirrors and chandeliers adorned the walls, aimed at amplifying the space and impressing the visitors and possible tenants.[63] The palazzo was hung with over 100 paintings, both classical and contemporary.

Fictional, and seemingly somewhat inaccurate, accounts of the time describe a courtyard bathed in light from stained glass windows that fell on pots of oleander, magnolia and orange trees. The carpeted marble staircase was said to lead up to a reception area with a marble-framed Venetian mirror and ottomans covered in velvet from Utrecht. There were marble statues from leading sculptors, and frescoes graced the ceilings. There was a billiard room, a library, and a grotto decorated with seashells.[64]

A more reliable account of an evening in Mergellina comes from John Orlando Parry:

At 12 we went to Barbaja and he took us in his carriage to Possilipo where his villa is situated on the side of the water and about half a mile from the end of the Villa Reale. ...Tis a most wonderful curious place ... He took us thro' magnificent apartments full of looking glasses, chandeliers, English fire-places, carpets, easy chairs, ottomans and every luxury one can imagine. From these splendid rooms you come into a lovely grotto or cavern, most beautifully fitted up – chandeliers, fire-places of shells, statues from the antique, also a fountain playing to cool this retreat in summer! The ceiling was arranged most curiously like icicles, and you almost fancied you felt the water dropping. I never saw anything so unique or curious. All this is cut from the solid rock as well ...You descend a staircase cut from the rock and paved with Lava – lined with statues, stuffed beasts which looked out of caverns on the side, and apparently going to eat you up!

This leads you into the theatre! In my life I never saw anything so beautiful or so elegant. This is entirely cut in the solid rock and is capable for holding nearly 300 people seated! It is lined with white marble and full of statues ... The stage is beautifully fitted up, everything complete – scenes, lights, &c. They have cut too, 8 Boxes on the sides out of the rock which are very curious.

All is fitted up in the most magnificent style and the effect of the blue and gold ornaments with lovely white marble forms a contrast the most elegant and brilliant. Near the stage is a canopy of blue and gold cords, surrounded by wreaths of roses under which any people of distinction sit when any play or festa [sic] is going forward! There is an orchestra, and at the back of the stage (which is very deep) there is a staircase that goes to the top of the hill ...

In this garden are all kinds of curiosities from Pompeii, and a number of statues & c. from Egypt; ruins of Temples placed in the most pictur-esque spots ... On the sides are two wooden figures, excellently carved, representing two Swiss Guards with real guns. They are as large as life and being painted &c. have the appearance of living men on duty! From the garden you pass the fountain again and come upon the terrace ... [which] commands a view of Naples, Vesuvius, the whole Bay and part of the Appenine Mountains![65]

Everything about the villa was designed for maximum impact when enter-taining. Barbaja's summer parties were choreographed to 'great scenographic effect',[66] and included among the guests the stars of his theatre productions as well as their composers. He added to the mix contemporary artists – among others, the painter Achille Vianelli – and proved to be the most gracious and charming host, wrote Parry:

> Barbaja was quite an altered man – he was quite affable and pleasant – & (what's more) very talkative. Everyone was wondering how it was I could so get the right side of such a man as Barbaja. – He said he would ask the King and Queen to come & of course if His Majesty came – the whole Court must!!! I fancied I was two inches higher really hearing all this kind of news.[67]

Barbaja entertained regularly at the Villa Dattero. His parties made full use of the grottoes, and the villa was decorated specially for the occasion by Niccolini on a theme taken from the current theatre productions. There were copious amounts of food, the finest alcohol, and the very best available tobacco, which Barbaja brought back from Paris.[68] Parry's report from his concert at the villa is revealing:

> The theatre was, without exception, one of the most purely elegant and tasty things I ever beheld! It was now all in order – Seats were laid for 250 Every [sic] chair having an embroidered cushion and a mahogany footstool!! The whole length of this superb place was carpeted to the bottom of the orchestre [sic], the large Window was covered with light curtains of silk, (crimson) which, as the brilliant sun shone thro', gave to the marble walls statues and gold ornaments a most enchanting and almost magic hue!
>
> The stage was all lighted and the effect of the quantity of wax lights was most lovely as they looked like so many stars! There were Two handsome marble slab tables against the Scene, (which was a painting from one found at Pompeii) and on them two very handsome gilt candlebras of 7 lights each! There were also two on the Grand Piano-Forte with three lights each …The wings were all lit & the whole place was a perfect bijou!
>
> … At half past one [o'clock] the theatre was opened by [the] sound of trumpets!! The company then descended the staircase in the rock – (all wonder-struck & astonished at the novelty, beauty & elegance of the place). Their tickets were taken at the head of this staircase. – They had not been given before as Barbaja had upwards of [a] hundred of his friends to come & see the rooms &c but no one could descend to the theatre without

a ticket (which they could purchase at the door). All the company seemed to make but one exclamation as they entered the theatre – 'Oh ! How lovely & enchanting!'[69]

At the peak of his financial liquidity in 1817, Barbaja also built a house on the island of Ischia, some 30 kilometres from the mainland in the Bay of Naples. The villa 'Rostinale' was constructed in a small community called Casamicciola, located at the top of a hill with open vistas to the sea all around. The villa had two suites of 11 rooms on the upper two floors which were self-contained and could be let, while below Barbaja could host artists in relative privacy. Ischia had neither roads nor carriages then, and so the spot proved a tranquil and relaxing retreat both for him and for those he entertained.

By the 1820s, Barbaja was one of the richest men in Naples, with a lifestyle of riches and luxury comparable with none other. And with that lifestyle he was expected to have the appropriate art. Barbaja bought paintings not just because they looked good in his villas and for their decorative qualities, but also for the prestige attached to displaying a collection of old masters and prominent contemporary artists. Art to him was one of the many trappings associated with wealth, as he had seen on his own visits to the homes of the 'old-money' families with which he now socialised; he no doubt hoped that he too would be judged a man of exquisite taste.

Barbaja applied the same commercial sense to collecting art that he applied to everything else in his life. He invested in art 'when good occasions presented themselves',[70] which they did, notably when the French closed a dozen convents and 24 monasteries in 1808, and put their many priceless religious works of art onto the market, as well as during the severe recessions that frequently plagued Naples and forced many families into liquidation.[71] By 1830, he had built one of the premier art collections in Naples. He had acquired nearly 300 paintings from different schools and artists, ranging from the Renaissance to the neoclassical. Some of these were of exquisite quality and artistry – there were works from Durer, Holbein, Poussin, Caravaggio, Palma (il Vecchio) and Titian, as well as Neapolitan greats such as Aniello Falcone and Gaspare Vanvitelli[72] – but others were plainly forgeries. He displayed most of his collection in the Palazzo Barbaja on the Via Toledo, veritably plastering the walls of his apartment with some 200 paintings, many of which were very large.

His decision on what to purchase was not just the result of his own personal taste, for he was guided in his selection by his friend, the architect and designer Antonio Niccolini. As Director of the Real Istituto di Belle Arti (Royal Institute of Fine Arts) as well as architect for the royal household, Niccolini was the single most important player in setting the cultural tastes of the time in Naples, dictating what the Court would buy and what it would not. And wherever the Court bought, others would follow, including Barbaja, who had every intention of keeping up with art fashion, and in particular those artists patronised by the royal family.

5

Rising from the Ashes

(1816–1819)

On the night of 13 February 1816, during a rehearsal for a ball at the Teatro San Carlo, a fire broke out in the storage room for lights and torches. The few people that were present fled the building in terror, as the fire swiftly spread to the stage and then to the entire theatre. The blaze quickly devoured the wood, papier maché and blue and gold fabric chairs. Whipped up by the wind, the roof collapsed in flames. The royal family came running out of their palace and helplessly looked on in horror. Nothing could be done. The Government had disbanded the fire brigade in an effort to save money.

As the oldest theatre in Italy burned uncontrollably to the ground, the enormous red flames could be seen from miles away. The residents of the upmarket Vomero district overlooking the city near the Castello Sant Elmo watched a shocking spectacle of smoke and fire as they looked down onto the centre of their city. In just two hours, the splendid Teatro San Carlo was reduced to ashes, with little remaining but remnants of the theatre's front wall. The destruction of the opera house tore a gash in the Neapolitan soul, and no one was more affected than King Ferdinand himself. 'The blow,' wrote Stendhal,' affected him more deeply than defeat in a dozen pitched battles or the loss of the whole realm.'[1]

In Emil Lucka's novel *Der Impresario*, Barbaja rushes to the scene to ensure the gold stored in the vault under the theatre is rescued, and then directs the fire brigade to ensure the fire does not spread to the neighbouring royal palace as well. There was no fire brigade, of course, and it will probably never be known exactly what Barbaja did the night of the fire, but given the amount of money the gambling tables generated, he might well have been concerned to rescue the cash stored overnight at the opera house. His role in the reconstruction of the opera house, however, is undisputed.

The Bourbon royal family immediately resolved to rebuild the opera house and within two weeks the King had appointed Domenico Barbaja to manage the work. Barbaja was not only running the opera house profitably, he had also overseen the initial refurbishments. When he promptly made a personal commitment to the sovereign to rebuild the opera house within eight months, the shattered King quickly agreed. At 65 years old, he was concerned that he would not live to see his beloved theatre rebuilt. Ferdinand's son Leopoldo wrote about the rebuilding in a letter to his brother Prince Francis, then residing in Palermo:

> I also see the real pain that you have suffered with the destruction of the San Carlo, but I hope that it will be restored and that it will emerge even more beautiful than before. Signore Barbaja, the current impresario, who is a millionaire, has already committed to rebuild it during the course of this year.[2]

Barbaja not only promised to rebuild the Teatro San Carlo in even greater splendour in honour of his monarch, he also offered to construct the basilica of the Church of San Francesco di Paola, which Ferdinand had sworn he would build upon his return from Palermo to Naples in 1815 in gratitude for the restoration of his reign. St Francesco di Paola was a 15th-century friar who had reportedly floated on his cloak across the Strait of Messina between Sicily and the mainland when a boatman had refused him passage.

Leopoldo's reference to Barbaja's wealth was not accidental. By that time, it was generally considered that Barbaja had amassed a fortune far greater than the Neapolitan King.[3] Yet, in fact, Barbaja's role in the construction projects, contrary to many reports, was principally as a contractor. It was perhaps the frequent references to his wealth that caused chroniclers to assume he paid for the construction and gifted it to the sovereign. He actually just advanced part of the cost of rebuilding the Teatro San Carlo and was then compensated out of the future earnings of the gambling revenues, benefitting from a particularly lax contract.[4] Nevertheless, the fact that an impresario financed major architectural projects for the sovereign of a leading independent state speaks volumes about the state of finances in Bourbon Naples, and the enormous wealth that Barbaja had been able to amass.

The architect chosen by Barbaja to rebuild the Teatro San Carlo was – predictably – Antonio Niccolini. He was not only a close artistic and architectural adviser of the impresario, but he had furthermore become the favoured architect of the King. He would later build the Villa Floridiana in Vomero for the Princess Partanna, the morganatic wife of Ferdinand I. Niccolini also handled the expansion of the Capodimonte royal palace and was involved in countless projects for the royal palace in central Naples which was continually being renovated.

Niccolini immediately started work on the design for the new San Carlo, enlarging the size of the stage to accommodate ever bigger and more elaborate productions, and giving the theatre six levels of boxes and balconies arranged in a steep horseshoe shape around the stage. The seating was again upholstered in the traditional Bourbon blue and gold.

Barbaja put enormous pressure on the architect and the builders, turning the Teatro San Carlo into a 24-hour construction site with giant torches lighting it at night. He also took a hands-on approach to the design, ordering the architect to remove the ante-chamber of the boxes and ensuring that the layout allowed each box to enjoy privacy from the curious glances of other box-holders. If we are to believe the Austrian novelist Lucka, Barbaja said 'the theatre box is like the salon of a lady',[5] somewhere she can entertain, drink coffee and listen to music. But what Barbaja really wanted was to take control of the goings-on in that very salon. He wanted bigger boxes as they constituted one of his main sources of income, and he wanted to give the box-holders discretion without them needing to close the curtains. The main event was to be on the stage, no longer in the boxes. And the absence of an ante-chamber forced patrons to the *ridotto*, where they could gamble.

Modern stage equipment was fitted. Plumbing and lavatories were installed throughout the theatre, a dramatic upgrade from the buckets that were formerly provided, but not always used, in the halls of the theatre.[6] By many accounts, earlier theatres were filthy and stank dreadfully as a result of the patrons relieving themselves pretty much anywhere they felt like it.

Barbaja also instructed the architect to attach the seats in the stalls to the floor so as to put an end to the annoying shifting of chairs and benches during performances, and possibly also to stop the disorderly conduct it encouraged.

It was not long ago that melées in the stalls between French troops and Neapolitans had involved the throwing of chairs.

Concurrently with the work at the opera house, Barbaja planned the work on the Church of San Francesco di Paola. Inspired by the Roman Pantheon, the basilica was to be placed in the centre of what was then called the Largo di Palazzo, now the Piazza del Plebiscito. The church itself, which overlooks the large square facing the royal palace, was built in the *decennio*, but the semi-circular colonnade around it and the basilica were only added during the restoration of the Bourbons. King Ferdinand had chosen the Swiss architect Pietro Bianchi to design the basilica after he emerged victorious in a design competition for the project; he had also been recommended by the legendary sculptor Antonio Canova.[7]

Initially, work started with another contractor in 1816, but two years later, in 1818, Barbaja received the official contract to construct the basilica. Soon he was running a building site employing nearly 4,700 workers.[8] The King expected Barbaja to complete the project in eight to ten years,[9] but the construction at the Church of San Francesco di Paola proved much more challenging and complex than the Teatro San Carlo, both technically and politically. It was not completely finished until 20 years later and went through many ups and downs during the construction period.[10]

Winning the award for the basilica's construction demonstrates the uniqueness of Barbaja's position and business approach. Because he ran the royal opera houses and offered great opera – the entertainment preferred by the monarchy – he enjoyed unfettered access to the decision-maker, the King. 'In this world of closed and restricted opportunities, royal favours and royal concessions were the *sine qua non* of success,' writes the historian John Davis.[11] Where financiers and merchants had these direct links, they were able to cut through the stultifying bureaucracy, and Barbaja managed to turn such access into gold. During these years he could seemingly do no wrong. His relationship with the King was better than most: the impresario's course manners, direct approach and vernacular Italian enabled him to build an easy rapport with Ferdinand.

The basilica of the Church of San Francesco di Paola was widely considered a masterpiece, and became one of the dominant landmarks of the modernising Naples, a status it retains to this day. It did have its critics however. The Prussian architect, city planner and painter Karl Friedrich Schinkel, whose mark on Berlin is inescapable and who we will again encounter as a stage designer in the Viennese years of Barbaja, wrote in 1824 after a personal tour of the building led by Herr Bianchi himself that, 'overall his design vacillated between ancient and modern, as a result of which much is characterless'.[12]

An opera worth waiting for

Even before the fire at the Teatro San Carlo, Barbaja and Rossini had agreed on what their next opera would be: *Otello*, based on Shakespeare's *Othello*. Barbaja had introduced the composer to his chosen librettist, the nobleman Francesco Maria Berio, the Marquis of Salsa. Berio was more of a literary dilettante than a professional librettist, but he was well read and had a great admiration for English literature. He also had flawless royalist credentials. Hailing from one of the top Neapolitan families, Berio had left Naples for Portici[13] during the French decade, returning only when the Bourbons were restored. He re-opened his literary salon at his house in the Via Toledo which was situated near Barbaja's palazzo. The Palazzo Berio was equally impressive as Barbaja's residence, with an imposing doorway, a ballroom, a private theatre, a sculpture by the Venetian artist Antonio Canova, and a marble fountain with a sculpted deer's head. On the lower level was a shopping arcade, the arches of which were built to a design by the prominent 18th-century architect and architectural engineer Luigi Vanvitelli.[14]

At his palazzo, Berio entertained some of the leading names of the 19th century, among them Stendhal, Rossini, Canova and Lady Sydney Morgan, the Irish travel writer, who wrote of her visit:

> The conversazione of the palazzo Berio … is a congregation of elegant and refined spirits, where everybody converses and converses well … The Marchese is a nobleman of wealth, high rank and very considerable literary talent and acquirement, which extends itself to the utmost verge of the philosophy and belles lettres of England, France, Germany, and his native country. He has read every thing [sic], and continues to read every thing. And I have seen his sitting room loaded with a new importation of English novels and poetry … [At the salon] Rossini presided at the piano-forte accompanying alternatively, himself, Rosetti[15] in his improvisi, or the colbrun [sic], the prima donna of San Carlos, in some of her favourite airs from his own Mosé [*Mosé in Egitto*]. Rossini at the pianoforte, is almost as fine an actor as he is a composer.[16]

Barbaja's choice of Berio for the libretto of *Otello* was politically astute. Given the tragic ending of the story and the controversial plot of the black general who murders his loyal white wife in a fit of jealousy, the opera benefitted from the sponsorship of the prominent marquis, who enjoyed extremely close relations with the Bourbons, and whose name was helpful in guiding the libretto through the censors.

The time leading up to the opening of *Otello* was particularly stressful for Barbaja, since both he and the composer were living at the Palazzo Barbaja, and Rossini's progress on the opera was fitful. As Rossini increasingly fell behind schedule, and Barbaja pressed him to complete the work, the equally strong personalities of the two men were exposed and they clashed continually.

Rossini and Barbaja spent most meals together and Barbaja incessantly demanded to know how far Rossini had got with the new opera. Rossini came up with all sorts of excuses, and playfully teased the impresario for weeks, which then turned into months, without showing any signs of progress whatsoever.

Although he nagged him, Barbaja appears to have tried to make the composer comfortable, and the two shared an obsession with food. It was well known that Rossini loved to eat, and many of his letters to his parents detail his wish for them to send him his favourite mortadella, melon seeds and chocolate-covered sweets from Bologna.[17] He was also an accomplished amateur chef, but first and foremost he was a voracious eater. In particular, he liked *macaroni alla napoletena*, the best of which he ate at Barbaja's home.[18] Though we do not know much about Barbaja's culinary habits, and the stories about his employing Joachim Murat's former chef[19] are almost certainly invented, he is reputed to have had two Sicilian cooks.

As Rossini fell hopelessly behind schedule with his undisciplined and unruly work patterns, an exasperated Barbaja felt compelled to reimburse the box-owners their subscriptions. In a letter to the Duke of Noja in November 1816 he complained of Rossini's 'irregular conduct and incompatible behaviour during the last eight months … he even showed himself ungrateful and ridiculing my attention.'[20] Finally, after months of putting up with his star composer's prevarications, Barbaja's patience snapped. Rossini awoke one morning to find his servant's bell not responded to, and then discovered his front door had been locked and bolted from the outside. With only weeks to go before the scheduled rehearsal, Barbaja had locked the composer inside his apartment.

Looking out from his third-floor balcony onto the Via Toledo, Rossini eventually saw Barbaja leaning out from his own, lower balcony. 'Do you wish for anything?' the impresario asked innocently, looking up at the furious Rossini. 'Let me out at once!' the composer screamed. Barbaja calmly offered to release him the minute *Otello* was completed. After much loud bargaining from the balconies Rossini agreed that the overture would be delivered that very evening.

That night, while Barbaja was entertaining in his apartment, a messenger from Rossini's room upstairs delivered the finished overture of *Otello*, which Barbaja quickly asked one of his guests to play on the piano. The genius of the 'Swan of Pesaro' was apparent to all and Barbaja was overjoyed, but he did not relent on his strategy. Rossini remained locked in his apartment, and reportedly delivered an act a day, but was not released until Barbaja had the complete score. The impresario then freed the composer, offering his most humble apologies.[21]

Other stories recount that Barbaja tricked Rossini by luring him into his study for his favourite dish of macaroni, and then locking him inside the room until he had delivered the score, serving him nothing but macaroni for eight days. Years later Rossini wrote in a letter:

> I wrote the overture for Otello in a study of the Palazzo Barbaja, where I had been locked against my will by the most bald and most ferocious of all directors, with nothing more than a plate of macaroni, and with the threat of never being able to leave my room until I had written the very last note.[22]

If we are to believe the stories of the day, Rossini got even with Barbaja by sending him and the copyist who reproduced the score the same piece of music several times. As Barbaja could not read music, it was only during rehearsals, after publicly embarrassing himself in front of the orchestra and rehearsing artists, that he noticed that he had been had.

Otello debuted in December 1816 at the Teatro del Fondo, only a few blocks away from the construction site of the Teatro San Carlo, with the tenors Andrea Nozzari as Otello and Giovanni David as Rodrigo, and Isabella Colbran singing Desdemona. The opening was a reasonable, though not an outstanding, success. The two tenors' 'glorious rivalry' moved Stendhal, but he was dismissive of Colbran. In later years he would contrast her performance

with that of Giuditta Pasta, whom he thought, 'sings the part and above
all acts it, twenty times better than Signorina Colbran'.[23] While the music
was mostly appreciated by the audience, if not by all critics, the lyrics were
roundly disparaged due to the nearly unrecognisable link with Shakespeare's
play. Neapolitan critics did their valiant best to praise their native librettist, Marchese Berio, but others were not so kind. Byron, who saw a later
performance, was outraged: 'They have been crucifying Othello into an opera
(Otello by Rossini) – Music good but lugubrious – but as for the words!'[24]
Stendhal went to the opera some months later:

> 17 March, 1817. I debuted in the San Carlo with Rossini's Otello. Nothing
> could have left me colder. It really took some savoir faire for the author
> of the libretto to turn the most passionate of all the theatre tragedies into
> something so insipid. Rossini seconded him beautifully. The overture is of
> surprising freshness, delicious, easy to understand, and engaging for the
> ignorants, without having anything in common.[25]

But *Otello* gradually found audience favour and really took off when it
was reprised some months later at the newly rebuilt Teatro San Carlo,[26] by
which time the audience had become more familiar with the music and so
less concerned about the libretto. Even Stendhal changed his mind; he added
a footnote to the entry in his travel journal, when it was published in 1826:
'To punish myself for thinking like that in 1817, I insert this note. I was led
blindly by my indignation against the Marchese Berio, author of the execrable
libretto, who turned Otello into Bluebeard.'[27]

The opera proved Rossini's vehicle to gain the Neapolitan audience's
acceptance and he finally won their full support; while Barbaja learned that a
disappointing first night did not always translate into an unsuccessful opera.
In spite of his composer's vicissitudes and chronic tardiness, Rossini produced
operas that truly were worth waiting for. The impresario immediately tried
to convince Rossini to cancel all other commitments in favour of Naples.[28]

Otello remained an enormously popular opera until the end of the 19th
century, when it was eclipsed by Verdi's version of the play. Alas, Rossini's
casting of three principal tenors in one opera make it virtually impossible to
produce today. *Otello* was a landmark production, probably the first major *bel
canto* opera to have a tragic ending, a true *opera seria*. It is worth noting, and a
testament to the maturity of the Neapolitan audience, that Rossini was forced

to adapt the ending to a happier one for the audience in Rome. The opera led the way in establishing the fashion for tragic opera which was to become ubiquitous by the end of the 19th century – and Barbaja's strength in staging it should not be ignored.

Otello also launched two key tenors from Barbaja's *cartello*, Giovanni David (1790–1864), sometimes referred to as Davide, and Andrea Nozzari (1775–1832). David was one of the most employed and versatile tenors of the Barbaja stable. A native of Bergamo, he debuted in 1808 in Siena and then passed through La Scala to join Barbaja's Neapolitan stages in 1816. He soon became one of Rossini's favourite tenors, creating the *prima* roles in several Rossini operas. 'Davide,' wrote Stendhal, '... is the greatest tenor of Italy.'[29] In 1822 when he joined the Barbaja troupe in Vienna, he became a favourite of the audience there too. After a highly successful run, he eventually broke his contract with Barbaja in 1829[30] in order to join the Paris opera. To gain his freedom, David paid the impresario a separation fee of 8,000 ducats.[31] After an unsuccessful couple of seasons in Paris (for which he was paid the significant amount of 77,000 francs) he retired to Naples where he opened a singing school in 1840.[32]

David was all about technique. In fact, his singing was sometimes compared to the sound of an instrument, rather than the human voice. It was considered technically perfect, but utterly free of emotion. The French press wrote that 'it is impossible to be less of an actor' than David.[33] He competed for top billing with his colleague Andrea Nozzari, who had a more baritonal tenor.

Nozzari, the other tenor in *Otello*, was also from Bergamo. He learnt his spurs in Paris, before Barbaja signed him up for the Neapolitan stages in 1810. His highly developed vocal abilities were put to good use by Rossini, who wrote many operas especially for his voice, making him, along with Colbran, the most regular performer of Rossini's time at the Teatro San Carlo and the Teatro del Fondo. His vocal range also enabled him to give occasional performances as a bass-baritone, and he performed the title role of Mozart's *Don Giovanni*, a baritone part, at the Teatro del Fondo.[34]

Typically for the time, Barbaja only paid him 282 ducats per year in 1816, as opposed to the 500 ducats he paid Colbran.[35] Barbaja knew that it was the female voices that really mattered to his audience. Nozzari wisely retired from the stage when he felt the quality of his voice was beginning to decline, saying, 'I want to abandon the theatre, before the theatre abandons me.'[36]

~

Rossini's style of working would be a constant source of exasperation for Barbaja, as well as for other impresarios. Some years later, the impresario of the Teatro Valle in Rome, taking a page out of Barbaja's book, also locked the composer in his house and forbade him any visitors until he had finished writing the opera *Cenerentola* (Cinderella).[37] Yet, in spite of the frequent tensions, the Barbaja-Rossini relationship was a partnership of equals in the truest sense. They complemented one another beautifully: one well schooled and cultured, the other ignorant and under-educated; one who paid attention to every detail, the other driven by instinct; one musically sophisticated, the other without musical training but with a great sense of what the audience would like.

Rossini certainly knew how to manipulate Barbaja. Many years later, in a letter of advice to an aspiring young composer, Rossini wrote, 'Nothing excites your inspiration more than pressure, the presence of a copyist waiting for your work, and the urging of a panicked impresario who is tearing his hair out by the fistful. At my time, in Italy, all impresarios were bald by age thirty.'[38]

The new teatro

To this day Neapolitans look with amazement upon Barbaja's feat of reconstructing such a grand theatre in just nine months. The newly built opera house was even more grandiose, more lavish and more impressive than the old. Very little remained of the old San Carlo after the fire, but parts of the stone front were unscathed. Barbaja and Niccolini restored the colonnaded façade to look very similar to the original. Inside there was to be room for over 2,500 spectators; the stalls would hold 674 people in 19 rows of sofas and seats, and there was standing room for another 150 at the back. There were also six tiers of 30 boxes, each of which accommodated eight to ten people.[39] The new San Carlo was now the biggest theatre in Europe. It was also spectacular. Even Stendhal was in awe:

> There is nothing in Europe, and I do not say this lightly, which can even come close to give an idea of this. This auditorium, rebuilt in three hundred days, is a coup d'état. It bonds the people to the King to a much greater

extent than does the constitution given to Sicily, and which is desired in
Naples, which serves Sicily well. All Naples is drunk with delight. ... I am
so impressed by the auditorium, that I was charmed by the music and the
ballets. The auditorium is gold and silver, and the boxes are blue as the sky.
The balustrades of the boxes are ornamented with reliefs; these project
magnificently. The torches are grouped and interspersed with fleur de Lys.
Occasionally this ornament, which is of the greatest richness, is separated
by silver bas-reliefs. I think I counted thirty six.

   The boxes have no curtains and are rather spacious. I see five or six
people in all the first rows. There is a superb chandelier, glittering with
light, which makes all the gold and silver ornaments sparkle throughout.
The effect would not be possible if the ornaments were not all in relief.[40]

Barbaja had installed state-of-the-art lighting for both the stage and auditorium. The theatre was lit by a massive crystal chandelier with three rows of
oil lamps, 108 in all. Over 2,000 wax candles replaced the torches lit with olive
oil of the old building, creating a 'triumph of lights'.[41] Barbaja also introduced
the newly popular Argand lamp, which had been invented in France in 1780
as an improvement on the domestic oil lamp. It had been adapted for use in
the theatre, had a tubular wick and a cylindrical glass chimney, and produced
light equivalent to six to ten candles.

   Lighting the theatre required considerable skill. As the actors played to a
fully lit auditorium, getting it just right was a balancing act: the impresario
wanted the auditorium bright enough for the audience to be able to appreciate the splendour of his theatre, yet sufficiently dark to permit the performance to be clearly visible. By all accounts, Barbaja's lighting was absolutely
perfect.

   No expense was spared on the interior. The *ridotto*, with its large hall for
gaming and dancing, remained the main area for socialising, and there were
six dining and function rooms built beneath the main foyer.[42] In order to
prevent any risk of fire from the lighting store again, it was fireproofed and
encased in metal.[43]

   The cost of the reconstruction was massive. The restoration was rumoured
to have cost 180,000 ducats, and to have employed over 1,000 workmen,[44] but
in fact it was more: official records state that the reconstruction was paid for
from the public coffers and cost 230,000 ducats,[45] while still other sources claim
it was built at a cost of 241,000 ducats, part of which was borne by Barbaja.[46]

The re-opening celebration of the San Carlo was held on 12 January 1817, just 11 months after the fire had destroyed it. The evening was full of pomp and splendour, with the royal family present as well as many foreign dignitaries. Stendhal wrote of the occasion:

> Finally, the big day of the opening of the San Carlo. Follies, torrents of people, dazzling room. One must accept several kicks and rude pushes. I swore to myself not to get upset, and I succeeded. But I lost the two tails from my coat ...
>
> At first, I thought myself transported to the palace of some Oriental Emperor. My eyes were dazzled, my soul uplifted. Nothing more stylish and nothing more majestic, two things that are not easily united. This first evening is all about pleasure: I do not have the force to criticise. I am exhausted.[47]

Doing away with the curtains in the boxes, making the experience more immediate, less private, led some visitors to complain, however, as Stendhal noted:

> My friend from Milan introduces me in several boxes. The women complain about being too visible. This complaint is so incredible, I ask it to be repeated. Thanks to the profusion of lighting, these women are in continuous representation, an annoyance that is quadrupled by the presence of a Royal Court. Madame R*** [sic] sincerely misses the boxes with curtains of La Scala.[48]

The date of the opening had been selected in celebration of the birthday of Ferdinand I, and Barbaja chose a new Cantata by the composer Giovanni Simone Mayr to be performed for the momentous occasion. It was aptly named 'Il Sogno di Partenope' (The Partenopean Dream). The all-star cast included Colbran, Rubini, David and Nozzari, and in particular was to cement the young Rubini's emerging superstar status. Henceforth, he would be closely aligned with Barbaja, who chose him as lead for many of his productions.

Though the grandeur of the evening was unforgettable, the work was not a critical triumph. A short dance by members of the Austrian troops stationed in Naples was especially praised by the Germanic press, but locals probably thought otherwise. In any case, Barbaja was satisfied. The evening brought in 6,000 ducats.[49] His choice of Mayr did not please the royal household, however, because Mayr was not a pure Neapolitan composer in their eyes. The Government requested another opening in order to 'save the national honour',[50] this time with a work by a composer truly from Naples.

The Ministry of the Interior dictated that Barbaja put on a new opera by the totally unknown Carlo Saccenti, a Neapolitan. There was roaring demand for tickets for the star-studded performance despite the elevated prices, but it proved a disaster. In spite of the presence of a member of the royal family, Leopoldo, the Prince of Salerno, the crowd went mad with disapproval, booing uncontrollably and whistling with their fingers and through keys. The principal singer acknowledged the catastrophe and expressed relief that the audience did not throw their chairs at the stage.[51]

The next morning Barbaja marched to the Ministry of the Interior to complain that the performance had lost him 8,000 ducats, not least on account of the damage caused to the theatre by the crowds going wild in the boxes and stalls.[52] It appears that even the fixed chairs were not enough to rein in the Neapolitan crowd. It is probable that Barbaja did manage to obtain some concession from the Government, even if he did not receive any cash compensation.

The new theatre immediately became the talk of the town. Spohr was deeply impressed by the rebuilt Teatro San Carlo, and its suitability for ballets and pantomime. For opera, however, he deemed the house simply too large. Witnessing a performance with Colbran and Nozzari he acknowledged that the singers had enormous voices, but it proved challenging to hear them and it was difficult to judge the quality of the singing: 'Either they were screaming or you could not hear them at all.'[53] Stendhal shared his view:

> I cannot let go of the San Carlo. The architectural pleasures are so rare. For the pleasures of music, however, one must not look here: for one does not hear them. For the Neapolitans, it is different; they swear they can hear very well.[54]

In order to return to the better acoustics prior to the renovation, Spohr recommended the theatre remove the ornaments and extensive golden decorations, which he considered unnecessary and tasteless.[55] The *Allgemeine Musikalische Zeitung*, a Leipzig-based music journal with a large staff of often caustic writers spread around all the main European cities, was also unimpressed by the difficult acoustics and the old-fashioned and ornate decorations, and regretted the loss of the convenient ante-chambers to the boxes.[56]

Just two months after the re-opening, Spohr had an opportunity himself to perform in Naples:[57]

> Yesterday evening our Academy took place. Since Barbaja, the Impresario of the Royal Theatres, a completely selfish individual, charges too much for the use of the theatres (100 Neapolitan ducats for the Fondo, 200 for the Teatro San Carlo), I preferred to accept his offer to perform in the foyer of the Teatro San Carlo, which he offered to me for free, including lighting. This apparently selfless suggestion, however, was also calculated and to his advantage, since the foyer and the adjoining rooms are used for gambling, and he sought to attract the richest and most respected citizens of the city with my concert. I did not begrudge him this plan, since it brought me no disadvantage.[58]

Spohr's concert was held 'in a very beautiful room in the casino nobile',[59] and in addition to his own piece, featured music by Mayr that was sung by David and Nozzari. It was a big success, leading to demands for a second performance. In order to avoid having to arrange an extra concert, Spohr accepted Barbaja's suggestion of giving two concerts between acts at the Teatro San Carlo, for which he was paid 300 ducats. While he was concerned that the enormous auditorium and noisy audience would drown out the sound of his violin, the Neapolitans proved respectful and appreciative, remaining silent during his performance, and calling him out twice to the stage.[60]

Spohr took the opportunity of his extended stay in Naples to see several opera performances. He wrote enthusiastically about a special concert given by Angelica Catalani, who billed herself 'Prima Cantatrice del Mondo' (the world's best singer), at the Teatro dei Fiorentini, the smallest of the theatres under Barbaja's control. The whole city had been excited about her arrival:

> The arrival of Signora Catalani had all the music lovers of Naples in a great state of excitement. She took advantage of it and promptly arranged a concert in the Teatro Fiorentino with tickets at seven times the normal price ... Never has an audience been in such intense expectation as the Neapolitan audience that evening ... At long last she appeared, and there

was deathly stillness throughout the auditorium. Her bearing was cold and rather pretentious, and she greeted neither the court nor the rest of the audience, which made an unpleasant impression. Possibly she had expected in her own turn to be greeted with applause, which is not customary in Naples, and was piqued when there was none. Her first song, however, was fervently applauded, and she promptly became more friendly, remaining so the rest of the evening ... What I missed most in her singing was soul.[61]

He then attended a performance of *Elisabetta* with Colbran in the lead. The audience was aware of the competition between Catalani and Colbran, so the San Carlo quickly sold out.

Immediately upon entering the stage she was greeted by both loud whistles and turbulent applause. But since this time she really sang and acted beautifully, the clapping increased and the whistling disappeared, and at the end she was called out nearly unanimously. She is inferior to Catalani in terms of voice and technique, but she sings with true feelings and performs with passion ...[62]

Rossini's new romance

After the rebuilding of the theatre and a busy period producing operas for Rome (*La Cenerentola*) and for La Scala (*La Gazza Ladra*), Rossini returned to Naples. The next few years were to be some of the most fruitful for Barbaja, cementing his working partnership with both Rossini and Colbran. Rossini was to write an opera about the Saracen sorceress Armida for Barbaja, a subject providing ample opportunity to show off the San Carlo's state-of-the-art stage and technical capabilities, and offering, according to historian and musicologist Richard Osborne, 'precisely the kind of commercial opportunity Barbaja was too shrewd to ignore'.[63]

Barbaja pulled out all the stops to make *Armida* a spectacular production. He was especially keen to demonstrate to Rossini the superiority of his productions over those of his competitor at the Teatro Valle in Rome, in whose more modestly endowed theatre Rossini had premiered *Cenerentola*.[64]

Rossini's musical technique had matured since the first Neapolitan operas. His style was now increasingly influenced by the taste and suggestions of Barbaja as well as of Colbran, whose extraordinary voice allowed him to expand his musical style and explore more technically demanding composition. The enormous range, shimmering heights and the sheer agility of her voice in seemingly effortless *coloratura*, gave the composer a unique instrument to work with, though the audience – and probably Rossini as well – were well aware that Colbran's voice was now past its peak.

Stendhal, overstating the case with his usual acerbic wit and growing dislike of 'La Colbran', wrote that Rossini had recognised the problems with Colbran's voice, and sought to avoid the 'handicap' of it by putting greater focus on the 'resources of the orchestra, gradually transforming accessory into principal'.[65] He was probably exaggerating, but it is certainly true that Colbran's vocal ability was not what it once was. Her stage presence and allure as an artist and star of the musical stage, however, continued undiminished.

In July 1817, Rossini stayed at Barbaja's retreat on the island of Ischia, where he took the thermal baths.[66] While there was little to do there, the presence of Isabella Colbran and other friends made it more bearable, even rather exciting. This might even have been the beginning of Rossini's romance with the singer.[67] Though Colbran was still involved with Barbaja, Rossini's professional relationship with Isabella Colbran now took on a decidedly personal dimension. In a letter to his parents, he writes of his fondness for the prima donna. In September 1817 he refers to her as an 'excellent companion'.[68]

While it is hard to imagine a union between the under-educated, impulsive and garrulous impresario and the sensitive, highly religious and artistic singer – other than through the prism of a Hollywood romance between a rich, successful producer and his leading movie star – the attraction between Rossini and Colbran makes eminent sense. It is even possible that Colbran cast her spell on Rossini as early as 1807, when she debuted in Bologna where the then 15-year-old composer was attending music school. While no one can be sure just how far their relationship developed at this time, Rossini and she were now working much more closely together, while Barbaja's focus was elsewhere.

It was against the backdrop of this simmering romance between composer and prima donna that *Armida* premiered at the Teatro San Carlo on 9 November 1817. It was nothing like the success of Rossini's preceding two Neapolitan operas. Stendhal attributed the relative failure principally to the audience's disappointment with Isabella Colbran, whose voice was showing undeniable signs of strain. A certain degree of audience fatigue with her cannot be excluded either. She had starred in almost every Barbaja production for the past five years. Such an extremely heavy schedule would have meant that she was not only one of the most versatile and flexible singers, she was also one of the most overworked. And the stress was clearly beginning to tell.

Nevertheless, Rossini's *Armida* was remarkable. Stendhal enthused about the splendid duet between the Saracen sorceress and the crusader knight, writing 'Nothing but emotion could inspire music like the duet from *Armida*',[69] and many modern musicologists see *Armida* as the culmination of Rossini's musical maturity. Colbran's role in the genesis of the opera is also noteworthy. The Rossini biographer Richard Osborne suggests that 'as for her personal influence, would he have written music as erotic as much of *Armida* undoubtedly is if some kind of closer relationship was not already afoot?'[70] While the eroticism of the music can be debated, Colbran and Rossini were clearly spending much time together. Isabella's name appears in the original manuscript of *Armida*, where she has written her name in the margin of a page, the position of her signature suggesting that she was sitting opposite Rossini as he was composing.[71]

The critical reception of *Armida* mattered less to Barbaja, too, now that he had so much of which he could be proud. With the Teatro San Carlo having re-opened in record time and the planning for the basilica of San Francesco di Paola progressing well, the impresario now enjoyed the favour of the royal family and the full backing of the Bourbon King. He was, in Stendhal's words, '*le premier homme du Royaume*' – the first man of the kingdom.[72] He fully epitomised the Italian impresario who was 'a despot, a czar, a sultan reigning over his theatre with some divine right, having just like the most legitimate Kings no other rules than his own volition, and accountable for his adminis-tration to nobody but God and his conscience'.[73]

Barbaja was at the peak of his power, wealth and influence, and was one of the most prominent – and observed – men in the city. He was also by now inextricably associated by the public – for better or worse – with the Neapolitan royal household. He had become, in the words of many, the 'Viceroy of Naples'. By 1817, this close association was not as advantageous as it had been several years earlier. Change was in the air. The *Carbonari* were starting to grow in popularity. Originally a secret society organised to resist the French occupation and fight for Bourbon restoration, they had dropped their support for the Bourbons in disgust over Prince Canosa's vicious crackdown on anyone not a royalist after the restoration, and focused their efforts on establishing a constitutional government free of tyrannical and foreign involvement. Additionally, the left wing of the Neapolitan liberals was angered by continued foreign interference in their affairs. The Sicilians sought separation from Naples. It was not the best time to be linked with the Crown.

The years 1818 and 1819 were dominated by Barbaja's and Rossini's efforts to attract various composers and principal singers of international repute to Naples, aiming to further position the city as the centre of the European opera scene. Rossini wrote to a leading tenor, 'come to this beautiful climate and you can be assured of many engagements, this being the country of intelligent people with good musical taste'.[74] This might have been a slight exaggeration, given what was going on in the political arena.

By 1818, the Church had regained much of its previous power, and liberal groupings such as the *Carbonari* had been outlawed. Freedom of expression had again been suppressed and the gaps in society widened. According to Stendhal, the Neapolitan Government still managed 'to preserve a few rags and tatters of administrative discipline, a legacy from the French occupation', but, he went on, 'It is impossible to imagine any form of government of more abysmal insignificance, or with less influence to wield on the population.'[75] Despite the general chaos and administrative incompetence, the sovereign's obsession with opera and Barbaja's personal relationship with the King enabled the impresario to continue with his activities unabated.

Rossini was at the height of his creativity and Barbaja maintained his pressure on him to produce new work. He had negotiated with the Government the right for his theatres to remain open throughout the season, closing only for Passion Week and Easter. As such, he required a production that was sufficiently austere for Lent.[76] The biblical drama *Mosè in Egitto* (Moses in Egypt) proved well suited for the occasion.

This tragico-sacra drama tells of the love story between a Hebrew girl and the son of the Pharaoh, set against the backdrop of the exodus of the Hebrews from Egypt. The opera starred Colbran (as the Hebrew girl), Nozzari (as the Pharaoh's son) and the bass Michele Benedetti (in the title role). It opened to huge acclaim, causing one doctor later to complain about 'the occurrence of over forty cases of brain-fever of violent nervous convulsions among young ladies with an over-ardent passion for music, brought on exclusively by the Jews' prayer in the third act'.[77]

The format developed by Rossini and his librettist for *Mosè in Egitto* was revolutionary for its time and opened the door for oratorio-style operas by other composers.[78] Colbran's character did not have much to sing until the end of the second act, allowing the singer sufficient time to warm up, accommodating her growing vocal difficulties.[79]

Soon after *Mosè*, Rossini produced an opera for the Lisbon theatre, and then he set to work on his next San Carlo production, *Ricciardo e Zoraide*. Once again, Francesco Berio provided the libretto. The aristocrat's lyrics were execrable, even worse than those for *Otello*, and the libretto incomprehensible. But the music carried the opera through and *Ricciardo* was a critical success. The previously anti-Rossini *Giornale delle due Sicilie* praised Rossini in a mock letter from the Heavens from (the long-deceased) Neapolitan composer Cimarosa, for having 'finally renounced the barbarian manners and strange ornamentations and embraced true musical culture.'[80]

Barbaja started the 1819 season by launching a Cantata by Rossini in February to celebrate King Ferdinand's recovery from illness. As usual, Colbran took the lead. This was followed by another Cantata on the occasion of the visit of the Austrian Emperor Franz I on 9 May, starring Colbran, David and Rubini at the San Carlo. It was a family affair: the Austrian Emperor was married to Ferdinand's daughter Maria Theresa, and was therefore the son-in-law of the King.

Cantatas for such special occasions were great publicity as well as good business. Choral works with singers and orchestra, they were mostly performed with more modest stage sets and costumes than a full opera, and in a chamber music-like setting. They were easier, faster and far cheaper for an impresario to produce than a full-scale production. For a Cantata performed at the Teatro del Fondo on the occasion of the wedding of the Duchess of Berry, Barbaja invoiced the Ministry of the Interior the sum of 1,552 ducats. This broke down into 150 ducats for Rossini, who composed the music, and the same amount for the librettist; 250 ducats for the principal singer, Girolama Dardanelli – clearly demonstrating the premium singers could charge; and 600 ducats for Barbaja for the costumes, tools, printing, provision of complimentary seats, and other special charges related to the event.[81]

Performance of Cantatas also offered the impresario, composer and

principal performers an unrivalled opportunity to meet possible patrons. At
the Cantata written in honour of the visit of Emperor Franz I, the Austrian
sovereign was accompanied by his Chancellor, Klemens von Metternich, who
met Rossini after the performance. Some 40 years later, Metternich wrote to
Rossini, reminding him of their encounter and recalling his unusual creative
maturity for such a young man: 'you were the author of a new science, rather
than reformer of an old school'.[82]

Keeping up his frenetic schedule, Rossini premiered *Ermione* on 27 March
1819, again with Colbran, Nozzari and David. Stendhal termed it a 'demi-
failure' and an 'experiment', but he was probably being charitable. The opera
sank with a thud and was Rossini's first obvious failure at the San Carlo. It
provided the perfect opportunity for Barbaja's and Rossini's growing number
of detractors finally to attack.

The *Allgemeine Musikalische Zeitung* reported that Barbaja's and Rossini's
control over the Neapolitan newspapers and indirect influence over the
Italian media enabled them to keep the fiasco of *Ermione* out of the local
papers. There seems to have been some truth in this: the *Giornale delle due
Sicilie*, for one, failed to review the opening, helping to ensure that the failure
was not known in Milan until much later. The *Allgemeine Musikalische Zeitung*
also accused the pair of deliberately ensuring that Saverio Mercadante, a
promising young composer and a student of Rossini's enemy Zingarelli, did
not get any press coverage.[83] This is unlikely since Barbaja's quest for new
composers continued unabated.

For years, Barbaja had tried hard to coax the popular composer Gaspare
Spontini to Naples. His opera *La Vestale* (The Vestal Virgin) had triumphed
in Napoleonic Paris.[84] In 1810 Barbaja had offered him the then outrageous
amount of 1,000 ducats for a new opera, but the composer still refused
him.[85] In 1819 Barbaja tried again, and this time Spontini finally agreed and
signed up with Barbaja. Shortly afterwards, however, Spontini reneged on his
contract with Barbaja, choosing to take up an offer from the king of Prussia to
become Music Director of the Royal Theatre instead. King Frederick William
paid the contractual indemnity Barbaja demanded to release Spontini from
his obligations.

With a gap in his schedule following the cancellation by Spontini, Barbaja
was again under pressure to find new material. This time Rossini helped
Barbaja out. The composer quickly came up with the idea of reworking Sir
Walter Scott's poem 'The Lady of the Lake', and wrote the opera *La Donna*

del Lago in record time. Barbaja and Rossini lined up their usual favourites to star in the production, though Colbran was for the first time forced to tolerate another prima donna by her side, the contralto Benedetta Rosamunda Pisaroni – possibly the first admission that Colbran's voice was no longer what it had been.[86] The opera opened on 24 October 1819, and Stendhal was there to witness what took place:

> ... Rossini had introduced a hitherto unsuspected dynamic force into the supremely boring convention of the opera seria. It is quite possible, however, that his besetting laziness would have tempted him to sit back and rest on his laurels, had it not been for the implacable hostility shown by the public towards Barbaja and everything connected with his organization. But Rossini could not bear failure, and I have seen him physically ill when one of his works was whistled off the stage. ... The actual occasion arose during the *première* of *La Donna del Lago*, an opera based on a bad poem by Walter Scott.[87]

It was another fiasco. The tenor Andrea Nozzari was positioned too far to the back of the stage to hear the music properly:

> ... as he opened his mouth to deliver a bellow of sustained sound, the effect was magnificent, and the echoes could have been heard right outside in the Via Toledo. Unfortunately, however, since he was in the back of the stage, and the orchestra was in the front, he could not hear the instruments; and so his glorious *portamento*[88] just fell about a quarter of a tone below the required pitch. At this unhoped-for chance to storm the stage with wild derision, the whole audience went mad as hatters, and the yell of malicious glee which ascended from the pit is still ringing in my ears! – a cage-full of roaring and ravenous lions, and the doors flung open! – Aeolus unleashing the fury of the winds! ... *nothing* can give the least, the sketchiest idea of the rage of a Neapolitan audience insulted by a wrong note, and so given the chance to work off a long-standing score of accumulated hatred![89]

Rossini set off that same night for Milan, unashamedly spreading stories of a hugely successful *prima*. As it turned out, the Neapolitans fully embraced *La Donna del Lago* from the second performance onwards, when the staging difficulties had been ironed out, so Rossini's fib proved self-fulfilling. Though it was never deemed one of Rossini's greatest operas, the aria 'Tanti Affetti' (Many Affections) remains one of the most popular pieces for a qualified *coloratura* soprano wishing to show off her vocal skills. Notably, this bravura piece is situated at the end of the opera, by which time Colbran would have had enough time to warm up her voice. Stendhal and several Rossini biographers concur that the cool reception to *La Donna del Lago* had less to do with the music, and more to do with Barbaja and Colbran.[90] The growing hatred for King Ferdinand, with whom Barbaja's name was now inextricably linked, was rubbing off on the impresario. And Colbran, too, was seen by association as under the protection of the increasingly despotic King.

Stendhal and other diarists were certainly less than fair about the quality of Colbran's performance, and their claims that Rossini protected her above all others were unjustified, given that Rossini gave one of the two lead parts to the new *prima donna contralto*, Pisaroni.[91] In fact, Stendhal had little gracious to say about Pisaroni either, judging her 'one of the ugliest actresses imaginable'.[92] Pisaroni was clearly well aware of her physical shortcomings, as she tended to enter the stage backwards, only turning her heavily pock-marked face to the audience after she had begun singing, so that they were first impressed by her enormous and beautiful voice. She would also send impresarios considering contracting her a picture of herself showing the disfigurement from smallpox to make sure that they knew what they were hiring. Barbaja, for one, had no issues with her looks: her prodigious vocal talent helped fill the house.

Following *La Donna del Lago* Barbaja and Rossini continued their quest to attract fresh talent to Naples. Rossini did more than his fair share of the recruiting, and he was influential in the visit of the legendary violinist and composer Niccolo Paganini to Barbaja's stages in 1819. Rossini had first met Paganini when the virtuoso attended a performance of Rossini's *Aureliano in Palmira* (Aurelian in Palmyra) in Milan in 1813. Paganini had sought out a personal introduction to the famous composer, whom he deeply admired. Five years later, in 1818, Paganini met Isabella Colbran at a dinner party in Bologna,[93] and on Barbaja's behalf Colbran invited the violinist to perform in Naples. The impresario put all his theatres at the violinist's disposal for free: Barbaja knew that Paganini was in a totally different league from Spohr.

Having conquered the north of Italy, Paganini was keen to make his mark in the south. He had given a series of performances in Rome, with the ultimate goal of performing in the more challenging and critical theatres of Naples. But the Neapolitan public was principally interested in opera and opera singers, and instrumentalists could not be assured of a great deal of interest from its temperamental audiences. Paganini's self-confidence combined with the near unbelievable reports of his virtuoso skills had also raised Neapolitans' expectations. Perhaps on Barbaja's advice, therefore, Paganini opted not to perform in the large Teatro San Carlo, but chose instead the smaller Teatro del Fondo for his debut performance in March 1819.[94]

Paganini himself wrote that he created 'great uproar',[95] which must have been true as Barbaja quickly secured further bookings for the 'devil's violinist' for June and July of that year, this time at the San Carlo. Paganini spent several months in the south, and was performing in Palermo while Rossini was in Naples preparing the opera *Matilde di Shabran* (Matilde of Shabran) for the Roman Apollo Opera. Paganini had hoped to accompany Rossini when he travelled up from Naples to Rome in November, but he was unable to go north until January, so he rejoined his friend in Rome.

Paganini's timing could not have been better. Rossini had become exasperated by the obstacles that were being thrown in his way in Rome, a situation that was exacerbated when the planned conductor of the opera suddenly died. Paganini himself jumped into the breach to conduct the first few performances of *Matilde di Shabran*, and even played what was meant to be a horn solo on the violin, after the horn player fell ill before a performance.

Rossini and Paganini celebrated by joining in the carnival festivities incognito with two friends dressed up as blind musicians, busking for hand-outs from passers-by. Rossini exaggerated his already impressive physique by stuffing his clothing, and the stick-thin Paganini wore feminine attire to accentuate his sickly body to give it an utterly cadaverous appearance. For Paganini, this is unlikely to have been much of a costume: the German writer and essayist Heinrich Heine wrote that Paganini always looked as if he were on his deathbed.[96]

6

The End of Easy Money

(1819–1822)

The Barbaja-Rossini era saw the Teatro San Carlo at its zenith. Staff motivation was high, creativity was astounding, and the impresario attracted the best in the industry. Barbaja's raising of the standards of production had, however, one unfortunate side-effect: a spoiled and unforgiving audience.

The merciless and unforgiving Neapolitan audience has become part of operatic legend, though today this mantle has been proudly grabbed by the audience of La Scala. This reputation was largely built during Barbaja's reign, when the impresario brought sophistication and judgment to the already unruly and emotionally charged spectators. Their weapons were ear-piercing whistling, shrill laughter, demonstrative yawning and the occasional projectile. 'The Neapolitan audience is the most demonstrative and the most capricious,'[1] wrote the French tenor Gilbert Duprez in his memoirs. He described being whistled off stage during a performance when he sang with a sore throat. The week afterwards he challenged the audience, stepping provocatively to the front of the stage during a performance and pausing, before powering through his aria and bringing down the house.

Not all performers were so resilient. In 1837 Barbaja put on a new opera by the young composer Giuseppe Lillo, featuring a young French singer in her second performance on the stage. In the first act the audience was relatively disciplined, possibly due to the attendance of the king's mother. In the second act, however, its displeasure became so thunderous that the singer fainted from fright and had to be carried off the stage.[2]

Barbaja himself was an active and enthusiastic participant in this spectator sport:

> You should have seen the impresario at a première performance, sitting in a nice box near the stage, opposite the King. He was serious, impassive, turning once to the performers, once to the audience. If the artist flinched, Barbaja was the first to crucify him with the severity worthy of a Brutus, screaming 'Dog of a God' at such volume that the house trembled. If, on the other hand, the audience was wrong, Barbaja would rear his head like a viper, and yell at full voice: 'Son of a bitch. Will you shut up. You deserve nothing but the rabble.' If however, it was the King himself who failed to applaud appropriately, Barbaja just shrugged his shoulders and left the box mumbling under his breath ...[3]

Such harsh and vocal criticism was not reserved only for the singers. No composer was immune from the local intrigues that felled so many visiting artists from the north. In 1826 the minor composer Giuseppe Balducci wrote the opera *Tazia* for the San Carlo. It saw a single dreadful performance before being withdrawn. The orchestra and singers had conspired to make it a failure: the singers deliberately sang off-key, the musicians started playing at the wrong times and one trumpeter intentionally blew the wrong notes.[4]

Like every other opera house, then and now, the San Carlo also had its fair share of oddballs. Its house eccentric was the master hairdresser, who spent his whole career with the opera. A true fanatic of the tenor Rubini, he fashioned his own hair to look like that of the Italian tenor, and had nothing but spite for any other tenor, especially non-Italian ones. Gilbert Duprez tells a story of the hairdresser always waiting in the wings for him to go on stage. As soon as he had gone on, the hairdresser would hector him: 'go on Frenchman, sing, sing. You will never be anything more than a zephyr compared to my Rubini'.[5]

The royal theatres were also, however, a place of merriment, much of which was provided by Barbaja himself. His garrulous nature, short fuse and frequent temper tantrums that quickly fizzled out were as much a source of entertainment as of fear. Barbaja's language was course and full of rough Milanese slang and curses. He addressed everybody, even the king, with the informal '*tu*', much to the glee of those around him. Though the theatre staff and musicians admired the way in which he had turned round the fortunes of the Teatro San Carlo, his shocking lack of education about musical affairs provided a constant source of amusement.

Being a very early riser, Barbaja was usually the first in the theatre and he took a very active part in the day's events, looking in on rehearsals and auditions and other musical practices he did not fully understand. One day, he watched a young singer auditioning for the chorus of the San Carlo. The singer proposed singing either a short aria or a *solfeggio*, a vocal exercise in which the names of the notes are sung to their proper pitch. Barbaja chose the *solfeggio*, not knowing what it was. As the young chorister starting singing, Barbaja quickly interrupted her, 'Stop, stop immediately. They would jeer you off the stage if they heard you singing *do, re, mi* at the theatre.'[6] The reporter of that story also tells of Barbaja witnessing the orchestra tuning up before a full rehearsal. The irritated impresario rapidly intervened, wanting to save time: 'Stop that, stop that. You can tune before the actual performance.'[7]

A late 19th-century newspaper related this doubtful but characteristic tale, which likely falls into the category *'se non e vero, e ben trovato'* – the Italian equivalent of 'don't let the truth get in the way of a good story':

> A vocalist having complained that the piano to whose accompaniment she had been rehearsing her part was too high, Barbaja assured her that as soon as she had gone he would have it lowered. The next morning the instrument was as before, a good half-note above the proper pitch. The vocalist still maintained that the piano wanted lowering; upon which the manager flew into a violent passion, and calling in one of the carpenters asked him indignantly why when he had been told that the piano was too high he had not shortened the feet by two or three inches instead of only one.[8]

Programming was guided by strictly commercial considerations. Barbaja had no qualms about splitting up operas, for instance putting on one act of Bellini's *Norma*, followed by an act of *Assedio di Calais*, and closing with an act of *Puritani*.[9] For him, opera was all about satisfying the audience, never about educating it.

But some things were sacred to Barbaja. He was unrelenting in his demand for punctuality, especially when it came to the delivery of commissioned works. He would send emissaries to enquire about the progress of a promised opera, and letters ranging from the encouraging to the profane. In an admonitory letter from 1820 to Mayr, Barbaja reminded him of the tight deadline for the opera the composer had been commissioned to write, and in signing off sent regards from Rossini and Colbran twice:[10] an unsubtle way in which to put peer pressure on the tardy Mayr. Given their close friendship and Rossini's strong character, Barbaja usually held back when it came to dealing with him, much as his work habits exasperated the impresario.

Rossini was considered part of the Barbaja family and he was fond of the impresario's daughter. On the occasion of the wedding of the 18-year-old Carolina Barbaja to a young Neapolitan banker, Cesare Politi, which took place at the Villa Barbaja in Mergellina in May 1819,[11] Rossini dedicated the composition 'Andante e Tema con Variazioni' for harp and violin to her. The composition includes variations on 'Di Tanti Palpiti' from *Tancredi*.[12] Carolina, like other educated women of the period, probably knew how to play the harp.[13]

Relations between Carolina and Isabella Colbran, however, were a different matter. While Carolina was certainly well aware of and accustomed to the comings and goings of Colbran at her father's household, what was initially a cordial friendship deteriorated over time. 'A disagreement related to gossip has emerged between Barbaja's daughter and La Colbran resulting in the two no longer seeing one another without others', wrote Rossini.[14] Whether she was jealous of the singer's relationship with her father, or disapproved of Colbran's emerging association with Rossini, or if there were other, pettier issues, we will probably never know.

While there was plenty of local gossip about the Barbaja-Rossini-Colbran triangle, and there were reports of growing tension between Barbaja and Rossini, these were mostly unfounded. Rossini wrote to his parents in 1820 advising them not to believe all the gossip they might hear: 'I am in full friendship with Barbaja, and I am fortunate to enjoy his devotion.'[15]

Rossini was also, untypically perhaps for that era, open with his parents on some very personal issues, including the fact that he suffered from gonor-rhoea.[16] A later doctor's report diagnosed Rossini as having had the disease since he 'abused Venus from his earliest youth',[17] and he would continue to suffer it even after he 'tempered his passions for women, [and] stopped the abuse of liquor and heating foods'.[18] It would have been an unpleasant experience. Before antibiotics, gonorrhoea was treated with astringents, laxatives and purges. Side effects included diarrhoea leading to haemorrhoids, which doctors would occasionally bleed with leeches. If that were not enough, emollients (consisting of sweet almond oil, milk and mallow) would be introduced through a catheter into the urethra. Doctors generally ordered treatments in the great spas of Europe, including Marienbad, Karlsbad and, of course, Ischia.

Some sources indicate that Barbaja also 'abused Venus', frequented prostitutes and picked up gonorrhoea, but no proof survives, though that matters little. Barbaja probably succumbed to the temptation of the commercially available Venus as commonly as any other Neapolitan male. Just a few blocks away from the Teatro San Carlo and the royal palace was an area for prostitutes, a ghetto designed by the city planners to contain vice and keep such women from mingling and soliciting in residential neighbourhoods. This was not some dark, little street, however, but a large borough directly up the hill from Via Toledo in what was called the Spanish Quarter. Here literally thousands of prostitutes lived in small flats, *bassi* or full-scale commercial bordellos. The Teatro dei Fiorentini was also located smack in the middle of a red-light district, providing further temptation for Barbaja.

Health commissioners estimated that Naples had around 30,000 prostitutes in the mid-18th century.[19] As this would be around 10 per cent of the population, this number is certainly an exaggeration, probably an effort to boost the magnitude and importance of the commissioners' work. But the 'ladies of the night' were certainly in the thousands. Gonorrhoea and particularly syphilis ran rampant. During the *decennio*, the French referred to syphilis as *'le mal de Naples'* (the illness of Naples); the Neapolitans returned the favour by calling it the 'French disease'. Controlling venereal disease was an important task for the Government, which vacillated between moralistic clampdowns by the police and the more realistic approach of regular medical check-ups and registration.

In the 19th century, Naples was nothing if not sexually permissive. Artistic circles were more liberal than others, and Barbaja's moral compass would not have constrained him in any way. As with almost any man of means, he would have had his preferred venues and providers of sexual services. While cleanliness was important to him, the siren call from the Spanish Quarter is likely to have been irresistible. It is entirely possible that he contracted syphilis or another sexually transmitted disease; his retreat at Ischia was perfectly equipped for the treatment of the most common ills.

Political and gaming revolutions

The year 1820 was a politically complex and charged one. Ferdinand was under renewed pressure to introduce a constitution, especially from the *Carbonari*, who had amassed a significant force under General Pepe in Avellino, which was threatening to march on the city. King Ferdinand I of the Kingdom of the Two Sicilies was terrified by the prospect of yet another revolution. Rather than fleeing to Sicily again, the fearful King took to his bed and appointed his son Francis Vicar-General of the kingdom for a few weeks while he was incapacitated. On 6 July Ferdinand issued a declaration promising a constitution.

On 12 July, the *Carbonari* entered the city, accompanied by the regular troops, and passed by the royal palace. The troops were treated to a performance at the Teatro San Carlo that evening. It was attended by Carlo, the Duke of Calabria (and the oldest son of Ferdinand I).[20] A few days later Ferdinand I publicly took an oath of loyalty to the new constitution. In less than a month, the July Revolution of the *Carbonari* under General Pepe had achieved a constitutional monarchy, without even a shot having been fired.

The tremendous social and political upheaval did not go unnoticed at the Teatro San Carlo. Barbaja's close association with Ferdinand was well known and he suddenly found himself politically exposed. His renewed contract, though only some months old, was put on hold pending the promulgation of a new Regulation for the Royal Theatres. This upheaval resulted in a complete breakdown of the well-oiled machinery of the royal theatres.[21]

The Government ordered the arrest of those members of the theatres it deemed guilty of insubordination. Of even greater concern for Barbaja was the Government's reappraisal of whether to separate the gambling licence from the theatre *appalto*. Although this did not happen, in the revolutionary fervour the Government was soon forced to suspend gambling licences, threatening Barbaja's lavish opera productions, which were underwritten by the gambling proceeds.

Since the restoration in 1815, the Bourbon Government had been cautiously trying to impose its more rigid moral views, and gradually curtailing gambling in the theatres, in order that they focus on their true purpose of cultural performances. But eliminating gambling in the theatres was a gradual affair. Initially it was just a matter of rolling back the liberal Muratian licence, allowing gambling only in the foyer, and on the evenings of opera performances and during the time of the actual opera.[22] In 1820, the Government cracked down harder, and the National Parliament finally outlawed gambling for good.

Barbaja fought back in a carefully worded treatise,[23] arguing for the legal and financial importance of keeping gambling going, as well as the rationale of keeping the gambling and the theatre contracts linked. He pointed out that any reduction in the permitted time for gambling or its prohibition altogether would have a direct impact on the revenues of the theatres:

> Meanwhile the undersigned is prepared to provide the details that the National Parliament is requesting, he who for services rendered to the government in various areas, and precisely due to the residual cost of the construction of the San Giacomo,[24] as well as for the great project of San Francesco di Paolo has found himself spending an additional 140,000 ducats, has found his means totally exhausted. Without gambling, the theatre itself has suffered manifestly larger losses, as can be ascertained from the books. The reason: the [gambling] foyer attracted other patrons as well, who would then descend to the theatre, either fuelled by the earnings they made, or to console themselves and forget about the losses they incurred.[25]

Only two years earlier,[26] Barbaja had successfully negotiated the renewal of both the gambling and the theatre contracts, which had originally been granted for separate periods, bringing them in line. When the royal theatres contract had come up for renewal from Easter 1818, he had extended the lease by another four years, to Easter 1822. He had also been able to renegotiate the gaming contract, which was not due to be renewed until 1819, adding another three years so that it too ran until 1822. On the back of his successful rebuilding of the San Carlo, not to mention his helpful attitude in constructing the basilica of the Church of San Francesco di Paola, Barbaja had been given a loose contract permitting him to keep the gambling foyers open every day from ten in the morning to three the following morning throughout the season, even on holidays.

He had also been permitted to build the large gambling set-up at the San Carlo, which consisted of two banks of 'red and black', double banks of roulette, as well as 'bassette' (a card game). Gambling had become big business, and not just for Barbaja's own benefit. The impresario's theatres brought in 132,000 ducats per annum through the gambling concessions and employed over 700 people,[27] most of whom were the family breadwinners.

When he was told the gambling licences would be revoked, he complained bitterly to the Government, demanding it indemnify him with 4,000 ducats a month to cover the lost revenue, and declining any responsibility for the obligations to which he had committed himself.[28] While Barbaja put on a very spirited defence, the new regulations would ultimately spell the end of gambling in the royal theatres.

Barbaja and his partner did not initially fare quite as badly as one would suppose. In August 1821, possibly putting a more positive spin on the situation than was merited, Rossini wrote to his parents that the Government had given a generous indemnity to Barbaja (and by implication to Rossini) for the temporary loss of the theatre and the suspension of gambling, by which 'we do not lose, we even make a reasonable gain'. Barbaja had been successful in extracting the indemnity from the Government.[29]

However, the atmosphere of relative freedom at the San Carlo, under the protection of Barbaja, and therefore Ferdinand, changed. It was now a hostile, politically dangerous place marked by uncertain loyalties. The choice of Rossini's next opera, *Maometto II* (Mehmet II), which described the struggle of a Venetian colony against the Ottoman Sultan Mehmet II, certainly had political undertones. Barbaja sent the libretto to the censors in July 1820, but Rossini had been working on the opera since May. With the many delays caused by political interventions, as well as Rossini's usual laggardly work style, *Maometto* only saw the light of day in December, an unusually long gestation period for Rossini.

The librettist of *Maometto*, Cesare della Valle, the Duke of Ventignano, brought with him particular obstacles. He had a reputation of being followed by bad luck. In a city as superstitious and as credulous of the tricks of the underworld and the threat of the evil eye as Naples, the duke's involvement was unsettling even to Rossini. Barbaja, not concerned by such issues, had to intervene heavily to convince Rossini that Ventignano was a safe pair of hands.[30] The opera had its first performance on 3 December 1820 at the San Carlo. Musically and structurally ambitious, it was not a success, but the *Allgemeine Musikalische Zeitung*'s report of a 'fiasco'[31] sounds like an exaggeration.

The year 1820 proved to be the end of an era of almost careless frivolity for Rossini as well as Barbaja. The Naples they knew, loved and worked so skilfully was fundamentally changing. The abolition of the gaming franchise by the revolutionary government spelt the end of the days of easy money for them, and probably also for Colbran.[32] For Rossini, too, the political changes in Naples were a cause of concern, because of how his links with Barbaja would be perceived.[33] The death that year of Colbran's father in Bologna meant that Colbran, too, would need to make decisions about her future, which put Rossini under pressure to define the nature of their relationship.

For Barbaja personally, the loss of the gambling rights marked a dramatic deterioration of cash flow. At the peak of his success, he was estimated to be worth about 3 million francs by the French newspaper *La Presse*.[34] From 1819 onwards, Barbaja made no major property purchases, and he dramatically slowed down his fanciful and often capricious collecting of art.[35] Possibly anticipating a newly constrained period in his finances, Barbaja ordered a *catalogue raisonné* of his art collection to be drawn up, covering about two-thirds of his now nearly 300 paintings.

The upheavals and the suppression of gambling robbed the theatre – and Barbaja – of its financial lifeline. Until this time, Barbaja's energies had been singularly focused on the Naples stages, with only occasional visits to other Italian theatres. Now Barbaja was forced actively to start casting his eye elsewhere. Following reports of strong economic growth in Austria, and with the help of contacts made during the Austrian occupation, Barbaja started to direct his attention to another city, Vienna. He asked Rossini to compose his next opera, *Zelmira*, with that new market in mind.

Austrian order and finance

The constitutional experiment in Naples was to prove to be exactly that. Alarmed by Ferdinand's granting of a constitution and in terror at what he feared could become a liberal wave covering Europe, the Austrian Foreign Minister Clemens von Metternich decided to 'smother the revolution in its cradle'.[36] On 19 November 1820, Austria, Russia and Prussia issued the Troppau Protocol by which the three nations asserted their right to intervene against any revolution that threatened other states. Naples was of tremendous concern to Metternich on account of the insidious demands for constitutionalism and liberties, which the Foreign Minister's representative in Naples described as 'amounting to the destruction of Austria'.[37]

King Ferdinand was invited to join the three nations in discussions at Laibach[38] where they would outline the nature of their intervention in Naples. Entertainment for the Congress was provided by some of the leading artists in the continent, including the charismatic bass Luigi Lablache who duly impressed all the participants, including King Ferdinand, who subsequently invited the singer to join his Royal Chapel in Naples.[39]

Opera was clearly of greater interest to the King than politics. King Ferdinand soon fell foul of his hosts, due to his 'vacillating personality and unwillingness to work'.[40] He stood on the sidelines of the conference and then returned to Italy via Florence with money lent to him by the Austrian Emperor Franz – King Ferdinand did not have sufficient funds for the trip himself. Meanwhile the three nations decided to send an Austrian army to the kingdom to re-establish order.

Laibach was also the locale for another development of some importance to Barbaja's story. The conference was attended by Calmann Mayer Rothschild (known as Carl) of the influential Rothschild banking dynasty. Carl was the fourth of the five Rothschild brothers, and reputedly the least gifted of them all. The five sons of the patriarch Mayer Amschel Rothschild – represented by the five arrows on the Rothschild coat-of-arms and on the bank's logo – had spread throughout Europe in an effort to expand the banking empire. The brothers were in Frankfurt, Paris, London and Vienna, with Carl tasked to set up the bank in Naples, an increasingly interesting financial market.

There was a tremendous shortage of both capital and credit in Naples, and this resulted in interest rates reaching 12 per cent in the city, and shooting up to 30–40 per cent in the provinces.[41] In this attractive market the single largest and most important client was none other than the Bourbon Government itself.[42]

Carl Rothschild founded the bank C M de Rothschild & Figli in Naples in 1821. The Rothschilds were not alone in realising the potential of the city for international banking, and many other foreigners tried their hand as financiers in the kingdom. Among the more successful were the Swiss banking families Appelts and Meuricoffe (who competed fiercely), the latter also distinguishing itself through its leading collection of contemporary art; the French banker Degas (grandfather of the painter Edgar Degas); and the German-Danish banker Heigelin, who ran the German bank Cutler & Heigelin and acted as the Danish Honorary Consul General in Naples (he hosted the composer Louis Spohr during his Naples visit). Though the French-origin bank Falconnet was well known for being 'very obliging to Travellers',[43] the Rothschilds quickly gained top rank in the Neapolitan market, leading the way in international payments, capital markets transactions (such as stocks and bonds) and foreign currency services to both troops and travellers. The

singer John Orlando Parry made a visit to C M de Rothschild & Figli one of
his first stops when arriving in Naples.

Barbaja was not oblivious to the money that could be made from capital
markets transactions such as a sovereign bond issuance. He might not have
had the network, experience or resources of the Rothschilds and other
bankers, but he had one great advantage over them: his easy access to the
sovereign. The financing of the Austrian invasion of 1821 would bring Barbaja
to the centre of the European political economy.

Metternich was clear what needed to be done: Naples' experiment with
liberalism had to be put to an end by military force. All that remained to be
arranged was the financing of the military campaign. Carl Rothschild met
Metternich at Laibach and agreed to handle the payment of Austrian troops
in Rome on his behalf, a significant first step in the establishment of his
family's bank in Italy. King Ferdinand had agreed to issue a sovereign bond, a
public loan in favour of the kingdom, the proceeds of which would bankroll
the Austrian military campaign that would keep the King on his throne.
Metternich asked Carl Rothschild to handle the issuance and distribution of
the bond, as his bank would already be dealing with the regular payments of
the troops, and he was well connected and trusted in Viennese royal circles.[44]

Carl Rothschild had travelled to Florence for the preparatory discussions on the financing of the Neapolitan expedition, to meet the representative of the Neapolitan royal family and negotiate directly with the Bourbon
government. While he was the first to speak to the Bourbon Government,
the supposedly confidential terms of the loan quickly leaked out, and other
financiers tried to get a slice of the pie. Barbaja, who had also made his way
to Florence to lobby for the deal directly, approached the Austrian representative in Naples, Baron Vincent, with a letter of recommendation obtained
from King Ferdinand. The king favoured the Barbaja loan, knowing that the
House of Rothschild would always act in Austria's interests rather than his
own. But he was also keenly aware that he was king only by the grace of
Austria, and that Vienna was calling the shots.[45]

Rothschild held a significant advantage over its smaller competitors in
lobbying for the bond transaction. In a time when there was no easy access
to financial information on the issuers, especially not in the important yet
distant capital markets centres such as London, the quality and reputation
of the bank chosen by the issuer was of great importance.[46] Capitalisation of
the issuing bank was also of major importance, as the bank would often need

to step in if the issue were not properly subscribed or trading became erratic due to investor jitters caused by political unrest.

The Austrians, Russians and Prussians had good reason to be worried about Naples. There was a significant grassroots movement in support of constitutionalism, which was also in evidence on the Neapolitan stage. A patriotic drama favourable to liberalism and constitutionalism, *Amor di Patria* (Love of the Fatherland) had been put on at the Teatro dei Fiorentini and then at the Teatro San Carlo on 12 February 1821. Barbaja donated the proceeds of 400 ducats from the San Carlo performance to the patriotic cause, though it is unclear if this was done under duress or if he was just hedging his bets.[47] As a major beneficiary of the Bourbon monarchy, a more liberal regime might not have suited him too well; on the other hand the Austrian police in Naples suspected that Rossini was 'heavily infected by revolutionary principles'.[48]

From the safety of northern Italy, Ferdinand publicly denounced the recent constitution and welcomed the Austrians to Naples, while he waited out the tense period in Florence until the Austrian army had done its clean-up work. Austrian troops entered Naples unopposed on 23 March 1821, finding an already abolished constitution, a parliament professing loyalty to the king, and the *Carbonari* and revolutionaries around General Pepe having fled the kingdom. The troops were received by a cheering population – they tended to embrace every change in government.

Metternich was understandably displeased by his repeated need to intervene on behalf of an incompetent monarch: 'This is the third time I'm putting King Ferdinand on his feet ... he still imagines that the throne is an easy chair to sprawl and fall asleep in.'[49] Upon Ferdinand's return to Naples, Metternich urged moderation, aiming at 'excluding both despotism as well as the representative system'.[50] Ferdinand, however, soon reappointed the despised Prince Canosa as Chief of Police, and he unleashed his customary reprisals and bloody vengeance on the population, this time with the helpful assistance of Austrian bayonets.

Barbaja offered to lead a syndicate of mostly French financiers to issue the bond,[51] advancing 'thirty million to the Bourbon government at an issue price of 60%'.[52] Baron Vincent was unwilling to see the Rothschild offer undercut and told Carl Rothschild the terms of Barbaja's offer. Once he returned to Naples, Rothschild negotiated his terms directly with Vincent, and soon announced the bank's willingness to issue bonds worth 10 million ducats at a face value of 54 per cent, infuriating the Neapolitan Ministry of Finance, which was able to issue bonds with a smaller discount in other public markets. The Rothschilds eventually revised their offer to 60 per cent and raised 16 million ducats, selling the bonds in London and Paris. Barbaja had been outmanoeuvred.

In the event, the Neapolitan Government chose wisely. The bond issued by the Kingdom of Naples in 1821 and listed by the Rothschilds in Paris with cross-listing in London was deemed a success. Unlike many other govern-ments of the time (Greece, Portugal, Guatemala, Chile and Mexico), the Neapolitan issue was never in arrears, not least due to the Rothschilds' careful handling. The Rothschilds also had political clout beyond anything Barbaja was able to muster. The Vienna branch of the Rothschild family was trying hard – though ultimately in vain – to persuade Metternich to put an end to the Austrian occupation of Naples, which Naples was forced to finance by means of this bond.[53]

The sovereign bond firmly established C M de Rothschild & Figli as the leading foreign bank in Naples. Its long-term future, however, was no more secure than that of all the other foreign banks after the brief cosmopolitan era of Naples. C M Rothschild & Figli was run out of business with the demise of the Kingdom of the Two Sicilies and Bourbon rule in Italy in 1861.

The Viennese promise

The year 1821 started with Barbaja planning the season through to Lent 1822. But Barbaja's mind was elsewhere. The environment in Naples had swung back to the darkest days of political retribution and revenge, with the hated Head of Police, Prince Canosa, interfering in everyone's lives. The royal theatre's gambling tables were closed, robbing Barbaja of his ready source of cash. Rossini was in increasingly high demand in other cities – he was currently in Rome – and Barbaja had failed to secure other significant composers. The *Carbonari* were demonstrating against the increasing crackdowns by Govern-ment forces, their protests growing louder and ever more violent. Barbaja was in the thick of it all. Politics, however, was never of any real interest to him. He was a businessman and his sponsor was under pressure. Naples had become a much less attractive place.

The Barbaja-Rossini-Colbran trio had been experiencing some complete failures, and the resentment against all three was becoming more vehement. The press as well as the people on the street were more outspoken and direct in their criticism of the prima donna's increasing vocal shortcomings. Initially an admirer, Stendhal became one of her fiercest critics, writing that Colbran regularly sang off key and that her singing had become 'execrable'. He claimed she forced many patrons to flee the theatres and that she ruined performances by 'devastating and laying waste with the noble ruin of her voice'.[54] In one report on a performance, he commented: 'Last night La Colbran scarcely went wrong at all. She can't have been more than a semi-tone off key'.[55] Rather viciously, in a later review,[56] he wrote, 'one thing alone would have made the Neapolitans happy; not the gift of a Spanish constitution, but the elimination of Signora Colbran'.[57]

In 1821 Barbaja sent a succession of letters to the Superintendent of Theatres, the Duke of Noja, asking for more time for Colbran's voice to recover, as it seemed to be in a temporary crisis.[58] But the outcry was not just about an indisposed voice. Protesting against Colbran was tantamount to protesting against Barbaja. And protesting against Barbaja meant protesting against the King.[59]

Bourbon control had now been firmly reinstalled, courtesy of the king's relatives in Vienna. To the small middle class and the elite not directly linked to the monarchy, the Neapolitan Bourbon monarchy had lost all credibility. The silver lining for Barbaja was the sudden opening of a completely new market: Vienna. In July 1821 none less than Prince Leopoldo, the Prince of Salerno and the son of King Ferdinand, wrote from Vienna to his father, requesting his permission to invite Barbaja to Vienna to start an Italian season at the opera houses.[60] Italian opera had become all the rage there and Leopoldo felt Barbaja would help the expansion of Italian cultural hegemony.

Some observers suggested that by exporting some of its finest cultural assets, the leading lights of Neapolitan opera, including Barbaja, his singers and Rossini, the city was thanking the Austrian Government for the restoratory invasion and political support.[61] The move aimed to please Metternich, an Italian music enthusiast and a passionate Rossini fan: to obtain the production quality he desired, Metternich needed Barbaja.

Barbaja was attracted by the much richer city and its enormous resources, and he did not wait around for the sovereign's answer to his son. In August 1821 he put his deputy, Antonio Giamberini,[62] in charge of the royal theatres and

departed for Vienna, causing the theatre authorities in Naples to complain
to the Ministry of Interior about the impresario's abrupt departure without
the Superintendent's permission.[63] But Barbaja of course had the protection of the King, and was following a royal invitation. Barbaja certainly had
no intention of actually relinquishing control of the Neapolitan stages. He
just wanted to control new and more appealing ones, while retaining full
oversight of the stages as well as his *cartello* in Naples.

Leaving Naples on 28 August 1821, Barbaja set off on a strenuous journey.
His first stop was Bologna, where he visited Rossini's parents and dropped
off a letter from him.[64] Clearly, relations between the two men were still good
enough. Barbaja next reached Milan, where he probably caught up with his
wife Rosa. The two saw each other so infrequently that one cannot imagine
that they remained close. Rosa had stayed behind in Milan when both the
children moved to Naples, and from then on Barbaja had arranged for the
continuation of their schooling in Naples and then abroad. Never emotionally
or romantically overwrought, Domenico no longer had anything in common
with his wife back in Milan.

Of far greater interest to Barbaja in Milan was the possibility of assuming
the *impresa* of La Scala, in addition to that of Vienna.[65] Barbaja had always
wanted to control the stages of his home city, and had tried (without success)
as early as 1805 to acquire the concession for the Milanese royal theatres.[66]
During his weeks in Milan, Barbaja prepared himself for assuming the
control of the stages both there and in Vienna, as the authorities in Milan
were searching for a successor for the season starting in 1822. The *appalto* of
La Scala under the impresarios Carlo Balochino (Barbaja's former partner)
and Giuseppe Crivelli had fallen apart in March 1821. Barbaja knew both well.
Only a year earlier, in 1820, he had financially backed Balochino and Crivelli
in their attempt to get the *impresa* for La Scala and he had put up the security
down payment to help them.[67] He would deal with them again several years
later when, this time, he would successfully take over La Scala.

Barbaja then continued to Vienna, arriving on 29 September, when he
finalised his discussions with the Viennese authorities, and signed the contract
for the Kaerntnertortheater on 6 November 1821.[68] Three days later, Barbaja
rushed back to Milan, in time to present his application for the *appalto* for
La Scala at the end of the month. The impresario was armed with a letter
from the imperial Viennese Court, which strongly recommended Barbaja as
the right man to deal with the 'capricious behaviour' and 'insatiable' demands

of the singers and dancers at La Scala.[69] Given the strong influence of the Austrian authorities on their theatre officials in Milan, the letter would have carried a fair bit of weight. Barbaja lobbied hard to convince the Milanese theatre authorities but the proposal failed due to his demands for a hefty endowment.[70]

By early December, Barbaja had returned home to Naples where he faced a barrage of complaints from the Superintendent about his absence and the quality of his productions, all of which he defended with utmost vigour. Barbaja was to remain in Naples until his relocation to Vienna in early 1822.

About the time Barbaja was returning to Naples, Rossini wrote to his parents not only about his undying love for 'La Colbran', but also of his intention to marry her and take her into his family.[71] What had been a long, simmering affair had turned into a serious relationship.

Rossini had also decided not to extend his contract with Naples and Barbaja, and he was going through an extended farewell to the city. In late December, the San Carlo put on a final benefit concert for Rossini,[72] aptly named *Riconoscenza* (Gratitude).[73] Though the Cantata was written in honour of a royal visitor,[74] this performance would be for Rossini, as all subscriptions were to be suspended, the revenues instead going to the composer. The concert would be an homage from the composer to the city and audience that had truly launched him, but also a farewell from the Neapolitan audience to the man who had become its favourite composer.

The newspapers touchingly reported how sad Naples was to see the great composer depart after six years, and praised the benefit performance, which played to a full house and was attended by the king, the royal family, all the Government ministers and selected nobility. The benefit brought in 3,000 ducats. Rossini was by this time considered a true Neapolitan: he had exorcised the troubled spirits of the great Neapolitan composers of the past, and been fully taken to the hearts of the city's people.

The last opera Rossini wrote for Barbaja was *Zelmira*. The opera was planned for Vienna, and was Rossini's first commission intended for a foreign market. For Vienna, Rossini needed to write a 'serious opera for a serious company'[75] and to showcase the star singers. The opera had a sneak preview of sorts at the San Carlo on 16 February 1822. The performance was led by Colbran, Nozzari,

David and Antonio Ambrogi,[76] the hugely talented bass who had been signed by Barbaja in 1819. The King attended the emotionally heightened performance, which as the trio's final production was rapturously received. The king as well as the audience dreaded to see the departure of such an illustrious cast, which Barbaja was imminently to transfer to Vienna, along with the production.

In early March, immediately after the last performance of *Zelmira*, Rossini and Colbran left Naples, but not for Vienna. They headed straight for Bologna, where the couple was married on the Colbran family estate of Castenaso on 13 March 1822. The wedding was a low-key event attended by Rossini's parents, and the singers Nozzari, David and Ambrogi. Barbaja was not invited.

It is hard to know quite why Rossini took the step of entering a formal union with Colbran. He was famously cynical and aloof from emotional commitments with women. Also, at 37, Colbran was near the end of the childbearing age of the time, was seven years older than the composer and had only relatively recently emerged from a liaison with Barbaja. But she was intensely religious.

Barbaja was quick to shrug off their romantic interlude. But what really went on in his mind we will never know. The impresario and biographer Gino Monaldi wrote that while Barbaja was shocked when he heard of the involvement of the woman who had until so recently been his mistress with his leading composer and business partner, he did not so much as bat an eyelid before turning his attention away from his 'terrifying favourite' towards another of his prima donnas, the contralto Teresa Cecconi.[77]

Nevertheless he would resent the slight until late in his life. Paganini, who knew both parties well, wrote that 'Rossini's marriage to Colbran made a fool of Barbaja',[78] and Stendhal claimed that Rossini making off with the great impresario's mistress was 'a practical joke in the worst imaginable taste'.[79] The Austrian novelist Lucka concludes his novel *Der Impresario* with Barbaja and Colbran walking on a balmy Neapolitan evening and Barbaja suggesting that Rossini and Colbran would make a nice couple, consciously pushing her away from him, and opening the field for new adventures of his own.

The likeliest scenario is that Barbaja remained emotionally rather detached from the event. While Colbran was clearly special, and not just because of her prodigious talent and financial independence, she was one of a string of lovers and mistresses of the great impresario, which included singers, ballerinas, society ladies and prostitutes. It is unlikely that Colbran shared the liberal mores of the day. While occasional biographers have linked her romantically with Paganini[80] and even King Ferdinand,[81] this seems improbable given her religious beliefs.

It is more plausible that as a strong, successful artist of independent means Colbran longed for attention and warmth that Barbaja was unable to provide, and that the impresario was unwilling to commit to her. While Barbaja was happy for her to be taken up by a friend, he may have been taken by surprise when their relationship became so serious. He would certainly not have appreciated the public humiliation of her marriage to his business partner. In all likelihood, he decided to 'put a good face on it',[82] but later sought his revenge on Rossini among others by trying to retain the original manuscript of *Zelmira*, starting a bitter dispute.

The close and trusting association between Barbaja and Rossini came to an end, and the friendly written correspondence between the two men virtually went dead. While Barbaja and Rossini were contractually bound to work together for a few months in Vienna in the coming year, there was no question of Barbaja trying to entice Rossini to compose for him in Naples again. Rossini had no appetite to return to Naples, and he did not want Colbran to either.

The King of the Two Sicilies, as usual, remained out of touch and well above the private affairs of those in the theatres. In February 1823, when Ferdinand reviewed the list of artists planned for the upcoming season that had been prepared by Barbaja for the Superintendent, he asked his staff to let Barbaja know that while he approved of the programme, he would prefer it if Barbaja would again engage Rossini for the season, given the warm reception of all his operas.[83]

7

The Conquest of Vienna

(1822–1824)

In September 1821, the *Allgemeine Musikalische Zeitung* wrote of rumoured discussions for the *Intendanz* (German for *'impresa'*) of the Kaerntner-tortheater to be taken on by Barbaja in association with the ballet producers Louis Duport and Count Wenzel von Gallenberg.[1] Referring to Barbaja as 'Conte Barbaja', this was the first time the newspaper mentioned him directly. The city Barbaja would be moving to in February 1822 was going through a political, economic and cultural renaissance.

The Austrian Empire of the Habsburgs had had some major military set-backs with resulting losses of territory during the Napoleonic Wars. The capital had also endured two occupations by the Napoleonic armies. But ultimately the Austrians had regained their force and had played a leading role in Napoleon's downfall. Napoleon had died in 1821. Vienna was now the centre of the most powerful dynasty in Europe: the Austrian Habsburgs had blood ties to the rulers of Spain, France and, of course, Naples.

The Habsburg Austrian Empire brought together a vast collection of territories in southern Germany, Slovenia, Bavaria, Trieste, Bohemia, Dalmatia and parts of Hungary. But under Emperor Franz I, Vienna was still recovering financially from the enormous costs of the Napoleonic Wars and the impact of the Vienna Congress, which rolled back most of the French territorial expansion, redrew the European political map and defined the spheres of influence of Austria, Britain, France and Russia.

The construction boom in the city of 267,000 inhabitants had yet to begin.[2] St Stephen's Cathedral with its coloured, zigzag-patterned tiled roof was already the city's best known landmark. The Schoenbrunn Palace had only just been refurbished and given its characteristic coat of yellow paint. The famous Ringstrasse that today surrounds the core of historic Vienna had not yet been conceived. The city was still surrounded by those remnants of the old city fortifications that Napoleon's troops had not destroyed, and a wide tree-lined grass strip replaced the defensive walls. The Vienna State Opera that stands today was yet to be built.

Upon his first arrival in Vienna, Barbaja could have had no doubt that he had entered the political centre of the European world. The city was in a completely different league from Naples, yet in some respects it also fell short, as a leading English travel guide described:

> Vienna ... is small but heavily fortified; its Faubourgs,[3] however, are immense, and contain finer buildings than the town itself; in which the palaces are few, and not spacious; and the want of splendid streets, and squares, prevents it from appearing, to foreign eyes, a handsome city.[4]

Indeed, Vienna at the time appeared almost a rural city, with woods, vegetable gardens, vineyards and even game reserves close to the city centre. Though Vienna lacked much of the visual grandeur of Naples, there was also much that would have struck Barbaja as similar. The city was ruled by the imperial family which patronised and promoted the theatres; music was the heart and soul of the city; cultural salons were a local tradition; and coffee-shops were ubiquitous and full of the secret police (led by Count Sedlnitzky – the Austrian equivalent of Naples' hated Prince Canosa – and disrespectfully referred to as 'Metternich's poodle'[5]). The Viennese also shared the Neapolitans' enjoyment of all forms of entertainment and their appreciation of pomp and pageantry. Barbaja would also have noticed with glee that the Viennese served their coffee with a heavy dollop of cream on top, reminiscent of his very own Barbagliata.

The Neapolitans arrive

Barbaja set himself up in the Hotel zum Goldenen Ochsen on the Spiegel und Seilergasse, one of the best hotels in Vienna and an easy stroll from the Kaerntnertortheater. In a tourist guidebook from 1840 it is listed as among the top ten hotels in the city.[6] Barbaja would have noticed the exorbitant cost of accommodation. Viennese hotels were among the costliest in Europe, and significantly more expensive and less clean than their equivalents in Paris.[7] The guidebook also reminded the visitor that (this in 1840!) smoking was not permitted in the centre of the city, on bridges, on heavily trafficked promenades, and in front of the bastion and the sentry post.[8] The Metternichian love of order was alive and well in early 19th-century Vienna, and Barbaja must have been stunned by the contrast to the chaotic and colourful Naples.

The Viennese economy was principally focused on the production and trade of silk textiles, sugar refining and porcelain manufacturing. But the theatres also provided an important source of employment in the city. Vienna supported five major theatres, including the Kaerntnertortheater and the Burgtheater, in addition to the suburban Theater an der Wien, the Leopoldstadt Theater and the Josefstadt Theater.

The Viennese music scene of the early 1820s was considered the most innovative and modern in the world. The opera stages of Naples, Venice and possibly Paris outshone the Vienna opera houses, but in terms of orchestral composition, Vienna was the undisputed capital. Its music was considered more refined and more advanced and, after years of exposure to musical giants such as Mozart, Beethoven and Haydn, the audience was even more sophisticated than that of Naples. But the Viennese stages were in desperate need of a shake-up, having suffered dramatic declines in audience attendance, which had resulted in the regular issue of large numbers of free tickets. Barbaja was intent on showing the Viennese something they had never experienced. He would deliver the pomp of the Naples theatres and his very own brand of glamour, as well as his unique approach to management.

Barbaja made a characteristically high profile arrival in Vienna, ensuring the press knew all about him and his plans for the Viennese opera in advance. The newspapers were full of the impending arrival of Barbaja and his Italian troupe, and the upper classes were bristling in anticipation and excitement at what Barbaja planned to do with the Kaerntnertortheater, the favourite theatre of the Habsburg Court. 'Goodbye German opera', proclaimed a leading Austrian musicologist when he heard about Barbaja's arrival in his city, accusing Barbaja of 'creeping' close to Metternich and other important figures in the Government in order to attain his objectives.[9] The Vienna correspondent of the *Allgemeine Musikalische Zeitung* reported: 'after the carnival the Neapolitan company is expected. The stranger [Barbaja] promises much, time will tell how many promises he can keep. At least the audience can look forward to some entertainment'.[10]

Far from needing to 'creep' to Metternich, whom Barbaja had already met several years earlier in Naples at the Rossini Cantata, Barbaja enjoyed some influential local support. When, during this, his first visit to Vienna, Barbaja signed the contract to take over the *Intendanz* of the Kaerntnertortheater, he had already received the backing of another influential family.

The impresario had obtained the unlikely support of the Rothschilds, who, as we know, had several months earlier outmanoeuvred him over the Neapolitan sovereign bond. Barbaja, apparently the only party interested in assuming the *Intendanz* of the struggling Kaerntnertortheater, had been short of cash and initially unable to post the 50,000 gulden cash deposit. The Vienna branch of the Rothschild family offered to pay and guarantee the sum in order to safeguard 'the further continuance of an entertainment worthy of the dignity of the Imperial court and the capital city', permitting Barbaja to take over the opera house.[11]

The Kaerntnertortheater was a prestigious theatre in the centre of Vienna, originally built in 1709 and named after the adjacent city gate, the Kaerntner Tor (Carinthian Gate), which led southwards out of the city. Its official title was the Kaiserliches und Koenigliches Hoftheater zu Wien, the 'Imperial and Royal Court Theatre of Vienna'. Like so many of its great European counterparts, the original Kaerntnertortheater had been destroyed in a fire (in 1761). It had been rebuilt by the Imperial Court, which had bought the theatre from the municipal authority. It specialised in Italian-style operas performed in German to a mostly upper-class audience, as it was authorised to charge higher ticket prices than the other royal theatres. Box-seat tickets normally cost around 5 florin at the Burgtheater and 20 florin (the equivalent of 4.65 ducats) at the Kaerntnertortheater for Italian opera, and 8 florin for German opera.[12] Well-known for its splendid interiors, it was also known to be rather cramped and could get extremely hot. The German poetess and librettist Helmina von Chézy (1783–1856) found the Kaerntnertortheater torturously uncomfortable and 'tropically' hot.[13]

The contract that gave Barbaja the *Intendanz* of the Kaerntnertortheater as sole lessee for a period of 12 years featured several break clauses and detailed obligations.[14] There was also a cultural protection clause, which mandated that Barbaja put on a minimum of three German operas of high quality per week, to ensure that the Austrian cultural legacy would not be railroaded by the suddenly popular operas emanating from the Italian states.[15] He was also expected to put on at least three ballets per week, but he also had the right to put on Italian opera for several weeks.[16]

In his negotiations with Government officials regarding what his responsibilities would entail at the Kaerntnertortheater, Barbaja demanded several structural improvements to the theatre, including the installation of a comfortable lavatory.[17] Proper lavatories were clearly of concern to Barbaja; he had also introduced them in the San Carlo.

Barbaja also took a stake in a second theatre, the Theater an der Wien, as an associate of a Count Palffy. In Count Ferdinand Palffy, Barbaja had met his first Austro-Hungarian version of an impresario. A mining engineer and civil servant of Hungarian origins, Palffy invested most of his fortune into Viennese opera houses from 1807 onwards, until he took outright control of the Theater an der Wien in 1813, a theatre he controlled until 1826. Barbaja and Palffy's cooperation at the theatre lasted only five months until the two fell out.[18] Stylistically and commercially they were completely incompatible.

Apart from his short interest in the Theater an der Wien, Barbaja's principal focus in Vienna was the Kaerntnertortheater;[19] he also continued to oversee the Naples theatres, albeit mostly from a distance. He did not wait long to make his management felt. While improving the quality of the lead performers, Barbaja concurrently cut back the costs. He dismissed many of the theatre's staff members, especially the older ones, and reduced the salaries of the others. The dismissals drove many older musicians into unemployment, some even into poverty, though the municipality tried to give new positions to as many as possible in the Government-run Burgtheater orchestra.[20] Many of the old favourites of the Viennese stage saw their contracts cut as they were overshadowed by the new stars from Italy.[21]

Barbaja also dramatically raised the ticket prices for the Italian operas, something to which the audience quickly grew accustomed. 'Prices doubled, full house, thunderous applause', the German press reported.[22] Helmina von Chézy was less impressed: 'this lively and energetic Italian, who raised the box seats in the opera theatre to 80 florin [four times more than the standard 20 florin], which had never been done before, and still managed to incur a loss of 3 million florin for the season.'[23]

In order to ensure more reliable and predictable revenue, Barbaja introduced the 'Italian practice' of opera subscriptions to the Vienna opera houses, a first for Austria.[24] Prior to that, theatres mainly sold tickets on a one-off basis at the door. Barbaja made the primacy of his commercial interests perfectly clear. In 1823 he offered the well-known pianist Ignaz Moscheles unlimited use of the Kaerntnertortheater as a performance venue as long as the pianist split half the proceeds with him.[25] Not used to such pragmatic commercial arrangements, the pianist was understandably outraged.

The money he saved from the lower fixed costs Barbaja pumped into large productions, with decorations that were extravagant and lavish. He brought in the stars from his Neapolitan troupe, including Giovanni David, Andrea Nozzari, Domenico Donzelli and Luigi Lablache, and also took on the popular French soprano Josephine Fodor 'for one year, with the unbelievable salary of 50,000 francs',[26] as the shocked German press reported.

The outflow of marquee names from Naples was so significant that Barbaja started running into some weighty opposition back home. He signed the hugely popular bass Luigi Lablache for a three-year contract commencing Lent 1823. The contract stipulated that the singer, a dyed-in-the-wool Neapolitan and a key member of Barbaja's stable, would sing at the impresario's pleasure in cities and on stages dictated by him. Barbaja's assuming a theatre in Vienna clearly meant that the leading bass would be required to sing at the Kaerntnertortheater. King Ferdinand I, however, was also a vociferous admirer of Lablache,[27] and he had appointed the singer to the Royal Chapel after the Congress of Laibach in 1821, regardless of any other legal commitments the singer might have. Though the appointment to the Royal Chapel was largely honorific, when the time came for Lablache to depart for Vienna, the King became indignant and threatened to withdraw Lablache's passport. A contretemps ensued between Ferdinand and Barbaja, and discussions followed between the Ministry of the Interior, the Royal Deputation of Theatres and Spectacles and the deftly lobbying Barbaja, until it was resolved in the latter's favour. The Government realised it had no legal grounds on which to retain Lablache, and the passport was returned to him. Barbaja's only concession was to delay the basso's departure from Naples for a few months.[28]

Nevertheless, Barbaja had to continue to maintain a certain quality in Naples. In February 1822 he wrote a letter to the Duke of Noja to justify a casting decision, going to great lengths to explain that the absence of Colbran, Nozzari, Ambrogi and David would not harm the quality of the theatres, given the strong replacements he had lined up, which included Donzelli, Rubini and Comelli (Comelli was Rubini's wife).[29] Barbaja still depended on the Government's goodwill, as he needed the police to issue passports to his leading singers as well as to Rossini, which they could refuse to do if the King objected.[30] Valid passports for his many travelling artists were vital to Barbaja's business.

Rossini was Barbaja's trump card for the first season at the Kaerntner-tortheater. The composer's operas had been performed – mostly in German – well before Barbaja's arrival,[31] and he had already become a favourite with the audience, and was acknowledged as a major force of the local opera stage. But the frenzy for Rossini was upped a notch with the arrival of the composer himself, Isabella Colbran and five other leading singers on 23 March 1822. 'Rossini and Paganini: everything else was forgotten,'[32] wrote one of Schubert's biographers. Under Barbaja's direction, Rossini's operas now took the Austrian capital by storm. Reaching Vienna just a few days after their wedding,[33] the Rossinis would remain in Vienna, also staying at the Goldener Ochsen, until July 1822.[34]

For Barbaja, working with Rossini so soon after the composer's marriage to Colbran must have been awkward. For the Viennese audience, however, Rossini's presence was cause for celebration:

> … the Swan of Pesaro cast the Viennese under his spell. That extravagant and lascivious warlock shakes melodies out of his arm like the magician on stage produces doves and roses from nowhere …[35]

Colbran was a complete triumph as *Elisabetta* in June 1822, the reviewers writing that they had 'never before seen as beautiful acting from a singer'.[36]

Nobody was happier about the Italian cultural invasion than the Chancellor Metternich: 'What a good episode in my life is the establishment of the Italian opera here. It has at last succeeded and I have gained a real and important victory.'[37] Metternich wanted Rossini in Vienna not only for his spectacular musical abilities, but also because Rossini's operas suited the Chancellor's conservative values. Rossini's works did not incite rebellion, and they helped to put pressure on Germanic composers such as Beethoven, who had been writing music that was distastefully supportive of liberty and openness, such as his opera *Fidelio*, a celebration of freedom and liberalism and a call to overthrow tyranny.

Metternich was enraptured by the quality of the Italian cast, and wrote in detail in his memoirs about the performances and the singers, who included Colbran and his personal favourite, the tenor Giovanni David, 'who surpasses them all'.[38] 'At the head of all', wrote Metternich, 'is Rossini himself, with an orchestra and chorus which astonish everyone. It may be [easily] supposed what a delight this gives to a *melomaniac* like me.'[39]

The fronts between the supporters of traditional German opera and imported Italian fare began to solidify, and a competition over musical taste and direction ensued in the Viennese coffee-shops and salons. The Chancellor entered the fray firmly on the Italian side:

> This evening I was at the German opera for the first time. But a German voice is quite pitiable in comparison with the Italian. People don't open their mouths, and seem to think the nose is also an organ of the human voice.[40]

Barbaja himself, however, was not content to stage only Italian operas. He needed to develop some German productions as well. While in Vienna, Barbaja had heard of the promising composer Carl Maria von Weber, who was employed at the Saxon Court in Dresden. He had only recently garnered enormous success with his opera *Der Freischuetz* (The Free Shooter), which had premiered in Berlin in June 1821. *Der Freischuetz*, with its chilling scenes of the supernatural set in an orderly village at the edge of a dark forest, was a typically traditional German story about huntsmen.

The opera's structure and sophisticated orchestration was a watershed for German romantic music and influenced generations of composers, including Weber's great admirer Richard Wagner. The sets for *Der Freischuetz* in Berlin further underlined the 'German-ness' of the production. They were designed by Carl-Wilhelm Gropius and Karl Friedrich Schinkel. The former was a set designer with a strong interest in diorama, the latter Berlin's leading architect and city planner as well as official stage designer for the Prussian Court.[41] Weber also had revolutionary ideas on stagecraft and audience participation, some of which would certainly have resonated with Barbaja:

> Yes, the energy of expression must be added. The audience that appears at the art events is cold and disengaged and must be strongly attacked, be forced into participation and empathy, must be dragged vigorously into the artistic circle, because on its own it will not become excited.[42]

Weber fully understood how to capture the audience, and made generous use of the effects of modern lighting in his operas. Theatre illumination was still in its infancy. Most lighting was still by candles. Gas lights were only gradually introduced in the late 19th century, after being adopted much earlier in London theatres. The use of a darkened theatre to heighten the dramatic effect and concentrate the audience's attention was widely discussed and requested by reform-minded theatre directors in the early 19th century, but it did not really catch on until Richard Wagner demanded it for all his productions in Bayreuth in 1876. Fully understanding the dramatic effect that he could achieve with light, Weber had insisted in 1821 that the opera at Dresden purchase the most modern Argand lamps for his productions and that the stage machinery be renovated.

Weber's *Der Freischuetz* opened just at the time when debate between the Viennese nobility, with their love for Italian opera, and the academics and those opposed to the 'foreign invasion', who sided with supporters of German musical and cultural ideas, was raging most furiously. There was a veritable battle for the hearts and minds of the Viennese audience between the German and Italian schools. By successfully producing a quintessentially German yet enormously popular and emotionally engaging opera, 'Weber had achieved, in June 1821, for the German Opera, what [General] Bluecher[43] had done, in June 1815, for German independence' and scored 'a decisive victory … at this great battle in favour of German art' wrote Max Maria von Weber, the composer's son and biographer.[44] Aside from its critical acclaim, *Der Freischuetz* proved a financial boon to the Berlin theatres. It was possibly the opera's financial success, rather than the nationalist interest, that principally prompted Barbaja to contact the composer. He was also attracted to the spectacular staging opportunities that Weber's *Der Freischuetz* offered, with its pyrotechnics, suspense and eerie atmospherics.

The letter from the well-known impresario inviting the composer to write a new opera for Vienna helped Weber snap out of one his frequent bouts of depression. Weber had heard of Barbaja's reputation for developing talent and he admired the first-rate opera troupe that the impresario had pulled together in the city. After popping the champagne and celebrating Barbaja's invitation, he accepted his offer to meet up in Vienna. In their first meeting, they discussed Weber's ability to write an opera 'in the style of *Der Freischuetz*' for the 1822/23 season at the Kaerntnertortheater, and reviewed several possible librettos that Weber could set to music.

Weber was more than a little intimidated, not only by Barbaja's offer, but also by the long shadow cast by Rossini, as his son and biographer wrote:

On the one hand was the German, small, insignificant and weakly ... On the other, stood proudly the magnificent Italian, with his fine form, born to be a friend of princes; ... the husband of a beautiful singer, who had ruled monarchs by her witcheries; the winner of the grand prize in life's lottery; accustomed to see fortune, love, and honour dance round him like humble slaves.[45]

But Weber had no regrets about throwing in his lot with Barbaja, whom he initially found 'pompous but well meaning ... straightforward and honourable'. [46]

Leaving his family behind, Weber travelled to Vienna and put on *Der Freischuetz* to great acclaim. For the new opera, Barbaja and Weber settled on *Euryanthe*, a libretto written by the relatively unknown Helmina von Chézy, as the composer had fallen out with the librettist of his successful earlier works. The plot of *Euryanthe* about a wager relating to a seduction that goes wrong, was based on an equally ludicrous 13th-century French romance. The libretto was not a very promising piece of prose, but Weber felt he could turn it into an engaging piece of music, and he tried to compose something in the 'Italian' style. This meant it would be fully sung, rather than having the extensive spoken parts of *Der Freischuetz* or other German operas at the time.[47] As we have seen, Barbaja was not a friend of the dry recitative. He had encouraged Rossini away from it, and now he did the same with the German composer.

Despite constantly swinging in and out of depression, and taking any negative reports on his previous performances deeply to heart, Weber managed to put together *Euryanthe* under the careful guidance of Barbaja and his team. The interaction was not always smooth, and Weber's view of Barbaja grew to be that of a man whose

... vulgar, florid, sensual outward appearance was far from stamping him as a man of enterprise and genius; whilst his singular mixture of meanness and extravagance, of noble-heartedness and parvenu vulgarity, of generosity and harshness, seemingly unfitted him for a position so delicate and responsible ...[48]

During the year 1822, Barbaja seems to have virtually commuted between
Naples and Vienna, and with his frequent absences, he had to rely on capable
associates and deputies. In Naples, he relied on his experienced deputy, Giam-
berini. In Vienna, Barbaja started delegating much of his authority over the
Kaerntnertortheater to his associate, the elderly former ballet dancer Louis
Duport who, according to Barbaja, 'got through his business in a pirouette'.[49]
Barbaja and Duport vigilantly steered Weber through the casting process
and the production of his work, recommending and sponsoring the young
German soprano Henriette Sontag, renowned for her precocious talent as
well as her good looks.

The atmosphere on the opening night of *Euryanthe*, 25 October 1823, was
electric. The tickets had completely sold out. Weber's supporters were keen to
see the success of *Der Freischuetz* repeated with this dramatic new opera. They
felt the composer embodied the very soul of contemporary German opera.
His many detractors were just as eagerly sitting in the stalls hoping to witness
a disaster with this reputedly overlong opera that would bring down the
emotionally wrought composer. The famously caustic music critics of Vienna
were out in full force, their pens at the ready. Waiting in silence for the curtain
to rise, the tension was broken by comic relief when the librettist Chézy, who
was not only controversial and cantankerous but also obese, shoved her way
through the packed aisles to her seat in the stalls, shrieking loudly that she was
the poetess, and bringing down the house with laughter. When the composer
himself took the podium, however, calm fell on the house.

After a slow start, Weber began to entrance the audience, whipping the
astounded Viennese – even the Italian faction – into a frenzy. Vienna was
ecstatic. While the audience condemned the ludicrous story and libretto, the
music was enthusiastically embraced. Barbaja was delighted.

Some days later, in the café where Vienna's writers, artists and singers
congregated, Weber's new work was also praised – except by a few curmudg-
eonly music critics and by the always argumentative composer Franz Schubert,
who labelled the new opera 'unmusical'[50] and lacking in melody. The situation,
if one is to believe the sources of the time, was salvaged when the 53-year-
old musical giant Beethoven joined the discussion and said that he had been
told the opera was a huge success: 'Yes, the German can still hold his own
above all the Italian sing-song.'[51] He had not attended the performance 'due
to *these*', he told the assembly, pointing to his ears. Beethoven had been going
deaf for some time.

Barbaja's casting of Henriette Sontag also proved fortuitous. Professionally singing since the age of 15, and barely 17 years old when she premiered the
title role of *Euryanthe*, Sontag enchanted the audience and went on to have
one of the most remarkable stage careers of the time. Beethoven was quite
smitten with the young girl and immediately after the performance ended
asked, 'how did the little Sontag sing?'[52] About a year later, the by then totally
deaf Beethoven cast Sontag in the first performance of his Symphony No 9
and his Mass in D.

Barbaja had put Weber not only at the top of the ranking of the most
important stage of the Habsburg Empire, he had also manoeuvred the
German composer to score a win in the ongoing German-Italian musical
debate. Encouraged by this success, Barbaja engaged Franz Schubert to write
an opera for the Kaerntnertortheater the same year. Schubert, whose health
was already failing him though he had not even begun to write some of his
greatest masterpieces, already enjoyed an established reputation as an orchestral composer. However, as an opera composer the 27-year-old Austrian had
never met any success in spite of many attempts.

The fact that Barbaja engaged Schubert to write the opera *Fierrabras* for
his Viennese theatre 'was in and of itself an honour'.[53] Schubert was hopeful
it would lead to his breakthrough on the opera stage and help get him out
of the rut in which he currently found himself. He, too, struggled with bouts
of depression. But *Fierrabras* was a complete failure. Suffering from a weak
libretto as well an unfortunate dramatic structure, the opera did not see the
light of day. Nobody was willing to attempt the staging, very least the impresario who had commissioned the work. Though it was composed in 1823, it
was not performed until 1858, well after Schubert's and Barbaja's deaths, and
it quickly disappeared off the stage.

Though Schubert's *Fierrabras* never took off (nor did any of his 16 other
attempts to write operas), tales of Weber's success fed the popular press for
months. While Barbaja had put Rossini's operas on the front pages for many
months, it was also Barbaja who evened the score in the great musical debate
by promoting Weber. Some critics of course claimed that Barbaja deliberately pitted Rossini's operas against Weber's in an effort to fan the flames of
the German-Italian cultural competition.[54] More debate meant more press
coverage, and more press coverage encouraged greater ticket sales.

Whatever Barbaja's motivations, the year 1822 was seen as one of the
most brilliant in Viennese operatic history and the Milanese upstart could

be proud of his achievement. Dumas (père) wrote: 'He came to reign without contest of control over the Italian and the German audiences; that is to say two audiences: one is considered the most capricious, the other the most demanding in the universe.'[55]

⌁

Barbaja personally took day-to-day control of the Kaerntnertortheater in 1823, as Duport went on leave to take the baths in Karlsbad, the popular spa resort.[56] He was also soon assisted by Julius Benedict, a Jewish composer and conductor whom Barbaja had probably met through Weber, a former teacher of Benedict. Barbaja appointed Benedict as Musical Director of the Kaerntnertortheater in Vienna in 1823. His Italian seasons at the Kaerntner-tortheater went like clockwork. Being more or less transplanted from the Naples opera house, the well-rehearsed company put on tried and proven performances.

By then, however, back in Naples, King Ferdinand had begun to feel that Barbaja was neglecting what he saw as his principal responsibility, the Teatro San Carlo, and he demanded that Barbaja return some of the stars of the company, including David and Lablache.[57] While Barbaja tried to appease the King, he also requested passports for a new set of top artists from the Teatro San Carlo in order to bring them too to Vienna. In frustration, the King offered to double the ticket prices of the Teatro San Carlo to make Barbaja's return more attractive.[58]

The discussions between the King and Barbaja demonstrate the delicate interplay between the royal theatres and the impresarios, though few, if any, got away with the liberties Barbaja successfully claimed for himself. Barbaja's relationship with the King was a symbiotic one: though the King was clearly the strongest voice in the kingdom, he could not simply dictate terms to Barbaja; while Barbaja, on the other hand, still needed the royal patronage to be able to work successfully. Although Barbaja refused to return immedi-ately to Naples, one way for Barbaja to show his continued commitment to the Teatro San Carlo was to send stars like Giuditta Pasta there during his absence. Pasta was one of the new, favourite singers of King Ferdinand, as well as the audience. Barbaja also kept the authorities sweet by writing letters to the ever-present Duke of Noja explaining his compliance with his contractual obligations:

My objective is to raise awareness that my Impresa, honoured by the protection of the Government and without the benefit of Maestro Rossini in the last year, has resulted in a satisfied audience; the Impresa has not lost even a third of the amount it formerly lost every year. This encourages me to hope, that obtaining the continued support of the Government, my zeal will be crowned by a fortuitous success, and can help reduce the constant losses of the Royal Theatres, which, to my great satisfaction, I already see much diminished.[59]

Meanwhile in Vienna, the newspapers reported rumours that Barbaja was planning to renew his contract at improved terms and was lobbying those at the top of the Habsburg Court. At the same time, there were contradictory reports that Barbaja had asked to be released from his theatrical obligations. This was typical of Barbaja's Neapolitan negotiation tactics with the authorities.

This time, however, Barbaja would not be able to use the presence of Rossini or Colbran as the big trump cards in his negotiations. Mr and Mrs Rossini had left Vienna in July 1822, and were now in Venice preparing to put on *Semiramide*, the composer's latest work, as well as a revised version of *Maometto II*. Colbran sang in several performances at the Teatro La Fenice, but her voice was no longer up to the challenge. The Venetian audience proved that they could be just as vicious as the Neapolitans. The morning after one performance, the city was plastered with posters resembling traditional death announcements proclaiming, '*Pregate per l'anima della Colbran Rossini*' ('Pray for the Soul of Colbran-Rossini') – essentially 'Isabella Colbran: Rest in Peace'. The disaster put enormous pressure on the Rossini-Colbran relationship and spelled the end of Colbran's career.

Some weeks later, Barbaja tried to obtain the ownership rights for Rossini's *Semiramide*. The ownership issue was more clear-cut than with *Zelmira*, as Rossini had sold his rights in the original score to the Teatro la Fenice, which left the negotiations to the Viennese music publisher Artaria & Co. The publisher sent Barbaja a tightly worded contract selling him the performing rights to the opera, but limiting performances to the theatres of Naples and Vienna. The contract also snuck in a clause giving Artaria's wife a ticket to all performances at Barbaja's theatres, including the opening nights.[60]

The constant pressure and frequent and arduous travels were starting to take their toll on Barbaja, however, and he was now fighting long bouts of sickness. While no details of the nature of his illness are available, it was in all likelihood a respiratory ailment. Vienna's damp climate was well known to cause pulmonary disease and the General Secretary of the Kaerntner-tortheater noted the difficulties that the 'particularly rough spring weather'[61] could have on the Italian artists so used to a milder climate. Barbaja's extended illness was noted by the newspapers, as well as by the staff, and it was during these weeks that he again relied heavily on Duport.[62]

At the same time, his two star singers in Vienna, Fodor and David, announced that they wanted to leave the city,[63] putting additional strain on the exhausted impresario.

Rossini, meanwhile, had travelled to Paris in November 1823 to put on some performances and explore the possibilities of a musical directorship in the French capital. His arrival in Paris caused a similar sensation as his presence in Vienna had triggered a year earlier. By 1824, he would be taking up residence in Paris, where he assumed the musical leadership of the Théâtre-Italien (Italian Theatre). From being a junior partner and friend of Barbaja, Rossini now emerged as a business competitor.

Even before his move to Paris and while still in Vienna, Rossini already tried to strike a deal for the tenor Giovanni David to join him in Paris later in the year. David took pains to keep the negotiations secret from Barbaja, and ultimately chose to serve out his contract.

Once in Paris, Rossini was more blunt in his attempts to poach talent from Barbaja, and wrote to the singer Teresa Cecconi in Naples, asking her to join him.[64] An emerging singing star, Cecconi had entered the Barbaja stable in 1821, quickly rising to prima donna at the Neapolitan royal theatres. Her contralto voice boasted unusual clarity and impeccable diction and she was described by the press as captivating and having a mysterious force of enchantment.[65] Her charms were not lost on Barbaja, who had an intense romantic affair with the young singer. Persuading her to leave Naples would therefore prove much harder for Rossini. It was not the first time the composer and impresario would fall out – and it would not be the last.

8

Juggling Europe's Stages

(1824–1828)

When Barbaja returned to Naples in 1824 following his frenetic time in Vienna, he had already decided that he would not renew the contract for his engagement as impresario. His attention was elsewhere, the finances at the royal theatres were a growing problem with the gambling revenues now gone, and his personal affairs had been in better shape. His patron Ferdinand I was ailing and increasingly detached from affairs of state, which included the theatre.

Barbaja had already informed the Duke of Noja of his intention not to renew the concession. While the Government continued to provide the 95,000 ducat annual subsidy,[1] without the gambling revenues it had now become increasingly difficult for Barbaja to make a healthy profit.

Before Barbaja actually left this *impresa*, however, the royal theatre in Naples again grabbed the headlines. In February 1824 a fire suddenly broke out under the stage of the Teatro San Carlo. Only the extremely quick reaction of the stage hands saved the theatre from what could have been another catastrophic blaze.

The fire, however, raised the suspicions of the police, who suspected arson as the incident came so close to the expiry of Barbaja's management contract. Their main suspects were Barbaja himself, Francesco Tortolj (a nephew of the architect Antonio Niccolini and an up and coming young scenographer), the head of stage machinery and the head of the artificial fireworks unit of the theatre.[2]

The police believed that Barbaja might have wanted to create a new, lucrative reconstruction project for himself, which was of course hard to prove. But the police investigation revealed another problem: a significant accounting irregularity. The difference between what Barbaja had declared as costs for costumes in the corporate expense accounts and what they actually found in the theatre was dramatic, amounting to some 40,000 ducats of fictitious claims. The police alleged that Barbaja might have set the fire to avoid this being discovered during the customary inventory verification by the authorities at the end of the *stagione*.[3]

Pending a full investigation, Barbaja was placed under house arrest for a few weeks at his villa in Mergellina. Tortolj was less fortunate and was detained in a prison where he died miserably of cholera after three months. At the hearing in August 1824 the case was dropped for lack of evidence, and all charges were dismissed.

Before leaving for the north, Barbaja attended a benefit performance put on by the orchestra of the Teatro San Carlo in appreciation of the impresario's 14 years of uninterrupted service to the theatre.[4] The records are silent on whether Barbaja took a cut of the earnings, but the press reported that a violinist's widow who had fallen on hard times was one of the beneficiaries.[5] This gesture helped build Barbaja's spreading reputation for helping the financially downtrodden, something even Dumas (père) took note of: 'After having amassed his fortune cent by cent, Barbaja spent it on royal extravagance and generous acts of charity.'[6] Indeed, there are frequent passing comments in press reports relating to Barbaja's generosity, especially towards the poor.

Such charity did not extend to his successor, however, for whom Barbaja was determined to make life difficult. Even as Barbaja was leaving the royal theatres, he was working out the best way of regaining control of them – on his own terms. He made sure the Superintendent allowed him to publicise the fact that he was giving up the *impresa*:[7] Barbaja wanted to disassociate himself publicly from the failure he was plotting for his successor.

Barbaja's unlucky successor in Naples was Joseph Glossop, an Englishman who made his life and career in Italy. Glossop hailed from a wealthy English family of tallow-chandlers and was utterly stage-struck.[8] He invested around £30,000[9] of family funds to build the Coburg Theatre in London, named in honour of Princess Charlotte and Prince Leopold of Saxe-Coburg. The theatre later became the Royal Victoria, and is now known as the Old Vic; it is still active today.[10]

Attracted by the Italian stages, he set off for the continent in 1822. Glossop

– perhaps naïvely – was only interested in the theatrical aspects of the impresario's role. He married twice, both times to opera singers (one being Elisabetta Ferron).[11] In December 1823 Glossop contracted to be the *impresario* of Naples from 1824 to 1827, as well as of Milan for the season 1824/25, perhaps hoping to replicate the successes of Barbaja. On 30 May 1824, he began his *impresa* at the Teatro San Carlo.

Barbaja, meanwhile, began his campaign to destroy him. While publicly pretending to help Glossop, he threw manifold obstacles in his way. In the programme notes for the opening night of his first opera at the San Carlo, a performance of Rossini's *Semiramide*, Glossop complained about his long and arduous trip to Naples, and also about the lack of available singers (the good ones had all been taken to Vienna by Barbaja). He also apologised in advance if he were not able to put on a satisfactory season.

The Ministry of the Interior wrote of 'the pleasure manifested by his Majesty the King to see Signora Fodor and Signor Lablache at the beginning of the operation of this new *impresa*'.[12] Both were signed to Barbaja, and while he proclaimed himself delighted to let Glossop cast the two star singers from his stable, he only did so at an inflated rate and with severe performance limitations, restricting them to playing only three times a week, which was low for the 19th century. Claiming huge generosity and goodwill in loaning his singers, Barbaja then proceeded to threaten Glossop over delayed payment for the singers. The situation between the two quickly deteriorated, and they ended up in the commercial courts in a bitter dispute over rights to the musical archives, costumes and stage machinery.

While Barbaja was sabotaging his successor in Naples, Vienna was alive with chatter about the impending return of the Italian troupe. The Viennese press was cynical: 'Mr Barbaja will probably once again muster all his resources in order to ignite the easily combustible Viennese with his invincible legionnaires, and through the strong influence then again attain an advantageous concession contract for the following season.'[13]

Expectations were running high as Barbaja was reported to be bringing with him even more of his top singers, including G B Rubini, Antonio Ambrogi and Elisabetta Ferron.[14] The composer Saverio Mercadante would also join the company.[15]

In April 1824 Louis Duport, on behalf of Barbaja, who was still in Naples, wrote to Beethoven, asking the great German composer if there were any possibility of his writing a new opera for the Vienna opera house, provided

Barbaja kept the *Intendanz* beyond 1 December 1824, when his contract was due for renewal.[16] Beethoven had actually been planning to perform his Symphony No 9 in Berlin, since he felt that Vienna would not fully appreciate his work given the current frenzy for Italian music, but friends persuaded him otherwise. His agent wrote to Duport, asking for his cooperation in renting the Kaerntnertortheater for the performance, as negotiations with Count Palffy's Theater an der Wien had proved fruitless. Duport agreed, and Beethoven premiered the Symphony, with its 'Ode to Joy', on 7 May 1824 at the Kaerntnertortheater. The performance featured the young singers Henriette Sontag and Caroline Unger,[17] and was a resounding success.

By July, Barbaja was back in Vienna to submit his conditions for continuing to operate the concession of the Viennese Kaerntnertortheater, a topic of great interest to the city's café society. The rules dictated that the concession should go to the impresario asking for the smallest subsidy. Barbaja confused observers by claiming first that the subsidy of 140,000 florins was too little, then that he would be willing to work for a smaller sum, to be negotiated.[18] In the middle of the month the deadline for the concession of the Kaerntnertortheater expired. As no credible or competent alternative had turned up and the two Austrian contenders were unable to make sufficient down payment, everyone expected that Barbaja would take the reins again:

> Barbaja, around whom many strange rumours are circulating, is back here [Vienna] after returning to Naples to clear his name from a series of accusations [relating to the suspected arson at the San Carlo]. One expects him to retain the imprese after all, even if the subsidy will be reduced to a tenth.[19]

Even in distant Vienna, Barbaja kept half an eye on what was happening in Naples and continued to do his best to ensure that Glossop's Neapolitan *impresa* would struggle. Soon the newspapers were reporting that Glossop's *impresa* was doing very poorly: 'cabals are part of the problem … operas did not find the audience's pleasure, principally due to the choice of singers'.[20] This was to be expected given Barbaja's stranglehold on nearly all the top singers. The situation of the *impresa* was so worrying that composers started abandoning ship. Gaetano Donizetti, who was then composing for the Naples theatres, urgently tried to get assignments in other cities in order to escape the lamentable conditions.[21]

As Glossop's contract stipulated that he would forfeit the *impresa* after one year if the sovereign were not fully satisfied, it was widely expected that it would pass back to Barbaja. By the spring, Glossop was at the end of his financial resources; he had not even been able to make good on the 40,000 ducat down payment still owing for the *impresa*,[22] having already incurred a personal loss of about the same amount.[23] King Ferdinand practically begged Barbaja to return to the royal theatres. Barbaja humbly and graciously accepted, though naturally on much improved conditions, including permission for him to double the ticket prices for up to 40 performances.[24]

By Easter 1825 Barbaja was back in the saddle at the royal theatres of Naples, and with greater flexibility on the terms. He would remain in charge of them until 1840, with only one interruption in 1834–36. Barbaja had proved his point, showing the Government that it was impossible to run the theatres successfully under the conditions it imposed. This had unfortunately been done at the expense of poor Glossop, who fared so badly financially that he had to be bailed out by his family back in England and pawn his wife's jewellery.[25]

Barbaja's new tenure at the royal theatres in Naples would, however, be conducted under the patronage of a new king. King Ferdinand I of the Two Sicilies, Barbaja's benefactor and friend, had become less and less involved in state affairs, even in the theatrical affairs he so enjoyed, and spent most of his last months hunting. At 74 the King was content to leave the job of governing to his ministers and the Austrian troops, which he had requested remain in Naples to prevent 'new disorders'. He died on 25 January 1825 after a long day of hunting.

Barbaja cancelled all preparations for the elaborate 75th birthday of the monarch, and closed the San Carlo for a period of mourning. For Barbaja, just as for Naples, Ferdinand's death marked the end of an era. King Ferdinand I was succeeded by his son Francis, who inherited his father's weakness of character, but combined this with greater political ambition and an absence of personal flair. Sharing his father's obsessive fear of liberal tendencies, Francis infiltrated every possible institution with spies, who were to report on any liberal elements. Like his father, he did nothing to combat the pervasive corruption, crime and poverty, nor did he institute the necessary administrative reforms.

Known as Francis I, the king's first marriage was to his cousin, Archduchess Maria Clementina of Austria, daughter of the Holy Roman Emperor

Leopold II. When she died, he kept his choice in the family and married another first cousin, María Isabella, daughter of Charles IV of Spain. Maria Isabella went on to have 12 children with the King, while also satisfying her well-known appetite for young soldiers from the Royal Guard.

Francis's only remarkable achievement was to convince the Austrian troops to withdraw from Naples in July 1826, which greatly alleviated the financial pressures on the kingdom's Treasury. Once the last Austrian troops had left in early 1827, he brutally crushed an incipient *Carbonari* rebellion aimed at restoring the constitution, completely destroying the village where the rebellion originated. He then embarked on a witch-hunt lasting a year, culminating in executions, beheadings and the imprisonment of the leaders of the uprising: Francis I made his father seem like a benevolent monarch.

In November 1824, Barbaja's concession with the Viennese theatres had come to an end and he had cancelled all existing contracts, though most had little doubt that he would again extend his stay. 'Italian opera has become too settled to simply disappear again', reported a Viennese newspaper, which speculated that Barbaja's magic would in any case be working for the forth-coming marriage of Archduke Franz with Princess Sophie of Bavaria.[26] A month later, Barbaja had, as expected, extended his Viennese concession until February 1825, retaining his key singers with the exception of the tenor Giovanni David. The German press cynically commented that 'those of German tongue may get lost!',[27] but also recognised with a fair bit of envy that all the theatre boxes were sold out for the next three months, in spite of their elevated prices.

While Francis I was pushing to remove the Austrian troops from Naples, Barbaja focused on another busy season in Vienna. He needed to maintain the packed schedule of the previous year, which had featured 64 German operas (most of which were actually Italian operas merely sung in German) and 129 Italian operas.[28] Not content with the success in Vienna, Barbaja had planned a company tour to St Petersburg for spring 1825 to show his ensemble to the Russian Court, taking advantage of the good relations between the royal houses of Naples, Vienna and St Petersburg. The plan was scuppered, however, by the massive destruction brought about by the great flood of St Petersburg in November 1824, in which around 10,000 people perished. Two of his leading singers, Josephine Fodor and Luigi Lablache, had also refused to make the arduous journey to Russia. Barbaja was forced to cancel the tour.

This caused Barbaja to reconsider his Viennese plans, and he requested the authorities' permission to remain longer in Vienna, even offering to set up a French opera on the side. However, the Kaerntnertortheater was set to close for a season by Easter 1825, shortly after Barbaja's current contract ended, and they could not be moved. The Austrian press displayed its patriotism: 'This would be the best turn of events for Count Palffy's enterprise in the Theater an der Wien, since the competition with the truly extraordinary singing talent has most sadly brought down German opera.'[29]

It turned out quite differently, however. The Kaerntnertortheater remained open, Palffy went spectacularly bankrupt and Barbaja assumed responsibility for not only the Kaerntnertortheater but also for Palffy's Theater an der Wien in February 1825. Palffy, who had once been the most important figure in Viennese opera, was forced to sell his theatre in 1826, also losing his extensive mineral collection and library. He fled his creditors and died impoverished.

By May 1826, Barbaja had successfully signed the *impresa* for the Kaerntnertortheater for an additional three years.[30] He raised the money for the down payment from a variety of sources but, most controversially, took a loan from one of his singers, G B Rubini.[31] This was not only highly unusual for an impresario, but would also come back to bite Barbaja several years later.

Barbaja relied on Duport to launch the German repertory, while he pulled together the Italian company that was expected to start performing in autumn 1826. With control over both Viennese royal theatres, he bolstered the troupe by signing on more stars.

Similarly, he recruited local stars from the Viennese stages to take back to Naples and continued strengthening his *cartello* there, hiring the famously stubborn French prima donna Henriette Méric-Lalande, whom he engaged for a period of six years for the royal theatres.[32] In another move designed to strengthen the internationalism of his musical and management team, Barbaja sent the German Julius Benedict from Vienna to Naples in 1826. Barbaja deployed him in a variety of roles, including Musical Director, composer and cembalo player at the Teatro del Fondo. While he did a decent job, his own opera compositions had 'no impact'.[33]

Barbaja was also planning to commission new operas for the next Viennese season, when he hoped to show audiences a strong wave of fresh Italian talent. The Austrian newspapers were deeply concerned, claiming that this could signify the 'moral death for German art'.[34] As before, the impresario continued to exert relentless discipline in adhering to the letter of his singers' contracts. *The Times* of London related the following story of Barbaja and Lablache:

> At the time in question Lablache was singing here [Vienna] as a member of the Italian company under the Impresario Barbaja. An artist died, and Lablache was asked to sing a part in Mozart's Requiem, which he promised to do if Barbaja would allow him. As the old skinflint refused to give the permission demanded without indemnification, Lablache consented to pay 150 zwanzigers (5l.) as a fine. As Lablache had a truly Italian fondness for money, his resolution to do honour to his deceased colleague produced the greater sensation here.[35]

Clearly, at both Vienna and Naples, Barbaja ruled with an iron fist; determined as always to make his operas stages of the first rank. Neither, at the age of 50, had his ambitions decreased; in fact, he was now to make another great career leap.

Taking Milan

In spite of all his activities in Vienna and Naples, Barbaja had never lost interest in taking over the stages of Milan. Since Barbaja's youth in the Duchy, the city had shot ahead as a centre of commerce, developing a larger middle class and wider prosperity. Ceded to the Austrian Habsburgs at the Congress of Vienna, it was now part of the Kingdom of Lombardy Venetia, a constituent state of the Austrian Habsburg Empire. Ruled formally by Emperor Franz I of Austria, the kingdom was administered by a series of Austrian viceroys, who collected taxes for Vienna and imposed order in the territory. In the mid-1820s, the viceroy was Archduke Rainer Joseph (1783–1853), a son of Leopold II, Holy Roman Emperor.

While La Scala had not yet reached the importance it attained in the later 19th century, it was a much more formidable opera house than it had been in the 1790s when Barbaja was working the coffee tables opposite the theatre. When the composer Louis Spohr went to Milan he was struck by the fact that La Scala, the second largest theatre in Italy after the San Carlo, only had capacity for 3,000 people. In its large stalls and six tiers, the seats were not crammed together and he praised it for its generous use of space.[36] Spohr also liked the fact that it was the composer who led the performance while playing the first violin; there was no other visible leadership, other than the prompter, who whispered the text to the singers and possibly helped the chorus with the rhythm.

Stendhal agreed with the positive assessment, repeatedly pointing out his overall preference for La Scala over the San Carlo. The orchestra, he wrote, 'cringes before the singers, and is their humble, obsequious and most obedient servant',[37] contrasting it to less disciplined orchestras that drowned out the singers. Stendhal also preferred the Austrian-led government in Milan which he considered an 'oligarchic [as opposed to absolutist] monarchy' which was 'reasonable, economical and calculating',[38] and he particularly praised the Milanese for their love and understanding of music.

The directors of La Scala had been determined that the theatre would have the latest technology, especially in illumination. They had taken the lighting so seriously that the Austrian Milanese theatre authorities insisted on playing an active role in the decisions made, rather than leaving it to the impresarios, of whom they generally held a low opinion. Back in 1815, the Milanese authorities had contemplated hanging two Bohemian crystal candelabra under the canopy, one with 18, the other with 12 candles. But this proved impractical, and they then attempted to design a large Argand lamp to be hung from the ceiling. The engineers advised against this, given the damage the smoke would do to the ceiling, and the difficulty of replacing the oil, not to mention the fact that such a large lamp would obstruct the view of the box-holders. The Milanese authorities had written to Barbaja in 1820, asking for his advice, and requesting details of how the San Carlo had solved the problem.[39]

The authorities continued to make regular inspections of the lighting effects during dress rehearsals, counting the candles, and giving exact instructions on the type of oil to be used in the lamps in order to obtain the appropriate light and avoid smoke and unpleasant odours.[40] By day, the instructions were to keep all five tiers lit, with no less than 996 candles. During performances, the stalls required 1,024 candles to be lit. In the grand *ridotto* five oil lamps were to be lit, and in the atrium six Argand lamps.[41]

While Barbaja was building the reputations of the Naples and Vienna opera houses, Milan saw a revolving door of impresarios running the royal theatres. Clearly, La Scala lost out in not having the benefit of a stable

long-term impresario like Barbaja. From 1813 to 1815 the theatre was run by
Giuseppe Crivelli. From 1816 to 1820, a gentleman named Angelo Petracci
was in charge. From 1820 to 1821, the *appalto* was held by Carlo Balochino and
again by Giuseppe Crivelli. From 1821 to June 1824 the concession was held
by a syndicate including Giuseppe Crivelli and Giovanni Battista Villa, until
the Government ran it directly again until July 1824.

Giuseppe Crivelli's is the one name that repeatedly shows up, but little is
known about him. He is believed to have been a bit of a brute, having reputedly
once hired thugs to beat up a Milanese nobleman who had forced him to
repay a debt.[42] He slid in and out of the often murky world of the *appalti*
for La Scala between 1808 and 1832, sometimes working alone, sometimes as
part of a syndicate with Balochino, or cooperating with Barbaja.[43] He also
involved himself in the *impresa* for the Teatro la Fenice in Venice.

When Crivelli's last contract ended in mid-1824, competition was stiff
among those impresarios who were keen to get their hands on the glorious
Milanese theatre. Against all the odds and amid fierce competition, Joseph
Glossop won the *impresa* of La Scala with the backing of the Milanese
bankers Marietti Brothers. He signed up for a period of six years, from 1824
to 1830.[44]

The *impresa* of the Milan theatre brought Glossop as little success as
the Teatro San Carlo in Naples (which for a time he was running concurrently), and again at great cost. He lost an estimated 27,000 Austrian lire[45] and
was forced to forfeit the concession within two years.[46] The letter from a
senior Government official to the Viceroy Rainer Joseph was not flattering,
recommending Glossop's removal on account of his 'absence of means, or
lack of knowledge'.[47] Glossop ceded the contract to Barbaja, though how he
manoeuvred himself into this position so rapidly is not quite clear.

Within a period of 12 months, Barbaja had taken the royal theatres off the
hands of the inept Glossop in both Naples and Milan. It seems extraordinary
that Glossop had been so naive and incompetent as to lose two prestigious
concessions so quickly, and risk both his fortune and reputation. It is also
surprising that Glossop spent practically no time in Milan while he held the
impresa for La Scala: he much preferred living in Naples. Some researchers
have suggested that Glossop may have been nothing more than a frontman
for Barbaja,[48] taking over the helm of the theatres during the difficult times,
or simply being deployed to enable Barbaja to negotiate better terms with
the authorities. Barbaja's continued and apparently harmonious work with

Glossop's first wife, Elisabetta Ferron, might indicate that relations between the two impresarios were better than they appeared. But when considering the nasty and costly litigation between Barbaja and Glossop in Naples, this theory seems less than plausible.

Barbaja officially signed on as *appaltatore* of La Scala and the smaller Teatro alla Canobbiana on 20 March 1826, taking over the remainder of Glossop's contract, but giving Glossop a quarter of the profits during the remaining term.[49] Finally Barbaja was officially, openly in charge of the Milanese royal theatres. His earlier attempts, in 1805 and 1821, had either not been successful, or merely put him in the position of silent partner to other impresarios.

From the autumn of 1826 Barbaja held the *imprese* for the Milanese theatres jointly with Giuseppe Crivelli, the Villa brothers and Barbaja's old syndicate partner Carlo Balochino. The authorities respected Barbaja's requirement for frequent absences given his string of concessions, and recognised Carlo Balochino and Giovanni Battista Villa as his official deputies. The Marietti Brothers continued to provide the financial security. Gambling was still not permitted, but basic card games were allowed in the *ridotti*.

This was the first time Barbaja worked with the Villa brothers, who were prosperous Milanese with a rather more refined approach to business than the rough Crivelli. Antonio acted as artistic director for La Scala, while his brother, Giovanni Battista, supported Barbaja in the development of business and talent.[50]

Barbaja actively headed the syndicate himself for much of 1827, even though he spent little time in Milan. The letterhead of La Scala read '*Domenico Barbaja, Appaltatore degl'II RR Teatri di Milano*' (Impresario of the Royal Theatres of Milan), though the documents were usually signed by Balochino or G B Villa.[51] Artistically and commercially, however, Barbaja's golden touch just did not seem to take in Milan. Even at the end of the first year, the authorities were grumbling about Barbaja's performance, accusing him of not providing enough leading singers or composers.[52] Financially, too, the Milan *impresa* was a disaster. Barbaja assumed a loss of 70,000 Austrian lire in 1826 and wrote to the viceroy requesting release from fulfilling the full term of the contract. Immodestly pointing out the excellent job he had done, he signalled his willingness to assume the *impresa* for another year, provided the Imperial Government accept changes to the contract so as to avoid his facing financial ruin and the resulting inability to feed his children.[53]

Neither were the Milanese critics kind to Barbaja:

Never in the memory of the oldest opera-goer was our great theatre so little frequented; indeed, had it not been for the regular subscribers, the house might as well have been closed. Signor Barbaja here, as in Naples, proved very unfortunate in his speculations; he thought to make the same hit with [the tenor Giovanni] David as at Vienna, but was woefully disappointed.[54]

For the first time Barbaja also started to run into more serious competition from other impresarios, and one in particular. Alessandro Lanari, referred to as the 'Napoleon among Impresarios' or the 'God among Impresarios',[55] was an educated man, a prolific writer of letters[56] and a passionate music producer. He acquired the means to buy a theatrical tailor's, and supplied costumes for rental and sale to theatres all over Italy. With over 30 staff exclusively employed in costume tailoring, this was a significant business and represented a major source of income for the impresario.[57] He worked as a theatrical agent for many of the prominent performing artists at the time and was married to a successful singer. While Barbaja occasionally worked with a nephew or son-in-law, Lanari drafted in at least six relatives to his businesses, where they worked as costume designers, tailors, theatrical agents in remote towns or as private secretaries.[58]

Lanari managed *imprese* at many of the leading stages of Italy, including Rome, Naples, Venice, Bologna, Lucca and Milan, as well as his home in Florence. Notoriously tight-fisted – his detractors called him an 'avaricious pirate'[59] – and prone to eccentricities, Lanari was known to receive visitors while soaking in his bath, to which a renal condition forced him to retire with frequency. The Frenchman Gilbert Duprez, one of the star singers Lanari represented, wrote that this provided the perfect venue for fee negotiations: 'What? HOW much do you want for that season? How DARE you ask that from me? Can't you see what condition I am in???!!!'[60] In a remarkable career, he launched some of the most successful operas of the day, including Donizetti's *Elisir d'Amore* (The Elixir of Love, 1832) and *Lucia di Lammermoor* (1835) and Bellini's *Norma* (1831) and *Beatrice di Tenda* (Beatrice of Tenda, 1833). He was also responsible for the Italian premiere of Rossini's *Guillaume Tell* (William Tell, 1831), with Gilbert Duprez in the lead role. His career stretched into the early years of Giuseppe Verdi, for whom he premiered *Attila* (Attila the Hun, 1846), *I due Foscari* (The Two Foscari, 1844) and *Macbeth* (1847). But Lanari was unable to manage his finances; he would die practically bankrupt in 1862.[61]

Barbaja's frustrations with the Milan *impresa* were to continue; the authorities evidently turned down his request to leave early as he was still complaining to Rossini about his terrible fortune in September 1829. The Milan years were also the time of two of the biggest legal disputes in Barbaja's life.

Barbaja-Rossini disputes

The *Zelmira* dispute, which centred on the ownership and rights to the opera's score, dated back to the last weeks of the Barbaja-Rossini enterprise in Naples and went on until well into 1826.

Barbaja had commissioned the opera from Rossini, but the composer did not release the autograph copy and sold the rights to the Viennese music publisher Artaria & Co. Barbaja, who maintained he was the rightful owner of the score, responded by retaining around 6,000 ducats owed to Rossini from his share in the San Carlo revenues, which would have included some residual gambling income. Rossini was angered that Barbaja not only retained the monies, but also declined to pay interest on the withheld amount out of a 'pure desire for vengeance'.[62]

Barbaja, on the other hand, accused Rossini of having stolen the original manuscript of *Zelmira* from the impresario's archive, thereby robbing Barbaja of the licensing income from renting the score to other theatres. Rossini denied the validity of Barbaja's argument, stating a score belonged to the composer, and that only the copyist could sell the score. He added that it was customary that one year after the performance of a new opera, the commissioning impresario would return the original score to the composer.[63] Though Barbaja, for understandable personal reasons, might not have wanted to cooperate with Rossini, the latter's claim that it was standard procedure to return scores was certainly incorrect, and Rossini never returned the autograph copy of *Zelmira* to Barbaja.

The furious arguments and litigation that ensued between Barbaja and Rossini reveals another aspect of their characters: they were equally stubborn. This, and their increasingly ferocious competitiveness, pitched the two men into another high profile dispute, this time over a tenor.

By the mid-1820s Rossini had attained the status of 'Grand Old Man' of Italian opera and was at the height of his popularity. He had settled in Paris in 1824 where he contracted to act as Musical and Artistic Director for the Théâtre-Italien, starting in spring 1825. Rossini and the commercial director of the Paris Opera, the Viscount de la Rochefoucauld, engaged in an exchange programme with Barbaja, whereby the two theatres would swap singers between Paris and Naples. There was a ready exchange of talent, the stars including Josephine Fodor, G B Rubini and Giuditta Pasta. Barbaja and La Rochefoucauld handled all the details, including transport, lodging and board, as well as fees and benefits and the roles that were to be sung. Indeed, the singers were transferred between the two opera companies according to need, moved around like pawns on a chessboard. The English music journal *Harmonicon*, which lasted only for ten years but which was respected and influential, published the following rumour:

> It is known that at this moment there exists a private contract between Barbaja and Rossini, to engage all the artists of merit of every kind, that, by means of such a monopoly, they may lay under contribution all the theatrical directions of Europe, as well royal as noble, dictating their terms for artists, in the same manner as they recently did for Donzelli in Paris. … They are in reality, endeavouring to establish a monopoly of singers, whom, if they succeed, they will hire out like so much cattle.[64]

This was a gross exaggeration of the intentions, ability or reach of Barbaja and Rossini, but some of the negotiations between the impresarios really do sound like the cattle trade. While the exchange of Donzelli provided some remarkable creative highlights, the affair caused a major fracas between Rossini and Barbaja, and damaged the impresario's relationship with the singer.

Domenico Donzelli (1790–1873) was the third of the great Bergamasc tenors in Barbaja's *cartello*. He also developed a deep friendship with Rossini from his earliest contacts with the composer, who cast him in many of his operas, especially during his Paris years. He was best man at Rossini's second wedding.[65]

Settling into Naples for his studies, Donzelli became enormously popular for his exceptionally strong voice – probably similar to a latter-day Mario del Monaco or Franco Corelli – and delicate phrasing. He was what was known as a '*tenore di forza*'. Stendhal wrote that Donzelli's massive voice 'resembles a yell'.[66] His technique was also sound, and he could effortlessly support the high notes.

The importance of the singer's technique cannot be overestimated. Good technique, then as now, dictates the length of a singer's career and, with the evolution of the more forceful singing demanded by larger theatres, poor technique could even be a matter of life or death. During an 1821 performance in Rome,[67] the second tenor Amerigo Sbigoli tried to keep up with the colossal volume of the first tenor, Domenico Donzelli. In a passage where the second tenor repeats the same phrase immediately after the first tenor, Sbigoli was eager to provoke the same rapturous audience reaction that Donzelli had just achieved and forced his voice, bursting a blood vessel in his throat. He collapsed on stage and died a few days later.[68] The composer Donizetti witnessed this performance and was traumatised ever afterwards by the event.

Barbaja signed Domenico Donzelli up as a *cartello* artist from 1825 to 1830.[69] The impresario proposed to the Théâtre-Italien (essentially Rossini) to second the singer to Paris from March 1825 for six months. In exchange, Barbaja would get the rights for Naples to perform the next opera Rossini composed for Paris, which was to be hand-delivered to Barbaja by Donzelli within eight days of its premiere.[70] The French theatre was also to pay Barbaja 26,000 francs for Donzelli's performances.[71]

The deal did not work out, but Rossini nevertheless remained determined to bring the tenor to Paris. Since Barbaja declined to give his permission for this, Rossini encouraged the singer to break completely with the impresario. Rossini meticulously coached Donzelli through the separation process, explaining what he should say to Barbaja and how best to argue his case.[72] He had arranged for La Rochefoucauld to pay the indemnity for the broken contract, but cleverly provided Donzelli with arguments to negotiate a reduction in the fee.

The luring of Donzelli away from Naples caused Barbaja significant embarrassment at the Teatro San Carlo, unleashing a nasty fight with Rossini. After threatening La Rochefoucauld with legal action, Barbaja travelled posthaste to Paris in April 1826 where he probably tried to poach some of La Rochefoucauld's singers and attempted to force his own singers – who had originally gone there with the agreement of the impresario – to return to Naples. Donzelli wrote pleadingly to La Rochefoucauld to be kept out of the matter: 'The reason I left Mr Barbaja was exactly to escape the obligation of running from one end of Europe to another for him.'[73]

In June Barbaja met up with Donzelli. In typical Barbaja manner, while he praised the singer's talent and expressed his genuine interest in working with him in Naples irrespective of the cost, he also made vociferous threats that he could have him arrested and deported to Italy.[74] The rather shaken Donzelli had to be calmed down by the Parisian theatre management. For good measure, Barbaja followed this up with a lawsuit and Donzelli was compelled to pay a fine of 12,000 ducats for non-appearance and failing to return to Naples.[75] The dispute does not seem to have harmed Donzelli's pricing power: at 37,000 francs a season, he was the highest paid singer among his peers.[76] In autumn 1826, Donzelli moved to Paris where his career flourished.

The Donzelli dispute was certainly the nastiest altercation between Barbaja and Rossini other than that over the score of *Zelmira*, but there were many other contentious issues between them, not to mention the Colbran affair, which no doubt affected those around them too. Despite this, their underlying friendship remained intact. Indeed, for some time, they had both been quietly working towards some sort of rapprochement. Barbaja had also remained in contact with Rossini's parents in Bologna as a way of keeping the channels open.[77]

In July 1825 a tenor from the Théâtre-Italien wrote somewhat prematurely in a letter that Rossini and Barbaja were reconciled and had entered a mutually beneficial agreement, probably meaning the exchange of singers between Paris and Naples.[78] The Italian composer Ferdinando Paer, who was sharing responsibilities with Rossini in the Théâtre-Italien observed: 'As soon as Barbaja arrived [in Paris in 1825] and saw Rossini, the two of them embraced, and the sentimental part cancelled all the past wrongs between the two men … oh what a comedy!'[79] The soprano Giuditta Pasta wrote to her husband that quite obviously, 'Barbaja was still in love with Rossini'.[80]

About a year after the initial steps towards reconciliation,[81] Barbaja agreed through an intermediary to release the funds owed to Rossini, as well as to his wife, Isabella Colbran.[82] On 3 July 1826,[83] the two giants of Italian opera put pen to paper and drafted an agreement, finally and formally clarifying their financial affairs and putting aside their differences. Two days later, Rossini wrote Barbaja an emotional and highly personal letter asking him to drop all issues related to Donzelli so that they could put the dispute behind them. The final chapter of the truce came in February 1828 when Angelo Morro, Rossini's confidant in Naples, met Barbaja to sort out some remaining financial affairs for Rossini: 'I met with Barbaja. He always refers to you as "assassino", but you should take that as a compliment.'[84] Clearly, relations were back on track.

ROSSINI.

Gioachino Rossini, Barbaja's business partner, friend and occasional rival, and the defining Italian opera composer of the early 19th century.

Collection Reto Mueller

The Sicilian composer Vincenzo Bellini was discovered and promoted by Barbaja.
The two soon fell out over financial and artistic differences.

Collection Opera Rara

Gaetano Donizetti, the most prolific composer of the bel canto era, and a frequent collaborator of Barbaja in spite of their often tense relationship.

Author's Collection

The Naples-trained Saverio Mercadante worked as Music Director and composer for Barbaja.

Collection Opera Rara

Giovanni Pacini, an important composer of his time, worked as Music Director for Barbaja and stood up with humour against the impresario's bullying.

Collection Opera Rara

A. Conté dir. ed inc.

ISABELLA COLBRAN

Leading Spanish prima donna Isabella Colbran had a long lasting personal and professional relationship with Barbaja, before she left him to marry Rossini.

Collection Sergio Ragni

Luigi Lablache, the most admired bass of his generation, was a key member of Barbaja's stable of singers, performing in Naples, Milan and Vienna, as well as Moscow, St Petersburg, Palermo, Paris and London. He also gave singing lessons to Princess Victoria, later Queen Victoria.

Author's Collection

Spanish prima donna Maria Malibran only lived to be 28, but was a living legend on account of her vivacious personality, electrifying stage presence, musical talent and enormous vocal range.

Collection Opera Rara

Giuditta Pasta, a key member of Barbaja's stable, created the title role in some of Bellini's and Donizetti's most important operas, and was a favourite of King Ferdinand I of the Two Sicilies.

Collection Sergio Ragni

Respected, successful yet tormented French tenor Adolphe Nourrit worked for Barbaja in Naples before committing suicide in the impresario's palazzo.

Collection Sergio Ragni

Luigia Boccabadati was a leading prima donna in Barbaja's stable until she launched a successful lawsuit against the impresario, effectively ending her career.

Collection Sergio Ragni

Bergamasc tenor Giovanni David, a long-time member of Barbaja's stable and a favourite of the Milanese, Neapolitan and Vienna audiences.

Collection Opera Rara

Domenico Donzelli boasted a stentorian tenor, and enjoyed huge popularity under Barbaja's management. Rossini, who became a close personal friend, tried to lure him away from Barbaja, triggering a long lasting feud between composer and impresario.

Collection Sergio Ragni

The enormously popular Giovanni Battista Rubini was regarded as the best tenor of his generation and was a favourite of Bellini. His long cooperation with Barbaja ended over financial disagreements.

Author's Collection

Only known oil painting of Domenico Barbaja. In the background are Giovanni
Battista Rubini, Gioachino Rossini and Giuditta Pasta. It was probably painted
in the 1820s. The artist is unknown.

Collection Museo Teatrale alla Scala

After the Teatro San Carlo burned to the ground in 1816, Barbaja led the reconstruction, making it the most important opera house in Europe. It served as the headquarters for Barbaja's European operations.

Collection Sergio Ragni

Marble bust of Domenico Barbaja, provenance unknown, possibly a former part of a tombstone of the impresario. Barbaja's grave can no longer be located.

Collection Sergio Ragni

Barbaja's villa in Mergellina boasted dozens of rooms, a full-sized theatre and an enormous art collection. This design was originally conceived by architect, scenographer and artistic heavyweight Antonio Niccolini. Barbaja later built the house according to his own designs. *Collection Sergio Ragni.*

PALAZZO BARBAJA IN ISCHIA.

Barbaja's holiday retreat on the island of Ischia where he invited Rossini, Colbran and other leading artists from the Teatro San Carlo. *Collection Sergio Ragni.*

Flirting with Paris

The Englishman Glossop had amazingly still not quite given up on opera. There were rumours of approaches he had made to Rossini, hoping he could help facilitate a deal for Barbaja and himself jointly to take over theatres in both Paris and London.[85] Given the extremely bad relations between the two impresarios from their previous entanglements, this sounds doubtful. Barbaja, in any case, would not have touched Glossop unless Rossini took the lead. Also, by this time Glossop was out of cash, partly as a result of Barbaja's actions.

Nevertheless, there does seem to have been a fair bit of deliberation and discussion in early 1827 about how Rossini and Barbaja could jointly take over Paris, provided Barbaja gave up Milan.[86] The owners of the Théâtre-Italien in Paris were, in any case, keen to attract a decent impresario, as under Rossini's and Paer's artistic direction the theatre was incurring enormous losses.[87] Indeed, the French newspapers and the composer Alessandro Micheroux believed that 'only Barbaja was capable of providing the means to stabilise the theatre'.[88] He was also the only internationally experienced impresario to have a large troupe of top singers at his command.

In late February 1827, Rossini gave Barbaja a letter with the Paris director Viscount de la Rochefoucauld's terms for Barbaja to take over the Paris opera. The viscount had raised the subsidy to 120,000 francs in order to entice Barbaja. The timing was fortuitous. In March 1827 Barbaja's discussions with the Neapolitan authorities over the upcoming *impresa* renewal collapsed, as both the royal household and the ministries voted against him.

Aggravated by Barbaja's frequent absences, and tired of the subsidies he needed to pay to the impresario, King Francis had suddenly cancelled the *impresa* from Holy Week 1827 onwards for both stages, actually closing down the royal theatres. Suddenly Barbaja found himself impresario only at Milan and Vienna, unable to deploy all his singers.

As before, however, Barbaja played a waiting game. Depending on the progress he made in reviving negotiations with Naples – the king, he was confident, would soon come back to him, for who else was there with his reputation in Naples? – he would decide whether or not to pursue Paris.

Barbaja set off for Paris, ostensibly to sign the agreement for the Théâtre-Italien, 'having already given the orders to his singers in Naples to follow him like sheep to Paris'.[89] The Paris contract had been fully agreed and negotiated by Rossini and was only awaiting his signature. In preparation for this expected new *impresa*, Barbaja wrote to Rossini, begging him to compose an opera to open the Paris season he was to command. The discussions with Barbaja had also been leaked to the press, including *Le Figaro*:

> We have been assured that the directorial sceptre of the Théâtre-Italien, so heavy for M. Paer, will pass to the hands of M. Barbaja, who is already running theatres in Italy and Germany. We are not told if, like Caesar, he will be governing his kingdoms by prefects. Whatever the case, as long as they are well governed.[90]

Whether the Paris theatres needed Barbaja or whether he needed the Paris stage is not altogether clear. The impresario Benelli wrote that Barbaja was desperate to sign on in Paris, as he needed a stage for the many artists whom he had contracted for several years ahead.[91] Alas, to the great disappointment of Rossini, Barbaja did not come through on the Paris contract. A month after voting down Barbaja as impresario for the royal theatres, the Neapolitans changed their minds and in April 1827 sent a delegation to Barbaja asking him to renew his contract for the royal theatres. Barbaja accepted the 'contract that was very advantageous to my interests',[92] but sent his friend and deputy Louis Duport to Naples to run the theatres. Barbaja had too many links and obligations to turn his back completely on the Naples theatres, and he wanted to turn around the loss-making of the last two years both there and in Milan.[93]

As for Paris, Barbaja simply had too much on his hands to accept running yet another major stage. Managing Vienna, Milan and Naples was enough. The Frenchman Emile Laurent took over the Parisian *impresa*. In a rambling letter to Rossini (written in colloquial language, and demonstrably without the help of a secretary) delivered via the Rothschild Bank, Rossini's bankers, Barbaja extended his apologies and explanations, and tried to assuage Rossini's disappointment.

> … I ask you if I can honestly take on other Imprese, not without hiding from you the fact that my [financial] position is much changed from what it was in the past, in view of the losses I have needed to absorb in Naples, and in Milan.[94]

After he resumed control of Naples, public criticism of Barbaja mounted, specifically against the number of concessions that the impresario was now running. His detractors were increasingly vocal in their objection to Barbaja's approach to theatre management. In December 1827 an anonymous letter circulated throughout the theatre community:

> Let me discuss the causes for the downfall of the *opera buffa* … in Italy. Domenico Barbaja in Naples was the first to cause the downfall and destruction of the *opera buffa* in Italy which had been admired throughout the musical world for centuries. As the gambling insured that lady luck smiled on Barbaja and gave him plentiful financial means to attract the finest artists to Naples, and also attracted a large number of people and foreigners to the Teatro San Carlo, he also sucked a large number of gamblers and new beginners into the gambling halls, called ridotto, where they lost huge amounts of money. As Barbaja saw that the roulette and so-called rouge et noir did well, and with the exception of the Teatro Nuovo obtained the right over all Neapolitan theatres, he suddenly thought about renting out the Teatro dei Fiorentini to the comedians, and engaged over many years Mr. Casacello [sic], the only Neapolitan *buffo* and the mainstay of the Neapolitan *buffo* scene, in order to avoid any *buffo* spectacle in Naples whatsoever, and even leave the Teatro Nuovo idle. Once B. had obtained his goals, he engaged Rossini's help (who he gave part of the gambling revenues) to put on big spectacles in the Teatro San Carlo … However, as Barbaja's racket was stopped through the prohibition of all gambling, he thought of another speculation, namely the trafficking of artists.[95]

A second letter followed soon:

> The Hermit of Montmartre in Paris writes me the following: Barbaja came here on the anniversary of the peace reached between himself, Rossini and Colbran one year ago … A few days thereafter the secret discussions started between Barbaja and Rossini to discuss the possibility of obtaining the imprese of the Parisian and London theatres, in order to exchange, sell the artists, and to make the direction pay for this, while he promised the Pesarese Orpheus half of the profits. This plan was ruined by the Parisian administration that caught wind of it.[96]

The British press also weighed in, *Harmonicon* reporting that:

The Generalissimo Barbaja has resumed the management of the Teatro
Reale [in Naples], which was shut during last season; ... so that now
he waves the theatrical sceptre from Naples to Milan and Vienna, and
probably will, 'ere long, extend his ample domain as far as Paris and
London.[97]

Indeed, London was one of the options that Barbaja was exploring. The
King's Theatre was run by the English opera impresario John Ebers. When
visiting Paris, he had tried to strike a deal with Rossini and Barbaja to run
it jointly with him. Ebers wrote in his memoirs that 'Rossini was to handle
the music and the engagements would have been transacted by Barbaja, who,
from his numerous theatrical concerns, was better calculated than any other
man in Europe, to engage performers with advantage.' Ebers himself would
deal with the 'arrangement for the ballet, letting the boxes, and attending to
the subscribers'.[98]

Had he been impresario of Vienna, Paris, Milan, Naples and London,
Barbaja would have had under his control all the leading stages of Europe,
providing him with ample venues to deploy his stable of singers. The plan for
London never reached fruition,[99] but this did not stop Barbaja from seeking
other ways of employing his artists. One possible solution was temptingly
near home.

During 1828, the Neapolitan authorities took a strict line on maintaining
high morals during the fasting season, and they closed the theatres. Rome
was more tolerant, permitting the performance of sacral music. Barbaja was
loathe to lose the income from his Naples-based singers, and negotiated with
the Roman Government for his singers to perform sacral music at the Teatro
Argentina in Rome during the Neapolitan lull. In order to make the proposal
more attractive, he offered to contribute half his earnings to the reconstruction of the Papal Basilica of St Paul Outside the Walls, which had been
severely damaged by fire some years earlier. There is no information as to
whether the Roman authorities accepted this proposal.[100]

9

Finding Successors to
Rossini and Colbran

Barbaja could look with satisfaction on the wide network of stages he controlled. But there was one nagging concern that had been pre-occupying him for years: who would be the next composer to write operas that would attain Europe-wide fame like those of Rossini, and that could provide Barbaja with the financial rewards that Rossini's work had done in the past?

Rossini remained the undisputed giant in the world of opera and was the most frequently performed composer throughout Europe for much of the 1820s and 1830s. His operas were also the most regularly heard works at all the theatres Barbaja controlled. The impresario was aware, however, that apart from Rossini, he relied too heavily on middle-of-the-road composers, with no other really superlative musicians. Most of the composers he commissioned were writing music in the Rossinian style, and showed limited true originality or novelty: there had been little development in their music, orchestration, harmony or musical characterisation. During the 1820s, Barbaja therefore put a great deal of effort into commissioning works from younger, less well known artists, in the hope that one or two of them would break out to become the 'next Rossini'.

The number of composers he worked with was enormous. It included names like Saverio Mercadante (1795–1870), Francesco Morlacchi (1784–1841), Giuseppe Balducci (f. 1826), Carlo Coccia (1782–1873), Carlo Conti (1796–1868), Nicola Manfroce (1791–1813), Michele Costa (1808–84), the brothers Federico (1809–77) and Luigi Ricci (1805–59) and many others, most of whose work has not survived the test of time. But there was a young composer who showed enormous promise: Giovanni Pacini.

Pacini

The Sicilian-born composer Giovanni Pacini (1796–1867) was one of the most prolific opera composers of his time, and one of the first to make a conscious attempt to break out of the Rossinian mould. In 1825 Barbaja engaged Pacini to write two operas for him for the price of 1,200 ducats, not considered a very large amount. But Pacini needed the money for his new family, and wrote *Amazilia*, quickly followed by *L'Ultimo Giorno di Pompei* (The Last Day of Pompeii), which debuted in Naples in November 1825.

The rehearsals were not plain sailing. Barbaja made frequent appearances and screamed at Pacini in his usual manner: 'Who do you think you are speaking to, *assassino!*'[1] Pacini, unbridled, gave back as good as he got, calling Barbaja a rascal, upon which Barbaja calmed down and shuffled away, chewing his nails.

To Barbaja's total surprise, however, *L'Ultimo Giorno di Pompei* proved a triumph. The music, the staging and the story that hit so close to home captured the audience's fancy. After its remarkable opening night, Barbaja threw his arms around Pacini and offered him a nine-year contract in Naples as Music Director at the San Carlo. The *Ultimo Giorno di Pompei* became the impresario's cash-cow for the 1825/26 season, prompting Barbaja to write to a friend: 'In my long theatre career no other opera has filled the coffers in the same way as this opera. In 5 days over 5,000 ducats came in.'[2] Pacini himself reported with pride that his opera was so successful the theatre regularly had to turn people away.[3]

Pacini went to great pains to document that he obtained the same conditions for his new contract as the great Rossini. This is hard to verify but doubtful, as the gambling concession, for one, had long been abolished. But Barbaja did contract Pacini to write two operas a season, act as Musical Director for the theatres, and also to deputise for Barbaja in administrative matters when the impresario was travelling, which was increasingly the case with his sprawling empire.[4] This last he would do in cooperation with Barbaja's son-in-law Cesare Politi, who became an associate of Barbaja's from May 1825, frequently acting as the impresario's General Administrator.[5] For these services Barbaja paid Pacini 200 ducats a month, and provided him with lodging, food, transport, a home trip and the proceeds of one benefit gala per year. When in Naples, Pacini lodged in the Palazzo Barbaja on the Via Toledo.

Trouble was not long in coming, however. During one of Barbaja's extended leaves, when Pacini had been left in charge, attendance dropped dramatically and funds started to dry up. Pacini therefore decided on his own accord to put on his evergreen opera *L'Ultimo Giorno di Pompei*, which immediately attracted the crowds and refilled the coffers. Upon his return, the impresario – whom Pacini would cheekily refer to as 'our Sultan' – balled out Pacini with his habitual fury: '*Assassino*, how dare you go against my orders!!' To which Pacini retorted in similarly loud volume, 'Because, if I hadn't, you scoundrel, you would have found nails in the coffers, rather than money.' Barbaja's fury instantly vanished. 'Well, then it's OK, you rogue', he quietly muttered, and Barbaja ordered spaghetti for them to share.[6]

Barbaja was keen to deploy Pacini around his vast portfolio of concessions to compose and perform operas, and regularly ordered him to Milan and later also to Vienna; both not inconsiderable voyages. Pacini tells of a trip from Milan to Vienna taking 15 days in the coach, the delay largely due to the David family, who he was travelling with and who needed to put in frequent rest stops. Barbaja left Naples for Vienna five days after the Pacini and David carriage, and arrived there before them, seething about his artists' delay.

Barbaja tried hard to promote Pacini who remained under contract to him through to 1833. In an effort to spread the popularity of his operas, the impresario would occasionally release Pacini from his obligations, permitting the composer to accept appointments in Trieste, Florence and Venice. But Barbaja never hesitated to command him back when he needed him at La Scala or the San Carlo. His constant travelling around Europe at Barbaja's orders prompted Hector Berlioz, who had something nasty to say about pretty much anyone, to call Pacini 'a miserable eunuch'.

In many ways, Pacini's early career perfectly reflected the Barbaja business model. Barbaja discovered young artists, locked them into long-term contracts at low cost, gave them the platform to succeed, and then exported them to stages around Europe where he could further their reputation and enhance the earning potential for himself. Pacini was a well-known and successful artist for his time in many ways, but he was quickly overshadowed by another composer whom Barbaja was promoting: Gaetano Donizetti.

Donizetti

Gaetano Donizetti (1797–1848) was born in the northern Italian town of Bergamo, and studied with the composer Giovanni Simone Mayr, who treated Donizetti like a son and gave the young composer a thorough foundation, emphasizing the study of the German maestros Haydn, Mozart and Beethoven. Donizetti gave some early performances in Venice and Rome, but he took his first major step into the world of opera when he moved to Naples in 1822 at the invitation of Barbaja. He was just 24. Donizetti was to remain in the southern city until 1838 and he would come to consider Naples his second home. His arrival coincided with the forthcoming departure of Rossini and Colbran. The city and the Teatro San Carlo had experienced a dramatic musical resurgence under Barbaja's *imprese*, but by all accounts the theatre was in a state of flux that year, with Barbaja and Rossini focused on moving much of the company to Vienna.

Donizetti was struck by the apparent lack of professionalism at the legendary theatre. On seeing Rossini in performance during the great maestro's last days in Naples, he commented with some dismay at his behaviour, particularly since Rossini was performing an oratorio by Giovanni Simone Mayr, Donizetti's teacher and friend. 'Rossini complains jesuitically to the singers that they have not performed well, and then, at the orchestra rehearsal, he was standing there gossiping with the prima donnas instead of conducting.'[7] Neither was he impressed with what the singers were doing to his work. 'They are such dogs, one should chase them with shoes and not perform the music.'[8]

Barbaja had recruited Donizetti after hearing several of his successful operas. The composer's prodigious output also appealed to the impresario. Barbaja contracted Donizetti to write some new operas for the royal theatres, as well as to perform and conduct operas by other composers whose work had not yet been heard in Naples. The first opera Donizetti wrote for Naples, *La Zingara* (The Gypsy), opened at the Teatro Nuovo in May 1822. Barbaja chose this theatre as it specialised in *semi-serie* and *farse*. The impresario wanted to test-run the young composer in a smaller house, before exposing him to the more demanding audience and the larger stage of the San Carlo. The audience flocked to *Zingara*, which ran for 28 nights in a row, and was then reprised in July the same year, when it was performed a further 20 times.

The success of this opera opened the door to the San Carlo, for which Donizetti would write 16 operas. It took the composer a little while to find his feet in the royal theatres, and his first opera for the San Carlo, *Alfredo il Grande* (Alfred the Great, starring Elisabetta Ferron), was a flop. In these early years he had only modest success in other cities as well, as he was still struggling to emerge from the shadow left by the great 'Swan of Pesaro'. It is little surprise then that Stendhal wrote that 'Donizetti is a tall, handsome young man, but cold and without a shred of talent'.[9]

In the early 1820s, Donizetti travelled back and forth to Rome and other cities for commissions, a liberty permitted by his contract with Barbaja, similar to the arrangement the impresario had had with Rossini. Though his first breakthrough was still some years away, his exposure on many stages would help Donizetti become a crucially important composer.

In early 1827 Donizetti proposed to his future wife Virginia, and in order to get himself on a stable financial footing, he signed a three-year contract with Barbaja which called for four operas a year. For this he received a salary of 300 ducats per month. Additionally he was to assume duties as Musical Director of the Teatro Nuovo in Naples, a role similar in responsibility to the one held by Rossini at the San Carlo many years earlier, except at a much smaller theatre.

Returning to Naples from Rome in January 1827, Donizetti quickly set to work. His first opera under the Barbaja contract, *Otto mesi in due ore* (Eight Months in Two Hours) premiered at the Teatro Nuovo on 13 May that year, and the composer took full advantage of the superior technical capabilities of the theatre. The opera was a huge success, running for 50 performances. After the opening night performance, 'the maestro was called upon the stage, to be gazed at by the ladies, we presume, for he is quite a *beau garçon*',[10] *Harmonicon* reported.

L'Esule di Roma (The Exile from Rome) was perhaps the last of the series of experimental operas which Donizetti composed in these early years. Premiered in January 1828, it was rapturously received and Rossini was later reported to have said that this opera alone would have sufficed to make a composer's reputation.[11] Nevertheless, the opera marked the end of what Donizetti would later term the *'anni di galera'* (the galley years), in which the young composer churned out a prodigious amount of pedestrian work that enjoys no popularity today. Although his abundant output might belie it, the creation of every opera was a struggle and Donizetti suffered from nerves.

There was no arguing about his productivity, however: Donizetti could produce operas fast and he lived to write 69 of them. Often accused of being formulaic, Donizetti's first 32 operas are for the most part forgotten and unremarkable, but many of his later works remain popular to this day. Musicologists largely agree, however, that these early Neapolitan years were an important period in the development of his style and technique, including the interaction of text and music, the mastering of comedic musical effects and, of course, the first treatments of stories from English history that would see their full application in his later masterpieces.

Although he had only so far produced two of the proposed 12 operas contracted, following their success in January 1828 Donizetti signed a fresh contract with Barbaja, this time for two new operas, each at a price of 500 ducats. Barbaja also offered Donizetti the post of Musical Director for the royal theatres, starting in 1829,[12] a promotion from his smaller role at the Teatro Nuovo.

Donizetti was deeply honoured by being given this new role at the royal theatres, as the great Rossini had been the last Musical Director to have had any real impact, though he was well aware of the criticism he would face if he favoured his own works. He was to hold this post with only a few interruptions up until his departure from the city in 1838.

Donizetti's schedule must have been extraordinarily busy. In addition to his responsibilities for the Teatro Nuovo, the Teatro San Carlo and the Teatro del Fondo, he continued to compose and to perform in Naples, Rome, Genoa and Milan, and he finally found time to marry Virginia in June 1828. Soon the couple were expecting their first child, due in July 1829. The Donizettis travelled to Rome to deliver the child in Virginia's family home, and Barbaja granted the composer a six-week leave of absence. The child was born in early August but died after less than two weeks.

Barbaja was less than understanding and pressed Donizetti to return to Naples at the earliest opportunity. The young composer was livid: 'the blow you have dealt me asking me to return, dear Barbaja, is too cruel.'[13] Barbaja eventually, probably grudgingly, relented and extended his Musical Director's leave of absence so that he could remain with his wife in Rome. But the relationship between the two men would henceforth always remain fractious. In a letter of 1830, Donizetti described his excitement about his upcoming assignment at the Carcano in Milan, contrasting it to his arrangements with 'the Jew Barbaja'.[14] Nevertheless, Barbaja offered the young Donizetti the creative and economic stability on which his enormous musical reputation in both the *opera seria* and *opera buffa* would be built in the next decade, with Barbaja as well as with other impresarios.

Barbaja was still in need of new composers to write stand-out operas with the creative flair to ignite the audience's passions and capture Europe's imagination in the way Rossini had been able to, however. His wish for a new superstar composer was fulfilled by a young, pale and unusually handsome Sicilian with blue eyes, Vincenzo Bellini.

Bellini

The precocious Vincenzo Bellini (1801–35) was born into a musical family in Catania, the island's second-largest city, situated at the foot of the Mount Etna volcano. Reportedly playing the pianoforte at the age of three and able to write music at five, the gifted child quickly outgrew the limited teaching facilities in Sicily, and was sent to the kingdom's capital on a scholarship. In 1819 Bellini moved to Naples and was enrolled in the Collegio di San Sebastiano.[15]

In Naples Bellini studied under some of the finest musicians in Europe, including the legendary Zingarelli, who ruled the Naples Conservatory with an iron fist. As a top Conservatory student, the young Sicilian had plenty of exposure to the performances at the leading European opera stage and was allowed to attend operas at the San Carlo on a student pass twice a week.[16] It was there that Bellini saw operas by Rossini and witnessed the world-class cast of singers that Barbaja had assembled. His graduation work was an opera performed by an all-male cast at the Conservatory, which was well received.

This initial success brought the young Bellini to the attention of the management of the royal theatres, which by tradition extended the privilege of a Teatro San Carlo debut for the Conservatory's most promising student. The Duke of Noja, who sat on the board of the San Sebastiano and was also the Superintendent of the Royal Theatres (and Barbaja's de facto direct superior), had negotiated this deal to help promising conservatory students launch their musical careers. But Barbaja was the chief beneficiary: 'With a small investment he found among those young men the one who would lead him to large profits,' reported Florimo.[17]

The Duke of Noja and Barbaja commissioned Bellini's first commercial opera in 1825, helped arrange the librettist and paid the composer 300 ducats, the customary amount for student composers. The opera was to be called 'Bianca e Fernando'.

Tall, handsome and – most importantly – Neapolitan-trained and from the Kingdom of the Two Sicilies, Bellini was an attractive package. Barbaja and the Duke of Noja were confident enough in the talents of the young composer to schedule his professional debut opera to premiere on 12 January 1826 on the occasion of the birthday of Crown Prince Ferdinand, Duke of Calabria (the future King Ferdinand II).

Bellini wrote the opera for a first-rate cast including Luigi Lablache and Giovanni David. At the last minute, the proposed date was changed by King Francis I, as it coincided with the first anniversary of the death of his father, King Ferdinand I, and the premiere was pushed back by nearly half a year. The delay occasioned a change of cast, which meant that Bellini had to rewrite many passages of the opera to adjust to the rather different voices. Instead of Giovanni David, the newly scheduled tenor was Giovanni Battista Rubini. From this coincidental cooperation sprang a fortuitous partnership between Bellini and Rubini. Bellini would write three operas specifically for his voice[18] and their collaboration did more than anything else to launch Rubini's stratospheric career.

Bianca e Fernando finally saw the light of day on 30 May 1826, at a gala event at the San Carlo. The opera had been renamed *Bianca e Gernando*, rather than *Fernando*, to avoid using the deceased King Ferdinand's name. The opening was attended by the son of King Francis, the Crown Prince Ferdinand, the leading Neapolitan music publisher Guillaume (Guglielmo) Cottrau, Giovanni Pacini and Gaetano Donizetti. King Francis I was ill and did not attend.

While musicologists spend a fair bit of time isolating the moments of genius of this opera, it was an early and relatively immature work. But *Bianca* was well received by the audience and the press. Donizetti wrote to a friend that the opera was 'beautiful, beautiful, beautiful, especially for someone who is writing his first opera'.[19] This enthusiasm would wane in later years, when Bellini and Donizetti became fierce competitors.

In April 1827 Barbaja (possibly on the advice of Pacini, who was then still Musical Director of the San Carlo) sent Bellini to Milan where he had promised him a contract for La Scala, at a rate of 100 ducats per month for the period from April to October 1827.[20] Bellini made the seven-day journey by coach, travelling with Rubini and the tenor's wife Adelaide Chaumel, who fashioned herself Adelaide Comelli-Rubini on the Italian stage. It could not have been a pleasant trip in the snug carriage. Much as he liked and admired Rubini, Bellini despised Comelli and called her 'ambitious' and 'asinine.'[21]

Barbaja and his Milanese partner G B Villa took it upon themselves to match up the young Bellini with a competent librettist, and put Bellini in touch with the Milan-based Felice Romani, one of the most accomplished librettists of the day. Romani would write about 100 librettos for composers including Donizetti, Meyerbeer, Mayr, Rossini, and later even for Giuseppe Verdi. For Bellini, until their fall-out over the delayed delivery of a libretto,[22] Felice Romani became his closest lyric collaborator, producing the librettos for some of his most successful operas.

Bellini and Romani first started working on an opera earmarked for La Scala's 1827 season. *Il Pirata* (The Pirate), which debuted on 17 October 1827, was a triumph and became Bellini's breakout opera. It also marked the defining performance for the tenor Rubini, the role being written for and ideally suited to his voice. Today's tenors have a harder time with the challenging role.

The German newspapers praised the young composer:

Mr. Bellini has a special passion for German music [referring to his understanding of Mozart, Haydn and Beethoven] … Considering this is his second opera we wish to congratulate Sg Bellini, at least we can hope he will soon turn into a respectable composer.[23]

In addition to the talented librettist, Bellini had access to some of the best singers under the Barbaja contract, including Rubini, the soprano Henriette Méric-Lalande and the baritone Antonio Tamburini. The composer made musical history by coaching his singers, particularly Rubini, into singing with emotion and expression befitting their character, rather than focusing only on their vocal artistry and technical skill. He encouraged Rubini to 'accompany your singing with gestures.'[24]

After 15 performances of *Pirata* at La Scala in the autumn 1827 season, Barbaja planned to take the opera to his theatres in Vienna and Naples. Bellini, however, decided to remain in Milan rather than returning to Naples, feeling the north offered him greater professional promise. In Milan, he quickly established a circle of friends and, assisted by a letter of introduction from Zingarelli to some of the leading families, focused on penetrating Milanese high society.[25] He befriended the singer Giuditta Pasta, and launched headlong into a romantic affair with the estranged wife of a prosperous Milanese industrialist. He also grew close to the composer Saverio Mercadante, one of his earliest supporters in the city. With his prodigious talent and good looks, Bellini's appearance at a party was a society spectacle.

In Milan, his self-confidence grew alongside his success and the increasingly high-profile reception he was accorded.

He began to behave more like a diva than many a prima donna, making not only financial and artistic demands, but interfering with the impresario in the casting of his operas even well beyond the premiere.

Bellini had a protracted argument with Barbaja in 1828 over Barbaja's choice of casting Rubini's wife Adelaide Comelli-Rubini in a performance of *Pirata* in Vienna. Apart from despising her personality, Bellini considered her an inferior singer and felt she would damage the quality of the work.[26] Barbaja was furious over Bellini's meddling in his affairs, and wrote the composer an insulting letter.

When Barbaja arrived in Milan, the composer avoided him since he knew Barbaja would make a scene, and Bellini felt he would be unable to contain himself. He also did not want to seem overeager to strike a deal with the impresario. Instead he dropped off a letter at Barbaja's office when he knew he would not be there.[27] When he found the letter on his return, Barbaja was near apoplectic that the upstart composer had been avoiding him for four days.

One day Barbaja's partner Antonio Villa was talking to Bellini while standing under the portico of La Scala, recounting how Barbaja blamed Bellini for 'causing a revolution in Naples by not permitting the showing of *Pirata*,[28] when Barbaja happened to exit the theatre and see them both. The fuming Barbaja unleashed his usual load of expletives, and demanded to know why Bellini had not responded to his letter. Bellini, unfazed, answered that he had seen the missive but assumed from the unpleasant tone that it had actually been addressed to another person and had destroyed it. Barbaja snapped back that he would have the letter rewritten so that the composer could see it every day.[29]

Bellini deftly defused the argument, the two went to lunch, and over pasta the impresario sealed the deal for Bellini's next great opera, *La Straniera*.[30] Barbaja offered Bellini the choice of composing for Naples or Milan, the decision being predicated largely on the available singers. Bellini preferred Naples because of Rubini's presence, but ultimately opted again to remain in Milan.[31] This did not stop Bellini from trying to convince Barbaja to release Rubini from his Naples obligations, which Bellini thought possible as Barbaja controlled both theatres. But Barbaja would not budge and insisted Rubini complete his contractual obligations in Naples.[32]

The Adelaide Comelli-Rubini and *Pirata* debacle actually had a happy ending. Barbaja went ahead with *Pirata* at the Kaerntnertortheater, casting Rubini and his wife, as well as Tamburini. The performances were a big success, and launched Bellini's fame on the Vienna stages.

When Bellini got word, however, that Barbaja was planning to show the same Vienna cast at the Teatro San Carlo, the composer lost his cool, sending his Naples-based friend Francesco Florimo to change the impresario's mind. Florimo made such a nuisance of himself that Barbaja barred him from attending the harpsichord rehearsals which were being held at Barbaja's home.[33]

Barbaja persevered. Both Signore and Madame Rubini performed at the San Carlo and, after overcoming her nerves, Adelaide Comelli-Rubini excelled at the role in front of the royal family in May 1828. The performance was also attended by the then 76-year-old Zingarelli, who had accepted a ticket for a large box from Barbaja to witness the performance of his most famous disciple.[34]

Bellini was intensely competitive and jealous of his fellow composers, especially Pacini and Donizetti. In June 1828, fresh after the success of *Pirata*, he wrote to Florimo that 'in this year, I do not need Barbaja, and nor does he need me. I understand he has hired Donizetti and Vaccai for Naples, and for this city [Milan] … Pacini and Conti.'[35] Pacini, his fellow Sicilian-born composer, particularly drew Bellini's ire, and in his letters he refers to him as 'Sig. P...' or simply 'P...'. He wrote with fury about the perceived plagiarism of his *Pirata* in Pacini's opera *Cavalieri di Valenza* (The Knights of Valenza), describing parts of it as 'unbelievable crap'.[36]

Cavalieri's opening performance at La Scala in June 1828 was a flop, prompting Bellini to write with *schadenfreude*, 'Imagine Barbaja's curses after spending so much money' on *Cavalieri*. Barbaja had hoped in vain that it would turn into another money-spinner like *L'Ultimo Giorno di Pompei*. Pacini himself was so traumatised by the failure, which coincided with the death of his wife of three years, that he asked Barbaja for a leave of absence and a sabbatical from composing for both Milan and Naples for a year. Barbaja granted this after extracting financial compensation from the composer.[37]

Like Rossini, Bellini was not scared to take on Barbaja. He knew that he needed to charge more than the others since he was a slower composer. It took him about a year to pen a new opera, which, he wrote, he needed to 'spit blood' to compose.[38] But he could also sense when an impresario was in urgent need of his work. Sensing Barbaja's desperation for a new opera to be ready in 1829, he demanded a very high fee, and Barbaja acquiesced though he complained bitterly. Bellini also warned that he would charge Barbaja twice the fee if the opera, *La Straniera,* proved a hit, which it did. Bellini wrote to Florimo that Barbaja 'will be my friend as long as I do well.'[39]

The young Sicilian played the wily impresario like a Stradivarius. Following *Pirata,* Bellini contracted with Barbaja to write another opera for La Scala, to be produced at the end of 1828. He had originally demanded 1,135 ducats for the work.[40] On 16 June 1828 he signed to produce an opera starring Méric-Lalande and either Lablache or Tamburini: Barbaja, after 'much screaming',[41] had bargained him down to 1,000 ducats. But Bellini was satisfied with the price, which was twice what he had achieved for writing operas just a few years earlier, and a large sum by the industry standard.[42]

Bellini was well aware of the risks of producing a second opera in Milan following the success of *Pirata.* He also remembered Pacini's fiasco with *Cavalieri di Valenza.*[43] Bellini knew that Rubini had been crucial to the success of *Pirata,* and again asked Barbaja via Florimo as well as the Neapolitan music publisher Guillaume Cottrau to release Rubini from his obligations in Naples, in order to allow him to act in the *prima* of this new opera. Bellini emphasised that he also wanted to safeguard Barbaja's financial interests, by ensuring the opening would not prove a fiasco.

But Barbaja remained firm. Given the importance of developing promising new composers, Barbaja could not afford to be bogged down by one composer's capriciousness. While Bellini was more cantankerous than most of the other young composers Barbaja was grooming, and he refused to be bullied by the impresario, his launch again demonstrated Barbaja's business methods. Barbaja gave young composers the chances they needed, introduced them to the right librettists and singers, and exposed them to a large number of stages. And while continuing to develop and promote Bellini and Donizetti in the late 1820s, Barbaja had his eye on one other promising composer.

Vaccai

Nicola Vaccai (1790–1848) hailed from the Marche region near the Adriatic, and studied in Naples under the legendary composer Giovanni Paisiello. He started composing early, as well as studying and teaching voice, though his composing career took off later than that of most of his peers. Barbaja began actively negotiating with the promising composer in 1825. Though Vaccai's friends urged him to sign with the 'generous gentleman', no deal was struck.[44]

Only in 1828 did Barbaja finally sign up the composer for work at the Neapolitan royal theatres, offering him a fee and a room and full board.[45] Upon his arrival in Naples, Vaccai experienced Barbaja's magic at its best, witnessing a grandiose performance of Bellini's *Pirata* at the San Carlo that was performed on the name day of the Prince of Calabria, and which featured five times the normal level of illumination and was attended by all the principal royals.[46]

Vaccai spent only a short time living in the Via Toledo, because Barbaja moved him to another apartment as he was renovating the guest flat for his son-in-law Cesare Politi. Vaccai continued to dine at Barbaja's house on a daily basis, but he enjoyed the liberty of being a bit further away from the dominant impresario.[47] The great visual spectacle of Naples gradually unfolded itself to the young composer, who wrote that the kingdom was a 'most delicious country'.[48] As Vesuvius was again spewing fire, foreign visitors were eager to get close to the sight, and Vaccai joined a group of 12 people, including Barbaja's 27-year-old daughter Carolina, to ascend the volcano on horse and mule and observe the furious eruptions. Other than being kicked by a mule, Vaccai returned unscathed and he was duly impressed.[49] He was also quite proud that, unlike the English visitors who had had themselves carried up the mountain, his party had climbed it like mountain goats.

Vaccai's later years in Naples were marked by tensions with Barbaja. 'There is little satisfaction in being signed on with this beast of a man,' whined the composer, as Barbaja was forced to tighten the financial screws.[50]

Vaccai was one of those young composers who probably failed to live up to Barbaja's expectations in terms of the fame he achieved, though he benefited from the full resources at Barbaja's disposal. None of the works written for Barbaja achieved the sort of impact the impresario desired, and his operas remain largely unknown today, totally eclipsed by the big three *bel canto* composers. Nevertheless, his impact on opera is undeniable. No voice student can escape Vaccai's *Practical Method of Italian Singing*, which remains the bible of exercises for training the operatic voice, teaching breathing support and extension of vocal range and agility.

While Barbaja might not have found a single successor to Rossini, and nor did any of these younger composers attain the degree of fame that Rossini reached at his peak, from today's perspective it is clear that Donizetti and Bellini emerged as composers of remarkable longevity who have enjoyed widespread popularity to this day. Rossini, Bellini and Donizetti became the supreme masters of the *bel canto* and it was they who helped to make Barbaja's reputation. Others have fared less well over time. The operas of Vaccai, Pacini, Ricci, Morlacchi and many others are barely performed anymore, and in spite of many works of remarkable musical beauty and originality are known only to specialists today.

Barbaja's 'dogs'

As much as Barbaja needed to find the next Rossini, he even more urgently needed to find the next Colbran. Again, he learnt through his early experience with Colbran that it was economically more sensible to hire promising and talented young singers, rather than hire established, but expensive, artists. It was best to discover young talent, hire them into his *cartello* on a long-term contract, develop them and either use them in his own theatres or loan them profitably to others. With singers, however, this model was less reliable, as he often needed to compete with other impresarios for singers who had already established reputations.

Barbaja had perfected the system for expanding his empire since his days of running a sprawling gambling syndicate, and was now comfortable controlling his theatres remotely. Using his Partenopean base as his headquarters, Barbaja's influence reached 'like tentacles'[51] over an ever expanding base of European operations, using a rather novel commercial business model from Naples to the capital of the Habsburg Empire and beyond.[52] In essence, Barbaja and his opera troupe was one of Italy's most successful exports, and Naples had been turned into the nerve centre for European opera agents, composers, publishers, musicians, singers and dancers. In many ways, this can be considered the first time that Naples was the centre of any pan-European business empire.

After the abolition of gambling, most of Barbaja's revenues were derived from the stars of the stages, the leading singers of the early 19th century. In 1826 and 1827 Barbaja's artist management business was at its peak. The English opera impresario John Ebers wrote that he was unable to attract singers to the King's Theatre in London as 'all the good singers were in Barbaja's hands',[53] which made it difficult for other impresarios to compete. His business in handling singers was so successful in the late 1820s that Barbaja even considered focusing only on artist management, and totally giving up the *imprese*.[54]

Barbaja's artist management needs were complex: coordinating schedules, handling talents while fending off competitors, dealing with critics, and of course handling the ever-present law suits. But this saw Barbaja at his best. Corresponding with singers, musicians, agents and other impresarios required careful logistical arrangements in an age before telegraphic or electronic communication. Letter-writing was complicated and slow, but still the only means of correspondence. A letter from Naples to Paris would take six days, usually being taken by boat from Naples to Marseille and then by carriage to Paris.[55] Many letters were lost or stolen, and judging from the surviving correspondence between Barbaja and his operatic world, many letters seem to have been hand-delivered by friends.

Barbaja negotiated several long-term contracts with his principal singers, whereby he paid them a fixed contractual salary and pocketed the earnings from all their performances both at his own opera houses and at other opera houses, such as Paris, where they took on roles during the term of the contract.[56] Commercially this made eminent sense. It was estimated that of the 125,000 francs that Rubini (and his wife) were paid in a single year under Barbaja's contract, only about 60,000 francs actually ended up in the singers' pockets.[57] The rest went to the impresario.

Acting in the dual capacity of talent agent and opera impresario, Barbaja was able to rotate the singers under his contract smoothly around the various theatres he controlled. Most singers did not seem to mind. Barbaja's system exposed them to audiences in the top houses around Europe, the pay was good and engagements were guaranteed for a period of time. But some did not like this policy, especially those on long-term contracts, and they found the travelling uncomfortable and the conditions stressful. Some observers also objected fiercely, believing Barbaja's methods were 'resembling in nearly every respect the now happily-abolished slave trade'.[58]

Barbaja's operating methods certainly drew a lot of international commentary. *Era*, a London newspaper, reported:

The [normal] impresarii usually engaged their singers for a season. M. Barbaja for a year, but with the power of making them shift their quarters and pass them from one city to another. He then proceeded to engage artists for a term of ten or twelve years, for he had a marvellous tact for divining the future powers of an artist by those he displayed at his debut, and when he thought he recognized the latest seeds of real talent, he did not hesitate proposing a *scrittura* [engagement] contracting with him for this long period for a sum of £100 or £120 annually. The debutant, generally in want of money, accepted the offer the more readily, because another manager would not give him half this sum for his initiatory exertions. It is true he is no longer his own master, but who can prognosticate the future, and at any rate he has his £120 sure. The whole mind of Barbaja was employed to find out the mode in which he could employ his musical serf to the best advantage.[59]

Harmonicon roundly criticised Barbaja's tactics. It reported that Barbaja rented out the celebrated tenor Rubini for a whole season to the Genoa opera house at a profit to himself. He also swapped the Paris-based tenor Donzelli for the French ballet dancer Albert,[60] irritating Rossini to the point that Barbaja needed to rush post-haste to the French capital to assuage his friend. While in Paris, he tried to persuade the Académie Royale de Musique to accept his 'tenor David in exchange for Paul the dancer'.[61]

Some critics claimed that there was a secret pact between Rossini and Barbaja to monopolise the European opera scene, in order to dictate the terms of the great singers in the major opera houses. The *Allgemeine Musikalische Zeitung* reported: 'We hear word of an alliance between Barbaja, Rossini and those Milanese individuals who want to take concessions for the theatres in Naples, Venice, Milan, Vienna, Paris, London and heaven knows where else.'[62] They were thought to be swapping singers from lower-paying stages (like Naples), to higher-paying stages (like Paris), ruthlessly arbitraging the varying compensation structures of the stages, irrespective of contractual obligations.[63] Barbaja had such a large number of singers under contract it was easy for him to lose control. He reportedly offered one singer a contract, only to be reminded that he was already under contract with him. Never embarrassed, Barbaja retorted, 'Well, then go to Donizetti and tell him to write a new part.'[64]

On another occasion Barbaja was caught out when he had been negotiating with Josephine Fodor to spend the entire 1825/26 season in Naples, and had therefore foregone booking another prima donna of her calibre until the following year, when he had arranged for Henriette Méric-Lalande to come to Naples. Then word came that Fodor had secretly signed a contract with the Paris opera. Barbaja's initial efforts to persuade her to stay until the end of the season were in vain. In spite of suffering a period of poor health and not wanting to undertake the journey, Barbaja rushed off to Paris, where he managed successfully to negotiate an extension of Fodor's current contract with the impresario of the Paris opera house, permitting her to bridge the gap until the next prima donna arrived. However, in spite of the huge audience support for her in Naples as well as the charm offensive launched by Barbaja, the capricious Fodor announced she was unwilling to accept this and left Naples prematurely.

Her decision set the local journalists in motion. The once adored Fodor suddenly became the 'beautiful sounding street organ with neither good taste nor dignity, poor pronunciation, many screaming notes and no trills, no *messa di voce*'.[65] She arrived in Paris to face a relatively frosty reception, possibly also due to a well-orchestrated hate campaign instigated by her rival, Giuditta Pasta.[66]

Giuditta Pasta (1797–1865) was born as Giuditta Negri to a Jewish family in Como. Hers was a story of mediocrity transformed to technical brilliance. With a relatively coarse voice that often veered off-key, she spent several years in extremely hard training to discipline it until she met some early success in the 1820s in Paris and Rome. Shuttling between London and Paris, she managed to build a reputation as one of the most thrilling dramatic singing actresses of her generation, mastering most of the great parts of Rossini. Pasta was one of the few singers of the time who really tried to work her way into the character of a role. Stendhal claimed she was the only singer to inject the true grandeur and chivalry into the character of Rossini's *Tancredi*.[67]

In November 1826 Barbaja signed up Pasta with the much coveted title of Prima Donna Assoluta for the San Carlo, Teatro del Fondo and Kaerntner-tortheater for a period of five months. The sum of 42,000 francs in addition to travelling expenses, room and board was an absolute record, but Barbaja was dead-set on getting his money's worth from the singer, whom he relentlessly ferried around Europe. When Pasta returned to Naples for the 1828/29 season, she was described by the local press as '*la prima cantante del secolo*' (the premier singer of the century),[68] and she became a huge favourite of the King as well as the audience.

Pasta's career was extremely short and after about ten years at the top, her voice suddenly deteriorated, described by some critics as 'a wreck'. After an ill-advised comeback in St Petersburg, she retired to her home in Como.

In the late 1820s and early 1830s, however, Giuditta Pasta and Maria Malibran were the two undisputed queens of the European opera stages, as well as fierce rivals: Pasta with a carefully polished, prepared and trained voice she deployed with skill, intelligence and pre-meditation, Malibran with a tremendous natural gift she used effortlessly.

Maria Malibran (1808–36), daughter of the tenor and composer Manuel García, and who worked closely with Barbaja, was to become the most celebrated singer of her era. Her performances at a very young age, at the encouragement of her father and his friend Rossini, did not leave much of an impression. It was only in 1825 when she replaced an indisposed singer at short notice as the lead soprano part of *Il Barbiere di Siviglia* in London that her talent really rose to the fore.

In a concert with the castrato Gian Battista Velluti, Maria is reported to have matched the fabled singer tone for tone in all his improvised embellishments, and then thrown in her own in an effort to outshine him. She had full and total control over her voice throughout an effortless three octaves and complete tonal homogeneity.

Guided by her ambitious and strict father, she married an American of French ancestry in New York in 1826 and thereafter appeared as Maria Malibran. She was known for her on-stage magnetism, her wide repertory and her ability to master a role in just a few hours. Bellini spoke of her endearingly as 'that little devil of a Malibran who can memorise an entire opera overnight'.[69]

By 1831 Malibran was such a superstar that the Opera of Rome thought it appropriate to quadruple the ticket prices for her performance.[70] The audience did not react well. The same year, Barbaja was unsure whether he would bring her to Naples, as he was concerned Malibran would 'crush the ordinary cast' and sow discord among his other singers, given her extraordinary talent and cost. Barbaja was just as worried that he would incur a significant loss in case she did not prove to be the same crowd pleaser in Naples.[71] But Barbaja could not resist Malibran's appeal and arranged her debut at the Teatro del Fondo. The impresario had already sold all the boxes at the Teatro San Carlo to the regular subscribers, so he figured he could make more money by casting the attractive singer at the Teatro del Fondo, where he was able to sell individual tickets.[72]

Malibran's larger than life personality attracted a lot of attention, and not always the best of fortune. Her carriage was overturned in an accident in the middle of the Chiaia Boulevard in central Naples when a herd of wayward pigs ran into her coach. The pigs had been brought into the city to be slaughtered and roasted, but had escaped and rushed the boulevards. Malibran broke her wrist, but otherwise emerged unscathed. She cancelled some performances, but quickly came back to the stage, wearing a sling around her arm.

In 1832, Malibran spent about six months in Naples, residing in the Palazzo Barbaja at the same time as Pacini. Pacini was quite taken by the singer and grew ever fonder of Malibran, with her peerless artistry, her simplicity and openness to people of all backgrounds, as well as her fluency in five languages. Pacini did concede that she tended to become inebriated at the table, but equally he admired the Amazon-like qualities that made her as expert a rider as a fencer.[73]

By March 1834 the audience and the critics were completely won over. The *Allgemeine Musikalische Zeitung* reported with its trademark cynicism that 'we are soon running out of words of praise for the Malibran. Indeed, we find even the highest words of praise inadequate in face of her natural wonder.'[74] Rossini seemed to concur: 'During my time [I have met] many singers who were great artists ... but only three of real genius: ... Lablache ... Rubino [sic], and that spoiled child of nature, Maria Felicita Malibran.'[75]

Malibran's flourishing career was cut brutally short when she died at the age of 28 in 1836 as a result of injuries sustained in a riding accident. La Scala gave a Cantata in her honour. It was hastily composed by the musicians for whose operas the singer had done so much, including Donizetti, Pacini, Mercadante and Vaccai, but, sadly, was judged a dud.

Luigi Lablache was, in spite of his name, Italian. Discovered by the impresario in 1816, he was to become one of the busiest singers on the Barbaja roster. Born in Naples of French parents, he was a man not only of tremendous vocal resources, but also of enormous physical size (he was well over 6 feet), and he was recognised as one of the leading basses of his generation. His physique, strong stage presence, fine voice and acting made him one of the most sought after basses of the early 19th century, and he was called upon to create roles in many first performances for Bellini, Donizetti and others.

He possessed great personal integrity and empathy, and was a caring father to his 14 children. In his later years he became a leading singing teacher, fondly remembered even by Queen Victoria, who was a pupil of his in London. His bass had remarkable volume and profundity, but he also controlled the full range, from tragic *basso* to the entertaining *buffo*. His colossal size and physical strength are part of operatic lore. For entertainment, he would reach down from the stage into the orchestra pit and effortlessly pick up a contrabass by its neck before gingerly replacing it. He was also known occasionally to pick up a fellow singer and pack him under his arms to remove him forcibly from the stage, to the delight of the audience.

In London house concerts in the 1830s, even top-rated artists and singers like Malibran, Rubini and Lablache were expected to enter the building from the service entrance. In the drawing-room where the performance was being held, the artists were separated from the guests by a long cord. The German pianist and composer Franz Liszt, who was infuriated by this classist custom, wrote a series of articles in 1835 protesting against such undignified and humiliating treatment.[76] It was Lablache, however, who put an end to it. Speaking to one of the guests on the other side of the cord after a house concert at a wealthy patron's home, Lablache simply untied the cord, dropped it, and demonstratively stepped across the line. He had the physical presence and charisma to get away with this unchallenged. The cord was reportedly never again used in London house concerts.

At the height of his earning power, Lablache was well aware that not all singers could command equally magnificent fees as those his impresarios had negotiated for him. Many singers, in spite of having had a period of fame, ended up unemployed and destitute. A once famous *buffo* singer called Benedetti was such an example. In a gesture of generosity born of empathy, Luigi Lablache dedicated the income from his benefit concert of 1835 to Benedetti as well as to an impoverished former dancer. The evening prompted many a tear from the audience, and netted 861 ducats, of which two-thirds went to the two retired artists. One-third remained with the impresario. The *Allgemeine Musikalische Zeitung* commented that this reminded it of another 'cute Italian tradition', where the owners of restaurants routinely kept for themselves part of the tips given to the staff.[77]

Lablache celebrated many of his greatest triumphs as a member of the Barbaja *cartello*. He had a genuine friendship with the impresario, even after he switched to Barbaja's competitor Alessandro Lanari in 1835, Barbaja's imperious ways having become a bit much for him. The switch to the younger impresario was probably supported by many of Lablache's friends. The composer Lorenzo Borsini, for one, was so excited about Lablache's move from Barbaja that he wrote a 110-verse 'heroic-comical' poem, praising the bass and ridiculing the despotic impresario with acerbic wit. The poem was titled 'L'ultimo giorno di Barbaja' (The last day of Barbaja).

Adelaide Tosi was another of the stars of the Barbaja stable. Trained by the great castrato Girolamo Crescentini, she had a remarkable career on the

Milanese and Neapolitan stages. Barbaja signed the young Milanese singer in spring 1827 for a period of 14 years, an unprecedented length of engagement. Interestingly, at her own request, the contract precluded her from performing in any form in Milan.[78]

Tosi was by all accounts an elegant and capable singer, as well as a vicious and temperamental gossip. At times, her rants against Barbaja and other singers got so out of hand she would lose her voice.[79] In Madrid she had a tumultuous relationship with the composer Saverio Mercadante. The affair, however, went sour when Tosi became involved with the Neapolitan Count Ferdinando Lucchesi Palli.[80] Mercadante, usually the calm Southern gentleman, went to great lengths to discredit Tosi and destroy her career, and distributed an anonymous letter painting her as a drunken loose woman: 'Tosi is a whore. She failed in her duty, she got drunk, she had herself fucked all night by her Prince, and we had to pay without being able to enjoy an opera we like so much.'[81] Meanwhile, amazingly, Mercadante and Tosi continued working professionally together.

Mercadante's anger was possibly also driven by the extraordinary disparity between the fees paid to the singers such as Tosi and to the composers. In 1833, Mercadante became enraged when the French prima donna Henriette Méric-Lalande was paid nine times more for the season at La Scala than he had been for composing the opera in which she was to perform.[82]

As well as promoting the careers of the Italian singers, Barbaja signed up singers he had discovered in Vienna and took them to the Neapolitan stages. The Hungarian-Austrian singer Caroline Unger had already enjoyed much success in Vienna on the stage, before Barbaja brought her to Naples in 1825, though she is best remembered from her Vienna days for her part in the first performance of Beethoven's Symphony No 9. According to a popular anecdote, it was Unger who turned around the by now completely deaf Beethoven after the performance so that he could acknowledge the thunderous applause of the audience.

While initially a contralto, Barbaja encouraged Unger to extend the upper range of her voice, though the high notes sounded like 'dagger thrusts' to Bellini.[83] Barbaja cast her in the premiere for Bellini's *Straniera*, and Donizetti and Mercadante would both create roles for her voice.[84] Unger later also had a well-publicised affair with the writer Alexandre Dumas (père), who left her broken-hearted. It appears that Dumas, like so many at the time, was principally attracted to the idea of a romance with an opera star.

With dozens of singers under contract, it could at times prove challenging for Barbaja to keep them all fully employed. As he paid the singers a fixed fee, and made his revenues from deploying them as frequently as possible, he was highly motivated to have his troupe perform as frequently as they could. The more theatres he controlled, the greater a platform he had for his singers. With the large number of stages at his disposal, the composers he had been developing and the large *cartello* of singers, Barbaja had succeeded in constructing a pan-European artistic empire.

Finding a replacement for Colbran as the dominant singer from 1810 to 1820, therefore, proved an easier task than finding a replacement for Rossini. The sheer number of singers under his management gave Barbaja a wide palette of excellent artists to choose from. Disposing of his *cartello* as if they were performing circus animals, it comes as little surprise that Barbaja frequently referred to his singers as his 'dogs': he wrote to Rossini, 'Regarding the troupe, you tell me who you want, and I will put my dogs at your disposal.'[85] But as Barbaja would later learn, the 'dogs' could sometimes fight back.

The ordeal of travel

For composers as well as singers, part and parcel of being handled and promoted by Barbaja was to accept extensive travel. Barbaja himself travelled throughout Europe in search of the best composers and artists, and he, for one, does not seem to have minded the difficult journeying. As he managed theatres in three different cities, the opera singers and composers under contract to him also needed to get used to continual travel, and some would complain of the drudgery, however.

The trip from Rome to Naples took four days in Barbaja's time, featured frequent axle-wheel ruptures, and included the very dangerous road from Terracina (the last town in the Papal territories) to Fondi (the first town in the Neapolitan dominions) along the Roman Via Appia, where bandits would hide in the shrubbery and regularly attack travellers. The Neapolitan Government tried to put an end to the robberies by paying farmers to burn the shrubbery, giving the carriages better visibility. Inside Neapolitan territory, the Government stationed soldiers 'every quarter of an hour', about every 2 kilometres, to be on the lookout for robbers. If they caught them, they were usually hanged.[86]

There is no record of Barbaja ever having any encounters with bandits. Nevertheless, a story about Barbaja (in the form of a successful impresario called Balboya, most certainly modelled on him) being held to ransom and forced to perform by bandits found its way into the opera *La Sirène* (The Siren) by French composer Daniel Auber (1782–1871) in 1840.[87]

Barbaja's competitor Alessandro Lanari, however, was less fortunate. Travelling along the notoriously dangerous road in 1834, his carriage was attacked by a group of armed bandits. A furious fight ensued, leaving two of the aggressors dead and one heavily wounded.[88] Even by the late 1830s, security had not improved. Rossini's second wife, Olympe Pelissier, wrote that 'just thinking of that route gives me goose bumps all over my body'.[89]

The road to Naples led through some of the bleakest parts of Italy: 'The swampy soil and marshes on the right hand, with a string of barren mountains on the left, for scores of miles together, may amuse, but cannot delight a traveller,' wrote the English traveller Samuel Sharp.[90] Likewise, the lodgings were notoriously dirty and barely heated in winter: 'The road from Rome to this place [Naples] is bad enough, the inns are still worse … all the way to Naples we never once crept within the sheets, not daring to encounter the vermin and nastiness of those beds.'[91]

Along the road, travellers would pass large wooden pillars on which the severed arms and legs of robbers and murderers had been tied, the 'sad signs of Roman justice'.[92] The composer Louis Spohr pitied the Italian robbers, who were reduced to thievery on account of hunger and destitution. He could not understand how a country as lush as Italy, with its fertile fields, could not feed its population properly.

During the Napoleonic regime, Italians were forbidden from carrying knives on pain of being sent to work in the galley. Should a fight break out and somebody pull a knife, its wielder would be immediately branded a murderer and hanged without mercy. In post-Napoleonic times these rules could not be enforced, making journeys even more dangerous.

Passengers were not only exposed to criminal elements, but also to harassment by government authorities, with frequent passport controls and Customs inspections. In a continent with so many borders, passports were a necessity and they were thoroughly scrutinised by officials. Spohr reported that Customs and passport controls were often 'tending to the ridiculous', and he recounted with annoyance that he was once required to pay duty on his own violin he was carrying.[93]

These trips were not only physically arduous, they were also long and complicated. In order to travel from Venice to Bologna, travellers took a sailing boat which first passed through the lagoons and then into the open sea, before eventually entering the Po, where the boat was pulled along by horses on the riverside. More common routes involved only a *venturino* (carriage) with two or four horses. Singers and composers would usually buy the right to have a cabin for themselves and their family, and the price included dinner and lodging for the night. The *venturino* could, however, be slowed down by carrying up to three extra passengers outside, on the cabriolet. The fast route from Florence to Rome, via Siena, took six days; the longer route, via Perugia, took seven.

Travelling regularly between Vienna and Naples, usually alone in a *venturino*, gave Barbaja plenty of time to think, and worry, about the composers and singers he was promoting, as well as the neverending politics of the theatre. But the strenuous travel, the increasingly frequent disputes and a slowly declining cash flow were starting to gnaw at him.

10

Retreat from Milan and Vienna

(1828–1831)

For the past few years, Barbaja had largely left day-to-day management of the two theatres in Milan to his partners, Crivelli and the Villa brothers, as he commuted between Naples, Vienna, Paris and Milan. Unresolved problems at La Scala and the Teatro alla Canobbiana, however, meant that from 1827 he was forced to spend more time in the city and to make a greater contribution to the syndicate. Considering how long Barbaja had wanted to get his hands on the Milanese *imprese*, it is somewhat surprising to discover how little he enjoyed actually controlling them. In fact, Barbaja despised working in Milan and was growing to loathe his involvement in its 'cursed theatre':[1] he was losing a significant amount of money in the Milanese *appalto*.[2]

By August that year, the breakdown between Barbaja and La Scala was complete. The Austrian authorities in Vienna, who ultimately controlled the theatres through the viceroy and the local Commissioner of Theatres, told them that 'Barbaja is poorly fulfilling his contractual obligations and the audience is unhappy about it'.[3] Barbaja was no longer seen as fit for the job under the conditions set out in the contract.

Barbaja's contract with Crivelli and La Scala continued through to 20 March 1830,[4] but for all practical purposes as far as Barbaja was concerned it came to an end in 1828.[5] There are no details as to the exact terms of separation, nor do we know whether the decision to terminate his contract was stated as being final. Whatever the case, by 1829 Barbaja had delegated most of his authority to G B Villa,[6] and additional external impresarios also took part in running the theatres.

The difficulties surrounding the Milanese *imprese* also exacerbated a much less public arrangement: the tense contractual relationship between Rubini, his wife Adelaide Comelli-Rubini and the impresario. Two years had passed since Rubini had given a loan to Barbaja for the down payment required for the last Vienna *impresa*. The fiasco of the Milanese venture made the timely repayment difficult, and Barbaja was forced to ask for an extension on the repayment date at the very same time that he was trying to renegotiate the terms of Rubini's contract.

Barbaja's initial letters to the singer at this time bear all the hallmarks of his customary strategy of persuasion. 'My dearest friend Rubini … come to Naples where you are considered a messiah by the court and the audience.'[7] He then offered favourable terms not only for Rubini but also for his far less employable wife. When Rubini still refused to yield, Barbaja adopted a more pleading tone, referring to himself in the third person as he liked to do when making particularly contentious requests.

> Dear friend, you now know what that prick Barbaja would do if he had the name and the talents of his friend Rubini … but you have too much talent and too much friendship for your Barbaja to not want to help me out.[8]

Rubini, however, had little intention of helping out. Remembering the beginnings of his career when Barbaja had forced him into a rough deal, he neither extended the loan nor renewed his contract. The correspondence first turned frosty, then hostile. Rubini terminated his contract, withdrew his wife from the stage, quit La Scala and demanded immediate repayment of the loan. From Naples, Barbaja asked G B Villa to arrange repayment to Rubini, but not before he had raised an invoice for room and board for the year that the Rubinis lived at the Palazzo Barbaja during their sojourn in Naples.

Barbaja was upset by the acrimonious break-up with one of his star singers, blaming all problems on the faltering of his contract with Milan, though he remained actively involved in placing other singers at the city's theatres.[9] He also, reluctantly, retained some administrative responsibility until the end of his term in 1830, during which time a significant improvement was made to the well-being of the staff.

Towards the end of his *appalto* Barbaja changed the pension fund arrangements of the royal theatres. While the members of the orchestra had benefitted from this since 1782, Barbaja extended the fund to cover all staff of the theatres, regardless of function or seniority. The Pio Istituto Teatrale (literally the Pious Institute of the Theatres, but actually the pension fund) retained, managed and disbursed the funds, the money deriving from the regular benefit evenings at the opera houses. The impresario was obliged to hold these benefit evenings at his cost, and was forbidden from receiving any of the revenue. It is hard to ascertain whether Barbaja actively championed the extension of the pension fund, or whether he was simply in charge of the theatres at the time the Government approved the change and thereby instrumental in its implementation. In any case, it certainly contributed to his charitable image. But it did not make him like Milan any better.

By September 1829 Barbaja was literally counting the days until the end of his engagement:

dear rosini [sic] now is the moment If [sic] it is true that you have a pact of friendship for your Barbaja to show me some proof. i [sic] am not speaking of the disgrace that has followed me for the last Four years.. once I leave the Cursed theatre of milano... which is, thanks to the Supremebeing [sic] only another six months and thirteen days away and then I have finished this Wicked contract I promise you that I would rather work as an Executioner than work again as theimpresario [sic] inmilan [sic]. Then let us not think any more aboutmilan [sic] for My Compatriots have sufficiently stoned me. and I will never forget the Savaging and outrage I have Received [sic] From the Directors of the theatres ...

now dear giovachino [little Gioachino] I really Need [sic] an opera from you fornextyear's [sic] easter, either For the 30: march = or for the 6. July of the Same year which ever Suits you, whatever compensation you request I will pay you and I will Not argue with you about it and Will remain eternally grateful, all we want dear giovachino Is to see your Name in the programme of the year 1830: this will reanimate the treatro [sic] San carlo which has become a desert ... and all Naples still speaks Only of the great rosini [sic]... Therefore dear rosini come to my rescue ...[10]

At the same time as Barbaja was trying to extricate himself from the Milanese mess, he was also considering pulling back from Vienna. Even without them, and with his deputy managing the Naples theatres, he had enough close associates running European theatres to allow him to keep his stable of singers profitably employed. And Barbaja no longer had the energy nor the ambition to commute constantly throughout Europe – let alone anywhere else. A few months later, Mozart's former librettist Lorenzo da Ponte invited Barbaja to join him in the United States where he had just opened America's first opera company and was in need of an impresario. Barbaja turned him down without further thought.[11]

In April 1828 Barbaja ended his lessee arrangement with the Viennese royal theatres, well before the official expiry of the contract.[12] After lengthy negotiations the lease was taken over by Barbaja's old colleague Count von Gallenberg. Count Wenzel Robert von Gallenberg (1783–1839) was an Austrian ballet music composer and occasional impresario and theatre director. Married to Countess Guicciardi, to whom Beethoven had dedicated the *Moonlight Sonata*, he had moved to Naples in the *decennio*, and had helped to organise the festivities for Joseph Bonaparte there in 1805. He had also had some success with the ballets he composed, which were performed in between acts, often of Rossini's operas. His business sense was less inspired. When he took over the Kaerntnertortheater after Barbaja from 1828 to 1830, he lost his entire fortune in the undertaking. The Austrian Emperor Franz I personally intervened to terminate the lease, because of the poor financial state of the concession.[13]

In May 1830, the dancer and choreographer Louis Duport, Barbaja's former deputy in Vienna, assumed the lease for the Kaerntnertortheater, starting performances in September 1830 and holding it through to 1836, when Carlo Balochino and Bartolomeo Merelli jointly took over the Viennese royal theatres, running them to 1848. Duport's tenure, predictably, focused on ballet, but he would also oversee the first performances in Vienna of Donizetti's *Anna Bolena* and Bellini's *Norma*.

Bartolomeo Merelli (1794–1879), known as the 'Eagle of the Impresarios', became an increasingly important competitor of Barbaja. Like so many of Italy's musical greats, Merelli was from Bergamo, near Milan. He was an accomplished music scholar and librettist, and had studied under Giovanni Simone Mayr, the German composer and musician. He worked with Donizetti as a librettist from 1818 through to 1821, and only launched his career as an impresario in 1830 when he took over the *impresa* at Varese. At his peak, he ran *imprese* at Paris, St Petersburg and La Scala[14] and also arranged several Italian *stagioni* at the Kaerntnertortheater. In spite of his many successes, Merelli's reputation was mixed because he found the commercial aspects of running a business challenging. When running the Kaerntnertortheater, he enraged Donizetti by his 'flagrant misrepresentation of the merits of some of the singers he sent to appear'.[15] Later he ran a successful theatre agency, organising tours for some of the major singers of his day. An ill-conceived comeback as an impresario in Milan and Turin was to ruin him financially, and he died impoverished in his hometown of Bergamo.[16]

Balochino and Merelli oversaw some of the most celebrated times of the Viennese opera, although Balochino's Austrian detractors were continually to make derogatory comments about him, even claiming that he was actually a tailor and knew nothing of music at all. His origins may well have been as a tailor – a skill that would undoubtedly have proved useful in producing the glorious costumes and sets for the opera – but he was first and foremost an astute and carefully calculating businessman, though one with neither charm nor humour. And it was from Barbaja, his first associate, that he learned the art of driving a hard bargain.

Difficult years in Naples

Barbaja's frequent absences from Naples had left their traces, and sometimes he felt that he might be losing his touch. The year 1828 was not a prosperous one for the Barbaja *imprese* at the Teatro San Carlo and the Teatro del Fondo, and the impresario was forced to introduce unpopular salary reductions at the royal theatres, leading to regular clashes with the Duke of Noja as well as staff unrest. The San Carlo was also frayed by intrigues, many of which were blamed on Pacini.

Vaccai suggested that the audience was so negatively disposed towards Barbaja that every new performance was doomed to failure, leading to empty theatres and forcing Barbaja to give away up to 50 boxes an evening.[17] A new opera, *Alexi*, by the composer Carlo Conti, which premiered on the name day of the King,[18] was a disaster as both the composer and conductor had to be replaced mid-performance due to illness. Nicola Vaccai, who replaced Conti, had the Neapolitan premiere of his own opera some months later, on the occasion of the queen's birthday.[19] That also ended in fiasco as the stage machinery collapsed mid-scene, causing Adelaide Tosi to crack up while singing and the audience as well as the attending royal family to break out in laughter. The curtain was ordered to be lowered. We will never know whether the collapsing machinery was a deliberate act of sabotage by the machinists and carpenters who were being paid less by Barbaja than in previous years. The impresario, however, did not wait to find out: he had them promptly arrested and taken away to jail.[20] Vaccai also felt that Barbaja was increasingly upsetting some of the strongest stars in his *cartello*. Lablache and Meric-Lalande declined to extend their contracts and departed to London, while Rubini complained heavily.

While singers, theatre staff and administrators seemed to be conspiring against him, Barbaja still hoped to retain his golden touch with his composers. During the years 1828 to 1831, the two biggest composers were Donizetti and Bellini, and they were critical to the success of the San Carlo. 'Without those two composers', wrote the music publisher Guillaume Cottrau some years later, 'our theatres would go to hell.'[21] Barbaja was, however, not lucky enough to be responsible for some of their greatest triumphs during this period. Donizetti's fame was steadily growing, and he was becoming a real peer and competitor to Bellini, the reigning Sicilian superstar. Exacerbating their competitiveness, the two composers' opera premieres were often scheduled for the same theatres at around the same time.[22] One week Bellini's opera would dominate, the next, Donizetti's work outshone his rival's. The vitriol, however, was decidedly one-sided: Donizetti remained ever the calm gentleman with a genuine interest in Bellini's work; Bellini bad-mouthed virtually all his competitors, and Donizetti was no exception.

Bellini triumphed with *La Straniera* (The Stranger), another co-production with Felice Romani and his last opera written for Barbaja. The opera debuted on 14 February 1829 at La Scala and elicited the much coveted '*furore e fanatismo*',[23] the ultimate Italian acclamation in the opera world. The audience called Bellini 30 times to the stage for an ovation. The *Allgemeine Musikalische Zeitung* commented that Bellini was putting Italian opera back onto the right track after several years of compositorial aberrations, remarking with gratification that Bellini was orienting himself on the German model and influence. While it is true that Bellini was an admirer of Mozart and Beethoven, the more important fact is that Bellini had established his own style, and had successfully stepped out of the shadow of Rossini.

Barbaja was delighted about Bellini's colossal success with *La Straniera*. He was less happy about how this translated into the composer's bargaining power. Rather than enter into long-term contracts with any one impresario or theatre, Bellini now demanded 10,000 francs for the composition of his next opera. This was the twice the world record at the time, which had been charged by Rossini for *Semiramide* in 1823 (5,000 francs).

Donizetti, meanwhile, was back in Naples in October 1829, to prepare his new opera *Il Diluvio* (The Great Flood). Barbaja worked closely with the composer, keeping him professionally and personally motivated. On a business trip to Milan, he hand-delivered a golden tobacco box to Donizetti's father, a gift from the composer.[24]

Il Diluvio was remarkable for several reasons. The absurd staging featuring laughable sets that exposed the stage-hands to the audience in the upper tiers was greeted with cat-calls and whistles, which probably contributed to the critics' excoriating reviews in the press. At this point bad reviews were unusual for Donizetti in Naples; he usually enjoyed far greater journalistic support in Naples than in the north. Also unfortunately noteworthy was that the prima donna, Luigia Boccabadati, came in 20 bars too soon during the first act's finale. This is the first time we hear of this singer in connection with Barbaja, with whom she would later be embroiled in a nasty lawsuit. Donizetti was so angered by Boccabadati's poor performance, that he argued with Barbaja over her continued casting. This led to Donizetti breaking his contract with Barbaja, and ultimately to the dismissal of the soprano.[25] Mercadante shared Donizetti's view of the singer: he believed she possessed an 'agile voice but not of supreme quality' and a rather disadvantageous body, and referred to her as 'Bocapatate' – potato mouth.[26]

A difficult year was rounded off with a loss-making premiere for Donizetti's new opera *Il Paria* (The Pariah), and the decision of the authorities to postpone Vaccai's long-gestating opera *Saul* to Lent, because of its religious storyline.

In 1830 Bellini signed a contract with Crivelli & Co. – the group of impresarios that included Barbaja, Crivelli and Villa – for two operas to be given at La Scala.[27] At this time, of course, Barbaja was only marginally involved with La Scala and his partners, and it is likely therefore that he was just a silent partner in this, and a reluctant one at that. Easily tempted by a better financial offer, however, Bellini allowed himself to be bought out of the Crivelli contract by a rival group of impresarios that had set up a competing season at the smaller Teatro Carcano. The Litta-Marietti-Soresi group, composed of a duke and two businessmen, had offered the composer 10,440 francs, the equivalent of 2,000 ducats,[28] as well as 50 per cent of the rights to the score; allowing Bellini once again to surpass the maximum rate paid to date.[29]

Bellini generally split ownership of the score with the impresario, or with the music publisher Ricordi. Clearly believing that Barbaja and his partners could not offer him enough money, he went with the other impresarios.

La Sonnambula (The Sleepwalker) premiered in the Teatro Carcano on 6 March 1831. The production was the composer's fulfilment of his contract to write an opera for that year. He had originally proposed another opera, *Ernani*, but the libretto fell foul of the censors, and Bellini and Romani scrambled to put together the less politically sensitive *Sonnambula*.

Bellini was particularly nervous about *Sonnambula*, as it opened shortly after the wildly successful premiere of *Anna Bolena* by his rival Donizetti, who shared the same librettist. He need not have feared. It opened with both Pasta and Rubini (by this time no longer under Barbaja's management) in excellent voice, and brought down the house. The theatre was overcome with tears of emotion. *Sonnambula* still enjoys success today, though the tenor role is too challenging for singers less gifted than Rubini, and is customarily transposed to accommodate most contemporary tenors. The opera was also to cement a strong personal and professional friendship between Pasta and Bellini.

While Barbaja was shuttling between Naples and Milan, and trying to find ways fully to exit the miserable Milanese *impresa*, another reign was coming to an end in Naples. In May 1830 King Francis I and his wife had travelled to Paris to visit their equally embattled Bourbon relative, King Charles X. They attended a number of celebrations and parties, including a gala performance given for the Neapolitan King at the Paris opera. 'We are dancing on a volcano', an observer at the unusually solemn event was reported as saying,[30] and only a few weeks later Charles X was deposed.

Francis I had returned to Naples worn out and dejected. He died after a convulsion on 8 November 1830. It was a reign that had been short, brutal and unpopular.

Il Re Bomba

Francis I was immediately succeeded by his son Ferdinand, who fashioned himself King Ferdinand II of the Two Sicilies. Born in 1810 while his parents

(Francis I and his first cousin Maria Isabella of Spain) and grandparents (Ferdinand I and Maria Carolina of Austria) were in exile in Palermo, he initially seemed to have his grandfather's popular touch, and gained widespread support among the *lazzaroni*. He cut taxes and expenditure, granted a political amnesty to members of the opposition, and was possibly the first of the Neapolitan Bourbons to show real interest in reviving the economy. In 1839 he commissioned the first railway in Italy, to run between Naples and the royal palace at Portici. He modernised the army and equipped his navy with the first steamship in the Italian peninsula. Ferdinand II also drew together his disparate kingdoms by establishing the first telegraphic connections between Naples and Palermo.

In 1840, for the first time, the main public squares in Naples were lit by gas, bathing the city in a never before seen light at night, and in many ways opening up the piazzas to the type of night life we still see today. After Paris, Naples was one of the first European cities to have public gas lighting, and the Teatro San Carlo was immediately fitted with gas illumination.

By the 1840s, on the back of the improved infrastructure and relative order, the increasing prosperity could be seen in Naples' main streets, with the opening of expensive shops and cafés. The roads began to fill up with shoppers, and their many carriages blocked the main thoroughfares, especially the famous Via Toledo. Although he was writing some 40 years later, Dumas' description of the street provides us with a picture of what it must have been like then:

> Toledo is everyone's street. It's the street of restaurants, cafés, boutiques; it's the artery that feeds and transverses all the neighbourhoods of the city. It's the street where all the torrents of the streets are disgorged. The aristocracy passes in its carriages; the bourgeoisie sells its fine fabrics there; the peasants have their siesta there. For the nobleman, it's a promenade; for the merchants, it's a bazaar; for the *lazzarone*, it's a domicile.
>
> Toledo is also the first step made by Naples towards a modern civilization ... [a road that] connects the poetic town with the industrial city, a neutral territory to observe the disappearing remnants of the ancient world, as it is being invaded by the new world. Next door to the classic osteria with old curtains stained by the flies, an elegant French patissier exhibits his wife as much as his brioches and cakes. Opposite an artisan making antiques for the Englishmen's tastes ... And finally, the final link

of this characteristic fusion, the pavement of the Via Toledo is made of lava cobble stones from Pompeii and Herculaneum, and lit by gas like London or Paris.[31]

The roads leading out of town from the Via Toledo were equally busy. With up to 500 open carriages driving along the seashore promenade towards Mergellina,[32] the Riviera di Chiaia could become so congested on balmy summer evenings that one observer wrote of his great wish to have 'Toledo one month a year without carriages'.[33]

Neapolitans took great care of their appearance, and well-cut clothes were a matter of pride for the well-heeled. Tailors and haberdashers were commonplace in the city centre, and those for men developed a reputation far beyond the borders of the kingdom. In a city where social life was dominated by a royal court, impeccable presentation mattered; something John Orlando Parry noticed during his travels: '... I think I never saw so many pretty women as we met on the road from Portici to Naples. Every doorway, every window was full of them; twas really astonishing!'[34]

There was a distinct feeling of cosmopolitanism in Naples now, with its many immigrants from other parts of Italy, as well as from Germany and France. The young Carl Rothschild was successfully integrating the Naples branch into the greater European network of his family's bank. Barbaja's occasional counterpart, the music publisher Guillaume Cottrau, was another successful immigrant: following Joseph Bonaparte, he and his parents had moved from Paris to Naples. His father had been a senior government official under Louis XVI in Paris, and on moving to Naples assumed senior positions in Murat's government, including Division Head of the Ministry of the Interior. Guillaume's brother Felix became a celebrated painter; his work can be seen in the museum at Capodimonte, the summer palace of the Bourbons outside Naples.

Guillaume Cottrau joined and later ran the most important music publishing company in the city, B Girard & Co. Eclipsed later by the dominant Milanese publisher Ricordi (still in existence today as the leading publisher of opera and part of Universal Music Group), B Girard was dominant in 19th-century Naples. As well as composing many songs himself, Cottrau published a well-known compendium of popular Neapolitan songs, which in capturing much of the oral tradition would become historically important. Guillaume's son Teodoro was a well-known composer and librettist, among other things giving us the Italian translation and music transcription for the unforgettable and quintessential Neapolitan song 'Santa Lucia'.

An enthusiastic account of Neapolitan everyday life from the 1840s describes the B Girard store as a major tourist attraction on Via Toledo.[35] Decorated in 'good taste in the Egyptian style', the store boasted a big bronze plaque on its inside wall listing the illustrious composers whose works the firm represented. It looked like a roll-call from the Barbaja years: Rossini, Donizetti, Bellini, Mercadante, Pacini. Inside, the walls were decorated with original drawings and cartoons of the singers of the day, including the pot-bellied Lablache, Malibran dishevelled in a death scene, and David in heroic tenor pose. Between the drawings and heavy oriental-style curtains, decorations and lanterns, the store displayed its enormous collections of opera scores, as well as piano, recital and other sheet music.

A coffee-shop culture also began to develop in earnest in the city, and Neapolitans started to insist that only they knew how to make a proper cup of coffee. There were countless coffee-shops, each catering to a different economic, social, cultural or political class. That for the cultural set, as well as those who cared to-see-and-be-seen, was the Caffè d'Italia on Via Toledo. In *Passeggiata per Napoli* (A Walk through Naples), the well-known travel guide to Naples written by the Sicilian dramatist and essayist Emmanuele Bidera (who was retained by Barbaja as a teacher of diction and house librettist at the San Carlo), the writer dedicates an entire chapter to the virtues and qualities of the Caffè d'Italia, and describes how the 30-year-old establishment was missed sorely after its closure in 1844. 'Oh my Caffè d'Italia. You fell like Arcadia. You fell like Barbaja fell and with it Italian music.'[36]

Much later, on the Piazza San Ferdinando (today's Piazza di Trento e Trieste) facing the Royal Palace, the Gran Caffè opened its doors. Given its unbeatable location opposite the palace and the opera, it should have prospered and survived, but it disappeared in the 1850s, to be replaced by a branch of the Banco di Napoli. In 1890, long after Barbaja's days, the Gran Caffè was replaced by a highly decorated and chic café called the Gambrinus. To this day, the Gambrinus remains *the* place for coffee, cakes and drinks.

∾

The optimism of a resurgent Naples was short-lived. Ferdinand II's early benevolence, tolerance and liberalism soon gave way to distrust and suspicion, and a repression and a general crack-down on all forms of freedom followed. The King was paranoid about any possible liberal movements. He believed that only a strong army and a wide network of spies and informants would guarantee the strength of his monarchy. He replaced an already over-zealous Minister of Police with an even more repressive one, and ensured that spies were placed in the university, schools, army barracks, churches, newspaper offices and of course in the theatres. The Minister of Police even spied on his own agents and on those closest to the King.

This retreat into repression was encouraged by Ferdinand II's first wife, Maria Cristina. Intensely religious as well as very beautiful, she would have much preferred to enter a convent than marry Ferdinand, but her parents' political opportunism prevailed, and she married the Neapolitan King in November 1832. She was accused of turning the royal household into a convent during her very brief time in Naples (she died in 1836). Spending many hours a day in prayer, she chastised her husband for the foul language he had picked up in the army, drove out the fashionable shorter dresses and generally turned back the clock on any liberal tendencies that might have emerged in or around the royal court.

Ferdinand II was particularly vigilant about any resurgent *Carbonari* tendencies. In 1837 he brutally suppressed the first riots in Sicily of liberals demanding the re-introduction of a constitution and a liberalisation of the regime. In the following years violent riots triggered by famine and economic hardship broke out in Calabria and Messina in Sicily.

The Sicilian riots would eventually culminate (after Barbaja's time) in an attempt at secession from Naples in 1848, the year that all Europe was overtaken by revolutionary fervour. There were further uprisings in Salerno and in Naples, and the overthrow of royal troops and lack of support elsewhere led the King, in January 1848, to agree a form of constitution. The fragile peace did not last long, however: when the King refused to grant real powers to parliament in May, the rebels rose again. King Ferdinand II responded forcefully, sending a flotilla to Sicily and, in September 1848, mercilessly bombing Messina over five days. The savage and gratuitous violence he unleashed on the city, even many hours after the people's surrender, earned the monarch the sobriquet '*re bomba*' (the Bomb King). Ferdinand brutally put down one further attempt by the liberals to obtain a proper constitution in Naples, with even more carnage. Under European pressure, he finally offered a restricted constitution and parliament, but by now the rebels were sceptical and distrusted their King. By 1849 royal troops had reconquered Sicily and the Kingdom of the Two Sicilies was once again in Ferdinand's vengeful hands.

The crackdown was as much cultural as military, and censorship of the theatres was at its most repressive during the reign of Ferdinand II. The censors consisted of a team of two who were accountable to the Ministry of the Interior for matters pertaining to literary value and decency, and to the Ministry of Police on issues of public order. One censor tended to be drawn from cultural circles, the other was usually a member of the clergy. They were at their most restrictive and retrograde in the late 1830s, when both censors were drawn from clerical circles.[37]

The censors saw their role as protectors of the dignity of the Crown as well as of the Church, and the King would often take a very direct interest in their decisions, sometimes even overturning them. The censors were not always consistent in their adjudication, and their standard depended on the personalities filling the roles at the time.[38]

The role of the Superintendent, the *de facto* supervisor of the censors, was a particular challenge during these years. Given the enormity of the Neapolitan theatre scene (at times the Superintendent was responsible for eight theatres,[39] in addition to the many performing 'academies'), he resorted to envoys who would work on-site in the theatres themselves to ensure that the Superintendent's orders were correctly observed and respected. Giuditta Pasta describes nearly being imprisoned for singing what were considered controversial words from the aria '*Cara Patria*' (Cherished fatherland) from Rossini's opera *Tancredi*. She was ordered to omit the word '*libertà*' (liberty) in all her songs.[40]

For Barbaja, one of the most difficult periods in his life was about to begin.

11

Counting the Losses

(1831–1836)

After his triumphs in Milan, Donizetti soon returned to Naples to fulfil his obligations to Barbaja. He wrote two unremarkable operas, and was keen to rid himself of the domineering Barbaja and the uncooperative Neapolitan censors:

> Tomorrow I hope to break my contract with Barbaja, since I am not free to choose whom I want in my new opera. So be it, for I desire it very much. … Already we are both free verbally, and tomorrow I bring the matter to a formal conclusion.[1]

Barbaja's increasingly threatening competitor Alessandro Lanari had approached Donizetti to write an *opera buffa*. Lanari now had the concession for the Teatro Canobbiana in Milan for the season of 1832 in addition to that for his home theatre in Florence. The assignment became the unforgettable *L'Elisir d'Amore* (The Elixir of Love), one of Donizetti's most enduring comic operas.

His competitor Bellini, meanwhile, was ending his period in Italy (in autumn 1831), but not before having one more fall-out with Barbaja, who was planning to perform the composer's *Capuleti* in Naples with a cast that the composer deemed underqualified. Bellini complained bluntly in a letter to his friend Francesco Florimo:

> I think Barbaja is going crazy. A woman who is less than mediocre, who

cannot sing, who moves like a salami on stage, who the Venetians were happy to pay to keep her from singing; this woman will sing the protagonist's role in Naples?[2]

Bellini was so upset he threatened not to write anything for Naples until after 1833, when he expected a new impresario to be appointed after the expiry of Barbaja's current contract.[3]

In September 1831, he wrote directly to the Superintendent of the royal theatres discussing his desire to return to Naples and the San Carlo, his native country as well as the stage where he had celebrated his first successes, and arguing that Barbaja was making it impossible since he refused to pay Bellini what he thought he was worth. Crivelli, he claimed, was offering him 12,000 Austrian lire (the equivalent of 2,400 Neapolitan ducats), half the rights to the score, and 200 additional ducats for the performance of the opera in Venice (where Crivelli also controlled the theatre). He demanded that Barbaja offer him 3,000 Neapolitan ducats for a new opera for the San Carlo to be performed in December 1832, in addition to travel, lodging, his choice to work with his favourite librettist Felice Romani, freedom to choose the story from pre-approved topics and one month's rehearsal time. Finally, he would only start work in September, 'as I cannot work in the heat'.[4] He fired a last shot at Barbaja, complaining of the impresario's proposal to stage his opera *Capuleti* with a cast he found inferior. 'If the intrepid Barbaja should prove resistant to my desires, that would make it certain that he feels no interest in me personally, and therefore I should retract the agreement to compose the opera.'[5]

While negotiating with Naples, Bellini was also working on what would be his biggest success, *Norma*, the story of the druid priestess who betrays her country and religion for love. Bellini was 30 years old when he wrote *Norma*, just a few months after launching *Sonnambula*. The period of preparation was fraught with concerns about an impending cholera outbreak, which threatened to close down the theatres.[6] Then, only a few days before the opening night, the impresario Crivelli, who had commissioned the opera for La Scala, died.

Bellini wrote *Norma* for the singers Giuditta Pasta, Giulia Grisi and the tenor Domenico Donzelli, tailoring the title role especially for his friend Pasta's vocal agility and dramatic intensity, and creating what is now known to be one of the most harrowing roles in the soprano repertoire. He was paid

3,000 ducats and half the royalties from the rights. *Norma*, interestingly, had a disappointing – even disastrous, if we believe Florimo – first night at La Scala in December 1831, for which Bellini predictably blamed intrigues arranged by Pacini and his clique. It was only after the second performance that the audience changed its mind, and *Norma* became the darling of the Milanese audience, which demanded it be played 40 nights in a row.[7] Even Richard Wagner, who abhorred most Italian composers of his day, praised Bellini for his passionate music and his ability to match the music to the lyrics.[8]

In March 1832 the music publisher Cottrau wrote to a friend:

> … we would like to engage Bellini [in Naples] to write an opera, but his demands are too high for Barbaja. In Barbaja's place, I would happily risk a large fee for such a genius. It seems to me that Sonnambula is a good precedent.[9]

While there is no record of Barbaja's reaction to *Norma*'s success, it is safe to assume he was fuming at missing out on yet another hit from the composer he had launched.

Some months later, Bellini left Italy to prepare operas in London and Paris. Paris was a particular draw for him, not only because he had been impressed by the success Rossini had been able to achieve with the Théâtre-Italien, but also because he liked the French copyright laws, which permitted him to collect royalties on performances of his operas year after year – as long as they were composed in French. Needless to say, the already infamous Parisian nightlife also held many attractions for Bellini's more carnal and social desires.

Rossini proved to be critical to Bellini's success. The *éminence grise* of the Italian opera scene in France lived in an apartment at the top of the Théâtre-Italien. He introduced Bellini to all the right people and gave him valuable guidance on composition as well as production – though he also belittled the young Sicilian upstart behind his back.

Moving initially in the refined *haute société*, Bellini was increasingly attracted to the *demi-monde* and the dark underbelly of the city. He would have been quite a sight. The French composer Hector Berlioz referred to Bellini as a 'little punk'.[10] Heinrich Heine, the German journalist and poet, who met Bellini frequently, wrote of his thin and frail-looking body, his wavy and seemingly carelessly unkempt waft of blond hair, and his fashionable clothing topped by his handsome face. He looked every bit the effete dandy with a gait that was 'so maidenly, so elegant, so ethereal!' In sum, Heine wrote, 'The whole man looked like a sighing swain en *escarpins*'.[11]

While Rossini was heavily promoting Bellini in Paris, the city was hit by a cholera epidemic and a large part of the population fled to the countryside. Not so Bellini and Malibran. It was murmured that the two were having an affair.[12] There is little to support this as Malibran, rather than ask Bellini directly, needed to resort to asking the composer's friends to influence him to write some music for her. She confessed in a letter to Cottrau in November 1833 that she in fact desired nothing more than for Bellini to write an opera for her. Considerately, Cottrau did not point out to Malibran how close Bellini was to Pasta, who would certainly have opposed any such plan.[13]

In fact, the young composer was busy writing another opera for a completely different cast, *I Puritani* (The Puritans). This opera would be Bellini's last, and Barbaja had no involvement in it. It premiered at the Théâtre-Italien in Paris, and benefitted from generous support from the great Rossini himself.

Much of the recent excitement in the operatic world now seemed to be happening in cities or on stages that Barbaja did not control. After a long period of continuous success, the impresario was facing growing difficulties and increasingly intense disagreements with his singers, his composers and even his friends. And the increasingly sour atmosphere on and behind the stage was also to be seen in the courtrooms.

Fighting publishers, performers and peers

Barbaja had always felt strongly about punctuality. He also felt strongly about the letter of the law. From his earliest days as an impresario, he had had no compunction about dragging a dispute into the courts, no matter how small the issue. The step from the stage to the courtroom was but a short one for the impresario. 'From 1826 to 1838 the courtrooms of the Bourbon Kingdom were practically an ideal extension of the theatrical stages,' writes one of Donizetti's biographers, 'a venue for intrigues and machinations, with its own protagonists, dramas and farces.'[14]

While Barbaja's exposure to the courts was certainly extreme, other impresarios, including Lanari, were no strangers to the courts either. Also, Naples was famous for its veritable addiction to litigation. The respected Prussian historian and publicist J W von Archenholz reported in 1787 on the Neapolitans' enormous appetite for litigation and their tendency to use the courts to gain possession of other people's property under the veil of legal legitimacy. 'There is probably no other city in the world with as many law suits as Naples,' he wrote. 'Therefore it is also teeming with lawyers here, as well as countless tribunals.'[15]

Barbaja's early opponents in the courtrooms were composers and publishers fighting over copyrights, sub-contractors and vendors, and singers who had been remiss in their duties defending themselves against suits taken out by the impresario. At a later stage, Barbaja even took the Government, represented by the Superintendent of the Theatres, to court.

In the days before copying became an easy and common mechanical process, original autograph manuscripts by great composers and writers were valuable, not only for their intrinsic worth but because they might represent the only 'true' version of the original work. Copyright in a work either remained with the artist or, more often, was shared between him and the publisher or even a commissioning impresario, who usually also dealt with the contractual issues regarding a work's publication and with performance rights and royalties. Original scores were reproduced by copyists in a strictly controlled manner for performances, but as the copyists' version spread with productions in different theatres, errors and variations crept in, and the value of the correct, autographed original score increased.

There were also pirated copies to contend with. Piracy usually took the form of the unauthorised orchestration of a purchased piano score, by which an unscrupulous impresario could avoid paying for the full score or the performance rights held by the publisher, composer or even another impresario. The musical result of such a pirated orchestration could be disastrous, and often had very little to do with the composer's original. Both Bellini and Donizetti would suffer tremendously from pirated versions of their works. Impresarios would also occasionally simply swap scores on a no-cash basis, avoiding any royalties whatsoever, as Barbaja did with his associate Crivelli in 1828.[16]

Music publishers began to appear in Italy in 1810, at first living largely off the sale of vocal scores and adaptations of music for solo instruments from new operas. They also rented out hand-copied scores to theatres and occasionally printed scores for the wider community. However, it was not until 1838 that copyright in Italy was widely observed professionally, and copyright laws only began to appear from 1840 onwards.

In Austria, the sale of piano and voice adaptations of popular operas was a big business. The music publisher Artaria was one of the most prominent advertisers in the Viennese daily *Wiener Zeitung*, printing frequent half-page notices advertising its scores as the 'only authorized editions' of currently popular operas.

In 1834, Barbaja sold his Donizetti archive to the music publisher Gennaro Fabbricatore for 1,200 ducats, and the composer was shocked that his entire Neapolitan work could be sold for so little money.[17] Donizetti later wrote to the publishing house Ricordi, which had contacted him seeking clarification on ownership rights to one of the scores:

> I sold my opera Roberto Devereux to Barbaja, ceding to him all proprietary rights imaginable, and I also know for certain that Barbaja ceded and sold those same rights to G Fabbricatore, director of the copyists. If you purchased my score of Roberto Devereux from him, you are the legitimate owner, through the legitimate transmission of rights from me to Barbaja, from the latter to Fabbricatore, and from Fabbricatore to you. I can't see where any doubt might enter.[18]

Things were not always so clear cut. In an absolutely exasperating series of suits and counter-suits between 1836 and 1840, Barbaja litigated against the music publishers Cottrau and Fabbricatore over copyrights and reproduction rights to the Donizetti operas. Interim damages were awarded to all sides. Though Barbaja won in the end, and Fabbricatore was ordered to comply with his obligations to Barbaja as well as to bear all legal costs, it cannot be considered much more than a pyrrhic victory to a maddening, and what must sometimes have seemed an interminable, series of suits.[19] In a legal fracas that extended beyond the impresario's death (and also that of one of the plaintiff's), the same publishers, Guillaume Cottrau and Gennaro Fabbricatore, were to sue Barbaja's children, Pietro and Carolina, over the failure to deliver the score of Donizetti's (practically forgotten) Cantata *Cristoforo Colombo*. This time the publishers won.

∼

The year 1831 started out as that of the ballerino. Barbaja won a dispute over an orally agreed fee with a choreographer who had served the royal theatres for 16 years.[20] A few months later he was again in front of the Tribunal of Commerce, this time facing a young ballet dancer who had triumphed at his performance in front of the royal family, but who had then been cheated out of his fee by Barbaja in spite of an oral commitment. The tribunal judged in favour of the dancer.[21]

A more complex legal tussle was with the businessman Raffaele Finizio, to whom for a period Barbaja sub-contracted the *impresa* of the royal theatres. Barbaja remained the impresario on record with the authorities, however, and Finizio did not receive a separate concession contract from the Government. In all likelihood, Finizio had already bought the sub-concession from Barbaja to run the theatre's machinery and decorations, and this additional arrangement permitted him to step up to greater commercial opportunity and responsibility.[22] There is no documentation on Barbaja's reasons for agreeing to the new arrangement, but it is likely that he was simply slowing down and thus happy to pass on some of the commercial burden. At 51, he was no longer a young man.

The agreement gave Finizio commercial responsibility for putting on performances in the two royal theatres from 1829 to 1833.[23] Barbaja was to pay him a fixed fee of 24,140 ducats, and this was also to cover the staging of the performances and ongoing expenses, including consumables such as oil, tallow[24] and wax, all of which were used in prodigious quantities to provide lighting for the theatre. Excluded from the contract were the 'English Pantomime', the dressage display by horses and various other sideshows which were not part of any formal arrangement with the Government and which Barbaja would continue to run himself. Barbaja kept the box-office revenues, though it is possible that Finizio might have had a share.

As it happened, Finizio's *impresa* covered the period of the wedding of King Ferdinand II to Maria Cristina of Savoy in November 1832 and the festive first visit of the Queen Consort to the Teatro San Carlo on 3 December that year. For this special gala event, the Superintendent instructed Finizio to install special lights and ornaments on the stage and in the auditorium. When Finizio presented the bill for the special outfitting to the Superintendent afterwards, the latter protested fiercely against paying the charges. This led to a high-profile legal case between Finizio and Barbaja and the Superintendent that lasted nearly eight years. The amount under dispute, 304.77 ducats, was roughly equal to two months' rent for a large furnished apartment in the prime Chiaia district. Even half that amount would have bought thousands of tallow candles,[25] and the visual impact of the stipulated additional lighting must have been striking. It sounds trifling to be the cause of a lasting dispute of such nature, but Barbaja considered himself a man of principle: he would not have hesitated to pursue payment, regardless of the amount under dispute, and if that meant a protracted lawsuit, so be it.

The Superintendent claimed it was Barbaja's responsibility to pay, since putting on performances, including gala performances, was part of his contract. He also argued that since Barbaja derived the economic benefit of the gala – he had doubled the ticket prices for the evening – he should also bear the additional costs incurred. Barbaja, on the other hand, claimed that he had no liability in the matter as the Superintendent made his request for the special arrangements to Finizio, and if the *impresa* were responsible it should be Finizio who should carry the financial burden.

The Tribunal of Commerce, and later the High Court, decided in favour of Barbaja. The document outlining this court case lays out the facts on both sides, and makes an independent recommendation.[26] Yet while the writers clearly took the legal arguments seriously, they might have been less than impartial, as one of them, the jurist, philosopher and sometime writer of medical treatises, Pasquale Borrelli, was a close friend of the impresario. He would some years later write the principal eulogy for Barbaja's funeral.

This dispute is of interest for many reasons. It demonstrates the often tense relationship between the Superintendent and the impresario, it shows Barbaja's willingness immediately to seek legal redress through the courts, and it also proves the utter detachment of the royal household from the realities of everyday life. Disputes resulting from the costs of the pageantry required for the royal court often had to be settled through protracted legal battles by commoners in the commercial courts.

Ironically, Queen Maria Cristina, who was of Sardinian and Austrian royal blood and whose wedding occasioned the expensive illumination, was never comfortable with the pageantry surrounding the royal court. Though pretty, she was timid and reserved, as well as extremely religious. As importantly, she was one of the few royals who truly had no interest at all in opera. In fact she 'detested the theatre'.[27] Indeed, the king had to force his wife to attend the opera, explaining to her that 'in Naples, opera is the profession of many, the delight of everyone, and one of the glories of the Kingdom that would certainly languish without the royal protection'.[28] The queen barely lived long enough to see the completion of the legal battle. She died shortly after giving birth in January 1836, just a month after the Tribunal of Commerce passed judgment.

From 1826 to 1827 Barbaja was battling the father and son singing duo Carlo and Raffaele Casaccia over unpaid dues. The father, Carlo Casaccia, was a wildly popular *buffo basso*, who principally performed at the Teatro dei Fiorentini and Teatro Nuovo, even before Barbaja's arrival in Naples. Singing exclusively in the Neapolitan dialect for audiences consisting mostly of commoners, he was considered an institution at the Fiorentini and was nicknamed 'Casacciello' by his adoring public. Barbaja and Rossini recognised his comic genius, and Rossini wrote a Neapolitan dialect role especially for him into *La Gazzetta* (The Magazine). The opera premiered at the Fiorentini in September 1816 and was Rossini's only *opera buffa* written for Naples.

In 1823 Barbaja engaged the Casaccias on a six-year contract as '*primi buffi assoluti*' (the leading buffo singers), promising the father 6,000 ducats a year (500 for the son), in addition to four candles per night (!) in each of their backstage dressing-rooms as well as a discretionary gratuity at the end of every year for performances at the San Carlo. Barbaja believed the singers had breached various performance clauses and refused to honour his side of the contract. The Casaccias took Barbaja to court, and won, twice. The impresario was compelled to repay the owed money, cover the Casaccias' legal costs and, for good measure, to give the singers 648 wax candles.[29]

Barbaja also saw no shame in suing one of his lead singers, Antonio Ambrogi, for performing without his permission at a theatre in London. Appearances at other theatres without Barbaja's consent were expressly forbidden in all his singers' contracts, though the temptation is understandable as London stages paid four times what the Neapolitan ones did.[30]

During the same period that Barbaja was fighting a ballet dancer, a choreographer, multiple singers, a fellow impresario and the Superintendent, he also faced an especially daunting adversary: the litigious *prima donna*. Luigia Boccabadati, a popular singer with a relatively short career, participated in five world premieres for Donizetti and was a favourite of Barbaja before her disastrous performance in *Il Diluvio*, described earlier. The legal dispute lasted from summer 1831 to late spring 1832 and involved at least 12 court appearances.

The soprano had joined Barbaja's troupe in February 1829, freshly inspired by her legal victory over a Roman impresario, where she had successfully argued that a singer – as a liberal artist – should be paid on the basis of a fee for a season, rather than receiving a daily payment for rendered performances – as a 'mechanical' employee. In Naples, she failed to turn up for numerous performances for reasons of illness, causing Barbaja to file a suit against her for missed performances. The legal case distracted both singer and impresario, working its way all the way up to the Supreme Court. What started as a dispute over missed performances because of sickness deteriorated into arguments over the validity of the stage manager's attendance record for the singers (the singer argued the records were biased, as the manager was Barbaja's employee), the income from her benefit performance (which was given during Lent, at prices cut by a third) and delayed salary payments.[31]

While Barbaja ultimately emerged the loser in these exasperating lawsuits,[32] they demonstrate the impresario's absolute doggedness when it came to defending what he considered his legal rights. The singer, who was paid a monthly stipend of 650 ducats and was living quite comfortably in a fully furnished apartment in the Palazzo Barbaja on Via Toledo as part of her contractual agreement, was awarded damages. But Barbaja made sure that 'Bocapatate's' career in Italy was finished. She rarely sang at a major house again.[33]

Losing the concession

By 1831 the Neapolitan theatre authorities were already contemplating alternatives to Barbaja to run their theatres. A classified advertisement appeared in *The Times* of London that year:

ROYAL SUPERINTENDENCE of THEATRES and PLAY-HOUSES of NAPLES.–The present Lease of the Royal Theatres of Naples, St. Carlo and Fondo, conducted by Mr. D. Domenico Barbaja, expiring on Saturday, in Passion Week, 1833. the [sic] Prince of Ruffano, Superintendent of the Theatres and Play-houses, has to make a new engagement, agreeable to an order from his Excellency the Minister for the Home Department, and will therefore receive TENDERS from the present time till the end of March, 1832, for the LEASE of the afore-mentioned THEATRES, commencing at Easter, in the year 1833. Any person wishing to engage in the above-mentioned undertaking can address, post paid, enclosing the securities required, to the aforesaid Superintendent of Theatres, at the Theatre Royal, of Fondo.-Naples, the 2th October, 1831.[34]

It is doubtful that any serious candidate responded to the advert, but clearly it was proving difficult for the authorities to find a suitable replacement for Barbaja. The impresario extended his concession through to the spring of 1834. In January 1833 *Allgemeine Musikalische Zeitung* reported:

> Domenico Barbaja kept, as was expected, the concession for the coming opera year for the royal theatres which he has already been running for a quarter of a century. Colossal theatres, such as Teatro San Carlo and Scala, must in spite of the support they are given by their respective governments, be managed by a very experienced impresario, and Barbaja is certainly up to it more than anyone else.[35]

This was, however, to be the last annual extension of Barbaja's contract in Naples for a while. After another year full of disagreements, suits and arguments, he would hand back the *impresa*. Why the Superintendent[36] and the royal household decided to try an alternative to Barbaja is not entirely clear. Perhaps they had simply grown tired of his imperious and autocratic manner; the recent lawsuit with the Superintendent related to the Finizio case is unlikely to have made him many friends among the Neapolitan nobility either. Nor, it seems, was Barbaja himself over-enthusiastic about renewing the concession.

Knowing his *impresa* was to come to an end with this season, Barbaja put on a relatively safe schedule, with many reprises of the popular operas of Rossini and Bellini. It would not have been Barbaja's style quietly to fade away, however. One of his parting gestures was to cast Maria Malibran in a large number of operas right up to the very end of the *impresa* in March 1834. Malibran was also a symbolic choice for Barbaja. The singer, technically a contralto but with easy access to the soprano register, was vocally not so dissimilar to the young Colbran. Spanish, like Colbran, and a favourite of Barbaja since her first performances for his *impresa* in the early 1830s, Malibran embodied all the star qualities that Barbaja cherished.

The publisher Cottrau speculated that Barbaja extended Malibran's stay in Naples right to the very end of his contract in order to damage the next *impresa* and 'crush them by the contrast'.[37] His agenda became clearer a few weeks later, as news emerged that Malibran had been engaged by Barbaja to sing 40 performances at the Teatro San Carlo and two benefits at the next carnival for a fee of 80,000 francs,[38] an enormous amount of money by the standards of the day. Even Cottrau was stunned by the amount: *N'est-ce pas fabuleux?*[39] In retrospect it looks more as if this enormous financial commitment was a farewell bouquet that Barbaja deliberately dumped in the lap of his successors, as the next impresario would have to honour both her performance schedule and her fee.

And this was not all. Just weeks before Barbaja was to hand back the *impresa*, on 12 April 1834,[40] Donizetti signed a contract for an opera for the San Carlo. This was to be the controversial *Maria Stuarda*,[41] a topic that Barbaja knew was unlikely to be approved by the censors, and that would cause an additional headache for his successors.

At the end of the Naples *stagione* in May 1834, Barbaja stepped down in favour of a cooperative *impresa* of several rich local nobles, bankers and merchants, the Società d'industria e belle arti (Society of Industry and Performing Arts). It took over the creative and administrative matters of the theatres as well as all the ancillary businesses for the 1834/35 season. The Società was a relatively novel financial structure, a limited liability company which dangled the prospects of cash dividends as well as benefits in the form of daily theatre seats before its shareholders. Led by the Prince of Torella, a local nobleman, the *impresa* engaged the services of Barbaja's competitor Lanari, who wore the three hats of salaried manager and administrator, shareholder and provider of artists under contract.[42] Other names featuring in the Società were Raffaele Finizio running the machinery and decorations, Eduardo Guillaume in charge of costumes and Vincenzo Flauto taking control of the theatre's printing press. Finizio had already clashed with Barbaja; the other two would cross swords with him just a few years later.

The Società did its best to maintain the quality of the performances[43] and put together a lavish season, lining up leading singers such as Malibran, the French superstar tenor Gilbert Duprez, Ambrogi and the ever popular Lablache,[44] now part of Lanari's *cartello*. But the new theatre management was fraught with bickering and in-fighting and struggled to keep the audience engaged. Lanari, who was based in Florence and barely – if at all – visited Naples, did not get involved in the day-to-day operations. The Società was managed by a committee that was unable to make decisions and was in sore need of the guiding hand of an authoritarian impresario. The schedule planning was so disorganised that if a singer fell ill, no replacement was readily found.

During the Società's *impresa* the audience was reported as being unenthusiastic or even responding with outright mockery to the uninspiring schedule. But mostly the Neapolitans were bored and undisciplined, often leaving the performance 'even before the ballet' to enjoy the night in Toledo, Posillipo or Santa Lucia.[45]

Malibran made an ill-advised attempt to dance a mazurka in one opera, causing much ridicule among the audience. The Società also dared to commission *opere buffe* for the hallowed Teatro San Carlo, which was only supposed to show *opere serie*, a transgression which *L'Omnibus* reported as being as 'scandalous as seeing indecencies in a sacred temple'.[46] As if things were not bad enough, Mount Vesuvius erupted once again in the summer, spewing ashes over the worried denizens of Naples.[47]

After an extended absence of over a year, Donizetti returned to Naples in March 1834. He had been appointed Professor of Composition at the Naples Conservatory as well as music tutor to the daughter of the Prince of Salerno, the King's uncle. The composer immediately set to work to complete the commissioned *Maria Stuarda*. The libretto was submitted to the censors in July, and in the absence of any definite prohibition the composer and the director went ahead with the production. Soon the rehearsals began, with specially prepared stage sets and costumes. In September, however, as orchestral rehearsals were being held, the censors summoned the librettist to make changes to the text. Though annoyed, the Prince of Torella smoothly handled the discussions with the Superintendent and arranged for changes to be made. Donizetti adapted the music accordingly.

Another contretemps occurred during the orchestral rehearsal that caught the attention not only of the censors, but also of most of the city's musical establishment. The soprano Giuseppina Ronzi de Begnis (playing Mary Stuart) and Anna del Sere (playing Queen Elizabeth) got carried away, Ronzi so realistically delivering the lines accusing del Sere's character of being an 'obscene and unworthy whore' that the latter felt personally offended and physically attacked her. An arts newspaper from Bologna published a report worthy of today's tabloids:

Elizabeth [del Sere] takes Mary Stuart [Ronzi] by the hair, slaps her, bites her, then pounds her face with her fists, and nearly breaks her legs with her kicks. Mary Stuart is stunned, gathers courage, boldly fends off the attack and then seizes the offensive, until del Sere falls over fainting, and needs to be taken away to bed.[48]

Ronzi easily outweighed del Sere. The singer was known for her fiery temper and competitiveness, as well as for being *'fort grasse'* (very fat), although this did not dispel rumours that she was a mistress of King Ferdinand.[49] Donizetti once compared her unfavourably with Malibran as 'having the bigger ass'.[50] The women were eventually reconciled and gave a rapturously received dress rehearsal. This was, however, the only performance *Maria Stuarda* was to see in Naples. It never made it to a premiere. The King personally intervened after the dress rehearsal and forbade the opera to go ahead.[51]

It was widely reported that it was actually Queen Maria Cristina who prevented the performance of *Maria Stuarda*. Allegedly, she had watched the dress rehearsal and been so shaken by the events on stage, especially the scene in which Mary Stuart is led away to be beheaded, that she had fainted in the royal box.[52] Though the story is unlikely to be true (not least since the queen hated the theatre and would have had no reason whatever to attend a dress rehearsal), it made a great telling in the Neapolitan coffee-shops. Nor was it lost on café society that the queen was a direct relative of Mary Stuart, albeit several generations removed. In fact, it was indeed the King who intervened, even though the censors had approved the various changes to the opera. The debacle led to a change in the system: thereafter, performances with a tragic ending were not permitted to be performed at royal galas.[53]

The Società was by now teetering on the edge of bankruptcy, and threatening to close the company in an effort to avoid the costs associated with the next opera (Donizetti's *Lucia di Lammermoor*). It barely managed to keep the season going until the end of the contract at Easter 1836. By early that year it had, according to the *Allgemeine Musikalische Zeitung*, 'lost over 100,000 Saxon thaler, and more seriously, also its honour, since libel, satyrs and law suits against them are keeping the press busy'.[54] Hearing that the Società was failing at the Teatro San Carlo, Bellini wrote to his friend Florimo complaining about the standard of productions, as well as about the impresario Lanari, who was still fronting the Società: 'Send my congratulations to the Società, who I see are starting to run a theatre just like Barbaja, if not worse.'[55]

Suffering from shortage of funds, the opera management was now forced to cancel the contract it had issued, and which had been agreed by Bellini and Lanari (representing the Società d'industria e belle arti), engaging the composer to write three operas at a fee of 13,000 francs per opera.[56] Likewise, cash flow problems forced it to cancel all payments, causing the soprano Fanny Tacchinardi-Persiani to refuse to sing out of protest.[57] With his prima donna refusing to appear for rehearsals, Donizetti became increasingly exasperated, and lodged formal complaints, referring to the Società as a 'cage of madmen'.[58] The desperate situation became almost comical when the King himself intervened to try to keep the Società alive.

In May 1835, Donizetti wrote to a friend:

> … many people want to call Barbaja back to act as director for the royal commission. Then the fat would be in the fire. Lanari would get angry. Barbaja would not want him as director, and the whole affair would end in a brawl.[59]

The Società finally managed to pull together the production of Donizetti's *Lucia di Lammermoor*, which opened at the Teatro San Carlo on 26 September 1835. Lanari had recruited the star tenor in his *cartello*, the Frenchman Gilbert Duprez, for the opera. He had already cast him in early Donizetti operas, and the French tenor had developed a close friendship with the composer, who had written the tenor part in *Lucia* especially with Duprez in mind. The star of the evening, however, was the soprano Fanny Tacchinardi-Persiani, whom Cottrau referred to as 'a delicious and surprising singer, with a perfect sound, excellent manners and a lively spirit'.[60] *Lucia* was an enormous success, the *Allgemeine Musikalische Zeitung* writing that 'the calls for the maestro and the singers after the premiere would simply not end'.[61] Shortly afterwards, however, the Società d'industria e belle arti unceremoniously went out of business. It was relieved of its duties at carnival 1836.[62]

Barbaja, in the meantime, had been having a relatively relaxing year. Having surrendered the Naples *imprese*, he had kept himself busy with two brilliant musical academies at his villa in Mergellina, taking full advantage of the spectacular setting and elaborately decorated theatre of his seaside home. He showcased some of the exciting talent he had worked with during his various European *imprese*, including Caroline Unger and Adelaide Toldi.[63]

He was behaving as if he were retired. He looked on in concern at the

Government's interference and micromanagement of the royal theatres, while congratulating himself on avoiding the senselessness of the censors. He must have felt a certain *schadenfreude* on hearing that the Società had failed so miserably, and so quickly.

12

Death is in the Air

(1836–1841)

From 1833 onwards, Barbaja would face dark times. Naples, like most of Italy, was confronted with a terrifying new threat: cholera. The disease had originated in the Ganges Delta in India, and through trade and colonisation had spread to the Middle East and then into Russia and beyond, becoming one of the biggest pandemics to affect Europe. The first of several waves arrived in the early 1820s; the second, in 1831, entered the United States and South America through immigration and was even more devastating. There were further outbreaks in the 1850s, the 1860s, and the 1880s and 1890s, killing millions worldwide; in Russia alone over 200,000 lives were lost. The work of John Snow (in Britain) and others led to better sanitation and prevention and the disease gradually died out in many countries (though it continues, of course, to be a problem in the developing world).

An extremely virulent malady, in the 19th century cholera was as terrifying as it was painful. Devastating its victims in a matter of hours, it caused agonising pain, compulsive and bloody vomiting, and often led to a quick and painful death from dehydration and organ failure. Naples provided the ideal environment for the disease to spread. It was not only the largest city in Italy, it was also the most overcrowded, with about a tenth of the population living in small, windowless *bassi* that sometimes accommodated up to ten people each. In the poorer sections of the city, sanitation was rudimentary and even the wealthier parts relied on antiquated sewage systems from the 17th century. In the stifling and crowded heart of Naples sewage would occasionally overflow into the streets and marketplaces. The stench was horrific.

At this time, it was generally assumed that cholera was contracted through the lungs from noxious vapours; it was hauntingly referred to as *'aria di notte'* (night air). It was not until the 1880s that it was fully accepted that the disease spread not through air breathed into the lungs, but via the oral-faecal route, through contact with contaminated food and water. The authorities thus addressed the crisis with forced quarantine and basic medical treatment, but failed to address the root cause of the disease – sanitation. As a result, after a period the cholera would die down for several months or years, until the next unexplained outbreak, which would spread like wildfire.

The large number of corpses lying in the streets and the appearance of millions of rats, swarming to scavenge, exacerbated the hysteria in Naples. A shocked Swedish doctor reported with horror on the Neapolitan scene in 1884:

> Intoxicated by the sulfur fumes and carbonic acid, they rushed about the slums like mad dogs. They did not look like any rats I had ever seen before, they were quite bald with extraordinary long red tails, fierce blood-shot eyes and pointed black teeth as long as the teeth of a ferret.[1]

Hundreds of people were severely bitten by the rats and numerous small children were literally eaten alive. The cholera epidemic of the mid-1830s swiftly killed nearly 100,000 people in the Kingdom of the Two Sicilies.

After the cholera epidemic of the early 1830s had subsided and moved north in 1835, a maritime cordon was established to prevent all communication between Barcelona and Civitavecchia, the seaport near Rome. Troops were stationed at the borders and nobody was permitted to pass before spending 14 days in quarantine on the border with Tuscany, and 21 days on the border with Rome. Naples was – somewhat naïvely – considered 'a veritable hermitage surrounded by our gardens and our excellent air'.[2]

In 1836, Donizetti travelled from Venice to Milan and then on to Naples, in one of those bone-crunching, tortuous and seemingly neverending trips. As the vehicle was overloaded, the first part of the voyage took four days. During the second part, he was forced to spend a two-week quarantine period in Rome to ensure that he was not infected by the recent outbreak of cholera.[3] Back in Naples, he wrote an exasperated letter to a friend: '… we are now so restricted by the sanitary measures around the advancing cholera, it is nearly impossible to raise so much as an arm'.[4]

In Paris, meanwhile, Bellini had been enjoying unparalleled success. In January 1835 *Puritani* had premiered at the Théâtre-Italien. The composer was paid 12,000 francs and a third of the royalties – an absolute record for the time.[5] Rubini, Lablache, Giulia Grisi and Antonio Tamburini, perhaps the four leading voices of their era, later to become known as 'the *Puritani* quartet', were considered ideal casting, and the Parisians greeted *Puritani* with unbridled enthusiasm. King Louis-Philippe named Bellini a Chevalier de la Légion d'Honneur and the 'City of Lights' was at the young Sicilian's feet. The King of Naples, refusing to be upstaged, quickly followed suit and awarded Bellini the Cross of the Order of Francesco I (in absentia).

Bellini soaked up the adulation. In spite of his recent frail health, he went to numerous parties and dinners in Paris, and took part in experiments of the occult, then considered a kind of popular parlour game. The superstitious Bellini was, however, terrified of the *jettatore*, the man who could cast an evil eye. His always delicate mental state was not helped when the German writer Heinrich Heine – who even looked like Bellini's image of a *jettatore* with his thick-rimmed black glasses – pronounced that Bellini was of such genius that he would probably suffer a premature death, just like Mozart and Raphael. His words were eerily prescient. After a summer spent on the outskirts of Paris, Bellini died of amoebic dysentery in September 1835, alone in a friend's house. He was not even 35 years old.

The composer's death shocked Europe and led to a tremendous outpouring of grief. Rossini organised the funeral proceedings in Paris and arranged the Mass at Les Invalides. This was attended by all the great names of Italian opera, including three leading Italian composers working in Paris: the legendary Luigi Cherubini (1760–1842) who was much admired for both his operas and sacred music, Ferdinando Paer (1771–1837) who also worked with Rossini at the Théâtre-Italien, and the Neapolitan opera composer Michele Carafa (1787–1872). Among the many singers, Lablache, Rubini and the prominent French tenor Adolphe Nourrit stood out. The Teatro San Carlo, with suitable Neapolitan pathos, put on a performance of *Norma* in Bellini's honour where all the ladies dressed in black.

Bellini's private life is to this day a topic of much speculation. Linked to various women in relationships that all proved impossible, including the daughter of the singer Giuditta Pasta and possibly even Maria Malibran, he also had a strong lifelong friendship with Francesco Florimo. Florimo, later Bellini's first biographer, was to destroy much of their correspondence in an attempt to deliberately mould the composer's image. It is he who is responsible for making Bellini out to be a more collegial and less competitive composer than he in fact was. Most contemporary observers were less complimentary about the acid-tongued dandy.

Whatever Bellini's sexual preferences, he was a man of his times, whose radiant good looks and obvious genius attracted a great deal of sexual interest. Whether he really was permissive is of little relevance: he left behind a brilliant, though small, operatic legacy as well as legions of sobbing female fans, hundreds of letters that would later be destroyed by Florimo and a stunningly large collection of clothes and gloves. While Barbaja did not have the privilege of producing Bellini's most enduring operas, the impresario could take credit for his discovery, his early mentoring, and his introduction to the librettist Romani. We cannot help but wonder if some of Bellini's bargaining skills and sheer greed were not also learnt from the master himself.

Reclaiming the San Carlo

After the disastrous seasons of the Neapolitan Società d'industria e belle arti, Barbaja was brought back to run the royal theatres, for which he again assumed control in May 1836. It was patently clear that he was – in spite of his advancing years and declining power – still the best man for the job. Judging by the correspondence of Donizetti from this period, Barbaja took his time before accepting the new *impresa* while he negotiated for better terms with the Government.

Barbaja took a more cautious approach with the *impresa* this time, sharing it with a local nobleman Prince Ottajano (a distant relative of the Medici family) and Vincenzo Flauto (a professional printer and occasional impresario).[6] The three assumed the *impresa* jointly as a limited company. Barbaja kept the association going until 1840, by which time the partners had fallen out dramatically.[7] His last four years as impresario of the royal theatres were not to be happy ones.

Expectations were not overly high that even Barbaja could lift the Naples theatres out of their present malaise. Donizetti wrote to a friend that, 'Everything is going well according to Barbaja. Everything is going badly according to the audience which however is running to subscribe out of faith in the past of the old impresario.'[8] The *Allgemeine Musikalische Zeitung* reported: 'The Teatro San Carlo, which next to La Scala and La Fenice is the biggest theatre in Italy, is now not what it used to be, even with the veteran Barbaja at its head.'[9]

Many of Barbaja's best singers had been poached by other impresarios, and Lanari especially was steadily encroaching on them. A few years earlier he had written to Rubini saying that he had heard Barbaja was willing to offer the tenor 60,000 francs per annum. 'I can offer you that same sum for the year 1835. If you are indeed free from your obligations in Paris, I can flatter myself knowing that you would prefer [working for] me rather than Barbaja'.[10] Barbaja's *cartello* was no longer a dominant supplier of operatic talent.

Theatre management had become more difficult because of the dramatically higher cost of the artists. The supply of performers had also tightened, permitting singers and composers to charge much more, not least since Italy was now supplying singers not only to Spain, Portugal, Germany and Paris, but also to Corfu, Dalmatia, Odessa and even America. 'Plus,' reported *Allgemeine Musikalische Zeitung*, 'Italy is drowning in theatres!'[11]

Strangely, the Società lived on to fight another day. Despite the tough times, the partners recapitalised and assumed the *impresa* of the Teatro Nuovo for the 1836 season. The Società put a salaried impresario, Filippo Pellegrini, in charge, but the new management committee was no less incompetent than the last. Soon, the Società was again teetering on the brink. Fortunately, Donizetti intervened. Repaying it for launching his most popular opera, he composed two new ones for the Teatro Nuovo in quick succession and gave them to the Società free of charge.[12] These two comedic operas, for which Donizetti wrote both the libretto and the music, enjoyed reasonable success.

At the royal theatres, meanwhile, Barbaja struggled to raise the quality of performances. Poor attendance was exacerbated by bad spring weather, and this was followed by another outbreak of cholera. Donizetti began work on *L'Assedio di Calais* for Barbaja, an ambitious work that tells the story of the siege of Calais at the beginning of the 100 Years War.

The genesis of this opera was strange. Barbaja had hoped Donizetti would produce another hit along the lines of *Lucia di Lammermoor*. Donizetti himself was determined to include an extensive ballet, revealing his ambition for a new career at the Théâtre-Italien in Paris.[13] The French theatres were in the habit of offering large ballets incorporated within the operas, rather than in between acts as was the custom in Naples. Some months earlier, Donizetti had received an invitation from Rossini to write an opera for the Théâtre-Italien in Paris. The Parisian theatre had now surpassed the Teatro

San Carlo in terms of reputation, and Donizetti was obviously keen to spread his success to Paris; he planned *L'Assedio* as a dry run for an eventual move to the Théâtre-Italien.

Even more unusual is that Donizetti wrote the male lead role for a contralto, as would have been done in the 18th century. This was because Barbaja had been unable to produce a creditable tenor for Donizetti to work with – the composer described the three available tenors as 'almost useless'.[14] Giovanni David's agent had not responded to Barbaja's request for him to join him (David's voice was already well past its prime) and there were few other real alternatives as most of Barbaja's male stars had deserted him. 'This impresario has lost his mind,' wrote Donizetti. 'The people are not coming to the theatre, and he just curses.'[15]

L'Assedio scored a reasonable success, but received nothing like the response Donizetti had achieved with *Lucia*. The opera featured many elements designed to appeal to a French audience, including the subject, the chorus and the dances.[16] Barbaja, for one, was not satisfied and withheld some of the payment due to the composer. As a result the two were soon facing off in the Tribunal of Commerce, Barbaja accusing the composer of sub-contracting part of the work to a student and disappointing the audience by producing an opera only three hours long.[17] The legal proceedings also reveal that Donizetti was to be paid only 2,000 ducats by Barbaja for *L'Assedio*, even though he had been given 2,500 ducats by the Società for *Lucia*. While Donizetti graciously said that he accepted the lower fee out of respect for the personalities involved, Barbaja's explanation was more matter-of-fact (written in his customary third-person): 'The Società spent the money of the share-holders. Barbaja spent mostly his own money.'[18]

In the view of both local and international critics, the Neapolitan theatre scene had once again hit a low point in 1836. The great impresario was past his prime. Much of the talent had moved to Milan, Paris or London. The quality of the performances was considered shockingly low when compared to the 1820s and early 1830s. The programme consisted mostly of reprises of older operas, and featured very few outstanding vocal performances. Many criticized the Superintendent and his staff, who were overwhelmed by the enormous workload.[19] They were so busy supervising eight theatres, full-time, and ensuring that the king's and the censor's wishes were respected that quality had become less important. But Barbaja took the brunt of the criticism.

Donizetti, for one, made sure he continued composing for many different

stages and accepted an assignment from Lanari for Venice towards the end of
1836. But luck did not follow him. In December that year, the famous Teatro
la Fenice, where Lanari held the *impresa*, went up in flames and was totally
destroyed, shocking the world of opera. All productions were transferred to
Venice's Teatro Apollo. Lanari asked all artists to accept a reduction in fees
by a quarter, and Donizetti was one of those affected.

Barbaja was also struggling to keep his contracting business together. The
Church of San Francesco di Paola remained under construction nearly 20
years after work had begun. As a result of the rising costs and the delays, the
Ministry of Finance recommended cancelling the contract with Barbaja. The
impresario contacted the King directly, asking him to intercede on his behalf:

> The Just Ferdinand of Glorious Memory [Ferdinand I] used to call me by
> name: Don Domenico, <u>come stai [how are you]</u>? How's business? King
> Francesco [Francis I], also of Glorious Memory, Your Majesty's royal
> Genitor, used to call me his Treasurer when he was still Duke of Calabria,
> and if your Majesty were to order that the accounts be examined, he would
> see that from 1818 onwards Barbaja loaned over D.90,000 to his Royal
> Highness the Duke which was later paid back without any interest being
> charged.[20]

The letter served its purpose, and Barbaja retained the contract.[21] But
Barbaja's first year back at the helm had been far from easy: 1836 had been a
dreadful year. The next four would be little better.

After travelling in the first months of the new year, Donizetti was back in
Naples in April 1837 to fulfil his obligation to Barbaja to deliver two new
operas for the San Carlo. The first was to be *Roberto Devereux*. A few weeks
after Donizetti's return, Zingarelli, the composer and legendary Director of
the Naples Conservatory and guardian of the old school of Neapolitan music,
died at the age of 85. Donizetti composed a *Requiem Mass* for him in a record
three days.[22]

As Professor of Composition at the Conservatory, Donizetti was named its
interim head, and it was widely expected that he would be formally appointed
by the King to the top role. The composer himself passionately hoped to obtain

the position, which would provide him with stability as well as prestige. But as a non-Neapolitan, he faced opposition from Mercadante (who considered himself Neapolitan) and Florimo (who as usual was intriguing behind the scenes), as well as the music critics of the influential journal *L'Omnibus*.

In June that year, the cholera epidemic again reached Naples. Deaths rapidly rose to 300 people a day, and the city filled with anxiety and fear.[23] Some members of the royal family fled the epidemic and decamped to Manfredonia, a town on the Adriatic coast. The theatres were intermittently closed and the churches were ordered to say prayers. 'The cholera monster is taking its toll. Yesterday evening 80 victims,' wrote Donizetti.[24]

On top of his already busy schedule, Donizetti was called upon to write a Cantata for the birthday of the King's second wife, Maria Theresa. The day before the performance his own wife, Virginia, died. Though this was probably the result of a severe syphilitic infection rather than cholera, the general health panic in the city forced burial within a day of her death.[25] The death of his wife was a severe blow to Donizetti and it would forever colour his view of Naples. After her body had been removed, he locked her room in their Naples apartment, leaving it untouched, and never entered it again. To pour bad news on top of bad, the Teatro San Carlo had also once again caught fire, though this time it had been kept under control.[26]

In August 1837, Donizetti, wanting to focus on his role as Director of the Conservatory, wrote to the authorities asking them to release him from his responsibilities as Musical Director of the royal theatres, a post he had held since 1829. He felt that the role had become 'totally useless'.[27] For one thing, he was upset that Barbaja had let his box at the theatre while he had been away tending to his ailing wife during her last illness. Also, Donizetti was angered by Barbaja's constant bullying and hectoring, and disturbed by the recent legal tussles with him over payment of the fees due for *L'Assedio di Calais*.[28] While Donizetti won the legal dispute, it had done little to endear him towards the gruff impresario, who was constantly interfering in the creative process and also controlling the use of ballets in the opera. He felt his voice carried no real weight in the musical decisions at the San Carlo and the Teatro del Fondo.

In October, after an unusually long wait, Donizetti received the censor's approval for *Roberto Devereux*, an opera that tells the story of the romance between Queen Elizabeth I and Robert Devereux, the Earl of Essex. The opera opened at the San Carlo on 28 October 1837 and was a triumph, considered artistically and musically on a par with *Lucia di Lammermoor*.

Giuseppina Ronzi de Begnis was well up to the challenging lead soprano role with its dramatic intensity and complicated vocal passages, and duly impressed. *L'Omnibus* was ecstatic: 'Great music from a great master, in the greatest theatre in the world, in front of the most demanding and intimidating audience on earth.'[29] The *Allgemeine Musikalische Zeitung*, which reprinted this quote, volunteered that the owner of *L'Omnibus* happened to be a good personal friend of Donizetti's. Other Neapolitan journalists also believed the reviewer might be exaggerating, and the publisher was forced to issue a second, more nuanced critique, which was positive nevertheless. The German newspaper liked much of *Roberto Devereux*, and admitted that Donizetti, along with Rossini and Bellini, had now become one of the 'immortal' Italian composers.[30] The score and publishing rights were accordingly popular, and the publishers Cottrau and Fabbricatore immediately started arguing with Barbaja over who owned the rights.[31] The opera enjoyed continued popularity until well into the 21st century.

While this success lifted Donizetti's spirits, it did not change the difficulties he was having obtaining a decision on his appointment as Director of the Naples Conservatory. King Ferdinand II received Donizetti and promised that a decision would be forthcoming shortly, but many weeks passed without any further response.

There was little else now to keep the composer in Naples. He was contracted by Barbaja to compose just one more opera for the San Carlo, to open in May 1838. For this, Donizetti had been working on *Poliuto*, an idea originally suggested by the tenor Adolphe Nourrit. It was the story of Poliuto (Polyeuctus), a secret Christian convert who is apprehended and condemned to martyrdom by the Roman pro-consul, a fate which his wife decides to share with him even though she is in love with the pro-consul. A libretto with such a story was bound to face some obstacles from the censors. Barbaja, however, as usual had other concerns. He was embroiled in a dispute over the leasing of the theatre's costumes.

Costumes were of great financial, and therefore also of great speculative, value. During the earlier suspected arson at the San Carlo in 1824, the police had had grounds to believe there had been over-invoicing of costumes by Barbaja. This time, in 1837, there was another angle to the disagreement. After vociferously objecting to his Head of Costumes, Eduardo Guillaume, Barbaja brought his own nearly worthless collection of old costumes into the San Carlo and entered them in the accounts at four times their value.

With the help of a nephew whom he had strategically placed in charge of costume inventory, he mixed his private collection with the existing costumes of the San Carlo, making it impossible to separate them. Barbaja then forced Eduardo Guillaume to sign for the acquisition of his costumes, at their now inflated, full value.[32]

The costume fiasco would came back to bite Barbaja a few years later, but right now he was more concerned with the financial impact the cholera was having, the meddling of the censors and his deteriorating relationship with one of his best, and last, composers. At least he could take credit for employing one of the leading singers of his generation, Adolphe Nourrit, a friend and student of Donizetti's.

Death of a tenor

The Frenchman Adolphe Nourrit had been the principal tenor of the Paris opera house for years, just as his father had been before him. Nourrit had what would now be called a very elegant, even intelligent voice, which was 'polished to the point of affectation',[33] and he relied on the *falsettino* (a head voice) to sing higher notes, such as the famous high C. But in 1836 he began to encounter serious competition at the Paris opera with the arrival of Gilbert Duprez.

Duprez had returned to Paris from an early career in Italy with an exciting new technique that emphasised greater forcefulness and volume in the voice and what is called a chest-voice high C. Opera lovers refer to Rossini's *Guillaume Tell* (William Tell) and the aria 'Asile Hereditaire' (Home of my Forefathers) in which Duprez first demonstrated and popularised this chest high C as the benchmark for this new singing technique and style. Duprez, in a sense, put a generation of French singers' technique into obsolescence. Long established among a large number of Italian singers, Duprez's technique resulted in a more virile sound that became the standard for all tenors for the future, displacing the French tenors' previous focus on clarity of line and turn of phrase. Henceforth, and to this day, all tenors are expected to sing the upper registers with a chest voice; a *falsettino* would now be jeered off the stage. The strain it places on the voice, however, may have contributed to the relative brevity of Duprez's singing career (and that of many other tenors after him).

When Nourrit was forced to share the Paris opera's top billing with the headline-grabbing Gilbert Duprez, he fell into a serious depression and consequently started to develop vocal problems. Nourrit decided to leave Paris to travel around France, but he encountered some less than friendly audience response due to his hoarseness. In a panic after a concert in Marseille, the singer attempted to commit suicide but was restrained by friends.[34]

In March 1838, Nourrit moved to the operatic heartland of Naples in order to take lessons with Donizetti, who had encouraged the tenor to join him there. Working with Nourrit would give Donizetti an opportunity to interact with a highly educated and cultured musician. The composer was also keen to get closer to someone who might give him pointers on developing his career in Paris, the city where the maestro's ambitions had lain for some time. Nourrit's objectives were to cure his vocal health problems and to try to learn the secrets of the elusive chest high C. Donizetti knew a fair bit about the risks of the wrong technique, having witnessed the on-stage demise of the tenor Amerigo Spigoli, and he was well positioned to help Nourrit improve his chest-supporting technique.

Nourrit was well aware that his technique needed adjustment. He had been heavily courted by Barbaja's competitor, the La Scala impresario Bartolomeo Merelli, but instead decided to go to Naples to resolve his vocal difficulties with Donizetti's help. Barbaja was dangling a performance of Rossini's *Guillaume Tell* for the San Carlo, but the singer knew it was unlikely to be approved by the censors, as the theme of a popular uprising against the dictatorial Habsburg government would probably be distasteful to the Bourbon rulers. He also felt it was more politic to sing works by Donizetti, who was now the dominating musical force in the city.

Under pressure from Barbaja to sign with him, the singer requested more time to improve his Italian. 'Eh, you speak better Italian than I,' replied Barbaja. 'He was not wrong about that ...' found Nourrit, 'for the jargon that he speaks is of no country. It is a mixture of Milanese, French and Neapolitan, in which there is very little good Italian.'[35] In April 1838, Nourrit signed an 11-month contract with Barbaja for the modest amount of 600 ducats a month plus half the revenues of a Teatro San Carlo performance outside the subscription series.[36] With this contract, according to some of his French compatriots, Nourrit sold his liberty to the 'most despotic of all despots in Italy'.[37]

But what mattered to Nourrit was that Barbaja had promised him a debut in a new Donizetti opera at the San Carlo. Nourrit was initially very positive about the imminent re-launch of his career. He was certain the audience would accept him as his voice would now be 'Naples trained', and he told his wife how happy he was with Barbaja's treatment of him: 'He is a strange man, very amusing, very gruff and basically not too tight-fisted for an Italian impresario.'[38] He was also very pleased with his lodging in the Palazzo Barbaja on Via Toledo. He had taken over the third-floor apartment only recently vacated by Lablache, the one where Rossini had lived while composing his operas, on the floor above that occupied by the impresario himself.

The vehicle Donizetti chose to launch Nourrit in Italy, singing in Italian in a role specifically written for his voice, was *Poliuto*. Both Donizetti and Nourrit would have a lot riding on it. The opera was intended to help position Nourrit as the upcoming star tenor of the Teatro San Carlo, as Barbaja had been unable to secure a strong tenor for a while. He had actually instructed the librettist to write a piece for a weaker tenor, until Nourrit had become available to sing a lead role in Naples.[39]

Censorship was at its most restrictive when Donizetti's librettist submitted the story for *Poliuto* to the Superintendent. The opera was turned down personally by the King in August 1838, only a few days after Donizetti had performed a Cantata he had composed in honour of the safe delivery of Queen Maria Theresa's first child. The King vetoed the libretto on the grounds that the glories of martyrdom belonged in the Church and not on the stage.[40] No amount of bargaining, negotiating, twisting and turning by Barbaja could change the monarch's mind.

Donizetti scrambled to come up with another opera as he was contractually obliged to create one acceptable to the censors. Given the timing and the continuing difficulties with the censors, he chose *Pia de Tolomei* (Pia of Tolomei), an opera which had already premiered elsewhere but was new to Naples. Barbaja was quick to complain formally to Donizetti about not fulfilling the terms of his contract. 'I always maintain that the music is not prohibited, just the libretto, and I have no part of that,'[41] the composer countered. He challenged Barbaja to provide him with a new libretto the next day, reminding the impresario that the librettist had been provided by Barbaja himself.[42] The dispute eventually ended up with the Tribunal of Commerce, where Donizetti was judged as having failed to provide a brand new score, and ordered to pay a fine of 300 ducats – but this did now allow him to extract himself from his contractual obligations to Barbaja.

The prohibition of *Poliuto*, the ongoing tensions he faced with Barbaja, the many sad memories associated with his wife's recent death, along with the fact that it was now obvious that he would not secure the appointment as Director of the Conservatory of Naples conspired to make Donizetti decide to leave the city. With the passing months, it had become as clear to the composer as it was to the foreign press that 'the Neapolitan *vox populi* and the government would prefer to give this [Directorship] to a Neapolitan, which means Mercadante'.[43] Having received neither a decision nor any response whatsoever to his enquiries, Donizetti finally tendered his resignation from the Conservatory to Ferdinand II in June 1838. He would, however, remain in Naples for some months, until departing for Paris in October. After nearly 16 years and with some ill feeling, Donizetti left Barbaja and his Naples days behind him and moved to the warm embrace of the Parisian audience.

For Nourrit, the refusal of *Poliuto* would prove more tragic. Without the right vehicle for his comeback, he considered cancelling his contract, but Barbaja encouraged him to pull himself together and give his voice the necessary time to recover. For Barbaja, the *Poliuto* debacle was just the latest in a long list of setbacks to his business, and to his confidence in the future commercial and artistic viability of the Neapolitan opera scene. *Poliuto* was only one of several operas that were forbidden, delayed or simply lost in the bureaucratic quagmire of Ferdinand II's Government.

Putting disappointment aside, therefore, Barbaja decided to put on another opera for Nourrit, *Il Giuramento* (The Oath) by Mercadante, and the French tenor made his Neapolitan debut in this opera in November 1838.[44] Nourrit was in good voice and was duly celebrated by the audience, giving his self-esteem a small boost, and Barbaja was delighted. Writing to Rossini after the fourth night, he boasted that he had never made so much money in Naples from four performances[45] – though he might have been exaggerating to wind up his old friend.

Barbaja continued casting the Frenchman frequently in relatively run-of-the-mill operas, causing the singer to complain. Nourrit also struggled to become accustomed to the rigorous Italian work style of four performances a week with rehearsals every morning, and rehearsals both morning and evening if there were no performance that night.[46] Nourrit did notice with satisfaction, however, that the entire company of the San Carlo tended to calm down in his presence. The choristers and orchestra musicians were not their usual rowdy selves in the presence of the educated and sensitive foreign visitor.[47]

As a result of the singer's frequent appearances in less than satisfactory operas and the heavy workload, the relationship with Barbaja gradually soured, and Nourrit announced his intention to leave Naples and return to France. He felt that he and Barbaja would 'not be parting as friends' and that Barbaja was using his old trick of trying to 'demolish in the eyes and ears of the public those artists who have decided to leave Naples'.[48] By casting Nourrit and an unpopular prima donna in a poorly received and 12-year-old Mercadante opera, Nourrit felt Barbaja was planning to drive both of them to their professional deaths. While the singer himself was clearly dissatisfied, the critics felt otherwise. *The Times* of London wrote on 2 February 1839:

> Nourrit continues to be much admired at Naples. At a concert lately got up by Barbaja, director of the Royal Theatre, he sung with a young French lady of great promise ... Notwithstanding the immense heat which prevailed in the concert-room, [the soprano and] Nourrit ... delighted the hearers. The engagement of Nourrit at San Carlo is one with which that admirable artist has constantly more reason to be satisfied.[49]

On 7 March 1839, Nourrit took part in a benefit concert, and was warmly received by the Neapolitan audience. Clearly in brittle mental health, he took the ovation as mockery and returned to his lodging at the Palazzo Barbaja under a dark cloud. In the early hours of the morning he left his wife in their bedroom alongside their young daughter, walked out of the apartment in a daze, and leapt to his death from the third floor of the building into the courtyard below.[50] He was just 37 years old, and left behind a heavily pregnant wife and five children.[51]

Barbaja was shaken by Nourrit's suicide. It had happened under his contract, for his theatre and in the courtyard of his very own palazzo. The singer's death was reported in astounded tones by the European press, and musical circles were devastated by the news, especially in Paris where Nourrit had celebrated his greatest success. 'Today, we have not the courage to laugh or to joke,' wrote *Le Figaro*. 'The sinister news we have received from Naples has likewise frozen us from pain and shock.'[52]

In an unusually cruel twist of fate *Poliuto*, renamed *Les Martyrs* (The Martyrs), saw the light of day in Paris in 1840 with Nourrit's fierce rival Gilbert Duprez triumphing in the title role.[53]

∽

Rossini, who had returned to Bologna, took the news of Nourrit's suicide very much to heart and fell into a melancholy state. In addition to his old colleague's sudden death, Rossini had recently lost his father, and his own health was also taking a turn for the worse. Now living with his French mistress (and future wife) Olympe Pelissier (having separated from Colbran in 1837), Rossini suggested a change of scenery. The couple decided to visit Naples and call on Barbaja. A visit to the city might also rekindle in the composer the energy of his glory days in southern Italy. He had not composed an opera in ten years.

Rossini and Olympe travelled to Naples and stayed in Barbaja's magnificent Mergellina villa in July and August 1839, the same villa where Rossini and Colbran had first become close. There is little information about the composer's stay in Posillipo, but no doubt the two now elderly men spent a lot of time on the famous balcony, drinking, chatting, laughing and talking about the good old days when Barbaja and Rossini had cast their spell over the city.

The publisher Guillaume Cottrau also visited the house many times and one evening Rossini, still up to his old pranks, served the publisher an 'orangeade de sa façon'[54] on Barbaja's balcony while wearing his night-cap. We can only guess that this was orange juice with liquor. There was some talk that Rossini was planning to write a new opera for the Teatro San Carlo, Giovanni di Montferrato.[55] One thing we can be entirely sure of: prodigious quantities of macaroni alla napoletana were consumed in the Barbaja household that month. Olympe Pelissier wrote to a friend in Bologna of the 'astounding stories' she heard from the 'King of the Impresarios'. 'Barbaja is truly a one of a kind character. He has a big heart but no education at all.'[56]

The old frustrations still plagued Barbaja. He was exasperated with the Superintendent, and in September 1839 he wrote to the authorities listing four recently disallowed operas and asking for approval of the libretto for Mercadante's latest work. He warned them, 'if you prohibit this ... as well, I will certainly no longer know how to live up to my obligations of the contract'.[57] In another letter Barbaja complained to the Superintendent:

> ... in the current critical position of the impresa, where nothing is permitted to be performed ... it should not come as a surprise to His Excellency, if from one day to the next he will no longer find me in Naples, as leaving here is preferable to failing in my obligations towards the Royal Government and the Audience, not to mention that in my 30 years of running

Theatres I have never been so disappointed, and that includes the last four years where I have been concurrently running Six theatres.[58]

To make matters worse, one of his business partners in the *imprese*, Vincenzo Flauto, pressed charges against Barbaja in 1839. Flauto hurled a laundry list of accusations at the impresario, accusing him of abusing the finances of the theatres, and mishandling contracts, singers and costumes.

Financially, the year 1839 was also a disaster. Barbaja's *impresa* was unable to meet its many financial demands, and the Government was forced to intervene with an extraordinary cash injection to ensure the theatres were able to pay their staff in full.[59] The decline of the Neapolitan theatres did not escape the European press:

> The now total collapse of the local opera has become a point of relative 'consolation' to the other houses in Italy, which are also not exactly doing well. At the end of this theatre season the famous impresario Barbaja will step down, then it [the total collapse] will happen. The conservatory is also not in good shape. Donizetti is still in Paris and is then expected in Milan. The issue [of the succession for the conservatory] will probably be decided when Mercadante is next here.[60]

The late 1830s spelled the end of the golden age of Neapolitan opera, of which Barbaja had been its staunchest promoter and defender. The impresario simply did not have the same hold over Ferdinand II that he had had over his grandfather, and the King's retrograde conservatism had made it increasingly impossible for Barbaja to work his magic. On 18 June 1840, Ferdinand II formally announced that Saverio Mercadante would become Director of the Naples Conservatory. *Campanilismo*, bell-tower politics, had won.

In retrospect, it seemed that Donizetti's decision to leave Naples had been the right one: in Paris the composer was achieving the same transfixing effect that Rossini had achieved in Vienna nearly two decades earlier. The ever acid-tongued Hector Berlioz wrote that Donizetti 'seems to treat us like a conquered country; it is a veritable invasion. One can no longer speak of the opera houses of Paris, but only of the opera houses of Monsieur Donizetti.'[61]

Neither was Donizetti missing out on much at the San Carlo. While he was celebrating success on the Paris stages, Barbaja was directing an uninspiring repertoire in Naples. In the spring of 1840, the impresario finally and

definitively relinquished his *imprese* of the royal theatres, the Teatro San
Carlo and the Teatro del Fondo. It had been a nearly 30-year relationship but
Barbaja stepped off the stage of the San Carlo with barely a whimper. Opera
in Italy was now dominated by new names. 'Lanari in Florence, Camuri in
Bologna, Merelli in Milano are now the three dominant impresarios in Italy'
commented the *Allgemeine Musikalische Zeitung*. 'The Nestor of all Impresarios finishes his career this spring.'[62]

Barbaja's losses mount

The new *impresa* at the Teatro San Carlo was held by the former head of
costumes Eduardo Guillaume, a ballet master, a dancer and several other
prominent Neapolitans. They had one small success with a new Pacini
opera, but otherwise they had little to show for their efforts. The critics were
not impressed with the declining quality of the famous opera house; the
programme at the theatre had shrunk to as few operas as had once been
forbidden by the authorities. The *Allgemeine Musikalische Zeitung* sadly
likened the contrast between the old San Carlo and the current opera house
to that between 'tropical vegetation' and 'crippled polar shrubs'.[63]

Barbaja, however, refused to disappear completely from the scene. Within
months of his resignation there were reports that he had re-emerged as the
'secret impresario of the Teatro Nuovo who can, and will, probably play some
unpleasant tricks'[64] on the new impresarios of the royal theatres. There was no
real danger of that, however. The Teatro Nuovo, which Barbaja was managing
jointly with his nephew Antonio Ventura,[65] did not have much of an orchestra,
nor was Barbaja's touch much appreciated. As the smallest and most populist of
the four principal Neapolitan theatres, traditionally the Nuovo was dedicated
to the operas of the Neapolitan greats and the *opera buffa* – not Barbaja's speci-
ality. Expectations from the theatre were not very high.

Barbaja's cantankerous and mercurial personality had not visibly softened
over the years either. He commissioned his old associate Pacini to compose
the opera *L'Uomo del Mistero* (The Man of Mystery) for the Nuovo, but the
composer's copies of the score for the first two acts were lost en route from
his residence in Lucca. In his usual panic about missed deadlines, Barbaja
suspected that Pacini was gaming him and deliberately delaying the dispatch
of the scores. In a handwritten note in coarse colloquial Milanese he wrote
to admonish him:

We have the third. August. You were due to deliver your opera to Naples this July. Dear Pacini, I never would have thought you would treat a friend like Barbaja this way. That you would send a messenger with the first and second acts. Your behaviour is not fitting of the honest man for whom I have always held you. You know that I have always liked you much.[66]

That Barbaja at over 60 years of age would seek all the stress and pressure of running another opera house, and a decidedly second-tier one at that, might lead one to think him an incorrigible workaholic unable to let go his previous status and power. There was, however, a much more mundane reason: money. The impresario had suddenly found himself in dire financial straits.

While Naples was enjoying a general air of prosperity, the man with the Midas touch was facing a serious cash shortage. Details of the genesis of his financial difficulties are not known, but he was certainly no longer able to support his previously lavish lifestyle. There had been no gambling revenues for some time, practically all of his star singers had left to work for different impresarios, he had been embroiled in many costly law suits and his special relationship with the Bourbon Court had gone cold under Ferdinand II. The impresario had started to incur significant debts.

In early November 1840 Barbaja attempted to sell 37 paintings from his large art collection to a syndicate of 17 buyers.[67] The sale was aborted for unknown reasons. At the end of that month, he approached the Ministry of the Interior, which had already sent several delegations of experts to inspect and value the collection, to invite them to take another look and either acquire several paintings for the collection of the Real Museo Borbonico, or at least permit him to sell them abroad, an act which required sovereign approval. He attached the *Catalogue Raisonné* that had been put together in 1819. The fact that Barbaja addressed the Government, specifically the king, shows the absence of other Neapolitan buyers for an acquisition of this magnitude.

In his first letter to the king, Barbaja writes of the need to raise funds to put in order his 'untenable position'.[68] Interestingly, the inspecting commission from the royal household was led by none other than Barbaja's old friend Antonio Niccolini, who by this time was not only the preferred architect and scenographer of the court as well as Head of the Real Istituto di Belle Arti, but also official art adviser to the royal court, which had put him in charge of valuations.

A few months later, in March 1841, Barbaja again wrote to the king, offering to sell him 300 paintings and revealing his need to raise funds urgently 'as an honest man to meet the significant financial commitments' he was facing.[69] The letter had its effect and the King instructed the Antiquities Department to make a valuation swiftly. By April, Barbaja's desperation is visible in the shaky handwriting of another pleading letter detailing his pressing financial obligations, including an imminently due bill of exchange of 600 ducats. The letter assumes a begging tone and is rambling and orthographically often unintelligible:

> Your sacred majesty. That great beast Barbaja entertained you for four years with his annoyance and bestiality [sic] but … remains deeply attached to you, and remains a gentleman. Please permit the sale of my paintings, which will certainly sell abroad and will permit me to move on and extricate myself from the hands of the usurers and enemies, of which there are not few, who have got together to ruin me.[70]

The King instructed the commission to accelerate its work, and in early August 1841 the court offered to buy 17 paintings for 5,150 ducats, payable in two instalments. Furthermore, it identified three additional landscapes for acquisition for around 600 ducats together. The commission also granted Barbaja permission to sell the rest of the collection abroad.

The agreement must have come as a profound relief. Barbaja's growing financial worries, the years of hard work, the constant travel and the frequent heavy living had taken its inevitable toll. The once vigorous impresario was now an old man with far less energy, his ambition sapped. While he would continue to carry some responsibilities for the Teatro Nuovo, in the last year of his life Barbaja would spend an increasing amount of time at his villa in Mergellina.

Death in Posillipo

On 16 October 1841 Barbaja was at home in Mergellina. He had long planned to make some repairs to the house, an on-going project which was an ever-lasting source of joy and entertainment. The Villa Barbaja in many ways was an extension of himself. Mostly constructed to his own design, it was playful, icon-oclastic, majestic, pretentious and known by everyone in the neighbourhood.

That day there were several workmen in the garden, preparing the ground for some new masonry. Barbaja felt energetic, and walked over to help the workers remove some fresh earth. Suddenly he felt a sharp pain and fell over backwards.[71] The stroke left him in a coma for two days. Domenico Barbaja died at midnight on 18 October 1841. He was 63 years old.[72]

News of the great impresario's death came as a shock and it immediately became the talk of the city of Naples. The religious service was held a few days later in the Church of Santa Brigida, only a few metres away from Barbaja's Palace. Those in the congregation reported that requests for people to join the service far exceeded the space available in the small church. Once news spread that a ceremony was to be held in Barbaja's honour, hundreds of people who had been beneficiaries of the impresario's generosity or for whom he had done favours came forward, asking that their names be mentioned in the eulogy.

The memorial service was held on 12 November in the same church. It was organised by Antonio Niccolini.[73] The windows of the church were covered and the sole source of light was 1,000 large candles assembled in the centre of the Santa Brigida.[74] Mozart's *Requiem* was played, conducted by Saverio Mercadante and performed by about 400 teachers, students and musicians. One of the eulogists might not have been exaggerating when he said that, judging by the spontaneous offers to join the performance, they could 'easily have tripled the size of the orchestra'.[75] There were more than 1,000 artists, those from the world of literature and Naples' cultural circles, as well as friends and paupers in the funeral cortège to the Campo Santo cemetery where Barbaja was put to rest.[76] As the cortège went along the Via Toledo, the throngs of people were so thick that the carriages could not pass through.

Barbaja's death was well reported in Italian publications. The press described the funeral as being one of the grandest held in Naples. It was attended by all the singers and orchestra members of the royal theatres and the Teatro Nuovo, the Italian and French acting troupes, high-ranking officials in gala uniform and countless singers. It was reported that, surprisingly, many of the mourners were from humble backgrounds. Of particular note were the large numbers of old and sick singers who came to pay their respects to the great impresario who gave them their careers. Many needed to be carried or supported by others. A Bologna-based newspaper wrote that it was the 'most moving display we have ever seen',[77] while the Naples correspondent of the *Allgemeine Musikalische Zeitung* contrasted Barbaja's large funeral with its throngs of mourners, speeches and eulogies to the near anonymous funeral of Mozart, where nobody was in attendance.[78]

Pasquale Borrelli, the jurist and philosopher (who had earlier written the judgment on the legal suit regarding Finizio's claim) delivered the principal funeral eulogy. In his speech, he took pains to explain that Barbaja directly benefitted a very large number of people and that he had cut through class barriers. He talked about how Barbaja's business ventures provided an income for many hundreds of families of servants, workers and artisans, not to mention the artists, that he employed.

He also mentioned the many acts of kindness that Barbaja performed by financially helping out people in need, intervening to obtain the release of those in jail, helping the down-and-out and infirm, and ensuring employment for the children of his servants. He emphasized, too, that Barbaja never fired old actors or performers, even if they were no longer able to work. Predictably, he also drew attention to Barbaja's legendary punctuality, his fulfilment of promises made and his reliable delivery of any agreed payments – something clearly not always the case at that time.

Borrelli's eulogy focused on three principal aspects of Barbaja's legacy: the development of Naples as the leading operatic centre in Europe; the reconstruction of the Teatro San Carlo after the 1816 fire in record time (not least thanks to his efforts to 'personally help out' with the construction work),[79] as well as his part in the construction of the basilica of the Church of San Francesco di Paola and the building of the villa in Mergellina; and, most importantly, he characterised Barbaja as a man who made up for the many deficiencies of the nation. As Italy had for many decades no longer been able to rest on the laurels of antiquity, and neither could it boast the economic, maritime or military might of other European countries, Barbaja had focused on what Italians did best: opera. Thanks to Barbaja, 'Neapolitan music became an element of civilisation of our species'.[80]

As with any other successful businessman, Borelli said, Barbaja had his fair share of enemies, but those 'hyenas' were motivated by jealousy. He admitted that Barbaja's 'manners could be crude, impetuous and more frank than what was appropriate for the occasion'.[81] But, he emphasized, most of Barbaja's works were done for the glory of God.

There were mild political undertones in the praise he gave for the 'august King Charles III' as well as the late 'magnanimous Ferdinand I'. When talking about the difficult last years, there was no need to mention which king had dragged down the quality of the theatres. Everyone in the audience would have known to whom he was referring.

As was to be expected from such a cultural city, there was an outpouring of creative tributes and emotion from Neapolitan artists. One poet, simply calling himself 'Tirteo Decumano',[82] wrote a canticle extolling Barbaja's virtues in rhyme, highlighting his tremendous achievements in raising the Neapolitan stages to prominence, rebuilding the Teatro San Carlo, putting on spectacular welcome performances for King Ferdinand upon his return from Sicily as well as for the King of Prussia (he probably meant the visit by the Austrian Emperor Franz I), and buying Giuditta Pasta out of her punitive contract with another impresario, thereby delivering the much-loved singer to the Neapolitan stage to please both king and people.[83] With levity and grace, it characterised Barbaja's unique style:

Il burbero benefico fu detto!	He was called the charitable ruffian
Ah, l'indole natia niunu puo mentire!	Ah, the native character nobody can deny
La bile avea sul labbro! il miel nel petto!	He had bile on his lips, but honey in his heart[84]

The dedication engraved on the tombstone, written by Borrelli, quickly made its way around Europe, and was quoted in many obituaries:

DOMENICO BARBAJA	DOMENICO BARBAJA
PRINCIPE DEGLI IMPRESARI TEATRALI	PRINCE AMONG THEATRE IMPRESARIOS
PREFERI IL PIACERE DEL PUBBLICO AL PROPRIO INTERESSE	HE VALUED HIS AUDIENCE'S PLEASURE OVER HIS OWN INTERESTS
D'INCARICO SUPERIORE	FOLLOWING A HIGHER CALLING
RILEVO DALLE CENERI IL TEATRO MASSIMO	HE RAISED THE TEATRO MASSIMO FROM THE ASHES
FE' SORGERE IL TEMPIO DI SAN FRANCESCO DI PAOLA	HE BUILT THE TEMPLE OF SAN FRANCESCO DI PAOLA
E NON PERCIO DIVENNE PIU RICCO	AND NOT BECAUSE IT MADE HIM RICHER
ROZZO NELLE PAROLE, NOBILE NEI FATTI	ROUGH OF WORDS, NOBLE OF DEEDS
EBBE FORTUNA MAGGIORE DEL SUO STATO	HIS FORTUNE OUTGREW HIS HUMBLE BACKGROUND
ED ANIMO MAGGIORE DELLA SUA FORTUNA	AND HIS SPIRIT OUTSHONE HIS FORTUNE
FU SEGUITO NELLA TOMBA DALLE LACRIME DI MOLTI DAL DISPIACERE DELL'UNIVERSALE	HE IS FOLLOWED TO HIS GRAVE BY THE TEARS OF MANY AND UNIVERSAL SADNESS
VISSE ANNI 63	HE LIVED FOR 63 YEARS[85]

The international press from England, Scotland, Germany and France picked up on a widely distributed report on Barbaja's death and funeral, *Era* in London writing:

> A hundred acts of beneficence are cited, which honour the memory of the deceased, who left behind him a fortune estimated at a million and a half of francs. More than 8,000 persons, among whom were remarked the most distinguished members of the aristocracy of the scientific and commercial world, attended his funeral of a man justly surnamed 'Le Bourru bienfai-sant' [the generous ruffian].[86]

Providing more detailed commentary, it continued:

> Barbaja, the most famous impresario in Italy, whose death we noticed in a preceding number, was the support and Mecaenas of all the musical artists who enjoy at present the highest reputation. ... He had a passion for building almost as remarkable as that for music ... By a monstrous alliance of sacred and profane architecture in his passion for piling stone upon stone, when he had no longer theatres to erect, he constructed churches, of which two still attest his activity and zeal. In his latter days he could not repose from his directorial labours without being tormented by the desire of again busying himself with music, the theatre and the administration.[87]

Several months after the event, some of the first extensive retrospectives on Barbaja's life started appearing in the international press. *Era* again summed up the situation pithily:

> A funeral service, composed by Mercadante [sic], has been lately cele-brated at Naples to the memory of the director, Barbaja. All the artists united in its execution, and this last adieu chanted in the most melodious voices in Italy, to airs which the genius Mercadante had inspired, filled the illuminated church with sweet harmony, and seemed an appropriate farewell to an impresario so devoted to the musical art. The whole city was present at the ceremony, from the gentlemen composing the Scarlet Guard of the King, to the Lazzaroni whom the venerable deceased had often relieved.
>
> It will not be forgotten that Barbaja numbered among the artists whom he pensioned, and held at his disposal, Rubini, Tamburini, Lablache,

Nourrit, Barhoillet; Mesdames Malibran, Sontag, Garcia, Pasta, Grisi, Persiani, – all the great luminaries of song.

The ceremony over, the crowd dispersed, and returned to the wonted festivities of the Carnival, and the following day Barbaja was thought no more of.[88]

The newpaper was surprisingly prescient. After such an extraordinary life, it is hard to understand how quickly the memory of Barbaja's achievements disappeared.

Epilogue

Barbaja's Legacy

The shock and flurry of news reports of Barbaja's passing were soon replaced by the realisation of how unique his talent had really been. Following Barbaja's death, the royal theatres passed into the hands of a costume designer, a singer, a dancer, and then a revolving door of impresarios from various backgrounds, none of whom had any lasting impact. The memory of the domineering and bullying impresario who had had an enormous impact on the world of opera slowly gave way to a less specific idea of his simply being a 'legendary impresario'. But the royal theatres of Naples would never again attain the importance, prominence and success they enjoyed during Barbaja's *imprese.*

Barbaja's drive, dedication, passion and sheer willpower had coalesced to create near miracles in the opera world of the *bel canto* period. He had helped Naples become the nerve centre of music and made the royal theatres the most admired stages in Europe. He had shepherded the Viennese Kaerntnertortheater to one of its greatest moments in history, producing unforgettable music and showing the inimitable artistry of the greatest singers on the continent. And he had helped Milan turn from an operatic backwater into a leading Italian stage, though La Scala's greatest period was only just about to begin.

Barbaja had also revolutionised the way Neapolitans, and many Europeans, enjoyed music and opera. Tearing away the closed curtains and truly opening up the boxes to the activities on the stage, he had turned the operatic performance from a sideshow into the main act.

Barbaja's ebullient personality and inimitable language also became part of his legacy, and his colleagues would joke about them for years. In 1844 Donizetti wrote a letter to a fellow musician (defending his view on a recently performed opera): '... and if I was wrong on that point, I would admit it to the entire musical world and I would publicly declare that I am the first beast (after Barbaja if he were still alive)'.

Like the fading memory of Barbaja's achievements, the Kingdom of the Two Sicilies continued its gradual decline. The last decade of Ferdinand II's reign was marked by further misgovernment and the deterioration of relations with Britain and France, leading to diplomatic isolation. Finally, this and general administrative incompetence led to the invasion of the armies of Piedmont and in 1861 the victory of the Red Shirts under Garibaldi, who united Italy into a single state. But King Ferdinand II did not live to see that. He died in May 1859, but not before inculcating his son and successor, Francis II, with his dearly held values of Catholicism and disdain for constitutionalism.

The 126-year Bourbon rule of Naples left behind a weak industrial manufacturing base, economic structures more befitting the 17th century, deep social divisions, and continuing poverty and over-population. Yet it also gave the city some magnificent architectural structures – among them Barbaja's own beautiful Teatro San Carlo and the basilica of San Francesco di Paola (which was finally finished in 1836 and inaugurated by Pope Gregory XVI).

Family legacies

What happened to Barbaja's legendary wealth is difficult to ascertain. It is safe to assume, however, that the financial difficulties of the last year of his life were ones of cash flow, rather than a permanent change of fortune. Barbaja died a millionaire, albeit a rather illiquid one. He left behind only £60,000 to his two children, considered a very moderate amount.[2] But he still owned at least three spectacular Neapolitan properties and a priceless art collection.

Barbaja did not live long enough to receive even the first instalment of the king's payment for the 17 paintings from his art collection. His children, Pietro and Carolina, would have been the beneficiaries. The three additional paintings were ultimately not purchased. Barbaja's children tried to obtain a better price than the 600 ducats originally offered, claiming they had interested new buyers, but the Government called their bluff and pulled out from the acquisition.[3]

In 1874, the remaining 231 paintings were put up for sale by Barbaja's son, Pietro, who commissioned a catalogue of the works in French. He successfully sold many works, including 'a genuine Tiziano' which fetched over 55 million lire,[4] with paintings going to private and public collections. Of those left, some were dispersed among family members. Others cannot be traced, a considerable number, according to a descendant, being 'sold off in earlier generations, the rest stolen some years ago'.

The great impresario's children seem also to have inherited their father's litigious nature. One of Donizetti's Cantatas, *Cristoforo Colombo*, was barely performed after its first night in 1838. Barbaja had held back the work for legal reasons, and it became the subject of a lengthy legal dispute between the estates of the publishers (Cottrau and Fabbricatore) and Pietro and Carolina. In 1849 the courts found in favour of the publishers and the Barbaja estate was ordered to pay damages to cover income lost because of the Cantata's non-publication and non-distribution.[5]

The sale of Barbaja's assets left his principal beneficiaries comfortably off, and his daughter Carolina also contested the claims of her husband Cesare Politi, Barbaja's occasional associate, over inheritance and related financial issues.

Barbaja's wife, Rosa Gerbini, who was relegated to such a small part in the impresario's life, died in Milan in 1849 at the age of 71. She left behind valuable Milanese properties, and is listed in the registry of deaths as 'financially well-off'.

Today, finding traces of Barbaja's magnificent properties is less easy than you would imagine. I had assumed his residential palazzo would not be difficult to find given its historical prominence. Alexandre Dumas (père), for one, made the Palazzo Barbaja on Via Toledo sound extraordinary:

> Everything on Via Toledo must be seen ... one must focus on three palaces that are the most outstanding and remarkable; the palace of the King at one end, City Hall at the other end, and in the middle, the palace of Barbaia.[6]

It did not take me long to find the palazzo at 205 Via Toledo, the main road leading through the old part of Naples. It was a terribly average-looking building with grey masonry set off by salmon colour paint, like hundreds of others in Naples. A helpful municipality sign identifies the building as the 'Palazzo of Domenico Barbaja' and as the residence of Gioachino Rossini, but further research quickly revealed that this palazzo was never occupied by either, and that the real Palazzo Barbaja[7] was torn down in the 1880s to make way for the spectacular Galleria Umberto II shopping arcade further up the road.[8]

The seaside villa in Mergellina remained in the possession of the Barbaja family until the 1970s, and it still stands. There is no plaque or inscription to identify its former owner, and it is now dwarfed and concealed by buildings of varying colour, style and taste that were built alongside it over the decades. The peaceful street that used to meander in front of the building is now a major road leading to Posillipo, and the small square in front of the building is dominated by a large restaurant. It is nearly impossible to imagine the glamour that the villa used to possess, but the views from the terraces remain astounding.

The splendid villa in Ischia passed to Barbaja's nephew Ventura. It is now owned and occupied by the municipality but, again, is not marked as having once belonged to the great impresario.

Barbaja's musical legacy

Barbaja's musical legacy has been much longer lasting. It is fair to say that the careers of the three great *bel canto* composers, Rossini, Bellini and Donizetti, were begun and developed by Barbaja, though their talent was so prodigious that another impresario equally might have launched them. While numerous composers have produced operas for Italy's principal opera houses and their impresarios, the intimacy of the relationship, the proximity of the professional interaction and the sheer intensity of the artistic collaboration that Barbaja maintained with Rossini, Bellini, Donizetti, and even with Pacini, was of a nature that no other impresario would ever repeat. The relationship between Barbaja and Rossini was especially close, and after Barbaja's death it continued with the impresario's son, Pietro, with whom the composer maintained warm relations. The *opere serie* that Barbaja and Colbran pushed Rossini to write were to found his reputation as a first-rate composer and were significant for the development of Italian opera, with an influence extending as far as Verdi and Puccini.

The 'old guard' of the golden era of *bel canto* singers – García, Colbran,

David, Rubini, Nozzari, Donzelli, Ambrogi, Nourrit, Pasta, Malibran and Sontag – would always have been stars, but without Barbaja, they would never have shone as bright or as far. Barbaja's unique *cartello* structure, indefatigable energy, peripatetic nature, and fearless expansion to other European stages brought the singers to a wider audience than would otherwise have been possible. Today these names are all but forgotten by any except the compulsive opera lover. But in the late 19th century, they were frequently referred to as 'so much better than the contemporary singers' and held up as models.

The opera houses at which Barbaja worked are also his testament. While today's La Scala is a busy, vibrant and bustling opera house with an enviable tradition, the less generously sponsored San Carlo projects an image of yesterday's charm and slightly faded glory, though the authorities are putting much effort into rebuilding the house's reputation and repertoire.

The auditorium is still breathtaking, now with a sea of red velvet upholstery, which replaced the blue upholstery favoured during the Bourbon era. A seemingly endless number of boxes in a horseshoe is clasped together by the deep stage and orchestra pit on one side and the royal box, flanked by two life-sized golden angels, on the other. The colossal ceiling painting of Apollo presenting to Minerva the world's greatest poets, is as impressive today as it was in Barbaja's time.

The old foyer, the *ridotto*, is still used for functions and has floor to ceiling windows that open onto the leafy gardens at the back of the royal palace. Opposite the windows, and flanked by pilasters, are enormous mirrors that reflect the brown-pink polished marble floor. Large chandeliers light the hall, picking out the geometrical yellow moulding on the otherwise white ceiling.

Even today, the sheer grandeur and enormity of the *ridotto* stun the eye. It is easy to imagine the bustle and magnificence that must have radiated on an evening in 1820 with a packed audience: the elegant ladies in their sweeping gowns with puffed elbow-length sleeves, whose stiff fabrics gave them the appearance of gliding round the room, their bejewelled shoulders and fashionable mid-length gloves revealing just enough skin; the gentlemen in their dark tail-coats and – even if they could ill afford it – tightly tailored trousers; the decorated military officers in uniform. These were the colourful and stylish gamblers who would chat, mingle and crowd around the roulette and card tables. And amid them all would be Barbaja, overseeing everything, hopping from table to table, greeting the players, chatting with his stars, shouting at the staff, and lording over the room like a captain over his ship.

Walking around the opera house and among its back offices, I discovered magnificent rooms that appeared to have been untouched for nearly 200 years, with large wooden meeting tables, oversize oil paintings, and old windows flung open. I could easily imagine the imperious Barbaja holding staff meetings there. From here it was but a short walk to the auditorium and the boxes, from which he could look out at the audience, or even see his favourite singers sitting and waiting for his instructions, just like in the painting in the Museum of La Scala.

Final visits to Naples

In *Passeggiata per Napoli* the writer and librettist Emmanuele Bidera describes his melancholy walk through the Campo Santo cemetery where Barbaja was put to rest:

> Oh Barbaja. If you could raise your head. If you could see to which miserable condition the Italian and even more the Neapolitan music scene has deteriorated, where all things conspire to its annihilation. You would say: Let me sleep eternally in order not to witness such desecration. Oh grateful Neapolitans, you should erect a tombstone in honour of this great man, upon which saying: Here lies Domenico Barbaja, the Napoleon of the music impresarios.[9]

The very same could be said today. Barbaja's grave cannot now be found. Neither cemetery officials, nor the records of the Campo Santo cemetery, nor living family members have any information on the whereabouts or existence of his grave and tombstone. My research assistant and I spent hours walking around the cemetery focusing on graves we had identified as being near Barbaja's, but we had little to show for our efforts. Perhaps the grave had been cleared out for another coffin and tombstone, had collapsed during an earthquake or had simply become so overgrown by vegetation that it was beyond recognition and discovery.

$\sim$

I walked around central Naples one final time, and stopped to listen to three buskers singing Neapolitan songs – by Cottrau – in the Via Toledo. They were standing in front of the Palazzo Berio, opposite the so-called 'Palazzo Barbaja'. A middle-aged woman played the violin accompaniment. An elderly gentleman in a dirty shirt with an astounding tenor sang the songs, intermittently joined by a very old passerby in a simple floral dress, clutching a ragged handbag under one arm, and using her other hand to fan herself wildly. The talent was amazing.

As I continued down the Via Toledo, the impact of Barbaja could not escape me. The Teatro San Carlo, the basilica of San Francesco di Paola, the palazzo on the Via Toledo, the apartment where Rossini lived, the road to the legendary villa in Mergellina. To me, at least, the spirit of Barbaja was everywhere.

Appendix 1

Cast of Characters

Singers

Ambrogi, Antonio (1786–?). Italian bass

Boccabadati, Luigia (1800–1850). Italian soprano

Catalani, Angelica (1780–1849). Italian soprano

Cecconi, Teresa Anna Maria (fl. 1821). Italian contralto

Chabrand, Margherita (fl. 1820). Italian soprano. Rival to Isabella Colbran

Colbran, Isabella (1785–1845). Spanish soprano, Barbaja's mistress and later Rossini's wife

Comelli-Rubini, Adelaide (1794–?). Real name Chomel, French soprano, wife of G B Rubini

Crescentini, Girolamo (1762–1846). Italian castrato

David/Davide, Giovanni (1790–1864). Italian tenor

Del Sere, Anna (fl. 1834). Italian soprano

Donzelli, Domenico (1790–1873). Italian tenor

Duprez, Gilbert (1806–1896). French tenor

Ferron, Elisabetta (Elizabeth Fearon). British soprano married to impresario Joseph Glossop

Fodor, Josephine (1789–1870). French soprano

García, Manuel (1775–1832). Spanish tenor and composer

Grisi, Giulia (1811–1869). Italian soprano

Lablache, Luigi (1794–1858). Italian bass

Malibran, Maria (1803–1836). Spanish soprano, daughter of Manuel García

Méric-Lalande, Henriette (1798–1867). French soprano

Nourrit, Adolphe (1802–1839). French tenor
Nozzari, Andrea (1775–1832). Italian tenor
Pasta, Giuditta (1797–1865). Italian soprano
Pisaroni, Benedetta Rosamunda (1793–1872). Italian contralto
Ronzi de Begnis, Giuseppina (1800–1853). Italian soprano
Rubini, Giovanni Battista (1794–1854). Italian tenor
Sontag, Henriette (1806–1854). German soprano
Tacchinardi-Persiani, Fanny (1812–1867). Italian soprano
Tamburini, Antonio (1800–1876). Italian baritone
Tosi, Adelaide (1800–1859). Italian soprano
Unger, Caroline (1803–1877). Austro-Hungarian contralto/soprano
Velluti, Gian Battista (1780–1861). Italian castrato

Composers

Bellini, Vincenzo (1801–1835). Italian composer
Benedict, Julius (1804–1885). German composer and Musical Director
Cimarosa, Domenico (1749–1801). Italian composer
Donizetti, Gaetano (1797–1848). Italian composer
Mayr, Giovanni Simone (1763–1845). German composer and teacher
Mercadante, Saverio (1795–1870). Italian composer, Director of Naples
    Conservatory
Meyerbeer, Giacomo (1791–1864). German composer
Pacini, Giovanni (1796–1867). Italian composer
Paganini, Niccolò (1782–1840). Italian composer and violinist
Porpora, Nicola (1686–1768). Italian composer and teacher
Rossini, Gioachino (1792–1868). Italian composer
Schubert, Franz (1797–1828). Austrian composer
Spohr, Louis (1784–1859). German composer and musician
Spontini, Gaspare (1774–1851). Italian composer
Vaccai, Nicola (1790–1848). Italian composer
van Beethoven, Ludwig (1770–1827). German composer
von Weber, Carl Maria (1786–1826). German composer
Zingarelli, Niccolò Antonio (1752–1837). Italian composer, Director of
    Naples Conservatory

Librettists and essayists

Berio, Francesco Maria, Marchese di Salsa (1765–1820). Neapolitan
   aristocrat, man of letters and librettist

Bidera, Emmanuele (1784–1858). Sicilian-born poet, diction coach and
   librettist at the San Carlo

Borrelli, Pasquale (1782–1849). Jurist, philosopher and writer of medical treatises

Cottrau, Guillaume (Guglielmo) Louis (1797–1847). French born, Naples
   based music publisher and composer

Florimo, Francesco (1800–1888). Italian composer, musicologist and librarian

Romani, Felice (1788–1865). Italian librettist

Schmidt, Giovanni (1775–1839). German poet, Court librettist in Naples

von Chézy, Helmina (1783–1856). German writer and librettist

von Kotzebue, August (1761–1819). German dramatist

Impresarios

Balochino, Carlo (1770–1851). Italian impresario and occasional associate of
   Barbaja

Caracciolo, Giuseppe, Prince of Torella. Neapolitan aristocrat (fl. 1834).
   Spearheaded the "Societa d'Industria"

Crivelli, Giuseppe (?–1831). Italian impresario, worked mostly in Milan and
   Venice

Duport, Louis (1781–1853). French choreographer, deputised Barbaja as
   impresario in Vienna

Ebers, John (c.1785–c.1830). English opera impresario, managed the Italian
   opera at the King's Theatre in London

Glossop, Joseph (1787–1852). English aristocrat and opera impresario. Ran
   the San Carlo and La Scala intermittently

Lanari, Alessandro (c.1790–1862). Italian impresario and costume
   entrepreneur. Competitor of Barbaja

Merelli, Bartolomeo (1794–1879). Italian impresario, composer and librettist,
   and competitor of Barbaja

Palffy, Count Ferdinand (1774–1840). Austro-Hungarian impresario in Vienna

Ricci, Francesco Benedetto (fl.1805). Milanese opera impresario and
   businessman

Ventura, Antonio Felice. Barbaja's nephew (fl. 1840); worked at the Teatro
   San Carlo and Teatro Nuovo

von Gallenberg, Wenzel Robert (1783–1839). Austrian musician and ballet
    composer

Opera administrators

Carafa, Giovanni, Duca di Noja (Duke of Noja). Superintendent of the
    Royal Theatres 1812–1826
Longchamps, Charles. Superintendent of the Royal Theatres 1809–1811
Ruffano, Prince Francesco di. Superintendent of the Royal Theatres 1828–1837

Designers and architects

Bianchi, Pietro (1787–1849). Swiss architect
Niccolini, Antonio (1772–1850). Tuscan architect and scenographer
Tortolj, Francesco (?–1824). Nephew of Niccolini, scenographer
Vanvitelli, Luigi (1700–1773). Neapolitan architect of Dutch ancestry. Son of
    painter Gaspare Vanvitelli

Rulers and royal houses

Naples and Sicily

Charles III (1716–88), King and of Naples and Sicily (1735–59) and then
    King of Spain (1759–88). Son of King Philip V of Spain and Elizabeth
    Farnese. Father of Ferdinand I.
Ferdinand I of the Two Sicilies (1751–1825) formerly Ferdinand IV of Naples
    and Ferdinand III of Sicily. Ruled intermittently: as Ferdinand IV of
    Naples 6 October 1759–23 January 1799; 13 June 1799–30 March 1806; 3
    May 1815–8 December 1816; as Ferdinand III of Sicily 6 October 1759 – 8
    December 1816; and as Ferdinand I of the Kingdom of the Two Sicilies 8
    March 1816 to 4 January 1825. Married to Maria Carolina of Austria and
    Lucia Migliaccio of Floridia.
Francis I of the Two Sicilies (1777–1830). Son of Ferdinand I. Became Duke
    of Calabria after death of his brother Carlo. Ruled 1825–30. Married to
    Maria Clementina of Austria and Maria Isabella of Spain.
Leopoldo, Prince of Salerno (1790–1851). Son of Ferdinand I, brother of
    Francis I.

Ferdinand II of the Two Sicilies (1810–1859). Son of King Francis I and
   Maria Isabella of Spain, ruled 1830–58. Married to Maria Cristina of
   Savoy and Maria Theresia Isabella of Austria. Known as 're bomba'.

Austria

Maria Theresa, Empress of Austria (1717–1780). Ruled the extensive
   Habsburg dominions from 1740–80. Married to Franz I, Holy Roman
   Emperor, who ruled from 1745–65.
Maria Carolina of Austria (1752–1814). The thirteenth child of Empress Maria
   Theresa, the sister of Emperor Joseph II of Austria and of Queen Marie
   Antoinette of France. Wife of King Ferdinand I of the Two Sicilies.
Marie-Antoinette (1755–93), Queen of France 1774–92. Daughter of Franz
   I, Holy Roman Emperor, and Empress Maria Theresa. Married to
   King Louis XVI of France. Deposed and executed during the French
   Revolution.
Franz I, Emperor of Austria (1768–1835). Son of Leopold II, Holy Roman
   Emperor, and Maria Luisa of Spain. Grandson of Franz I and Maria
   Theresa. Ruled the Holy Roman Empire 1792–1806 as Franz II, the last
   Holy Roman Emperor, until he dissolved it after the defeat by Napoleon
   at Austerlitz. Founded Austrian Empire in 1804, becoming Franz I.
   Ruled the Austrian Empire 1804–35.
Prince Klemens Wenzel Metternich (1773–1859), Austrian Statesman and
   crucial participant of the Vienna Congress of 1815. In office as State
   Chancellor 1821–48.

France

Louis XVI, King of France (1754–93). A member of the House of Bourbon,
   he ruled only from 1791–2. Married to Marie-Antoinette. He was
   deposed and executed during the French Revolution.
Joseph Bonaparte (1768–1844). Older brother of Napoleon, he ran the
   Kingdom of Naples as King Joseph 1806–08.
Napoleon Bonaparte (1769–1821). Political and military leader of France and
   French Emperor 1804–15.
Joachim Murat (1767–1815). Married to Caroline Bonaparte and thus
   brother-in-law of Napoleon. Ruled the Kingdom of Naples 1808–15.

Appendix 2

The Bourbons and the Habsburgs 1638–1859

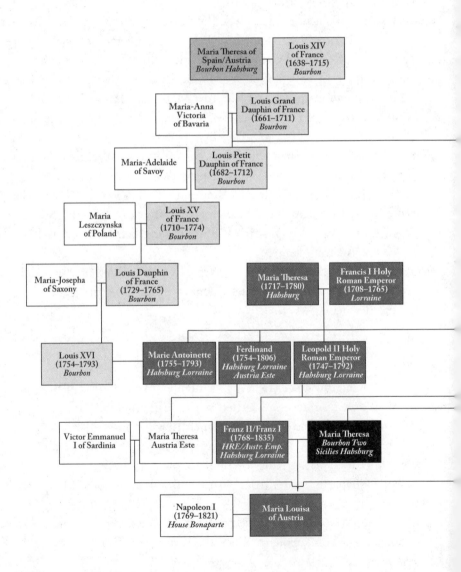

MAIN RELATIONSHIPS
Bourbons and Habsburgs 1638–1859

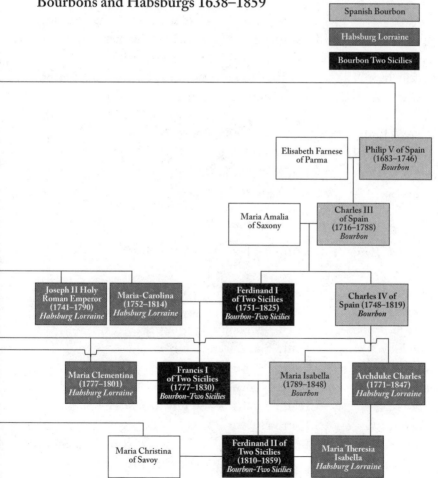

Appendix 3

The Barbaja Operas

This list is not comprehensive, but gives only the operas of the most prominent composers working with Barbaja. It does not include the dozens of Cantatas, hymns, ballets and other musical pieces commissioned by the impresario, nor does it include Neapolitan, Milanese or Viennese *prime* of operas performed first elsewhere. The date given is the date of first performance.

Vincenzo Bellini

Bianca e Fernando	Teatro San Carlo	30 May 1826
Il Pirata	Teatro alla Scala	27 October 1827
La Straniera	Teatro alla Scala	14 Fbruary 1829

Michele Carafa

Gabriella de Vergy	Teatro del Fondo	3 July 1816

Gaetano Donizetti

La Zingara	Teatro Nuovo	12 May 1822
La Lettera Anonima	Teatro del Fondo	29 June 1822
Alfredo il Grande	Teatro San Carlo	2 July 1823
Il Fortunato Inganno	Teatro Nuovo	3 September 1823
Don Gregorio	Teatro Nuovo	11 June 1826
Elvida	Teatro San Carlo	6 July 1826
Emilia di Liverpool	Teatro Nuovo	28 July 1824
Gabriella di Vergy	Teatro San Carlo	Composed 1826, first performed 29 November 1869 (three versions)

Otto mesi in due ore	Teatro Nuovo	13 May 1827
Il Borgomastro di Saardam	Teatro del Fondo	19 August 1827
Le Convenienze Teatrali	Teatro Nuovo	21 November 1827
L'Esule di Roma	Teatro San Carlo	1 January 1828
Gianni di Calais	Teatro del Fondo	2 August 1828
Il Giovedi Grasso	Teatro del Fondo	28 February 1829
Il Paria	Teatro San Carlo	12 January 1829
Elisabetta al Castello di Kenilworth	Teatro San Carlo	6 July 1829
I Pazzi per Projetto	Teatro San Carlo	6 February 1830
Il Diluvio Universale	Teatro San Carlo	28 February 1830
Imelda di Lambertazzi	Teatro San Carlo	5 September 1830
Francesca di Foix	Teatro San Carlo,	30 May 1831
L'Uomo Nero	Teatro del Fondo	18 June 1831
Fausta	Teatro San Carlo	12 January 1832
Sancia di Castiglia	Teatro San Carlo	4 November 1832
Maria Stuarda	Teatro alla Scala	Commissioned and composed at the Teatro San Carlo July 1834, first performed 30 December 1835 (after Barbaja)
Il Campanello	Teatro Nuovo	1 June 1836
L'Assedio di Calais	Teatro San Carlo	19 November 1836
Roberto Devereux	Teatro San Carlo	28 October 1837
Poliuto	Paris/Teatro San Carlo	Composed July 1838. Premiered as I Martiri, Paris, 10 April 1840. Performed 30 November 1848 Teatro San Carlo

Nicola Manfroce

Ecuba	Teatro San Carlo	13 December 1812

Giovanni Simone Mayr

Medea in Corinto	Teatro San Carlo	28 November 1813
Cora	Teatro San Carlo	26 March 1815
Mennone e Zemira	Teatro San Carlo	22 March 1817

Saverio Mercadante

L'Apoteosi d'Ercole	Teatro San Carlo	19 August 1819
Anacreonte in Samo	Teatro San Carlo	1 Januray 1820
Gli Sciti	Teatro San Carlo	18 March 1823
Costanzo ed Almeriska	Teatro San Carlo	22 November 1823
Doralice	Kaerntnertortheater	18 September 1824
Le Nozze di Telemaco ed Antiope	Kaerntnertortheater	5 November 1824
Podestà di Burgos, ossia Il Signore del Villaggio	Kaerntnertortheater	20 November 1824
Ipermestra	Teatro San Carlo	29 November 1825
Elena da Feltre	Teatro San Carlo	1 January 1839

Francesco Morlacchi

Boadicea	Teatro San Carlo	January 1818 (no exact date)

Giovanni Pacini

Amazilia	Teatro San Carlo	6 July 1825
L'Ultimo Giorno di Pompei	Teatro San Carlo	19 November 1825
La Gelosia Corretta	Teatro alla Scala	27 March 1826
La Niobe	Teatro San Carlo	19 November 1826
Gli Arabi nelle Gallie	Teatro alla Scala	8 March 1827
Elvezi	Teatro San Carlo	12 January 1833
L'Uomo del Mistero	Teatro Nuovo	9 November 1841; commissioned by DB, but performed after his death

Gioachino Rossini

Elisabetta	Teatro San Carlo	4 October 1815
La Gazzetta	Teatro dei Fiorentini	26 September 1816
Otello	Teatro del Fondo	4 December 1816
Armida	Teatro San Carlo	9 November 1817
Mose in Egitto	Teatro San Carlo	5 March 1818
Riccardo e Zoraide	Teatro San Carlo	3 December 1818

Ermione	Teatro San Carlo	27 March 1819
Donna del Lago	Teatro San Carlo	24 September 1819
Maometto II	Teatro San Carlo	3 December 1820
Zelmira	Teatro San Carlo	16 February 1822

Franz Schubert

Fierrabras	(not performed)	1823

Nicola Vaccai

Alexi	Teatro San Carlo	6 July 1828
Giovanna d'Arco	Teatro San Carlo	19 August 1828
Saul	Teatro San Carlo	11 March 1829

Carl Maria von Weber

Euryanthe	Kaerntnertortheater	25 October 1823

Appendix 4

A Note on Currency

Many different currencies were used in 19th-century Italy. In Naples the principal mode of payment was the Neapolitan ducat, but Roman scudi and francs were also frequently referred to in contracts and letters. Other parts of Italy used the Milanese lire, later placed on a par with the Milanese franc, making it interchangeable. Visitors from other parts of Europe referred to the French Louis d'or, the French franc, the svanzica or the Saxon thaler. Barbaja regularly dealt with different currencies in the same piece of correspondence, and banks routinely handled a wide range of currencies.

The Neapolitan ducat, in existence since the 13th century, was issued as a silver coin by the Bourbons in the 18th century. It was divided into ten *carlino* (named with reference to King Charles III), and one hundred *grano* (a grain), which was the smallest unit, made of silver or bronze. In today's money, it is easiest to think of a ducat as worth around £15 in terms of purchasing power, though different calculation methods provide divergent values for the currency. The exchange rate in the 1830s was approximately 1 ducat to 5.22 French francs. As the £/FF exchange rate held steady for most of the 19th century at £1 = 25.221FF, we can assume that 1 ducat = £0.2070 in 1830s currency. The Measuring Worth Calculator on www.eh.net which is supported by the Economic History Association calculates that £0.2070 in 1830 would be worth £14.70 in today's pound sterling in terms of purchasing power.*

---

*Another way to value the ducat is to compare it to the Italian lira, to which the ducat was converted at the time of Italian unification in 1861. The exchange rate was set at 4.25 lire to 1 ducat. The new lira was defined on its introduction as 290.322 mg of gold. Given the current (July 2012) gold price of around $52.1 a gram, 290mg – or 1 lira – equates to £9.6/$15.1, and 1 ducat to £2.30/$3.60.

In the 1820–30s, 1 ducat bought 3.5 litres of oil or 4.5kg of meat. Bread was fixed at 4 grana per loaf. A cup of coffee at a coffee shop cost 3 grana. The average wage for a manual labourer was 5 ducats per month, that is, 60 ducats a year. A private cook could earn up to 192 ducats a year; a senior government official in the Bourbon government up to 6,000. A top musical director at the San Carlo opera house would be paid around 2,400 ducats a year, while a successful composer could be paid around 1,900 ducats for a single opera. Popular opera singers could command around 6,000 ducats per season, while a leading prima donna could demand up to 19,000.

Notes

Introduction

1. Alexandre Dumas (père), *Le Corricolo* (Michel Levy, Paris: 1872) p 40
2. Bruno Cagli and Sergio Ragni, *Gioachino Rossini: Lettere e Documenti* (Fondazione Rossini Pesaro, Pesaro: 2004) Vol I, p 184
3. Jutta Toelle, *Oper als Geschaeft. Impresari an italienischen Opernhaeusern 1860–1900* (Baerenreiter Verlag, Kassel: 2007) p 8
4. The opera houses of Italy are brought to life by the German artist Matthias Schaller (born 1965), who photographed 150 of the nation's opera houses, depicting both those in small towns such as Faenza (home to the Fayence pottery) and the three opera houses in Naples. His work provides a strong visual representation of the ubiquity of opera houses, as well as their varying styles.
5. Toelle, *Oper als Geschaeft*, p 7
6. Samuel Sharp, *Letters from Italy, describing the Customs and Manner of that Country, in the years 1765 and 1766. An Admonition to Gentlemen who pass the Alps, in the Tour through Italy* (R Cave, London: 1767) p 82
7. Remo Giazotto, *Le Carte della Scala. Storie di Impresari e Appaltatori Teatrali (1778–1860)* (Edizioni Akademos & Lim, Pisa: 1990) p 18
8. Guillaume Cottrau, *Lettres d'un Melomane; pour servir de document a l'histoire musicale de Naples de 1829 a 1847. Avec un preface de F Verdinois* (A Morano, Rome: 1885), p 13
9. Cottrau, *Lettres d'un Melomane*, p iv
10. John Rosselli, *The Opera Industry in Italy from Cimarosa to Verdi. The Role of the Impresario* (Cambridge University Press, 1984) pp 76, 77

Chapter 1

1. In 1500, Milan fell under the control of the French for 12 years, until the
    Sforza gained power and held onto it for the next three years with the help
    of mercenaries from the Swiss Confederacy. The Battle of Marignano of 1515
    saw a decisive French victory over the Swiss forces, and the House of Valois
    controlled Milan for the next decade, until they were routed by the Spanish
    Habsburgs in the Battle of Pavia of 1525. The victorious Habsburg Emperor
    Charles V abdicated in 1556 in favour of his son Philip II and his brother
    Ferdinand I. The Spanish-born Ferdinand I moved to Vienna and obtained
    control of the Holy Roman Empire, centred on the Austrian hereditary lands.
    Philip II was handed control of his father's Italian possessions, including
    Milan. The territory fell into decline and one of the last large-scale outbreaks
    of the plague halved Milan's population of 130,000. With the death of the
    ineffectual Charles II, the great-grandson of Philip II, the Spanish Habsburg
    line was extinguished. The resulting 1701 War of Spanish Succession saw the
    return of the French, who however only held on to the old Spanish Habsburg
    territories in northern Italy until 1706, when they were defeated by the
    Austrian line of the Habsburgs. Austrian control of Lombardy, and the capital
    Milan, was ratified in the 1713 Treaty of Utrecht.
2. His sisters were Annunciata (1774–?), Rachele (1784–1819) and Cecilia (1795–
    1825). There are no available records on the Barbaglia family and their economic
    circumstances: the first detailed population census was conducted in 1811.
3. Dumas (père), *Le Corricolo*, p 40
4. In 1793
5. It was previously known as *Caffé delle Sirene* (Café of the Sirens)
6. Count Hubner, quoted in Gaia Servadio, *Rossini* (Constable & Robinson,
    London: 2003) p 69
7. Giuseppe Rovani, *Cento Anni* (Stabilimento Redaelli dei Fratelli Rechiedei,
    Milan: 1868) p 550
8. What happened to Rosa is not clear. She is never mentioned in any
    correspondence. The only available information about her is from the 1811 and
    1835 censuses and the death registry.
9. In 1812
10. Desmond Gregory, *Napoleon's Italy* (Rosemont Publishing, Massachusetts:
    2001) p 64
11. First permitted in 1778, then forbidden again in 1788, allowed again in 1802
    and finally completely outlawed in 1815. Henri Blaze de Bury Stendhal, *Life of
    Rossini*, trans. Richard N. Coe (French ed. 1823; Calder & Boyars Ltd, London:
    2010) p 506

12. Stendhal, *Life of Rossini*, p 444
13. Stendhal, *Life of Rossini*, p 152
14. Some sources indicate that Barbaja obtained the *appalto* on 24 April 1806, notably Giazotto, *Le Carte della Scala*, p 45
15. Giazotto, *Le Carte della Scala*, p 47
16. Giazotto, *Le Carte della Scala*, p 43
17. Giazotto, *Le Carte della Scala*, p 42
18. Giazotto, *Le Carte della Scala*, p 45
19. Rosselli, *The Opera Industry in Italy*, p 30
20. '*Assassino*' literally translates as murderer or assassin in modern Italian. In the Milanese slang Barbaja spoke, the meaning was more akin to 'crook', 'villain' or 'rogue', and certainly was not meant to denote an actual killer.
21. Giovanni Pacini, *Le mie memorie artistiche* (G G Guidi, Firenze: 1865) p 51
22. He also took over the Viennese Kaerntnertortheater from 1835–48. Rossini, *Lettere e Documenti*, Vol 1, p 279
23. Giazotto, *Le Carte della Scala*, p 47
24. Henri Blaze de Bury Stendhal, *Rome, Naples et Florence* (Delauney Librairie, Paris: 1826) p 161

Chapter 2

1. During the War of the Spanish Succession in 1713, the Spanish ceded the Neapolitan territories to the Austrians, but the Austrians were only able to hold on to the territories for two decades. With the victory of the Spaniards (under the Bourbon Crown) over the Austrians (under the Habsburg Crown) in the Battle of Bitonto of 1734, the Spanish Bourbons once again wrested control of Naples and Sicily away from the Habsburgs.
2. Treaty provisions did not permit Charles to hold all three titles.
3. A total population of 341,047 according to the census of 1807, and 381,664 in 1816 according to the later census: John Mazzinghi, *A Guide to the Antiquities and Curiosities in the City of Naples* (Agnello Nobile, Naples: 1817) p 5
4. Stendhal, *Rome, Naples*, p 245; Commerce, however, was not a major part of city life. Until 1826, the government census did not even have a category for merchants or financiers, these professions were simply labelled 'proprietors'. Financiers, however, were to later take up a significant role in the development of the city.
5. 6 October 1759–23 January 1799; 13 June 1799–30 March 1806; 3 May 1815–8 December 1816
6. 6 October 1759–8 December 1816, and finally as Ferdinand I of the Kingdom of the Two Sicilies from 8 March, 1816 to his death on 4 January 1825.

7. Letter from Emperor Joseph of Austria, quoted in John Santore, *Modern Naples. A Documentary History 1799–1999* (Italica Press, New York: 2001) p 7

8. Stendhal, *Life of Rossini*, p 154

9. Santore, *Modern Naples*, p 19

10. Harold Acton, *The Bourbons of Naples (1734–1825)*. (Prion, London: 1998) p 262

11. Acton, *The Bourbons of Naples*, p 263

12. Santore, *Modern Naples*, p 55. Quotes from: *The Confidential Correspondence of Napoleon Bonaparte and his brother Joseph* (D. Appleton, New York: 1856) Vol I, p 80–81

13. Mariana Starke, *Information and Directions for Travellers on the Continent* (John Murray, London: 1828) p 269

14. Starke, *Information and Directions for Travellers*, p 298

15. Starke, *Information and Directions for Travellers*, p 298

16. The schedule could differ from city to city. The Naples theatres remained closed for 18 days (referred to as a double Novena) each May and September. The ritual, the Novena of San Gennaro, was named after the patron saint of Naples, who was supposed to protect the city from the eruption of Vesuvius. Phials reported to contain the blood of San Gennaro would be on show during the holidays.

17. Stendhal, *Life of Rossini*, p 444

18. Louis Spohr, *Selbstbiographie*, Vol 2 (Georg H. Wigand, Kassel: 1860) p 17

19. This seems to have been a popular description of Italy. Cottrau's editor F Verdinois also refers to Southern Italy as the place 'ou fleurit l'oranger'

20. Spohr, *Selbstbiographie*, Vol 2, p 2

21. Spohr, *Selbstbiographie*, Vol 2, p 35

22. August von Kotzebue, *Erinnerungen von einer Reise aus Liefland nach Rom und Neapel*, Vol 2 (Heinrich Froelich, Berlin: 1805), p 93

23. Kotzebue, *Erinnerungen*, Vol 2, p 130

24. Kotzebue, *Erinnerungen*, Vol 2, p 129

25. Kotzebue, *Erinnerungen*, Vol 2, p 95, 124

Chapter 3

1. Tobia R Toscano 'Il rimpianto del primato perduto. Dalla Rivoluzione del 1799 alla caduta di Murat' in Bruno Cagli and Zino Agostino, *Il Teatro di San Carlo 1737–1987. L'Opera, Il Ballo,* (Electa, Napoli: 1987) p 81

2. Napoleon Bonaparte in Confidential Correspondence 1:95–6, quoted in Santore, *Modern Naples*, p 62

3. von Kotzebue, *Erinnerungen*, Vol 2, p 157

4. As part of his drive for greater efficiency, he ordered the 1806 merger of two conservatories into a single Royal School of Music, which was overseen by a jury consisting of several significant musical professionals, including Giovanni Paisiello, the noted Neapolitan-trained composer.

5. Napoleon Bonaparte in Confidential Correspondence 1:320, quoted in Santore, *Modern Naples*, p 69

6. In later years, Barbaja would put on many other Mozart operas including *Don Giovanni* (1812), *Nozze di Figaro* (1814) and *Cosi fan tutte* (1815) in the Teatro del Fondo. This contradicts the apocryphal story in Emil Lucka's book, which describes Barbaja, upon the suggestion of a friend that he should put on some Mozart operas, immediately offering to invite the composer to Naples. Mozart had died in 1791. Emil Lucka, *Der Impresario* (Donauverlag, Vienna: 1948) p 31

7. Paologiovanni Maione and Francesca Seller, *I reali teatri di Napoli nella prima meta del ottocento. Studii su Domenico Barbaja* (Santabarbara, Bellona: 1994) p 22

8. Domenico Barbaja, *Sull' Oggetto de Giuochi d'Azzardo in seguito del contratto per atto pubblico e solenne de' 19 febbraio 1818. Pro Memoria.* (Tipografia Flautina, Naples: November 1820) p 15

9. Maione and Seller, *I reali teatri di Napoli,* p 27

10. Maione and Seller, *I reali teatri di Napoli,* p 27

11. Paologiovanni Maione and Francesca Seller, *Domenico Barbaja a Napoli (1809–1840). Meccanismi di Gestione Teatrale.* Gioachino Rossini 1792–1992. Il testo e la Scena. Convegno internazionale di studi (A cura di Paolo Fabbri, Pesaro: 1992) p 404

12. Franco Carmelo Greco and Renato Di Benedetto, *Donizetti, Napoli, l'Europa,* (Edizioni Scientifiche Italiane, Napoli: 2000) p 78

13. Rossini, *Lettere e Documenti*, Vol I, p 81

14. Rossini, *Lettere e Documenti*, Vol I, p 81

15. Rossini, *Lettere e Documenti*, Vol I, p 83

16. Exactly when Barbaja obtained control of the Teatro dei Fiorentini is not clear. So far no documentation has been produced. See Rossini, *Lettere e Documenti*, Vol I, p 110

17. Napoleon, who had marched into Russia in June 1812 with his *Grande Armée* consisting of about half a million men, became bogged down in the Russian winter amid logistics breakdowns, leading to a humiliating and demoralising retreat in December of the same year. The defeat destroyed once and for all his reputation for military genius.

18. Gregory, *Napoleon's Italy*, p 104

19. The San Carlo always remained open, with the exception of the period 1816–17, when the theatre burnt down and was subsequently rebuilt, and the years 1874–5 when lack of funds forced a temporary closure.

20. Charles Burney, *The present state of music in France and Italy* (J Robson, London: 1773) p 347

21. Burney, *The present state of music*, p 348

22. Burney, *The present state of music*, p 351

23. Kotzebue, *Erinnerungen*, Vol 2, p 87

24. Sharp, *Letters from Italy*, p 78

25. Sharp, *Letters from Italy*, p 79

26. Sharp, *Letters from Italy*, p 82

27. Kotzebue, *Erinnerungen*, Vol 2, p 138

28. Most of his reports dated from after the fire and reconstruction of 1816/17.

29. Stendhal, *Rome, Naples*, p 254

30. Spohr, *Selbstbiographie*, Vol 2, p 15

31. John Orlando Parry, *Victorian Swansdown: Extract from the Early Travel Diaries of John Orlando Parry, Entertainer* (ed. Cyril Bruin Andrews) (John Murray, London: 1935) p 125

32. In some theatres, though not at the San Carlo, the partitions between the boxes were removed in the top tier and the 'lower classes' – comfortable but not affluent – were admitted.

33. Rosselli, *The Opera Industry in Italy*, p 41

34. Starke, *Information and Directions for Travellers*, p 504

35. Jeremy Commons, 'L'eta di Donizetti' in Cagli and Agostino, *Il Teatro di San Carlo 1737–1987*, p 187

36. Stendhal, *Life of Rossini*, p 191

37. Paologiovanni Maione and Francesca Seller, *Il Palconscenico dei mutamenti: il teatro del Fondo di Napoli 1809–1840* (Lim Editrice, Lucca: 1997) p 106

38. Parry, *Victorian Swansdown*, p 159

39. Parry, *Victorian Swansdown*, p 157

40. Toscano, 'Il rimpianto del primato perduto', in Cagli and Agostino, *Il Teatro di San Carlo*, p 86

41. Toscano, 'Il rimpianto del primato perduto', in Cagli and Agostino, *Il Teatro di San Carlo*, p 100

42. Toscano, 'Il rimpianto del primato perduto', in Cagli and Agostino, *Il Teatro di San Carlo*, p 86

43. See Nicolas Clapton, *Moreschi and the Voice of the Castrato* (Haus Publishing, London: 2008)

44. Burney, *The present state of music*, p 210

45. Burney, *The present state of music*, p 210
46. Stendhal, *Rome, Naples*, p 147

Chapter 4

1. Cagli and Ragni, *Rossini, Lettere e Documenti*, Vol 1, p 44
2. There is no proof that Barbaja actually travelled to Bologna to meet Rossini and discuss his engagement – this might have happened by letter. Yet the impresario Gino Monaldi certainly believed negotiations took place in Bologna, where the impresario came 'on both feet' to beg the young composer to join him in Naples. This certainly makes for a better story: Gino Monaldi, *Impresari Celebri del Secolo XIX* (Licinio Capelli, Rocca S. Cassiano: 1918) p 28
3. Quoted by Bruno Cagli, in Cagli and Agostino, *Il Teatro di San Carlo*, p 140
4. Stendhal, *Life of Rossini*, p 152. Azevedo claims Stendhal exaggerated the amount of money Rossini made from his share of the gambling business – Stendhal claimed it amounted to 30–40 *Louis d'or* a year. Azevedo also asserts that Rossini was paid 2,400 ducats a year as Musical Director in addition to the 1,000 ducats a year which he earnt from his interests in the gambling business; he also claims Colbran had a share in the business: Alexis Jacob Azevedo, *G. Rossini. Sa vie et ses oeuvres* (Heugel, Paris: 1864) p 90. Pougin reinforces Azevedo's claims about Rossini's income. Arthur Pougin, *Rossini: Notes – Impressions – Souvenirs – Commentaires* (A Claudin, Paris: 1871) p 35
5. Rossini, *Lettere e Documenti*, Vol IIIa, p 196
6. Rossini, *Lettere e Documenti*, Vol I, p 366
7. Rossini, *Lettere e Documenti*, Vol I, p 367, footnote #6. 'all said 3000 ducats… corresponding to 5 carats of interest in the theatre and gambling impresa etc' While a carat is the unit of measurement of the alloy of gold (ie pure gold is designated 24 carat), it was also used as a unit of participation in a business, with 24 being the equivalent of 100% ownership. As such, we can deduce that Rossini's share was 5/24, equivalent to 20.8 per cent.
8. Cagli and Agostino, *Il Teatro di San Carlo*, p 148
9. Stendhal quoted in Rossini, *Lettere e Documenti*, Vol 1, p 366
10. As related by Alexandre Dumas (père) in 'How Rossini's opera of Otello was composed' published in *Estafeyette Paris* and translated in *The British Minstrel, and Musical and Literary Miscellany*. Vol 2 (W Hamilton, Glasgow: 1844) p 106
11. Austrian involvement reached its peak in 1816, when Count Nugent of Austria was put in charge of the Neapolitan forces and remained until their withdrawal in 1818.
12. Acton, *The Bourbons of Naples*, p 666. No original source given.

13. The first contract was 7 July 1809; the second was 8 May 1812 and the third was 8 March 1815; all three were during the French *decennio*. This third contract of March 1815 with the Duke of Noja gave Barbaja the concessions for a further three years, up until Palm Sunday 1818. Bruno Cagli, 'Al gran sole di Rossini', in Cagli and Agostino, *Il Teatro di San Carlo*, p 139

14. Baroness du Montet, in Acton, *The Bourbons of Naples*, p 722

15. Maria Carolina did not die a happy woman. She saw power slip from her hands several times and her husband increasingly preferred to spend time hunting rather than with her. The final straw was when the man she blamed for her kingdom's demise, Napoleon, took her granddaughter Maria Louisa as his second wife in 1811.

16. The name 'Two Sicilies' harked back to the Middle Ages, when the Kingdom of Sicily was divided after the War of the Sicilian Vespers of 1285. Prior to that, the Kingdom of Sicily consisted of not only the island of Sicily, but all of the Southern portion of the Italian peninsula, including what today is Campania (with Naples as its capital), Calabria and Apulia. After 1285, the erstwhile King of Sicily only retained control of the peninsular part of his territory, which he continued to call the 'Kingdom of Sicily'. The victors of the war, the Aragonese (hailing from what is today the eastern coast of Spain) also referred to their realm as the 'Kingdom of Sicily'. As such, there were two concurrent kingdoms of Sicily.

17. Rubini was later to become one of the most celebrated tenors of his day.

18. Spohr, *Selbstbiographie*, Vol 2, p 19

19. Azevedo, *G. Rossini. Sa vie et ses œuvres* (Heugel & Cie, Paris: 1864) p 93

20. Florid vocal embellishments

21. Stendhal, *Life of Rossini*, p 168

22. Cagli and Agostino, *Il Teatro di San Carlo*, p 138

23. In a Cantata by Raimondi, *L'Oracolo di Delfo* (The Oracle of Delphi).

24. Colbran is sometimes referred to as a soprano, and sometimes as a mezzo-soprano; a testament to her wide vocal range.

25. Rossini, *Lettere e Documenti*, Vol I, p 202

26. Rossini, *Lettere e Documenti*, Vol I, p 397

27. Azevedo, *G. Rossini. Sa vie et ses oeuvres*, p 95

28. Stendhal, *Life of Rossini*, p 163

29. John Ebers, *Seven Years of the King's Theatre* (William Harrison Ainsworth, London: 1828) p 211

30. Marguerite Blessington, *The Idler in Italy*. Vol 2 (Henry Colbourn, London: 1839) p 85

31. Acton, *The Bourbons of Naples*, p 432

32. Eduard Maria Oettinger, *Rossini. Ein komischer Roman* (Costenoble und Remmelmann, Leipzig: 1851) p 34
33. Stendhal, *Life of Rossini*, p 164
34. Stendhal, *Life of Rossini*, p 157
35. After a few performances of *Elisabetta*, Rossini departed to Rome, where he was commissioned to write *Il Barbiere di Siviglia* (The Barber of Seville) which premiered at the Teatro Argentina in February 1816. Though not a Barbaja opera, it was to become Rossini's most famous, enduring and defining work.
36. Rossini, *Lettere e Documenti*, Vol 1, p 224
37. Monaldi, *Impresari Celebri del Secolo XIX*, p 26
38. Rossini, *Lettere e Documenti*, Vol I, p 283
39. Rossini, *Lettere e Documenti*, Vol I, p 180
40. Manuel García I (1775–1832); not to be confused with his son Manuel García II (1805–1906).
41. He was widely admired not only for his own compositions but also for his work with the celebrated castrato Farinelli as well as later collaborations with Joseph Haydn.
42. Including his daughters Maria Malibran and Pauline Viardot, as well as Adolphe Nourrit and Henriette Meric-Lalande.
43. 'Monsieur, singing is not something that can be taught' (author's translation). Quoted in Lady Morgan's Memoirs, Vol 2 (W H Allen & Co, London: 1863) p 176
44. Dumas (père), *Le Corricolo*, p 39
45. Dumas (père), *Le Corricolo*, p 40
46. Dumas (père), *Le Corricolo*, p 40, also Rossini, *Lettere e Documenti*, Vol 3, p 211
47. Rossini, *Lettere e Documenti*, Vol 1, p 102. García was a prolific composer of operas. Barbaja actually did produce three of his operas, with varying success. The last one, *Jella e Dallaton*, was a dud in spite of the lavish production, and contributed to García's frustration with both Naples and Barbaja.
48. Rossini, *Lettere e Documenti*, Vol 1, p 97
49. Dumas (père), *Le Corricolo*, p 40
50. Lorenzo Bianconi and Giorgio Pestelli, *Opera Production and its Resources* (University of Chicago Press, Chicago: 1998) p 112
51. Quoted in William Ashbrook, *Donizetti and his Operas* (Cambridge University Press, Cambridge: 1982) p 158
52. A Signore Morabito
53. Ashbrook, *Donizetti and his Operas*, p 34
54. Dumas (père), *Le Corricolo*, p 40
55. Stendhal, *Life of Rossini*, p 176

56. Parry, *Victorian Swansdown*, p 202
57. Starke, *Information and Directions for Travellers*, p 503
58. Simona Pollio, 'La Collezione Barbaja. Tesi di Laurea in Museologia e Storia del Collezionismo', MA thesis (Istituto Universitario 'Suor Orsola Benincasa' Napoli, Napoli: 1998/99) p 82
59. Starke, *Information and Directions for Travellers*, p 501
60. Rossini, *Lettere e Documenti*, Vol 1, p 373
61. Emmanuele Bidera, *Passeggiata per Napoli e Contorni* (Aldo Manuzio, Napoli: 1844) p 313
62. Much of the description of the villa and the layout is drawn from Pollio, 'La Collezione Barbaja.'
63. Pollio, 'La Collezione Barbaja', p 86
64. Oettinger, *Rossini.*
65. Parry, *Victorian Swansdown*, p 203
66. Pollio, *Collezione Barbaja*, p 88
67. Parry, *Victorian Swansdown*, p 206
68. Rossini, *Lettere e Documenti*, Vol III, p 57
69. Parry, *Victorian Swansdown*, p 210–12
70. Pollio, *Collezione Barbaja*, p 106
71. Pollio, *Collezione Barbaja*, p 131
72. the father of the architect Luigi Vanvitelli

Chapter 5

1. Stendhal, *Life of Rossini*, p 154
2. Rossini, *Lettere e Documenti*, Vol 1, p 153
3. While there is no direct documentation to support this, it is often reported that Barbaja also acted as financier to the King. See the letter quoted later in the text by John A Davis, *Merchants, Monopolists and Contractors* (Arno Press, USA: 1981) p 273
4. Rosselli, *The Opera Industry in Italy*, p 186
5. Lucka, *Der Impresario*, p 201
6. Rosselli, *The Opera Industry in Italy*, p 10
7. Bianchi went on to become one of the preferred architects of the Neapolitan Bourbons, involved in numerous projects including the throne room in Caserta.
8. Lodovico Bianchini, *Storia delle Finanze del Regno di Napoli*. Vol 7 (Francesco Lao, Palermo: 1839) p 29
9. Stendhal, *Rome, Naples*, p 197

10. While construction of San Francesco di Paola was ongoing, Barbaja was also involved in work on the Chiesa di San Carlo all'Arena, to which he donated a marble altar: see Pollio, *La Collezione Barbaja*, p 51

11. Davis, *Merchants, Monopolists*, p 272

12. Quoted in Hanno-Walter Kruft, *A History of Architectural Theory. From Vitruvius to the Present* (Princeton Architectural Press, Princeton: 2003) p 297

13. Portici is a small port town at the foot of Mount Vesuvius, about 8 kilometres south-east of Naples. It was the site of a Bourbon royal palace.

14. The retailers in the arcades included the famous Swiss pastry store Spiller, Telli & Co. which opened in the palazzo in 1826 and stayed in business – albeit at other addresses and in various permutations – despite the inevitable squabbles among the Caflisch family who owned it, until it finally closed its doors in 1979. The arcades also housed *L'Omnibus*, Naples' leading journal dedicated to the arts.

15. the celebrated poet and 'improvisatore'

16. Sydney Morgan, 1821, quoted in Rossini, *Lettere e Documenti*, Vol 1, p 28

17. Rossini, *Lettere e Documenti*, Vol 3a, p 296, 363

18. Francesco Mastriani, *I Misteri di Napoli* (G Nobile, Napoli: 1870) p 53

19. Oettinger, *Rossini*. p 21

20. Rossini, *Lettere e Documenti*, Vol 1, p 184

21. As related by Dumas (père) in 'How Rossini's opera of Otello was composed' The British Minstrel, and Musical and Literary Miscellany. Vol 2, p 106

22. Rossini, *Lettere e Documenti*, Vol 1, p 184

23. Stendhal, *Life of Rossini*, p 226

24. Quoted in Richard Osborne, *Rossini. His Life and Works*. (Oxford University Press, Oxford: 2007) p 46

25. Stendhal, *Rome, Naples*, p 199

26. Azevedo, *G. Rossini*, p 129

27. Stendhal, *Rome, Naples*, p 198

28. Rossini, *Lettere e Documenti*, Vol 3a, p 153

29. Stendhal, *Rome, Naples*, p 178

30. Rossini, *Lettere e Documenti*, Vol 3, p 581

31. *Allgemeine Musikalische Zeitung*, 1830, Vol 32, p 76

32. Rossini, *Lettere e Documenti*, Vol 1, p 61

33. F J Fetis, Revue Musicale, Sautelet & Cie. Paris, 1828, Vol 2, p 521

34. Rossini, *Lettere e Documenti*, Vol 1, page 140

35. Rossini, *Lettere e Documenti*, Vol 1, page 140

36. Cottrau, *Lettres d'un Melomane*, p vii

37. Spohr, *Selbstbiographie* Vol 1, p 346

38. Rossini, *Lettere e Documenti*, Vol I, p 184

39. Mancini and Ragni, *Donizetti e i teatri napolitani*, p 163

40. Stendhal, *Rome, Naples*, p 242

41. Giazotto, *Le Carte della Scala*, p 95

42. Mazzinghi, *A Guide to the Antiquities*, p 15

43. Parry, *Victorian Swansdown*, p 153

44. Mazzinghi, *A Guide to the Antiquities*, p 15–17

45. Bianchini, *Storia delle Finanze del Regno di Napoli*. Vol 7, p 672

46. Mancini and Ragni, *Donizetti e i teatri napolitani*, p 163

47. The visit took place in February 1817: Stendhal, *Rome, Naples*, p 170

48. Stendhal, *Rome, Naples*, p 174

49. *Allgemeine Musikalische Zeitung* Vol 19, 12 March 1817, p 196

50. Ragni, Sergio, *Rossini a Napoli. La Conquista di un Capitale* (Ente Autonomo Teatro di San Carlo, Napoli: 1991) p 23

51. Rossini, *Lettere e Documenti*, Vol I, page 152

52. Sergio Ragni, *Rossini a Napoli. La Conquista di un Capitale* (Ente Autonomo Teatro di San Carlo, Napoli: 1991) p 23

53. Spohr, *Selbstbiographie*, Vol 2, p 13

54. Stendhal, *Rome, Naples*, p 174

55. Spohr, *Selbstbiographie*, Vol 2, p 9

56. *Allgemeine Musikalische Zeitung* Vol 19, 12 March 1817, p 195

57. 11 March 1817

58. Spohr, *Selbstbiographie*, Vol 2, p 22

59. Spohr, *Selbstbiographie*, Vol 2, p 22

60. Spohr, *Selbstbiographie*, Vol 2, p 25

61. Spohr, quoted in Henry Pleasants, *The Great Singers. From the dawn of Opera to Caruso, Callas and Pavarotti* (Simon & Shuster, New York: 1981) p 117

62. Spohr, *Selbstbiographie*, Vol 2, p 31

63. Osborne, *Rossini*, p 257

64. Azevedo, *G. Rossini*. p 141

65. Stendhal, *Life of Rossini*, p 172

66. Ischia would be only one of many of Rossini's regular spa destinations. He later went to Montecatini, Bad Wildbad, Bad Kissingen and Baden-Baden.

67. Rossini, *Lettere e Documenti*, Vol 3a, p 181

68. Rossini, *Lettere e Documenti*, Vol 3a, p 185

69. Stendhal, *Life of Rossini*, p 131

70. Osborne, *Rossini*, p 256

71. This fact was noted by the musicologist Philip Gossett

72. Stendhal, *Life of Rossini*, p 154

73. Dumas (père), *Le Corricolo,* p 39
74. Bruno Cagli, 'Al gran sole di Rossini', in Cagli and Agostino, *Il Teatro di San Carlo,* p 153
75. Stendhal, quoted in Santore, *Modern Naples,* p 87
76. Bruno Cagli, 'Al gran sole di Rossini', in Cagli and Agostino, *Il Teatro di San Carlo,* p 152
77. The doctor's complaint refers to a later version of the opera which was rewritten for the 1819 Lent season. Stendhal, *Life of Rossini,* p 16
78. Bruno Cagli, 'Al gran sole di Rossini', in Cagli and Agostino, *Il Teatro di San Carlo,* p 153
79. Philip Gossett: 'Rossini's Spanish Muse', Liner Notes to CD, Joyce di Donato, *Colbran, the Muse.* 2009, p 7
80. *Allgemeine Musikalische Zeitung,* Vol 21, 10 February 1819, p 83
81. Rossini, *Lettere e Documenti,* Vol 1, page 165. The wedding was in April 1816; this Cantata was *Le Nozze di Teti e di Peleo*
82. Ragni, *Rossini a Napoli,* p 50
83. *Allgemeine Musikalische Zeitung,* Vol 21, 10 November, 1819, p 758
84. Today, Spontini's music would be all but forgotten were it not for the attention that Maria Callas lavished on it.
85. Rossini, *Lettere e Documenti,* Vol 1, p 386
86. Musicologists including Reto Mueller indicate that this might also have been Rossini's attempt to re-introduce a contralto in a leading role, a practice that was frowned on by the French.
87. Stendhal, *Life of Rossini,* p 387
88. The vocal technique of bridging the interval between two notes so that there is no break, often with gentle anticipation of the second note.
89. Stendhal, *Life of Rossini,* p 388
90. Notably Azevedo, *G. Rossini,* p 153 and Stendhal, *Life of Rossini,* p 387
91. Azevedo, *G. Rossini. Sa vie et ses oeuvres,* p 153
92. Stendhal, *Life of Rossini,* p 423
93. G I C de Courcy, *Paganini. The Genoese,* Vol 1 (University of Oklahoma Press, Oklahoma: 1957) p 175
94. Jacques Gabriel Prod'homme, *Niccolo Paganini, A Biography* (Carl Fischer, New York: 1911) p 192
95. Prod'homme, *Paganini,* p 192
96. Heinrich Heine, *Florentine Nights,* trans. Charles Godfrey Leland and Hans Breitmann (Mondial, New York: 2008) p 24

Chapter 6

1. Gilbert Duprez, *Souvenirs d'un Chanteur* (Calmann Levi, Paris: 1880) p 113
2. *Allgemeine Musikalische Zeitung*, Vol 39, 7 June 1837, p 372. The singer in question was a Sigra Favelli. The King's mother was Maria Isabella of Spain.
3. Dumas (père), *Le Corricolo*, p 40
4. Jeremy Commons, 'L'eta di Donizetti' in Cagli and Agostino, *Il Teatro di San Carlo*, p 220
5. Duprez, *Souvenirs d'un Chanteur*, p 117
6. Jacques Marquet de Norvins, *Italie pittoresque* (Alphonse Pigoreau, Paris: 1850) p 77
7. Norvins, *Italie pittoresque*, p 77
8. H Sutherland Edwards, in *The Lute*, 1 June 1884, p 126
9. *Allgemeine Musikalische Zeitung*, Vol 39, 7 June 1837, p 372
10. Rossini, *Lettere e Documenti*, Vol 1, p 421
11. Rossini, *Lettere e Documenti*, Vol 1, p 372
12. This piece of music was described by Philip Gossett, who dated it between the summer of 1819 (when Carolina married) and the spring of 1822, when Rossini left Naples for Vienna. It might also have been written as a farewell to Barbaja's daughter, according to Gossett.
13. As suggested by Philip Gossett, who discovered the piece.
14. Rossini, *Lettere e Documenti*, Vol 1, p 373
15. Rossini, *Lettere e Documenti*, Vol 3a, p 277
16. Osborne, *Rossini*, p 70
17. Herbert Weinstock, *Rossini. A Biography* (Alfred A Knopf, New York: 1975) Appendix B. Doctor's Report from 1842
18. Weinstock, *Rossini*, Appendix B. Doctor's Report from 1842
19. Lucia Valenzi, *Donne, Medici e Poliziotti a Napoli nell'Ottocento. La prostituzione tra repressione e tolleranza* (Liguori, Napoli: 2000) p 12
20. Santore, *Modern Naples*, p 115
21. Bruno Cagli, 'Al gran sole di Rossini', in Cagli and Agostino, *Il Teatro di San Carlo*, p 156
22. Maione and Seller, *Domenico Barbaja a Napoli*, p 405
23. Domenico Barbaja, '*Sull' Oggetto de Giuochi d'Azzardo in seguito del contratto per atto pubblico e solenne de' 19 febbraio 1818. Pro Memoria*' (Tipografia Flautina, Napoli: 1820)
24. The aborted contract for Barbaja to build the Government offices of the Secretariat of State, referred to as 'Fabbriche di San Giacomo'.
25. Barbaja, '*Sull' Oggetto de Giuochi d'Azzardo in seguito del contratto per atto pubblico e solenne de' 19 febbraio 1818. Pro Memoria*', p 12

26. Signed in February 1818, though did not take effect till Easter that year.
27. Barbaja, *'Sull' Oggetto de Giuochi d'Azzardo in seguito del contratto per atto pubblico e solenne de' 19 febbraio 1818. Pro Memoria'*, p 12
28. Maione and Seller, *Domenico Barbaja a Napoli*, p 411
29. Rossini also asked his father to send 6 mortadelle and 12 salamis to Barbaja's address. Rossini, *Lettere e Documenti*, Vol 3a, p 296
30. Azevedo, *G. Rossini*, p 160
31. *Allgemeine Musikalische Zeitung*, Vol 23, 10 January 1821, p 28
32. Azevedo, *G. Rossini*, p 90
33. Rossini, *Lettere e Documenti*, Vol 3a, p 267
34. *La Presse*, Paris, 25 October 1838. Three million French francs were equivalent to £119,000 which in today's money would be worth somewhere between £7.4m to well over £100m depending on which economic measure is applied, see www.eh.net.
35. Pollio, *La Collezione Barbaja*, p 121
36. Metternich, quoted in Santore, *Modern Naples*, p 117
37. Count Egon Caesar Corti, *The Rise of the House of Rothschild* (Cosmopolitan, USA: 1928) p 242
38. Today's Ljubljana, the capital of Slovenia; this was an integral part of the Habsburg Austrian empire in the 19th century.
39. Francesco Florimo, *Cenno Storico sulla Scuola Musicale di Napoli*, (Lorenzo Rocco, Napoli: 1869) p 2076
40. Santore, *Modern Naples*, p 123
41. Davis, *Merchants, Monopolists*, p 18
42. This meant, of course, that many banking families had taken a hit during the French *decennio*, unless they had been able to adapt quickly to the new regime. In turn, most of those financiers who supported the French monarchy were punished for their misplaced loyalty once the Bourbons returned to power following the restoration of 1815.
43. Starke, *Information and Directions for Travellers*, p 501
44. Corti, *The Rise of the House of Rothschild*, p 244
45. Corti, *The Rise of the House of Rothschild*, p 246
46. Marc Flandreau and Juan H Flores, *Bonds and Brands: Foundations of Sovereign Debt Markets, 1820–1830*). The Journal of Economic History, Cambridge. 2009. Vol 69, p 646–684. Abstract p 6
47. Rossini, *Lettere e Documenti*, Vol 1, p 482
48. Rossini, *Lettere e Documenti*, Vol 1, p 482
49. Quoted in Acton, *The Bourbons of Naples*, p 711

50. Prince Richard Metternich (ed), *Metternich: Memoirs of Prince Metternich*. Vol 3. Translated by Mrs Alexander Napier (Richard Bentley, London: 1881) p 516
51. Then, just as today, sovereigns would access the capital markets in order to raise funds. Bonds were the most commonly used financial instrument for this purpose and they were issued on behalf of a borrowing sovereign by leading merchant banks (such as Rothschild or Barings) with a pre-determined duration (e.g. 10 years), as well as a coupon (the yearly payment the bond would provide its investors, expressed as a percentage) and at a determined issue price. The relationship between the issue price and the coupon percentage defines the actual yield of the bond to the investor when the bond is first launched in the capital markets. If the issue price is low (for instance 83) on a 6 per cent coupon bond, the actual yield to investors is 7.14 per cent. This makes the issue more attractive to investors (who enjoy the benefits of a 'run-up' when the bond trades up from say 83 to 90 between its issue and its first day of trading), but less attractive to the issuer who needs the funds and must make the coupon payment. The large discount (in our example 83, rather than, say, 90) represents money left on the table by issuers. As such, quality bond issuers seek to attain as high an issue price as possible, and as low of a coupon payment they can get away with.
52. Corti, *The Rise of the House of Rothschild*, p 245
53. Flandreau and Flores, *Bonds and Brands*, p 19
54. Stendhal, *Life of Rossini*, p 155
55. Stendhal, *Life of Rossini*, p 452 Stendhal further wrote: '...to utter rude thoughts about La Colbran is to speak sedition against the King.'
56. In 1820
57. Stendhal, *Life of Rossini*, p 171. Sergio Ragni points out that Stendhal's extreme views of Colbran might have been motivated by the writer's friendship with the singer Giuditta Pasta. Also, Ragni's research reveals that it was unlikely that Stendhal actually witnessed all the described Colbran performances, nor that he met Rossini on all the dates he suggests in his writing. See Sergio Ragni, *Isabella Colbran, Isabella Rossini* (Zecchini, Varese: 2012) pp 145, 146
58. Rossini, *Lettere e Documenti*, Vol 1, p 476
59. Monaldi, *Impresari Celebri del Secolo XIX*, p 28
60. Rossini, *Lettere e Documenti*, Vol 1, p 521
61. Bruno Cagli, 'Al gran sole di Rossini', in Cagli and Agostino, *Il Teatro di San Carlo*, p 159
62. Sometimes referred to as Giambanini
63. Rossini, *Lettere e Documenti*, Vol 1, p 524
64. Rossini, *Lettere e Documenti*, Vol 3a, p 299

65. Giazotto, *Le Carte della Scala*, p 66
66. Handwritten Memorandum from the Office of the Director of Theatres and Public Performances in Milan. '1805.1807. Per un nuovo appalto'. 1805. Collezione Biblioteca Trivulziana. Archivio Storico Civico, Milan
67. Giazotto, *Le Carte della Scala*, p 64
68. Rossini, *Lettere e Documenti*, Vol 1, p 531
69. Giazotto, *Le Carte della Scala*, p 70
70. Giazotto, *Le Carte della Scala*, p 68. Barbaja requested an endowment of 250,000 lire. The winning bidder had requested only 216,000 lire.
71. 30 November 1821: *Rossini, Lettere e Documenti*, Vol 3a, p 302
72. on 27 December 1821. Ragni, *Rossini a Napoli*, p 67
73. Rossini later adapted *Riconoscenza,* his Naples farewell concert, for multiple uses, including as an homage to Austrian Emperor Franz I at the Congress of Verona, and in memory of the famed sculptor Antonio Canova.
74. the Duchess of Lucca
75. Osborne, *Rossini*, p 297
76. Rossini, *Lettere e Documenti*, Vol 1, p 264
77. Monaldi, *Impresari Celebri del Secolo XIX* , p 32
78. de Courcy, *Paganini*, Vol I, p 212
79. Stendhal, *Life of Rossini*, p 153
80. Servadio, *Rossini*, p 50
81. James Anderson, *Bloomsbury Dictionary of Opera and Operetta* (Bloomsbury, London: 1989) p 120
82. Bruno Cagli, 'Al gran sole di Rossini', in Cagli and Agostino, *Il Teatro di San Carlo,* p 161
83. Bruno Cagli, 'Al gran sole di Rossini', in Cagli and Agostino, *Il Teatro di San Carlo,* p 162

Chapter 7

1. *Allgemeine Musikalische Zeitung*, Vol 23, 26 September, 1821, p 668
2. Alice M Hanson, *Musical Life in Biedermeier Vienna* (Cambridge University Press, Cambridge: 1985) p 9
3. The ancient French term for suburb.
4. Starke, *Information and Directions for Travellers,* p 422
5. Hanson, *Musical Life in Biedermeier Vienna*, p 35
6. This is well before the Hotel Sacher (home of the famous Sachertorte) was built on the site of the Kaerntnertortheater.
7. Hanson, *Musical Life in Biedermeier Vienna*, p 15

8. Wilhelm Hebenstreit, *Der Fremde in Wien, und der Wiener in der Heimath: möglichst vollstaendiges Auskunftsbuch fuer den Reisenden nach Wien* (Carl Armbruster, Wien: 1840) p 26

9. Rossini, *Lettere e Documenti*, Vol 1, p 531

10. *Allgemeine Musikalische Zeitung*, Vol 24, 2 January 1822, p 15

11. Quoted in Corti, *The Rise of the House of Rothschild*, p 264. The Rothschild guarantee lasted for two years, until the first break clause in the contract.

12. Hanson, *Musical Life in Biedermeier Vienna*, p 63

13. Helmina von Chézy, *Unvergessenes, Denkwuerdigkeiten aus dem Leben von Helmina von Chézy. Von ihr selbst erzaehlt*, Vol 2 (Brockhaus, Leipzig: 1858) p 256

14. From 1 December 1821 to the end of November 1833. The long-dated contract had various break clauses: Rossini, *Lettere e Documenti*, Vol I, p 521 and Vol IIIa, p 316

15. This may sound familiar to residents of France, where the government imposes the airing of a minimum of one French for every three international songs on the radio and music television.

16. Michael Jahn, *Die Wiener Hofoper von 1836 bis 1848: Die Aera Balochino/Merelli* (Der Apfel, Wien: 2004) p 13

17. Maione and Seller, *Da Napoli a Vienna*, p 496

18. W E Yates, *Theatre in Vienna. A critical history. 1776–1995* (Cambridge University Press, Cambridge: 1996) p 98

19. from 1821 to 1828, with only one short interruption. From April 1825 to March 1826, the Kaerntnertortheater was run by an impresario called Hensler: *Allgemeine Musikalische Zeitung*, Vol 27, May 1825, pp 344, 349, and Jahn, *Die Wiener Hofoper von 1836 bis 1848*, p 13

20. Hanson, *Musical Life in Biedermeier Vienna*, p 25

21. Jahn, *Die Wiener Hofoper von 1836 bis 1848*, p 14

22. *Allgemeine Musikalische Zeitung*, Vol 26, 23 December 1824, p 857

23. Chézy, *Unvergessenes*, Vol 2, p 255

24. *Allgemeine Musikalische Zeitung*, Vol 24, 2 January 1822, p 15 and Hanson, *Musical Life in Biedermeier Vienna*, p 65

25. Hanson, *Musical Life in Biedermeier Vienna*, p 89

26. *Allgemeine Musikalische Zeitung*, Vol 24, 7 August 1822, p 527

27. According to historian Harold Acton: '…at a performance of *The Barber of Seville* he shouted, 'Bravo, lazzarone, bravo!' in his enthusiasm for Lablache. … The actor was delighted by the King's exclamations, which he had heard perfectly. Acton, *The Bourbons of Naples*, p 722

28. Maione and Seller, *Domenico Barbaja a Napoli*, p 417

29. Rossini, *Lettere e Documenti*, Vol 1, p 575

30. Rossini, *Lettere e Documenti*, Vol 1, p 583

31. From 1816–1822 at least 16 Rossini operas had been performed in Vienna. Rossini, *Lettere e Documenti*, Vol 3a, p 334

32. Anita Silvestrelli, *Franz Schubert* (Anton Pustet. Leipzig: 1939), p 162

33. Rossini, *Lettere e Documenti*, Vol 3a, p 331

34. Rossini, *Lettere e Documenti*, Vol 3a, p 345

35. Silvestrelli, *Franz Schubert*, p 162

36. *Allgemeine Musikalische Zeitung*, quoted in Rossini, *Lettere e Documenti*, Vol 3a, p 345

37. Metternich wrote in April 1822. Metternich, *Memoirs of Prince Metternich,* p 575

38. Metternich, *Memoirs of Prince Metternich,* p 576

39. Metternich, *Memoirs of Prince Metternich,* p 576

40. Metternich, *Memoirs of Prince Metternich,* p 587

41. Schinkel (1781–1841) worked in the German Neoclassical and later Neo-Gothic architectural styles and had a huge impression on Berlin's city landscape. His impact is still visible in today's Berlin.

42. Author's translation from Attila Csampai und Dietmar Holland (ed), *Carl Maria von Weber: Der Freischuetz. Texte, Materialien, Kommentare* (Reinbeck, Hamburg: 1981). Quoted in Thomas Baumann and Marita Petzoldt McClymonds, *Opera and the Enlightenment* (Cambridge University Press, Cambridge: 1995) p 84

43. Gebhard von Bluecher (1742–1819) was a Prussian field marshal known as 'Marschall Vorwaerts', or 'Marshal Forward' for his aggressive and direct military tactics. He fought Napoleon at Leipzig and Wellington at Waterloo.

44. Baron Max Maria von Weber (Freiherr), *Carl Maria von Weber. Life of an Artist.* Translation by J Palgrave Simpson (Chapman and Hall, London: 1865) p 225

45. Weber (Freiherr), *Carl Maria von Weber,* p 312

46. Weber (Freiherr), *Carl Maria von Weber,* p 247

47. Weber's *Der Freischuetz*, like Beethoven's only opera *Fidelio*, is strictly speaking a 'Singspiel', a structure which includes many, often long, pieces of spoken dialogue leading into the musical numbers.

48. Weber (Freiherr), *Carl Maria von Weber,* p 274

49. Weber (Freiherr), *Carl Maria von Weber,* p 267

50. Weber (Freiherr), *Carl Maria von Weber,* p 338

51. Weber (Freiherr), *Carl Maria von Weber,* p 339

52. Francis Rogers, *Some Famous Singers of the 19th century* (H W Gray, New York: 1914) p 74

53. Silvestrelli, *Franz Schubert*, p 161

54. Hanson, *Musical Life in Biedermeier Vienna*, p 66
55. Dumas (père), *Le Corricolo*, p 39
56. Carlovy Vary in today's Czech Republic – and still a spa. *Allgemeine Musikalische Zeitung* Vol 25, 30 July 1823, p 504
57. Maione and Seller, *Da Napoli a Vienna*, p 498
58. Ticket prices were one of the three main sources of income for the impresario; increases to ticket prices faced a lot of resistance, and an offer to raise prices was a major concession by a theatre proprietor.
59. Rossini, *Lettere e Documenti*, Vol 2, p 148
60. Rossini, *Lettere e Documenti*, Vol 2, p 169
61. Ignaz Freiherr von Poeck, *Darstellung des Zustandes der Oper und des Balletes im k.k. Hoftheater naechst dem Kaerntnerthore waehrend der Pachtung des Herrn Domenico Barbaja* (Wallishauser, Wien: 1825) p 46
62. Poeck, *Darstellung des Zustandes der Oper,* p 48
63. *Allgemeine Musikalische Zeitung* Vol 25, 30 July, 1823, p 504
64. Rossini, *Lettere e Documenti*, Vol 2, p 197
65. Rossini, *Lettere e Documenti*, Vol 1, p 413

Chapter 8

1. Franco Mancini (ed), *Il Teatro di San Carlo 1737–1987. La Storia, La Struttura* (Electa Napoli, Napoli: 1987) p 15
2. Mancini, 'La scenografia sancarliana all'epoca di Donizetti', in Franco Mancini and Sergio Ragni, *Donizetti e i teatri napoletani* (Elekta Napoli, Napoli: 1997) p 89
3. Mancini, 'La scenografia sancarliana all'epoca di Donizetti', in Mancini and Ragni, *Donizetti e i teatri napoletani*, p 99
4. on 10 April of 1824
5. *Allgemeine Musikalische Zeitung*, Vol 26, 5 August 1824, p 520
6. Dumas (père), *Le Corricolo,* p 39
7. Rossini, *Lettere e Documenti*, Vol 2, p 148
8. Glossop's grandson, Sir Augustus Henry Glossop Harris (1852–96), continued in his ancestor's footsteps and ran the Drury Lane Theatre in the 1880s with much greater success.
9. Giazotto, *Le Carte della Scala,* p 71
10. George Rowell, *The Old Vic Theatre. A History* (Cambridge University Press, Cambridge: 1993), p 14
11. Her English name was Elizabeth Fearon.
12. Quoted in Maione and Seller, *Domenico Barbaja a Napoli,* p 405
13. *Allgemeine Musikalische Zeitung*, Vol 26, 18 March 1824, p 187

14. Elisabetta Ferron was the first wife of Joseph Glossop, though there are questions about the legitimacy of the marriage. By this time, Glossop was probably already married to Josephine Bonneau de Meric.

15. Mercadante was acting as Music Director and putting on a season of Italian opera; one of the operas was supposed to be Donizetti's *Emilia di Liverpool*, through there is no record that it was ever performed. See Ashbrook, *Donizetti and his Operas*, p 32

16. While there is no record of Beethoven's initial letter and we cannot be sure of the full nature of the discussion, the tone of the reply indicates that it was Beethoven who reached out to Barbaja (and Duport), rather than the other way around.

17. Theodore Albrecht, *Letter to Beethoven,* Vol 3 (University of Nebraska Press, Nebraska: 1996) p 26

18. *Allgemeine Musikalische Zeitung*, Vol 26, 5 August 1824, p 527

19. *Allgemeine Musikalische Zeitung*, Vol 26, 30 September 1824, p 652

20. *Allgemeine Musikalische Zeitung*, Vol 26, 25 November 1824, p 783

21. Ashbrook, *Donizetti and his Operas,* p 33

22. Maione and Seller, *Domenico Barbaja a Napoli,* p 415

23. Mancini, *Il Teatro di San Carlo 1737–1987,* p 15

24. Maione and Seller, *Domenico Barbaja a Napoli,* p 415

25. Commons, *Il Carteggio Personale di Nicola Vaccai,* p 549

26. *Allgemeine Musikalische Zeitung*, Vol 26, 23 December 1824, p 852

27. *Allgemeine Musikalische Zeitung*, Vol 26, 23 December 1824, p 858

28. *Allgemeine Musikalische Zeitung*, Vol 27, 19 January 1825, p 46

29. *Allgemeine Musikalische Zeitung*, Vol 27, 19 January 1825, p 47

30. 1826–29

31. B Cassinelli, A Maltempi and M Pozzoni, *Rubini. L'uomo e l'artista.* Vol 2 (Cassa Rurale ed Artigiana di Calcio e di Covo. Commune di Romano di Lombardia: 1993) p 491

32. *Allgemeine Musikalische Zeitung*, Vol 27, 6 April 1825, p 233

33. *Allgemeine Musikalische Zeitung*, Vol 32, 12 May 1830, p 300. Benedict left Naples for Paris in 1834, later emigrating to the United Kingdom in 1838. He became Musical Director of the Drury Lane theatre and was knighted in 1871.

34. *Allgemeine Musikalische Zeitung*, Vol 27, 25 May 1825, p 350

35. *The Times*, London, 4 March 1858

36. Spohr, *Selbstbiographie*, Vol 1, p 276

37. Stendhal, *Life of Rossini,* p 450

38. Stendhal, *Life of Rossini,* p 450

39. Giazotto, *Le Carte della Scala,* p 84

40. Giazotto, *Le Carte della Scala*, p 83
41. Giazotto, *Le Carte della Scala*, p 84
42. Stendhal, as reported in Rosselli, *The Opera Industry in Italy*, p 189
43. Giazotto, *Le Carte della Scala*, p 48
44. from 1 July, 1824 to 20 March 1830
45. Giazotto, *Le Carte della Scala*, p 71
46. *Allgemeine Musikalische Zeitung*, Vol 28, 7 June 1826, p 383
47. Letter from August 1825: Giazotto, *Le Carte della Scala*, p 75
48. Giazotto, *Le Carte della Scala*, p 74
49. Giazotto, *Le Carte della Scala*, p 77
50. In February 1826, G B Villa wrote on behalf of Barbaja to the prominent German composer Giacomo Meyerbeer, discussing the opera which they had commissioned for April, which Meyerbeer was now unable to deliver until September due to other engagements. Given the repeated delays and the impresario's need to plan an orderly schedule, Barbaja offered to cancel the contract without any damages or consequences in an attempt to remain on good terms with the German composer. Asking only for a reimbursement of 800 lire that Barbaja had advanced to the librettist Rossi, Barbaja and Valle released Meyerbeer from any obligations. While Barbaja and Meyerbeer remained in touch and several Meyerbeer operas were performed at the San Carlo and Scala during his *imprese*, Barbaja did not launch any of his works.
51. Commons, *Il Carteggio*, p 280
52. Giazotto, *Le Carte della Scala*, p 77
53. The changes demanded included higher subventions and power of veto over the schedule and programme. Letter from Barbaja to Francis I, 18 June 1827, Collezione Biblioteca Trivulziana. Archivio Storico Civico, Milan.
54. *Harmonicon*, December 1826, p 249
55. Monaldi, *Impresari Celebri del Secolo XIX*, p 56
56. Unlike Barbaja, Lanari's life is well documented. Florence has a collection of over 15,000 letters and documents from the impresario.
57. Marcello de Angelis, *Le Carte dell'Impresario. Melodramma e costume teatrale nell'Ottocento* (Sansoni Editore, Firenze: 1982) p 72
58. Angelis, *Le Carte dell'Impresario*, p 15
59. Angelis, *Le Carte dell'Impresario*, p 9
60. Duprez, *Souvenirs d'un Chanteur*, p 85
61. Toelle, *Oper als Geschaeft*, p 64
62. Rossini, *Lettere e Documenti*, Vol 2, p 154
63. Rossini, *Lettere e Documenti*, Vol 2, p 154
64. *Harmonicon*, Vol 4–5, December 1826, pp 195, 250

65. Rossini, *Lettere e Documenti*, Vol 1, p 92

66. Quoted in Ashbrook, *Donizetti and his Operas*, p 30

67. The performance was of Pacini's *Cesare in Egitto*

68. Pacini, *Le mie memorie*, p 34

69. Rossini, *Lettere e Documenti*, Vol 2, p 514

70. Rossini, *Lettere e Documenti*, Vol 2, p 330

71. Rossini, *Lettere e Documenti*, Vol 2, p 357

72. Rossini, *Lettere e Documenti*, Vol 2, p 466 and 482

73. Rossini, *Lettere e Documenti*, Vol 2, p 514

74. Rossini, *Lettere e Documenti*, Vol 2, p 556

75. Greco and Di Benedetto, *Donizetti, Napoli, l'Europa*, p 166

76. Mancini and Ragni, *Donizetti e i teatri napoletani*, p 208

77. Rossini, *Lettere e Documenti*, Vol 3a, p 399

78. Rossini, *Lettere e Documenti*, Vol 2, p 378

79. Rossini, *Lettere e Documenti*, Vol 2, p 389

80. Rossini, *Lettere e Documenti*, Vol 2, p 389

81. in May 1826

82. Rossini, *Lettere e Documenti*, Vol 2, p 523

83. Rossini, *Lettere e Documenti*, Vol 3a, p 399

84. Rossini, *Lettere e Documenti*, Vol 3, p 318

85. Rossini, *Lettere e Documenti*,. Vol 3, p 143

86. Rossini, *Lettere e Documenti*, Vol 3, p 158

87. *Revue Musicale*, Vol 2 (Sautelet & Cie, Paris: 1828), p 64

88. Rossini, *Lettere e Documenti*, Vol 3, p 161

89. Rossini, *Lettere e Documenti*, Vol 3, p 200

90. *Le Figaro*, No 56, 27 March 1827, p 220

91. *Le Figaro*, No 56, 27 March 1827, p 200

92. *Le Figaro*, No 56, 27 March 1827, p 278

93. *Le Figaro*, No 56, 27 March 1827, p 279

94. Rossini, *Lettere e Documenti*, Vol 3, p 279

95. The writer of the letter signed it '"The Hermit of the Apennines" G D F Yoke. 27 June 1827'. We have no record of the real identity of the writer. *Allgemeine Musikalische Zeitung*, Vol 29, 19 December 1827; p 868. Author's translation.

96. *Allgemeine Musikalische Zeitung*, Vol 29, 19 December 1827, p 869. Author's translation.

97. *Harmonicon*, Vol 4–5, November 1826, p 235

98. Ebers, *Seven Years of the King's Theatre*, p 311

99. Rossini, *Lettere e Documenti*, Vol 2, p 621

100. *Morgenblatt fuer gebildete Staende.* 22 March 1826. This publication and story were brought to my attention by Reto Mueller

Chapter 9

1. Pacini, *Le mie memorie,* p 51
2. *Allgemeine Musikalische Zeitung,* Vol 28, 7 June 1826, p 380
3. Herbert Weinstock, *Vincenzo Bellini. His Life and his Operas* (Alfred A Knopf, New York: 1980) p 33
4. Pacini, *Le mie memorie,* p 50
5. Rossini, *Lettere e Documenti,* Vol 1, p 373
6. Pacini, *Le mie memorie,* p 52
7. Ashbrook, *Donizetti and his Operas,* p 25
8. Guido Zavadini, *Donizetti: Vita – Musiche- Epistolario* (Istituto Italiano d'Arti Grafiche, Bergamo: 1948) p 232
9. Quoted in Ashbrook, *Donizetti,* p 30
10. *Harmonicon,* Vol 4–5, 1827, p 235
11. Ashbrook, *Donizetti,* p 46
12. Zavadini, *Donizetti,* p 262. This meant that he replaced Pacini in this role, who had asked for a leave of absence
13. Quoted in Ashbrook, *Donizetti,* p 46
14. Zavadini, *Donizetti,* p 279
15. One of the former four conservatories in Naples; this was later merged into San Pietro a Majella, the former convent turned conservatory
16. Francesco Florimo, *Bellini. Memorie e Lettere* (G Barbera, Firenze: 1882) p 7
17. Florimo quoted in Weinstock, *Bellini. His Life and Operas,* p 35
18. *Pirata, Puritani* and *Sonnambula*
19. Florimo, *Bellini,* p 103
20. Florimo, *Bellini,* p 15
21. Florimo, *Bellini,* p 297
22. The libretto was for *Beatrice di Tenda* which became Bellini's only real flop
23. *Allgemeine Musikalische Zeitung* Vol 29, 19 December 1827, p 872
24. Weinstock, *Bellini. His Life and Operas,* p 40
25. Filippo Cicconetti, *Vita di Vincenzo Bellini* (Alberghetti, Prato: 1859) p 15
26. John Rosselli, *The Life of Bellini* (Cambridge University Press, Cambridge: 1996) p 63
27. Florimo, *Bellini,* p 341
28. Florimo, *Bellini,* p 344
29. Florimo, *Bellini,* p 344
30. Rosselli, *The Life of Bellini,* p 78

31. Florimo, *Bellini*, p 346
32. Philip Gossett, *Divas and Scholars: Performing Italian Opera* (University of Chicago Press, Chicago: 2006) p 359
33. Weinstock, *Bellini. His Life and Operas*, p 51
34. Weinstock, *Bellini. His Life and Operas*, p 472
35. Florimo, *Bellini*, p 341
36. 'porcheria incredibile': Florimo, *Bellini*, p 348
37. Florimo, *Bellini*, p 347
38. Florimo, *Bellini*, p 350
39. Rosselli, *Life of Bellini*, p 64
40. Florimo, *Bellini*, p 350
41. Florimo, *Bellini*, p 350
42. Florimo, *Bellini*, p 19
43. It appears Pacini's *Cavalieri* turned out to be nothing like the fiasco that Bellini describes. It ultimately had a very successful run at La Scala. See Weinstock, *Bellini. His Life and Operas*, p 54
44. Commons, *Il Carteggio*, p 555
45. Commons, *Il Carteggio*, p 709
46. Commons, *Il Carteggio*, p 721
47. Commons, *Il Carteggio*, p 723
48. Commons, *Il Carteggio*, p 723
49. Commons, *Il Carteggio*, p 728
50. Commons, *Il Carteggio*, p 742
51. Maione and Seller, *Da Napoli a Vienna*, p 494
52. Maione and Seller, *Da Napoli a Vienna*, p 493
53. Ebers, *Seven Years of the King's Theatre*, p 128
54. Rossini, *Lettere e Documenti*, Vol 3, p 143
55. Cottrau, *Lettres d'un Melomane*, p 43
56. *Allgemeine Musikalische Zeitung*, Vol 28, 26 July 1826, p 487
57. The British Minstrel, and Musical and Literary Miscellany. Vol 3 (W Hamilton, Glasgow: no year indicated), 1836, p 51
58. *Harmonicon*, October 1826, p 194
59. *Era* (London), 17 October 1841, Issue 160. *The Theatres of Italy. No. III.*
60. Albert was the stage name of the famous French ballet dancer François-Ferdinand Decombe.
61. Antoine Paul was one of the premier French ballet dancers of the time.
62. *Allgemeine Musikalische Zeitung*, Vol 27, 19 October 1825, p 697
63. *Harmonicon* October 1826, p 195
64. Servadio, *Rossini*, p 50

65. *Allgemeine Musikalische Zeitung*, Vol 28, 18 January 1826, p 36. 'Organetto' probably referred to a hurdy-gurdy with its grating bagpipe-like sound, rather than to a more pleasant street organ. It was certainly not meant as a compliment. 'Messa di voce' is the singing technique used to gradually and seamlessly raise and lower the volume of the voice while sustaining a single pitch.

66. Cottrau, *Lettres d'un Melomane*, p 12

67. Henri Blaze de Bury Stendhal, *Musiciens Contemporains* (Michel Levy Frères, Paris: 1856) p 286

68. Cottrau, *Lettres d'un Melomane*, p 12

69. 'quella diavoletta della Malibran' in Cottrau, *Lettres d'un Melomane*, p 43

70. Rossini's *Otello*

71. Cottrau, *Lettres d'un Melomane*, p 16

72. Maria De la Mercedes Merlin, *The Memoirs of Madame Malibran* (Henry Colburn, London: 1840) p 164

73. Pacini, *Le mie memorie*, p 82

74. *Allgemeine Musikalische Zeitung*, Vol 36, 17 September 1834, p 632

75. Framcesco Florimo, *Cenno Storico sulla Scuola Musicale di Napoli*, (Lorenzo Rocco, Napoli: 1869) p 2088

76. Prod'homme, *Paganini*, p 195

77. *Allgemeine Musikalische Zeitung*, Vol 37, 21 January 1835, p 51

78. This might have been a preclusion enabling her to sing in Milan without Barbaja's permission, rather than a prohibition from her singing there. *Allgemeine Musikalische Zeitung* Vol 28, 27 September 1826, p 637

79. Mancini and Ragni, *Donizetti e i teatri napolitani*, p 232

80. A major Neapolitan library is named after Lucchesi Palli

81. Quoted in Rosselli, *Singers of Italian Opera*, p 70

82. Ashbrook, *Donizetti and his Operas*, p 80. Singers mattered more than composers and were paid a multiple of the composer's fees. The composer's fee might have been around 3 per cent of the total outlay of a production, while the soloist's would account for about 50 per cent.

83. Quoted in Ashbrook, *Donizetti*, p 342

84. Gaetano Donizetti's *Parisina* (1833, Florence), *Belisario* (1836, Venice), *Maria de Rudenz* (1838, Venice) and Saverio Mercadante's *Le due illustre rivali* (1838, Venice) were all written for Unger's contralto. The majority of these were produced by Lanari.

85. Rossini, *Lettere e Documenti*, Vol 3, p 211

86. Spohr, *Selbstbiographie*, Vol 1, p 349

87. The story of the bandits is more probably drawn from the experiences of Manuel García and his troupe, who were indeed attacked by bandits in Mexico and forced to perform for their entertainment.

88. Angelis, *Le Carte dell'Impresario,* p 16

89. Paolo Fabbri, *Rossini nella raccolte Piancastelli di Forli. Carteggi e Documenti* (Libreria Musicale Italiana, Lucca: 2001) Letter from Pelissier to Antonio Zoboli, p 57

90. Sharp, *Letters from Italy,* p 64

91. Sharp, *Letters from Italy,* p 63

92. Spohr, *Selbstbiographie,* Vol 1, p 316

93. Spohr, *Selbstbiographie,* Vol 1, p 316

Chapter 10

1. Rossini, *Lettere e Documenti,* Vol 3, p 555. Letter dated 7 September 1829

2. Rossini, *Lettere e Documenti,* Vol 3, p 570

3. Giazotto, *Le Carte della Scala,* p 80

4. Crivelli himself died during the summer of 1831

5. Rossini, *Lettere e Documenti,* Vol 3, p 278

6. Rossini, *Lettere e Documenti,* Vol 3, p 555

7. Cassinelli, Maltempi and Pozzoni, *Rubini. L'uomo e l'artista.* Vol II, p 498

8. Cassinelli, Maltempi and Pozzoni, *Rubini. L'uomo e l'artista.* Vol II, p 503

9. Commons, *Il Carteggio,* p 100

10. Rossini, *Lettere e Documenti,* Vol 3, p 555. Author's translation

11. Letter from Lorenzo's brother Agostino da Ponte to Barbaja: Autograph letter of 19 August, 1829. Stanford University, Memorial Library of Music Collection, #239

12. Jahn, *Die Wiener Hofoper von 1836 bis 1848,* p 14

13. Jahn, *Die Wiener Hofoper von 1836 bis 1848,* p 14

14. Which he ran from 1836–1850

15. Ashbrook, *Donizetti,* p 16

16. Toelle, *Oper als Geschaeft,* p 24

17. Commons, *Il Carteggio,* p 738

18. 6 July

19. *Giovanna d'Arco* on 19 August 1828

20. *Allgemeine Musikalische Zeitung* Vol 30, 15 October 1828, p 700

21. Cottrau, *Lettres d'un Melomane,* p 29

22. Teatro Carlo Felice 1828, Teatro Carcano 1830–1831, Teatro alla Scala 1830–1831

23. *Allgemeine Musikalische Zeitung,* Vol 31, 6 May 1829, p 290

24. Zavadini, *Donizetti,* p 274

25. Ashbrook, *Donizetti,* p 615

26. Mancini and Ragni, *Donizetti e i teatri napolitani,* p 204

27. Herbert Weinstock refers to the Crivelli-Lanari-Barbaja society at La Scala
    and in Venice. Weinstock, *Bellini. His Life and Operas,* p 89: It is unlikely that
    Crivelli, Barbaja and Lanari would have cooperated in the same theatre. It
    is more probable that he was referring to Crivelli and Barbaja in Milan and
    Lanari in Venice.

28. According to Florimo

29. Rosselli, *Life of Bellini,* p 72

30. Santore, *Modern Naples,* p 132

31. Dumas (père), *Le Corricolo,* p 37

32. Mazzinghi, *A Guide to the Antiquities,* p 32

33. Bidera, *Passeggiata per Napoli e Contorni,* p 154

34. Parry, *Victorian Swansdown,* p 131

35. Bidera, *Passeggiata per Napoli e Contorni,* p 313

36. Bidera, *Passeggiata per Napoli e Contorni,* p 30

37. Commons, 'L'eta di Donizetti', in Cagli and Agostino, *Il Teatro di San Carlo,*
    p 187

38. The Neapolitan censors in the late 1820s and 1830s sincerely believed that plots
    should be morally uplifting, and that the depiction of violence onstage was
    detrimental to public welfare. The censors retained a marked preference, more
    insistent after 1832, for happy endings; as they believed that they affirmed the
    status quo and upheld the principle that benevolent intervention (preferably by
    the sovereign) could reconcile differences. Ashbrook, *Donizetti,* p 39

39. The royal theatres of San Carlo, the Teatro del Fondo, the Teatro Nuovo and
    the Teatro Fenice, as well as the Fiorentini, Partenope, San Ferdinando and
    San Carlino.

40. Lady Sydney Morgan, *Lady Morgan's Memoirs,* Vol 2 (W H Allen, London:
    1863) p 359

Chapter 11

1. Quoted in Ashbrook, *Donizetti,* p 69

2. Florimo, *Bellini,* p 393

3. Florimo, *Bellini,* p 395

4. Florimo, *Bellini,* p 396

5. Weinstock, *Bellini,* p 102

6. Weinstock, *Bellini,* p 101

7. Florimo, *Bellini,* p 33

8. Florimo, *Bellini,* p 41

9.   Cottrau, *Lettres d'un Melomane*, p 17

10. 'petit polisson' in Cottrau, *Lettres d'un Melomane*, p iii

11. Heine, *Florentine Nights*, p 23. Original German: *'Ein Seufzer en escarpins'*. *Escarpins* are 'dancing pumps'

12. Servadio, *Rossini*, p 145

13. Cottrau, *Lettres d'un Melomane*, p 22

14. Greco and Di Benedetto, *Donizetti, Napoli, l'Europa*, p 161

15. Johann Wilhelm von Archenholz, *Rom und Neapel: 1787*. (Manutius, Heidelberg: 1990) p 237

16. Commons, *Il Carteggio*, p 690

17. Zavadini, *Donizetti*, p 354

18. Quoted in and translated by Philip Gossett, *Divas and Scholars*, p 102

19. Greco and Di Benedetto, *Donizetti, Napoli, l'Europa*, p 159

20. Greco and Di Benedetto, *Donizetti, Napoli, l'Europa*, p 93

21. Greco and Di Benedetto, *Donizetti, Napoli, l'Europa*, p 95

22. A year later, Finizio would appear in the register of the *Società d'industria e belle arti* as 'appaltatore, Direzione del macchinismo e decorazione', indicating that stage machinery and decoration, just like costumes, was one of the many businesses that were sub-contracted by the impresario.

23. Signed on 24 February 1829

24. Tallow is rendered beef or mutton fat which was used to make candles as a cheaper alternative to wax.

25. Starke, *Information and Directions for Travellers*, p 503

26. Simone Tarsia and Pasquale Borrelli, 'Per Domenico Barbaja, impresario de' reali teatri contro la real soprintendenza degli spettacoli'. Biblioteca Lucchesi Palli, Biblioteca Nazionale di Napoli. 3633 nasi 2.el "c"r (3) 1828 (A) The printed document is dated 25 July 1828. This is certainly wrong, as it discusses legal issues that only arose in 1832. It is more likely that the document is from 1838.

27. Harold Acton, referenced by Jeremy Commons, 'L'eta di Donizetti', in Cagli and Agostino, *Il Teatro di San Carlo 1737–1987*, p 190

28. Commons, 'L'eta di Donizetti' in Cagli and Agostino, *Il Teatro di San Carlo 1737–1987*, p190

29. Greco and Di Benedetto, *Donizetti, Napoli, l'Europa*, p 162

30. Greco and Di Benedetto, *Donizetti, Napoli, l'Europa*, p 166

31. Greco and Di Benedetto, *Donizetti, Napoli, l'Europa*, pp 172–7

32. G Badolisani, 'Per la Signora D. Luigia Boccabadati contro il Signor Domenico Barbaja' (Nunzio Pasca, Napoli: 1832). Biblioteca della Societa Napoletana di Storia Patria; Giustizia, Decisioni Civili, fol 95. A printed brief of the legal argument by the defendant's lawyer, it was aimed to discharge

the singer's responsibilities and defend her point of view. Barbaja's lawyer was Simone Tarsia, who defended the impresario in many other cases.

33. Ashbrook, *Donizetti*, p 615
34. *The Times*, London, 1 November 1831
35. *Allgemeine Musikalische Zeitung*, Vol 35, 20 February 1833, p 101
36. Prince Ruffano in 1834
37. Cottrau, *Lettres d'un Melomane*, p 24
38. November to February: *Allgemeine Musikalische Zeitung*, Vol 36, 17 September 1834, p 632. The actual fee reflected in the accounts of the San Carlo is 19,020 ducats for the period from 10 November 1834 to 3 March 1835. See Francesca Canessa (ed), *Almanacco dei Reali Teatri S. Carlo e Fondo; Ristampa anastatica dell'edizione del 1835* (Edizione di Gabriele e Mariateresa Benincase, Roma: 1987) p 8
39. Cottrau, *Lettres d'un Melomane*, p 25
40. Ashbrook, *Donizetti*, p 84
41. Barbaja's impresa lasted until May 1834, so he must have signed Donizetti, but the ensuing events happened in the Societa d'Industria era.
42. Bianconi and Pestelli (ed), *Opera Production and its Resources*, p 123
43. *Allgemeine Musikalische Zeitung*, Vol 36, 17 September 1834, p 632
44. Duprez, *Souvenirs d'un Chanteur*, p 109
45. *Allgemeine Musikalische Zeitung*, Vol 37, 21 January 1835, p 50
46. Commons, 'L'eta di Donizetti' in Cagli and Agostino, *Il Teatro di San Carlo 1737–1987*, p187
47. In August 1834: Cottrau, *Lettres d'un Melomane*, p 28
48. Cottrau, *Lettres d'un Melomane*, p 28 p II
49. Howard Bushnell, *Maria Malibran: A Biography of the Singer* (Pennsylvania State University Press, Pennsylviania: 1979) p 140
50. Ashbrook, *Donizetti*, p 401
51. Maria Stuarda had a Neapolitan première of sorts under the name of Buondelmonte. The story and libretto were different, but the music practically the same. It was premièred at the Teatro San Carlo on 18 October 1834 with Ronzi and de Sere. Both ladies performed well and did not fight.
52. Commons, 'L'eta di Donizetti' in Cagli and Agostino, *Il Teatro di San Carlo 1737–1987*, p 191
53. Commons, 'L'eta di Donizetti' in Cagli and Agostino, *Il Teatro di San Carlo 1737–1987*, p 191
54. *Allgemeine Musikalische Zeitung*, Vol 38, 16 March 1836, p 172
55. Florimo, *Bellini*, p 415

56. Or two operas for 2,000 ducats and the retention of the entre ownership of the score, according to Florimo, *Bellini*, p 58
57. Ashbrook, *Donizetti*, p 97
58. Quoted in Ashbrook, *Donizetti*, p 95
59. in Ashbrook, *Donizetti*, p 95
60. Cottrau, *Lettres d'un Melomane*, p 53
61. *Allgemeine Musikalische Zeitung*, Vol 38, 16 March 1836, p 173
62. *Allgemeine Musikalische Zeitung*, Vol 38, 16 March 1836, p 174
63. *Allgemeine Musikalische Zeitung*, Vol 38, 13 Jan 1836, p 32. Adelaide Toldi d'Anvers was a French singer of noble extraction.

Chapter 12

1. Axel Munthe, *The Story of San Michele (E P Dutton, New York: 1957) p 158*
2. Cottrau, *Lettres d'un Melomane*, p 36
3. Ashbrook, *Donizetti*, p 107
4. Zavadini, *Donizetti*, p 417
5. Florimo, *Bellini*, p 53
6. Rossini, *Lettere e Documenti*, Vol 1, p 169
7. Commons, 'L'eta di Donizetti' in Cagli and Agostino, *Il Teatro di San Carlo 1737–1987*, p 184
8. Zavadini, *Donizetti*, p 415
9. *Allgemeine Musikalische Zeitung*, Vol 39, 7 June 1837, p 570
10. Giulio (Jarro) Piccini, *Memorie d'un impresario Fiorentino* (Loescher e Seeber, Firenze: 1892) p 131
11. *Allgemeine Musikalische Zeitung*, Vol 39, 7 June 1837, p 570
12. *Il Campanello* and *Il Betly*
13. Ashbrook, *Donizetti*, p 111
14. Zavadini, *Donizetti*, p 219
15. Zavadini, *Donizetti*, p 417
16. Ashbrook, *Donizetti*, p 389
17. Guido Olivieri, 'L'Archivio Storico del Banco di Napoli: Barbaja, Donizetti, l'opera napoletana' in: Mancini and Ragni, *Donizetti e i teatri napolitani*, p 125
18. Olivieri, 'L'Archivo Storico del Banco', in Mancini and Ragni, *Donizetti e i teatri napolitani*, p 125
19. Commons, 'L'eta di Donizetti' in Cagli and Agostino, *Il Teatro di San Carlo 1737–1987*, p 187
20. Davis, *Merchants, Monopolists*, p 273
21. Barbaja had negotiated successfully with the King once before. In 1832 when Barbaja applied for renewal of the contract, the sovereign said that Barbaja was

his preferred choice, and unless Barbaja himself offered to reduce the terms, the Ministry should accept the Barbaja contract as it stood: Davis, *Merchants, Monopolists*, p 273

22. Ashbrook, *Donizetti*, p 119
23. Ashbrook, *Donizetti*, p 120
24. Zavadini, *Donizetti*, p 433
25. Ashbrook, *Donizetti*, p 121
26. *Allgemeine Musikalische Zeitung*, Vol 39, 7 June 1837, p 372
27. Ashbrook, *Donizetti*, p 122
28. Greco and Di Benedetto, *Donizetti, Napoli, l'Europa*, p 142
29. *Allgemeine Musikalische Zeitung*, Vol 40, 14 February 1838, p 113
30. *Allgemeine Musikalische Zeitung*, Vol 40, 14 February 1838, p 114
31. Zavadini, *Donizetti*, p 455
32. Greco and Di Benedetto, *Donizetti, Napoli, l'Europa*, p 150
33. Rogers, *Some Famous Singers of the 19th century*, p 70
34. Rogers, *Some Famous Singers of the 19th century*, p 67
35. Nourrit, as retold by Henry Pleasants, *The Great Tenor Tragedy* (Amadeus Press, Portland, Oregon: 1995) p 57
36. Pleasants, *Tenor Tragedy*, p 65
37. Louis Quicherat, *Adolphe Nourrit: sa vie, son talent, son caractère, sa correspondance* (L Hachette, Paris: 1867) p 542
38. Pleasants, *Tenor Tragedy*, p 65
39. Commons, 'L'eta di Donizetti' in Cagli and Agostino, *Il Teatro di San Carlo 1737–1987*, p 191
40. Commons, 'L'eta di Donizetti' in Cagli and Agostino, *Il Teatro di San Carlo 1737–1987*, p 184
41. Zavadini, *Donizetti*, p 486
42. Quoted in Ashbrook, *Donizetti*, p 134
43. *Allgemeine Musikalische Zeitung*, Vol 40, 14 November 1838, p 774
44. Giuramento had premiered a year earlier in Milan.
45. Pleasants, *Tenor Tragedy*, p 94
46. Pleasants, *Tenor Tragedy*, p 95
47. Quicherat, *Adolphe Nourrit*, p 418
48. Pleasants, *Tenor Tragedy*, p 112
49. *The Times*, London, 2 February 1839, quoting a report from *Musical World*
50. Duprez, *Souvenirs d'un Chanteur*, p 152
51. *La Presse*, 19 March 1839, p 2
52. *Le Figaro*, 21 March 1939, p 4

53. In 1848 it had its first showing at the Teatro San Carlo, again under the title *Poliuto*.

54. Cottrau, *Lettres d'un Melomane*, p 70

55. *Allgemeine Musikalische Zeitung*, Vol 41, 14 August 1841, p 650

56. Fabbri, *Rossini nella raccolte Piancastelli di Forlì*, p 57. Letter from Pelissier to Antonio Zoboli. Author's translation

57. Commons, 'L'eta di Donizetti' in Cagli and Agostino, *Il Teatro di San Carlo 1737–1987*, p 192

58. Commons, 'L'eta di Donizetti' in Cagli and Agostino, *Il Teatro di San Carlo 1737–1987*, p 192

59. Mancini (ed), *Il Teatro di San Carlo 1737–1987*, Vol 1, p 16

60. *Allgemeine Musikalische Zeitung*, Vol 41, 23 October 1839, p 838

61. Quoted in Ashbrook, *Donizetti*, p 146

62. *Allgemeine Musikalische Zeitung*, Vol 42, 13 May 1840, p 424

63. *Allgemeine Musikalische Zeitung*, Vol 42, 29 July 1840, p 636

64. *Allgemeine Musikalische Zeitung*, Vol 42, 29 July 1840, p 637

65. Commons, 'L'eta di Donizetti' in Cagli and Agostino, *Il Teatro di San Carlo 1737–1987*, p 184

66. Commons, 'L'eta di Donizetti' in Cagli and Agostino, *Il Teatro di San Carlo 1737–1987*, p 184

67. Pollio, *Collezione Barbaja*, p 118

68. Pollio, *Collezione Barbaja*, p 147: 'la mia posizione sconnessata'

69. Pollio, *Collezione Barbaja*, p 148–149

70. Pollio, *Collezione Barbaja*, p 151

71. Perticari, 'In morte di Domenico Barbaja: accenti di dolore espressi al passaggio del suo feretro per Toledo nella sera del 19 ottobre 1841' (Rusconi, Napoli: 1841). Biblioteca Nazionale di Napoli. p 8. The poem is headed and filed in National Library of Naples as being by the poet Giulio Perticari. But since he died in 1822 it would have been difficult for him to write these lines, so it is more likely to be 'in his style'.

72. 63 is the number most frequently referenced: he was actually 64, if the baptismal certificate was accurate.

73. Pollio, *Collezione Barbaja*, p 55

74. Giornale delle due Sicilie, 16 November 1841

75. Pasquale Borrelli, 'Elogio funebre dedicato alla memoria di Domenico Barbaja' (Presso Lampati, Mendrisio: 1841). Biblioteca Nazionale Vittorio Emmanuele III, Napoli, p 10

76. *L'Omnibus*, 21 October, 1841

77. *Teatri, Arti e Letterature*. Bologna, 28 October, 1841

78. *Allgemeine Musikalische Zeitung*, Vol 44, 16 March 1842, p 240
79. Borrelli, *Elogio funebre*, p 19
80. Borrelli, *Elogio funebre*, p 15
81. Borrelli, *Elogio funebre*, p 22
82. Referring to the ancient Greek poet Tirteo, and Decumano in reference to the back alleys of old Naples.
83. Perticari, *In morte di Barbaja*, p 8
84. Perticari, *In morte di Barbaja*, p 5
85. Author's translation, with guidance from Reto Mueller.
86. *Era*, London, 7 November, 1841, Issue 163. *Le Bourru Bienfaisant* was a 1771 play by the Venetian playwright Carlo Goldoni (1707–1793), later translated as *Il Burbero Benefico*, and as *Il Burbero di Buon Cuore* by Goldoni himself.
87. *Era*, 21 November, 1841, Issue 165
88. *Era*, 30 January 1842; Issue 175

Epilogue

1. Zavadini, *Donizetti*, p 549
2. *The Hull Packet*, 5 November 1841, Issue 2968
3. Pollio, *Collezione Barbaja*, pp 165, 93
4. Pollio, *Collezione Barbaja*, p 143
5. Paologiovanni Maione and Francesca Seller, *Cristoforo Colombo o sia la scoperta dell'america di Donizetti* (Leo S. Olschki, Firenze: 2005) p 424
6. Dumas (père), *Le Corricolo*, p 39
7. at 210 Via Toledo
8. This was confirmed by Alfredo Buccaro of the University of Naples, Faculty of Architecture. The original Palazzo Barbaja on 210 Via Toledo was torn down in the 1890s. No illustrations could be found of the original palazzo. See also Aurelio De Rose, *I Palazzi di Napoli, Storia, curiosità e aneddoti che si tramandano da secoli su questi straordinari testimoni della vita partenopea* (Newton e Compton, Napoli: 2004) p 272
9. Bidera, *Passeggiata per Napoli e Contorni*, p 248

Bibliography

Archives

Biblioteca Livia Simoni, Museo Teatrale della Scala, Milan

Barbaja, Domenico and Melzi, Count Gaetano, Correspondence (1829–1833). Reference C297-C302

Barbaja, Domenico Barbaja and Pasta, Giudita, Correspondence (1816). Reference 10524

Biblioteca Nazionale di Napoli

Perticari, G, 'In morte di Domenico Barbaja: accenti di dolore espressi al passaggio del suo feretro per Toledo nella sera del 19 ottobre 1841' (Rusconi, Napoli: 1841).

Tarsia, Simone and Borrelli, Pasquale, 'Per Domenico Barbaja, impresario de' reali teatri contro la real soprintendenza degli spettacoli'. Biblioteca Lucchesi Palli, 3633 nasi 2.el "c"r (3) 1828 (A)

Borsini (da Siena), Lorenzo, 'L'ultimo giorno di Barbaja. Poemetto eroi-comico' (Tipografia Trani, Napoli: 1834)

Biblioteca Nazionale Vittorio Emmanuele III, Napoli

Borrelli, Pasquale, 'Elogio funebre dedicato alla memoria di Domenico Barbaja' (Presso Lampati, Mendrisio: 1841)

Barbaja, Domenico, 'Sull' Oggetto de Giuochi d'Azzardo in seguito del contratto per atto pubblico e solenne de' 19 febbraio 1818. Pro Memoria' (Tipografia Flautina, Napoli: 1820)

Biblioteca della Societa Napoletana di Storia Patria
Badolisani, G, 'Per la Signora D. Luigia Boccabadati contro il Signor Domenico
    Barbaja' (Nunzio Pasca, Napoli: 1832). Giustizia, Decisioni Civili, fol 95

Biblioteca Trivulziana, Archivio Storico Civico, Milan
Barbaja, Domenico, Letter to King Francis I from 18 June 1827.
Office of the Director of Theatres and Public Performances in Milan.
    Memorandum. '1805.1807. Per un nuovo appalto'. 1805.
Ruoli della Popolazione, 1811.

Harvard University, Houghton Library – Harvard Theater Collection
Gentile di Giuseppe, F, Collection of French and Italian opera ballet, 1694–1904.

Stanford University
da Ponte, Agostino to Domenico Barbaglia. Autograph letter of August 19, 1829.
    Memorial Library of Music Collection, #239

Books
Acton, Harold, *The Bourbons of Naples (1734–1825)* (Prion Books Ltd, London: 1998)
Albrecht, Theodore, *Letter to Beethoven,* Vol 3 (University of Nebraska Press,
    Nebraska: 1996)
Anderson, James, *Bloomsbury Dictionary of Opera and Operetta* (Bloomsbury,
    London: 1989)
Ashbrook, William, *Donizetti and his Operas* (Cambridge University Press,
    Cambridge: 1982)
Azevedo, Alexis Jacob, *G. Rossini. Sa vie et ses oeuvres* (Heugel, Paris: 1864)
Baumann, Thomas and Petzoldt McClymonds, Marita, *Opera and the
    Enlightenment* (Cambridge University Press, Cambridge: 1995)
Becker, Heinz (ed), *Meyerbeer, Giacomo, Briefwechsel und Tagebuecher.* Vol 2 (Walter
    de Gruyter, Berlin: 1959)
Benedict, Julius, *Weber* (Sampson Low, Marston Searle & Rivington, London: 1889)
Bianchini, Lodovico, *Storia delle Finanze del Regno di Napoli.* Vol 7 (Francesco Lao,
    Palermo: 1839)
Bianconi, Lorenzo and Pestelli, Giorgio (ed), *Opera Production and its Resources*
    (University of Chicago Press, Chicago: 1998)
Bidera, Emmanuele, *Passeggiata per Napoli e Contorni* (Aldo Manuzio, Napoli: 1844)
Black, John, *Donizetti's Operas in Naples 1822–1848* (The Donizetti Society, London:
    1982)

Blessington, Marguerite, *The Idler in Italy*. Vol 2 (Henry Colbourn, London: 1839)

Burney, Charles, *The present state of music in France and Italy* (J Robson, London: 1773)

Burwick, John, *The Journal of John Waldie Theatre Commentaries 1799–1830* (University of California, Los Angeles: 2008)

Bushnell, Howard, *Maria Malibran: A Biography of the Singer* (Pennsylvania State University Press, Pennsylviania: 1979)

Cagli, Bruno and Ragni, Sergio, *Gioachino Rossini: Lettere e Documenti* (Fondazione Rossini Pesaro, Pesaro: 2004)

Cagli, Bruno and Agostino, Ziino (ed), *Il Teatro di San Carlo 1737–1987. L'Opera, Il Ballo* (Electa, Napoli: 1987)

Cagli, Bruno, *Rossini a Londra e al Theatre Italien di Parigi* (Bollettino del Centro Rossiniano di Studi, Pesaro: 1981)

Canessa, Francesco (ed), *Almanacco dei Reali Teatri S. Carlo e Fondo; Ristampa anastatica dell'edizione del 1835* (Edizione di Gabriele e Mariateresa Benincasa, Roma: 1987)

Cassinelli, B, Maltempi, A, Pozzoni, M, *Rubini. L'uomo e l'artista*. Vol 2 (Cassa Rurale ed Artigiana di Calcio e di Covo. Commune di Romano di Lombardia: 1993)

Castile-Blaze, F H, *L'Opera Italien de 1548–1856* (Castil-Blaze, Paris: 1856)

Cavadini, Nicoletta Ossanna, *Pietro Bianchi 1787–1849. Architetto e archeologo* (Elekta, Milano: 1996)

Celano, Carlo and Chiarini, Giovanni Battista, *Notizie del bello, del curioso e dell'antico della citta di Napoli*. Vol 5 (L Chiurazzi, Napoli: 1870)

Cicconetti, Filippo, *Vita di Vincenzo Bellini* (Alberghetti, Prato: 1859)

Clapton, Nicolas, *Moreschi and the Voice of the Castrato* (Haus Publishing, London: 2008)

Commons, Jeremy, *Il Carteggio Personale di Nicola Vaccai* (Giancarlo Zedde, Torino: 2008)

Corti, Count Egon Caesar, *The Rise of the House of Rothschild* (Cosmopolitan, USA: 1928)

Cottrau, Guillaume, *Lettres d'un Melomane; pour servir de document a l'histoire musicale de Naples de 1829 a 1847. Avec un preface de F Verdinois* (A Morano, Roma: 1885)

Croce, Benedetto, *I Teatri di Napoli. Secolo XV-XVIII* (Uigi Pierro, Napoli: 1891)

Davis, John A, *Merchants, Monopolists and Contractors* (Arno Press, USA: 1981)

de Angelis, Marcello, *Le Carte dell'Impresario. Melodramma e costume teatrale nell'Ottocento* (Sansoni Editore, Firenze: 1982) de Courcy, G I C, *Paganini. The Genoese*, Vol 1 (University of Oklahoma Press, Oklahoma: 1957)

De la Mercedes Merlin, *Maria, The Memoirs of Madame Malibran* (Henry Colburn, London: 1840)

De la Rochefoucauld, François, *Mémoires de M. de la Rochefoucauld*, Vol 1 (Michel Lévy Frères, Paris: 1861)

de Norvins, Jacques Marquet, *Italie pittoresque* (Alphonse Pigoreau, Paris: 1850)

De Rose, Aurelio, *I Palazzi di Napoli, Storia, curiosità e aneddoti che si tramandano da secoli su questi straordinari testimoni della vita partenopea* (Newton e Compton, Napoli: 2004)

Di Vincenzo, Riccardo, *Milano al Caffè. Tra settecento e Novecento* (Hoepli, Milano: 2007)

Dumas, Alexandre (père), *Le Corricolo* (Michel Levy, Paris: 1872)

Duprez, Gilbert, *Souvenirs d'un Chanteur* (Calmann Levi, Paris: 1880)

Ebers, John, *Seven Years of the King's Theatre* (William Harrison Ainsworth, London: 1828)

Fabbri, Paolo, *Rossini nella raccolte Piancastelli di Forli. Carteggi e Documenti* (Libreria Musicale Italiana, Lucca: 2001)

Faraglia, N F, *Storia dei Prezzi in Napoli dal 1131 al 1860* (Nobile, Napoli: 1878)

Florimo, Francesco, *Bellini. Memorie e Lettere* (G Barbera, Firenze: 1882)

Florimo, Francesco, *Cenno Storico sulla Scuola Musicale di Napoli* (Lorenzo Rocco, Napoli: 1869)

Giazotto, Remo, *Le Carte della Scala. Storie di Impresari e Appaltatori Teatrali (1778–1860)* (Edizioni Akademos & Lim, Pisa: 1990)

Gossett, Philip, *Divas and Scholars: Performing Italian Opera* (University of Chicago Press, Chicago: 2006)

Greco, Franco Carmelo and Di Benedetto, Renato, *Donizetti, Napoli, l'Europa* (Edizioni Scientifiche Italiane, Napoli: 2000)

Gregory, Desmond, *Napoleon's Italy* (Rosemont Publishing, Massachusetts: 2001)

Grempler, Martina, *Das Teatro Valle in Rom 1727–1850* (Baerenreiter, Kassel: 2012)

Haine, Marie (ed), *400 Lettres de Musiciens au Musee Royal de Mariemont. Collection "Musique-Musicologie"* (Pierre Mardaga, Liege: 1995)

Hanson, Alice M, *Musical Life in Biedermeier Vienna* (Cambridge University Press, Cambridge: 1985)

Hebenstreit, Wilhelm, *Der Fremde in Wien, und der Wiener in der Heimath: möglichst vollstaendiges Auskunftsbuch fuer den Reisenden nach Wien* (Carl Armbruster, Wien: 1840)

Heine, Heinrich, *Florentine Nights,* trans. Charles Godfrey Leland and Hans Breitmann (Mondial, New York: 2008)

Heine, Heinrich, *Florentine Nights,* trans. Charles Godfrey Leland and Hans
    Breitmann (William Heinemann, London: 1906)

Heine, Heinrich, *Florentinische Naechte. Heinrich Heines saemtliche Werke in 12
    Baenden.* Vol 7–8. XX. (T Knaus, Berlin: date n/a)

Holden, Anthony, *The Man who wrote Mozart. The extraordinary life of Lorenzo Da
    Ponte* (Phoenix, London: 2007)

Istituto Banco di Napoli, Fondazione. *Dal Teatro San Bartolomeo al Teatro San
    Carlo. Documenti* (Istituto Banco di Napoli, Napoli: 2009)

Jahn, Michael, *Die Wiener Hofoper von 1836 bis 1848: Die Aera Balochino/Merelli* (Der
    Apfel, Wien: 2004)

Kimbell, David, *Vincenzo Bellini, Norma* (Cambridge University Press, Cambridge:
    1998)

Kruft, Hanno-Walter, *A History of Architectural Theory. From Vitruvius to the Present*
    (Princeton Architectural Press, Princeton: 2003)

Lablache Cheer, Clarissa, *The Great Lablache* (Xlibris, USA: 2009)

Lucka, Emil, *Der Impresario* (Donauverlag, Wien: 1948)

Maione, Paologiovanni and Seller, Francesca, *Cristoforo Colombo o sia la scoperta
    dell'america di Donizetti* (Leo S. Olschki, Firenze: 2005)

Maione, Paologiovanni and Seller, Francesca, *Da Napoli a Vienna. Barbaja e
    l'esportazione di un nuovo modello impresariale* (Oesterreichische Akademie der
    Wissenschaften, Wien: 2002)

Maione, Paologiovanni and Seller, Francesca, *Domenico Barbaja a Napoli (1809–
    1840).* (Santabarbara, Bellona: 1994)

Maione, Paologiovanni and Seller, Francesca, *I reali teatri di Napoli nella prima meta
    del ottocento. Studii su Domenico Barbaja* (Santabarbara, Bellona: 1994)

Maione, Paologiovanni and Seller, Francesca, *Il Palconscenico dei mutamenti: il teatro
    del Fondo di Napoli 1809–1840* (Lim Editrice, Lucca: 1997)

Mancini, Franco and Ragni, Sergio, *Donizetti e i teatri napoletani nell'Ottocento*
    (Elekta Napoli, Napoli: 1997)

Mancini, Franco (ed), *Il Teatro di San Carlo 1737–1987. La Storia, La Struttura*
    (Electa Napoli, Napoli: 1987)

Mastriani, Francesco, *I Misteri di Napoli* (G Nobile, Napoli: 1870)

Mazzinghi, John, *A Guide to the Antiquities and Curiosities in the City of Naples*
    (Agnello Nobile, Naples: 1817)

Metternich, Prince Richard (ed), *Metternich: Memoirs of Prince Metternich.* Vol 3.
    Translated by Mrs Alexander Napier (Richard Bentley, London: 1881)

Monaldi, Gino, *Impresari Celebri del Secolo XIX* (Licinio Capelli, Rocca S Cassiano:
    1918)

Morgan, Lady Sydney, *Lady Morgan's Memoirs,* Vol 2 (W H Allen, London: 1863)

Munthe, Axel, *Letters from a Mourning City. Naples, Autumn, 1884.* Translated from the Swedish by Maude Valerie White (John Murray, London: 1884)

Munthe, Axel, *The Story of San Michele (E P Dutton, New York: 1957)*

Newbould, Brian, *Schubert: The Music and the Man* (University of California Press, Berkeley: 1997)

Oettinger, Eduard Maria, *Rossini. Ein komischer Roman* (Costenoble und Remmelmann, Leipzig: 1851)

Orrey, Leslie (ed), *The Encyclopedia of Opera* (Pitman, London: 1976)

Ortlepp, E, *Grosses Instrumental- und Vokal- Concert. Eine musikalische Anthologie.* Vol 9 (F H Koehler, Stuttgart: 1923)

Osborne, Richard, *Rossini. His Life and Works.* (Oxford University Press, Oxford: 2007)

Pacini, Giovanni, *Le mie memorie artistiche* (G G Guidi, Firenze: 1865)

Parker, Roger, *The Oxford Illustrated History of Opera* (Oxford University Press, Oxford: 1994)

Parry, John Orlando, *Victorian Swansdown: Extract from the Early Travel Diaries of John Orlando Parry, Entertainer* (ed. Cyril Bruin Andrews) (John Murray, London: 1935)

Piccini, Giulio (Jarro) *Memorie d'un impresario Fiorentino* (Loescher e Seeber, Firenze: 1892)

Pleasants, Henry, *The Great Singers. From the dawn of Opera to Caruso, Callas and Pavarotti* (Simon & Shuster, New York: 1981)

Pleasants, Henry, *The Great Tenor Tragedy* (Amadeus Press, Portland, Oregon: 1995)

Poeck, Ignaz Freiherr von, *Darstellung des Zustandes der Oper und des Balletes im k.k. Hoftheater naechst dem Kaerntnerthore waehrend der Pachtung des Herrn Domenico Barbaja* (Wallishauser, Wien: 1825)

Pollio, Simona, *La Collezione Barbaja.* Tesi di Laurea in Museologia e Storia del Collezionismo (Istituto Universitario 'Suor Orsola Benincasa' Napoli, Napoli: 1998/99)

Pougin, Arthur, Rossini: *Notes – Impressions – Souvenirs – Commentaires* (A Claudin, Paris: 1871)

Prod'homme, Jacques Gabriel, *Niccolo Paganini, A Biography* (Carl Fischer, New York: 1911)

Quicherat, Louis, *Adolphe Nourrit: sa vie, son talent, son caractère, sa correspondence* (L Hachette, Paris: 1867)

Ragni, Sergio, *Isabella Colbran, Isabella Rossini* (Zecchini, Varese: 2012)

Ragni, Sergio, *Rossini a Napoli. La Conquista di un Capitale* (Ente Autonomo Teatro di San Carlo, Napoli: 1991)

Radomski, James, *Manuel Garcia (1775–1832). Chronicle of the Life of a Bel Canto Tenor at the Dawn of Romanticism* (Oxford University Press, Oxford: 2000)

Rogers, Francis, *Some Famous Singers of the 19th century* (H W Gray, New York: 1914)

Rosselli, John, *Singers of Italian Opera. The history of a profession* (Cambridge University Press, Cambridge: 1992)

Rosselli, John, *The Life of Bellini* (Cambridge University Press, Cambridge: 1996)

Rosselli, John, *The Opera Industry in Italy from Cimarosa to Verdi. The Role of the Impresario* (Cambridge University Press, Cambridge: 1984)

Rovani, Giuseppe, *Cento Anni.* Vol 1 (Stabilimento Redaelli dei Fratelli Rechiedei, Milano:1868)

Rowell, George, *The Old Vic Theatre. A History* (Cambridge University Press, Cambridge: 1993)

Santore, John, *Modern Naples. A Documentary History 1799–1999* (Italica, New York: 2001)

Servadio, Gaia, *Rossini* (Constable & Robinson, London: 2003)

Sharp, Samuel, *Letters from Italy, describing the Customs and Manner of that Country, in the years 1765 and 1766. An Admonition to Gentlemen who pass the Alps, in the Tour through Italy* (R Cave, London: 1766)

Silvestrelli, Anita, *Franz Schubert* (Anton Pustet, Leipzig: 1939)

Sinclair, J D, *An Autumn in Italy* (Constable & Co, Edinburgh: 1829)

Spohr, Louis, *Selbstbiographie,* Vol 2 (Georg H. Wigand, Kassel: 1860)

Starke, Mariana, *Information and Directions for Travellers on the Continent* (John Murray, London: 1828)

Stendhal, Henri Blaze de Bury, *Life of Rossini.* First published in French in 1823. Translated by Richard N Coe. (Calder & Boyars, London: 2010)

Stendhal, Henri Blaze de Bury, *Musiciens Contemporains* (Michel Levy Frères, Paris: 1856)

Stendhal, Henri Blaze de Bury, *Rome, Naples et Florence* (Delauney, Paris: 1826)

Stendhal, Henri Blaze de Bury, *Rome, Naples et Florence* (Michel Levy Frères, Paris: 1854)

Toelle, Jutta, *Oper als Geschaeft. Impresari an italienischen Opernhaeusern 1860–1900* (Baerenreiter, Kassel: 2007)

Valenzi, Lucia, *Donne, Medici e Poliziotti a Napoli nell'Ottocento. La prostituzione tra repressione e tolleranza.* (Liguori, Napoli: 2000)

von Archenholz, Johann Wilhelm, *Rom und Neapel: 1787.* (Manutius, Heidelberg: 1990; first published 1785)

von Kotzebue, August, *Erinnerungen von einer Reise aus Liefland nach Rom und Neapel,* Vol 2 (Heinrich Froelich, Berlin: 1805) von Chézy, Helmina, *Unvergessenes, Denkwuerdigkeiten aus dem Leben von Helmina von Chézy. Von ihr selbst erzaehlt,* Vol 2 (Brockhaus, Leipzig: 1858)

von Weber (Freiherr), Baron Max Maria, *Carl Maria von Weber. Life of an Artist.* Translation by J Palgrave Simpson (Chapman and Hall, London: 1865)

Weinstock, Herbert, *Rossini. A Biography* (Alfred A. Knopf, New York: 1975)

Weinstock, Herbert, *Vincenzo Bellini. His Life and his Operas* (Alfred A Knopf, New York: 1980)

Yates, W E, *Theater in Vienna. A critical history. 1776–1995* (Cambridge University Press, Cambridge: 1996)

Zavadini, Guido, *Donizetti: Vita – Musiche- Epistolario* (Istituto Italiano d'Arti Grafiche, Bergamo: 1948)

Periodicals

Allgemeine Musikalische Zeitung, Breitkopf & Haertel, Leipzig, 1799–1842

British Minstrel, and Musical and Literary Miscellany, William Hamilton, Glasgow, 1845

Caecilia, eine Zeitschrift fuer die musikalische Welt. B. Schott, Mainz, 1824

Donizetti Society, Articles. Donizetti Society, London, 1977

Era, London, 1841–42

Le Figaro, Journal Littéraire et d'Arts, Paris. 1827, 1839

Harmonicon, A Journal of Music, W Pinnock, London, 1826–28

Hull Packet, Hull, 1841

Istituto Banco di Napoli, Fondazione. Documenti, 2009

Journal of Economic History, Cambridge, 2009

Lute, London, 1884

L'Omnibus, Naples, 1841

La Presse, Paris, 1838–39

Morgenblatt fuer gebildete Staende. Cotta'sche Buchhandlung, Stuttgart and Tuebingen, 1807–65

Musical Quarterly, Oxford, 1939

Musical Standard, London, 1879

Revue Musicale, Fetis, F J (ed.): Sautelet, Paris, 1828

Wiener Zeitung, Vienna. 1820–26

Index